Fragments of Trauma and the Social Production of Suffering

New Imago: Series in Theoretical, Clinical, and Applied Psychoanalysis
Series Editor Jon Mills, Adler Graduate Professional School, Toronto

New Imago: Series in Theoretical, Clinical, and Applied Psychoanalysis is a scholarly and professional publishing imprint devoted to all aspects of psychoanalytic inquiry and research in theoretical, clinical, philosophical, and applied psychoanalysis. It is inclusive in focus, hence fostering a spirit of plurality, respect, and tolerance across the psychoanalytic domain. The series aspires to promote open and thoughtful dialogue across disciplinary and interdisciplinary fields in mental health, the humanities, and the social and behavioral sciences. It furthermore wishes to advance psychoanalytic thought and extend its applications to serve greater society, diverse cultures, and the public at large. The editorial board is comprised of the most noted and celebrated analysts, scholars, and academics in the English speaking world and is representative of every major school in the history of psychoanalytic thought.

Titles in the Series

Fragments of Trauma and the Social Production of Suffering: Trauma, History, Memory
Edited by Michael O'loughlin and Marilyn Charles
Relating to God: Clinical Psychoanalysis, Spirituality, and Theism,
by Dan Merkur
The Uses of Psychoanalysis in Working with Children's Emotional Lives,
edited by Michael O'Loughlin
Psychodynamic Perspectives on Working with Children, Families, and Schools,
edited by Michael O'Loughlin
Working with Trauma: Lessons from Bion and Lacan,
by Marilyn Charles
Hypocrisy Unmasked: Dissociation, Shame, and the Ethics of Inauthenticity,
by Ronald C. Naso
Searching for the Perfect Woman: The Story of a Complete Psychoanalysis,
by Vamık D. Volkan with J. Christopher Fowler
In Freud's Tracks: Conversations from the Journal of European Analysis,
edited by Sergio Benvenuto and Anthony Molino
Desire, Self, Mind, and the Psychotherapies: Unifying Psychological Science and Psychoanalysis,
by R. Coleman Curtis

Fragments of Trauma and the Social Production of Suffering

Trauma, History, and Memory

Edited by Michael O'Loughlin and Marilyn Charles

ROWMAN & LITTLEFIELD
Lanham • Boulder • New York • London

Published by Rowman & Littlefield
A wholly owned subsidiary of The Rowman & Littlefield Publishing Group, Inc.
4501 Forbes Boulevard, Suite 200, Lanham, Maryland 20706
www.rowman.com

Unit A, Whitacre Mews, 26-34 Stannary Street, London SE11 4AB

British Library Cataloguing in Publication Information Available

Library of Congress Cataloging-in-Publication Data

Library of Congress Cataloging-in-Publication Data Available

ISBN 978-1-4422-3185-6 (cloth : alk paper)

∞™ The paper used in this publication meets the minimum requirements of American National Standard for Information Sciences Permanence of Paper for Printed Library Materials, ANSI/NISO Z39.48-1992.

Printed in the United States of America

Contents

Acknowledgements

We wish to thank all of the authors for their contributions to this volume. Thanks to Jon Mills for accepting this book and its companion volume, *The Ethics of Remembering and the Consequences of Forgetting: Trauma, History, and Memory* in the New Imago Series. Amy King, our editor at Rowman & Littlefield , and her assistant Francinia Williams managed all aspects of the book production process with grace and ease. Special thanks to Dr. Errol Rodriguez from the Derner Institute of Advanced Psychological Studies at Adelphi University who has graciously assigned students from the master's program as graduate assistants. These students, Katrina Florio, Jacqueline Hrzich, Caitlin Lapine, Brendan McGann, Dolores Paul and Melodie Piciullo assisted willingly with proofreading, index preparation etc., and we are very grateful to them.

I

Fragments of Trauma

Fragments of Trauma

An introduction

Marilyn Charles & Michael O'Loughlin

In this volume, we offer you a kaleidoscope of perspectives that together highlight the problem of traumatic memory. Because trauma fragments memory, telling the story is impeded by what is unknowable and what is unspeakable. Each of the contributors tackles this problem of narrativizing memory that is constructed from fragments broken by trauma that has been passed along the generations. We hope that by offering you these fragments, a picture will emerge that illuminates the larger dilemma of the need for attending to precisely those whispers that most elude us within our own cultures, the chora that speaks from the side to invite a different narrative that opposes the prevailing myths.

When trauma is cultural as well as personal, it becomes even more invisible, as each generation's attempts at coping push the pain further below the surface. That pain, then, becomes increasingly ineffable, thereby haunting the succeeding generations. Each of the chapters locates the personal within the wider context of stories insufficiently told, leaving people suffering alone rather than available to one another for comfort, nurturance, and healing. We will see how cultural context helps to define what may and may not be known or spoken, and how meanings are shaped and altered as one culture interlocks with or avoids engagement with another. In each story, there emerges the theme of difference, a difference that cannot be encountered with interest, concern, or consideration but rather that turns back on itself and makes an accusation as though difference can only mean disparagement, violence, abhorrence, abjection.

In these chapters, we see themes emerge of knowing and unknowing—the terrible toll that trauma takes when there is no one with whom the trauma can be acknowledged and worked through. In the face of utter lack of recognition, what might be known together—thereby strengthening the bonds of human loyalty and compassion and respect—becomes hidden. As these meanings move underground, we hold on to them but cannot entirely believe in them. It is as though in pushing them beneath the surface we deny their validity. In that way, our failure to speak to these unaspirated truths becomes a betrayal of self and also of others. In the case of intergenerational and cultural trauma, we betray not only our ancestors but also the future generations who will come after us. In the face of unacknowledged trauma, we are confronted with the perennial choice of speaking or becoming complicit in our silence. What seems from one perspective protective becomes profoundly annihilative.

Psychoanalysis has highlighted the importance of a truth that can be spoken, one that requires an attentive, responsive, empathic ear through which to echo. Shoshana Felman (1995), for example, speaks of the importance of witnessing a truth that had not been spoken, of allowing truth to reveal itself through the process of narrativization. Opposing such difficult truths can, literally, drive a person mad, which makes it important that these various stories can be articulated and collected in this volume. History, like water, can pass over us, erasing the ridges and markers that might signal events that had occurred. With humans, however, unlike stones, what is erased at the surface level lives on in the unconscious, and it is precisely those memories that cannot be articulated that can most impede growth. At the extreme, the parent's unresolved mourning inhibits the child's ability to construct a coherent, resilient, sustainable self. When the trauma has occurred at the level of culture, the failure to recognize the markers of trauma can inhibit the development of an entire race, as we see in many of the chapters that follow.

In each chapter, culture is implicated in the possibility of a reparative or redemptive memory process. In some instances, the culture itself needs to face a heritage of injustice and invite a collaborative process in which members of the culture can find their own valued place. In other chapters, we see the theme of a failure of care come forward—whether in the inhibition of motherhood that makes care inaccessible, or the sequelae of those failures—that demand profound repair. We hope that, in reading these fragments that together describe ways in which people too often become isolated from one another at just those junctures when we need one another most, the reader will be reminded of the powerful thread that runs through our differences and joins us in the common dilemma of what it means to live well and with integrity, from wherever we are situated in the challenges facing us in relation to time and memory, reparation and redemption.

In the opening chapter, Marilyn Charles speaks to the fragmentation of life narrative that trauma can produce. Drawing on Raczymow's concept of "memory shot through with holes," as well as her own personal experience with trauma, and her ongoing clinical work with highly vulnerable sufferers, Marilyn offers a meditation on the gaps and losses that we encounter in people who have come in contact with trauma. Gaps and disruptions can be produced initially, Marilyn notes, not only through obviously traumatic violations of personhood, but also through disjunctures in parenting, and through the inheritance of affect regulation difficulties due to the presence of 'ghosts' of unresolved trauma from ancestors. Looking into her own history, Marilyn speaks of "the unaspirated voices of my ancestors," and speaks of her own hunger to create links, in the Bionian sense, that would allow the split-off parts of her family's experience to be pulled together into a new autobiographical narrative where traumatic fragments can be owned, examined, and claimed. Marilyn offers a poetic description of the process whereby painful narratives are split off, and slip out of the realm of speakable discourse, but nevertheless make their spectral presences felt, portending incomplete mourning:

> For example, I have a memory that is not my memory. It marks meanings that are compelling affectively, holding a truth that defies rational comprehension. I think I hold on to this memory in part as a way of trying to piece together fragments of a story to which I was exposed in various ways in childhood but that could not explicitly be told precisely because it could not be linked to my current experience. The exposure was to echoes of the past, the debris of wounds, slights, and losses that had not been passed along in the annals of our publicly acknowledged collective history. Such are the unaspirated lullabies that we croon unconsciously to our children through our own attempts at self-soothing. In some families, these melodies take the form of melancholic remembrances, transliterations of a dirge for a funeral that could not be attended. Likely, it was my intuitive recognition of the truth contained in these contours of meaning that made the issue of patterns so salient in my work and thought (Charles, 2002). The sense of a patterned order that might make inchoate meanings decipherable became a driving force in me (Charles, 2011a).

In the middle section of the chapter, Marilyn draws on Bion and Lacan to illustrate how the impasses and symptoms that adults experience are echoes of archaic object relational difficulties centered around earlier trauma. Illustrating her analysis with examples from her work at Austen Riggs Center with people with complex psychological difficulties, Marilyn illustrates the difficult path back to the narrativization of experience for people who have suffered emotional and cognitive fragmentation. She concludes with a case that illustrates the intimate process of engaging a patient with the gaps in his own narrative, the sequelae of unresolved mourning, and the process by which analyst and patient come together to try to establish an intersubjective rhythmicity that can allow the patient to pick up the narrative shards of his life and, in Winnicott's words. to "go on being."

Ingo Lambrecht, author of Chapter 2, is a clinical psychologist and shaman from South Africa who currently works with Manawanui Māori Mental Health Services in Auckland, New Zealand. His work is a powerful reminder of the cultural constitutedness of what we call trauma, and his chapter offers an exploration of how the dynamics of culture play out in a culturally informed, psychodynamic treatment setting. As Ingo notes,

> Working along the cultural-clinical interface holds complexities and depth that Western dominant mainstream mental health thinking, training and services often ignore or deny. It requires integrative thinking that reaches beyond the clinical taxonomies and formulations towards systems that involve political, historical and cultural processes.

Māori people still suffer the ongoing consequences of colonization, cultural genocide, and the comorbid effects of enduring poverty, all of which lead to the over-representation of Māori people in psychiatric inpatient units. The continued replication of colonial patterns of domination through the mental health services causes great complexity for clinicians and indigenous participants alike. Among the particular difficulties noted for clinicians is a tendency to idealize indigenous cultural values, and a failure to recognize the shadow side of these practices. In the case of the Māori, for example, while whanau (embeddedness of the individual in a web of familial relations) is frequently valorized, often little acknowledgement is given to the destructive and toxic aspects of Māori family relations. In addition, among Māori, sometimes a political correctness creeps in, whereby clients who are not viewed as sufficiently identified as Māori are discouraged from participation. Ingo offers illustrations from his work of how he seeks to approach individual clients "without memory or desire," to borrow Bion's phrase, so that he can work to understand the particular cultural positioning of each client vis a vis both Māori and dominant cultural values.

After a discussion that locates his clinical practice in relation to theories of intergenerational trauma, Ingo then explains te whare tapa wha (the house of well-being), a holistic model of Māori health or well-being:

> The Manawanui Māori Mental Health Service of the Auckland District Health Board has adopted the Māori mental health model. It is made up of the four pillars or aspects of well-being, namely whanau or the family health, hinengaro or mental health, tinana or physical health, and wairua or spiritual health (Durie, 2001). These four pillars hold the protective space of health and well-being for Māori and in fact, it could be argued, for most people. . . All four aspects of Māori mental health are considered to work together, and all aspects are necessary to achieve well-being. In this manner, Māori mental health is more clinically sophisticated than the common psychiatric medical model. This clinical-cultural interface avoids reductionism and also enhances clinical depth and range. In fact, all excellent clinical practice entails cultural and political sensitivities. Equally, in-depth and sensitive cultural work would include clinical aspects. Schizophrenia or psychosis within a Māori mental health model is not merely addressed as a brain disease or an intrapsychic process but requires the addition of understanding the whanau (extended family), the body (tinana), and the spiritual

(wairua), which leads to an integrated intervention to heal the mind (hinengaro).

Ingo devotes the concluding part of his chapter to a discussion of the holding function of wairua (the sacred), a process that requires explicit acknowledgement of ancestors, and the incorporation of uncanny, occult, and anomalous experiences, as well as altered states of consciousness that, in a Western paradigm, would be regarded as pathological. Ingo argues for a recognition in our trauma treatment practices of the importance of restoration of links to ancestors through the healing of tapu (taboo), and he concludes the chapter with a dramatic illustration of this process, working with a Māori client.

In *The Bluest Eye* (1970), Toni Morrison discusses the tragic racial identity crisis experienced by the young African American girl Pecola Breedlove, growing up in a racially polarized society, and with a mother, Pauline, who derives her greatest satisfaction from being a nanny and housekeeper for the white Fisher family. Cora Smith's work, reported in Chapter 3, brings this to mind with her exquisite description of the complex racial dynamics of the black servant class and the white master class in post-apartheid South Africa. How is the child of a black domestic servant, living in the home of a wealthy white employer, and often being actively "parented" by the white employer, to negotiate the treacherous complexities of class, race, and aspiration? This is the story Cora seeks to tell:

> As many black domestic workers currently live on the premises of their white employer's properties, they rear their children alongside their white employer's offspring. It is here that some employers have become involved with the children of their black domestic workers, from offering emotional and financial support, or sponsoring education at expensive private schools, to direct engagement with child rearing and allowing these children to live in their homes, be included on their holidays and be part of their families. It is at this interface that difficulties have emerged. In many instances, the biological mother/domestic worker has retained her status as employee while her son/daughter has transformed to "family member" of the employer's family, leaving a dangerous power differential between child and parent mirrored in the power dynamics between employee and employer. Although she is the biological mother, as domestic worker, she may be instructed to take orders, clean up after family members, and generally be in a subservient role in the presence of her own biological child. Her attempts at parenting can be undermined by the employer who has greater power and status in this context, leaving her child confused about his or her mother's role as parent and authority as well as his or her own role and position in this family context.

Cora draws on trauma theory, particularly intergenreatioanl trauma, writings on the politics of memory and forgetting, and critical discussions of race, particularly the workings of white privilege and dominance, to frame the complex processes at work here, and the ways in which the many versions of history are reenacted by the participants:

> employer mother, servant mother, and black child. A substantial portion of the chapter is taken up with a detailed discussion of the separate clinical treatments of three people inserted in just such a relation. There is a child, Brian/Karabo, his biological mother, the live-in domestic servant, Mavis, and the employer mother Emma, who for complex historical and personal reasons seeks to insert herself as Brian/Karabo's mother in loco parentis. Cora notes: "It is clear that each member of this tragic triangle is faced with unconscious enactments and demands as they grapple with their own pain at lack of recognition, feeling devalued, confused about their roles and identities. Each is struggling to establish him or herself as a subject, different but validated and worthy." Cora's story makes for compelling reading and offers a profound illustration of the interaction of political, historical, and familial dynamics as we live our lives from the tattered scripts we inherit, to paraphrase Fraiberg, Adelson and Shapiro (1975).

In Chapter 4, Jeff Moore and Christine Thornton explore the long-term consequences of institutional child abuse in Ireland. As the authors explain, from the middle of the nineteenth century through the end of the twentieth century in Ireland, collusion between the Irish Roman Catholic Church and the state led to the development of a series of containing institutions for children. These included orphanages, reformatories, and industrial schools. All too often these institutions became repositories for children who grew up in extreme poverty, as well as for children of unwed mothers, and children who were simply inconvenient. The numbers here were not insignificant, with in excess of 100,000 children committed involuntarily to such institutions, some for very lengthy periods of time, and some for their entire lifetimes. Jeff and Christine go on to outline the regime of austerity in many of these institutions, including harsh physical punishment, hard manual labor without compensation, and, of course, widespread sexual abuse, revelations of which exploded into the public arena in Ireland in the 1990s. The trauma these children experienced, the authors note, was greatly exacerbated by the exalted position the Catholic Church occupied in Ireland during that time. They note: "Victimised catholic children learnt that the perpetrators were God's representatives on earth and so, for some, submitting to the abuse was somehow 'God's will.' As a result some suggest, clerical abuse may create a special 'trauma bond' associated with the victim's faith." Jeff and Christine have spent considerable time working with the expatriate Irish community in the London Irish Center, and the second part of their chapter is a moving discussion of the experiences of Irish survivors of institutional child abuse, along with two detailed case studies from their work with immigrant counseling and psychotherapy (icap). While mindful of the resilience and adaptability many survivors, have shown, Jeff and

Christine's comments on the narrowed parameters that were placed on the lives of Bernadette and her peers is a sobering reminder of how deeply and pervasively the effects of the abuse entered their psyches:

> A theme evident in Bernadette's case study is that of re-institutionalization. After a childhood immersed in a total institution, the new-found freedom, or lack of structure, can be frightening. We know that many males joined either the Irish Defence Forces or overseas armies at some time during their lives. Some described the Army as providing security, shelter and a structured regime. Evidence suggests that many females sought other forms of institutionalized life in the UK, such as nursing or domestic service. Some managed to spend their whole lives working in one institution after another, often the only places familiar enough to be comfortable. As former residents of the schools age, some will again require institutional care. How these "homes" are constituted and managed will require careful thought by the Irish state, while those who have emigrated are likely to be cared for by people with little understanding of their past or its legacy.

Claude Barbre (Chapter 5) is interested in ghosts and he opens his chapter with a review of some of the contemporary literature on hauntology. Then he tells a personal story of a haunting:

> A personal example of such hauntings comes to mind. My mother's family were farmers since the 18th century near the eastern marshlands of South Carolina. When I was a child in the late 1950s, our family would drive from North Carolina several times a year to visit my grandparents' farm. I recall an ancient water mill not far from the county farmstead that dated back to the 1700s, and flecked among the edges of corn and tobacco fields, broken-planked shacks, their porches left to chance, half-listed into heavy seas of hedge and hyacinth. These dilapidated structures seemed to float from afar in the heavy air and dense humidity like swamped rafts on a tide of green shadows. Many of these fallen-down structures were at the end of overgrown dirt roads that bent into the distance beyond the field ponds and forest pines. My grandmother always told us not to stray down those old roads, saying there was "Nothin' there but snakes and bees and rusty nails—so stay away!". . .I recall one particular homestead that frightened me. It was surrounded by several moss-strewn oaks that seemed out of place in the broken pines, and although its front porch had retained frame enough to stand on, the doorless yawn of the dark entrance felt foreboding, forbidden, and uncanny. I remember a felt sense of unnamable presences there that the skin could see what the eyes could not. Each time I turned to run back to the pond and company, I would look over my shoulder expecting to see someone or some others watching me recede down the road. . . when I asked my grandmother about the house at the end of the dirt road, she would say sternly that I was not to go there, and that it was only the skeletal remains of an empty farmhouse of no use to us, to the world, to anyone anymore. Years later I visited my great aunt in a nearby town, and as we talked we eventually

> came around to stories and memories about the farm. I asked her about the far house at the end of the road by the two live oaks, telling her that it had always frightened me as a child, and that the ruins had always left me feeling uneasy. She looked at me hard. "I am surprised your grandmamma let you play there considering. All those ruins were old slave quarters, and in decay" she said curtly, "and I'm not surprised you were frightened of that particular house—you should have been frightened of that house." She paused, looking beyond me like someone was approaching but was not. "A lot of people died in that house" she said softly. She mopped her brow and rocked slowly. "My, My," she said in rhythm of the rocking. I could see her eyes brimming. "That was the birthing house used by the slaves long before I was born," she said, "and later some people lived in it, but mostly it fell empty. Many births and deaths were there. Other unspeakable things happened there as well, things not to be talked about. Now it is gone, gone, torn down, the planks used for the barn furnace to cure tobacco."

Claude use this story, and associations that are evoked in him by three recent features films on aspects of African American experience to explicate a sophisticated theory of trauma transmission and on the role of *revenants* in psychic life, drawing on the writings of Freud, Ferenczi, Abraham and Torok, and many contemporary psychoanalytic theorists of trauma to illustrate the ineluctable presence of history and of spectral presences in the human unconscious.

Apart from outright genocide, forcible removal, and the invariable cultural genocide that frequently accompanies it, appears to be one of the most nefarious techniques invented by humans to enforce subjugation. While examples can be found in every continent, none is perhaps more poignant that the case of the forced removal of indigenous children as part of the process of colonial expansion and appropriation of native lands. Examples abound from North America, but a remarkably similar process occurred in Australia in the twentieth century. Aboriginal children were forcibly removed, placed in custodial schools and then forced to live out their lives as domestic servants and farm labors for white Australians. Victims of this process, which caused catastrophic cultural and psychological damage, have come to be known in Australia as the Stolen Generations. Australian American author Janice Walters turns her attention to the effects of this process in Chapter 6.

When British colonizers arrived in Australia there was no recognizable national governance structure, as Aboriginal people had adopted a tribal structure. The British declared the doctrine of *Terra Nullius* to authorize the appropriation of lands that theoretically had never previously been subject to sovereign writ. After sketching out some of the historical background, Janice uses the writings of Freud and Klein to offer an understanding of the complex racial dynamics that pervade contemporary Australian society. Janice addresses the psychological legacy of the

Stolen Generations directly in the second half of the chapter. Drawing on intergenerational trauma theory, as well as on her own conversations with survivors, as well as field research by others, Janice offers a devastating portrait of the suffering that continues to travel down the generations of Aboriginal Australians, though, as with any comprehensive account of trauma, stories of resilience and courage reminds us of the indomitability of the human spirit and the dangers of essentializing all responses to trauma as the same. Here is an illustration of the intergenerational effects of the Stolen Generations

> Intergenerational trauma exists within this family. There is the trauma of being a stolen child, the guilt of being the child that remained and the burden of living with an emotionally unavailable mother. For Alice, Tara's youngest daughter, the process of transposition (Kaplan, 1995) has occupied her personal space and the need to be her mother's protector has impacted her identity. Alice married her non-Aboriginal childhood sweetheart and they have three children. Tara and Alice were bound by unspeakable terror when the skeleton that was locked tightly in the closet was revealed. Alice left her children with her husband believing they were better without her. She escaped to drugs and was full of anger, rage and shame. As she acted out these emotions, she was constantly re-traumatized and this ultimately led her to turn her anger and rage inward and to succumb to self-hatred and severe depression. The outside world became the enemy and she was unable to leave her mother's side. She became the unavailable, dead mother (Green, 1986) for her children. The ancestral ghosts (Fraiberg, Adelson and Shapiro, 1975) are now impacting a third generation. Tara's son, Ben, who was taken as an infant, is addicted to drugs. He, his wife and children are often homeless and his children are suffering the direct consequences of his traumatized past and their trauma laden present. On occasion, he and his family moved in with Tara. He brought drugs with him and this caused Tara and the other children to become distressed by his behavior, especially her sons who had given up drugs. She feels guilty and questions her competence as a mother, because the last time he asked she would not allow him stay with her. She no longer has contact with him and continues to worry about his wellbeing, wishing she had not lost him as an infant. . .

Janice concludes with a discussion of resilience and of the importance of creating healing structures that are respectful of Aboriginal cultural practices in promoting resilience and well-being.

In Chapter 7, Marie Hansen addresses the discursive construction of premenstrual syndrome (PMS) and its failure to recognize what she terms the "subtle trauma" at its core. Marie critiques the medicalization of menstruation within phallogocentric Western cultures and laments the severance of the connection between a woman and her body caused by the insertion of logos—and particularly, the logos of didactic education and the marketing discourse of the "feminine care" industry. Marie, however, begins by contextualizing the issue in personal terms:

> Growing up, I was given the message that menstruation is an unspoken secret, a bodily function that must remain profoundly concealed. Great lengths were taken to insure it remained hidden from view—from learning how to secretly carry menstrual products to school, to attempts to silently rip open tampons while in a public restroom. Not even other girls could be alerted to its presence. Used menstrual products were not casually disposed of like other garbage, but wrapped tightly in wads of toilet paper before being tossed into the can. No sign of blood was allowed to show, even in the trash. Although my mother never explicitly taught me this, it was a message that I received nonetheless. We do not speak of menstruation; we do whatever we can to keep it hidden. This is the same message that millions of western girls receive each year, making this rite of passage a silent one. This silence is perpetuated not only by the wider culture, but also within the home, in the strange silences of our mothers as they usher us quickly from the bathroom cupboard into a lineage of female shame.

Marie challenges the supposed biological etiology of PMS, and argues that, in view of the diverse range of presentations for what the West calls PMS, across cultures, it is best thought of as a culture-bound syndrome. As the quote above suggests, Marie views shame and silencing as key factors in the discursive construction of PMS as a shame-based disorder, and she argues that the kind of closeted sexuality education offered in schools, abetted by a femcare industry that has a vested industry in manufacturing a "hygiene crisis," is designed to keep women in the closet. This leads to the creation of a secretive culture that, as intergenerational trauma theory suggests, contributes to the unspeakability of menstruation, and hence to the perpetuation of the marginalization of a key component of women's experiences of their own bodies. In the final section of the chapter Marie invokes the work of Lacan, Kristeva, and Irigaray to retheorize women's subjectivity, and poses the question as to how, in a culture apparently obsessed with women's bodies, women can actually reclaim their corporeality and become feminine on their own terms.

In chapter 8, Karen Lombardi and Avigail Gordon explore the psychodynamics of trauma. They begin with a review of the origins of trauma theory in the psychoneurosis of hysteria and they argue that Freud's notion of confronting the possibility of death is a key concept in traumatic experience. They discuss Ferenczi's confusion of tongues, and then move on to Winnicott's fear of breakdown. Winnicott offered an understanding of fear of death not as literal, but as fear of "phenomenal death," and they note the cumulative trauma that can come from losses that shake the fundamental core of our subjective experience. Drawing on psychodynamic and intergenerational trauma theory, they address the failure of symbolization that gives the unspeakability of trauma its power. In the middle section of the chapter they use narratives from *Zeitoun* and *What is the what*, recent works by Dave Eggers, to illustrate the socio-political situatedness of trauma in the world. Here is an illustration of the unspeakability that is at the core of such suffering, what the authors refer to as "metaphorical death":

> Deng runs as softly and quickly as he can, his thoughts running with him: "Oh God of the sky, keep me safe tonight. Keep me hidden, keep me quiet. Run again. No. No. Yes, run. Must run to people. Must run, find people, then rest. Run now. Oh God of rain, let me find water. Let me not die of thirst. Quiet. Quiet. Oh God of the soul, why are you doing this? I have done nothing to ask for this. I'm a boy. I'm a boy." (pp. 97–98)

His boyhood ripped away from him, he finds people, some of them kind, some of them tormenters. Banding together with other young boys who must take charge of themselves, they trek to Ethiopia in hopes of escaping their war-torn land. On the way, he suffers terrible hunger, attacks by villagers, and the loss of many of his comrades through murder, starvation, collapse, and suicide. He speaks of the traumatic effects on the boys in his group, including the absence of narrative:

> One boy would not sleep, at night or during the day. He refused to sleep for many days, because he wanted always to see what was coming, to see any threats that might befall us. Eventually he was left in a village, in the care of a woman who held him in her lap, and within minutes he was asleep. There was another boy who dragged a stick behind him, making a line in the dirt so he would know his way home. . .A boy named Ajiing was even stranger; he saved all the food given to him. He saved the food—groundnut paste, mostly—in a shirt he had brought with him. He would only dip into the shirt once a day, to retrieve enough of the gummy mixture to cover his first three fingers. He would lick these clean and then tie his shirt back again. He was preparing for many weeks without food. But most of the boys only walked and spoke little because there was nothing to say. (p. 147)

Karen and Avigail conclude the chapter by reporting on an empirical study that attempted to assess the core subjective experience of trauma and then conclude with a clinical case example that illustrates both the complexity and resilience of struggles with internal loss.

Combining her deep musical sensibility and her passion for working with persons with significant psychological distress, in Chapter 9 Trisha Ready explores the uses of self-selected music on patients' capacities for containing their suffering. Her chapter consists of three in-depth case studies that, while not being dogmatic about the origins of psychosis, illustrate the embeddedness of psychosis in complex family dynamics and deeply rooted trauma and emotional communication difficulties. While psychiatric hospitals serve a vital function in managing acute psychosis, Trisha notes that they often come up short when it comes to providing a containing environment in which the precipitants to acute psychosis can be understood:

> A psychiatric hospital is an effective and essential resource for addressing acute and critical psychological states. At the same time, it is not the ideal holding environment (Winnicott, 1971) or psychosocial environment (Kegan, 1982), wherein young people such as Kevin, Steven or Lyaconnia could rehabilitate effectively. Kevin perceived the hospital as secure but not psychologically safe. He found relief from suffering but he could not sufficiently trust hospital staff to embrace treatment. I believe that a clinical professional working with these three young people, using music or another safe portal of communication, would need to establish a meaningful connection to help them to resolve shame and trauma from childhood and inherited generational traumas, as well as the social failures they were experiencing in adulthood.

Trisha's case studies are reminiscent of the work of Frieda Fromm-Reichmann and Harold Searles in her capacity to stay with acute suffering and to persist in seeking to create a state of reverie through music with patients whose acute suffering can easily elicit the opposite from a therapist:

> Just after finishing chart notes, I saw a frantic Lyaconnia standing at the nurses' station. Her pink hair was tangled and askew; she demanded in a loud voice: "Where is that woman who was trying to kill me?"
>
> "There you are," she said, "Were you trying to kill me with that song? What were you doing?"
>
> At that moment, all theories and aspirations about music's ability to serve a mothering function and to facilitate emotional expression evaporated. My initial response was panic: a combination of transference of Lyaconnia's terror of annihilation, mixed with my own fear that the hospital might terminate these pilot music sessions.

In illustrating the complexity of severe psychic distress, and its embeddedness in relational trauma, Trisha's work poses troubling questions about the predominance of narrow biomedical understandings of psychosis, and of exclusively pharmacological treatments—not to mention incarceration in prisons—as the predominant societal response in the United States to severe psychiatric distress. Trish invokes, for instance, the work of Yrjo Alanen and colleagues in Finland, work that involves both engaging the entire network of community supports (friends, family etc.) in assisting in the treatment process, as well as respectful engagement with persons with psychiatric distress to assist them in articulating the narratives of distress that are concealed in the enigmatic communications of psychosis. While using music as one particular therapeutic vehicle, Trisha's work underlines the importance of caring, receptive human beings who are willing to assist trauma sufferers in articulating the effects of their distress.

Cate Osborn, a clinical psychologist at Gunawirra, an organization that provides services to Aboriginal families in New South Wales, Australia states the problem of interest in no uncertain terms in the opening paragraph of Chapter 10:

> The true depth of the impact of dispossession, violence, loss of culture and separation from family on the lives of Aboriginal people, then and now, is largely unacknowledged. This is a traumatic legacy for both Aboriginal and non-Aboriginal Australians. We have not been able to come to terms with the cruel acts perpetrated by our recent ancestors. Instead, via a range of psychological and cultural devices, we have turned away from the reality and replaced it with a picture of heroism, benign "settlement" of "unclaimed" land, brave battles with the forces of nature, the "convict made good" and success against all odds. Our knowledge of the past remains unintegrated with our feelings about it. In this very important and fundamental way, we are unknowing.

The specific topic of Cate's paper is a therapeutic support group she runs for young Aboriginal mothers to assist them in reclaiming the mothering wisdom so cruelly usurped by forcible removal and conquest. She describes the terrifying emptiness many of the mothers experienced at the unbounded space the group offered, and Cate takes us with her on the journey as she assists these young mothers in getting in touch with the "the-baby-in-the-mother," as a vehicle in assisting them in developing attuned responses to their children. She speaks of the incredible dependency needs and vulnerabilities of the mothers, and uses Shengold's concepts of too muchness and not enoughness to illustrate the relation between the emotional needs of the mothers and their capacities for receptive parenting, in a manner highly reminiscent of the renowned work of Selma Fraiberg and her team with mothers similarly haunted by tragic and painful ghosts. A large portion of the chapter is taken up with three clinical vignettes, one of which featured the story of Anne:

> Anne is the mother of an eight-week-old girl and has come to the attention of child protection authorities due to her history of substance abuse and concerns that the baby is not putting on weight. Her partner is in prison and she lives with her mother with whom she has a very conflicted relationship. The little girl has been diagnosed as having "failure to thrive". Several years ago Anne had a little boy who died of SIDS and her oldest daughter is in the care of her grandmother. Many levels of support and treatment have been provided, as the pair is seen as being seriously at risk. As well as attending the group, Anne sees a psychotherapist at the Centre and is visited regularly at home by health workers. The baby needed a feed and Anne's breast milk supply is low so she is supplementing with bottle feeds. As she gave the baby the

> bottle, I saw that Anne had her knees slightly apart, so that the little bottom of the baby lying across her lap dipped down between them. The baby's neck was arched back and her head unsupported. Anne was not looking at the baby at all and she had a faraway, blank look on her face. I felt more alarmed as I noticed that the baby was not protesting at all, no struggle, no cry, just weak little sucks on the bottle. There was an urgent need to intervene but I was concerned that Anne could very easily feel criticised and undermined. I felt that I was watching a disaster unfold and was close to becoming a "failure to thrive" as a therapist. I simply said that I could see she was in another world and I wondered where she was. She didn't answer me but she did look at the baby and draw her knees together to make a safer lap. A little later I noticed her holding the baby firmly and protectively and making eye contact. I took this opportunity and said, "she looks very comfortable with you holding her like that." This time, Anne responded with a smile and continued to hold the baby lovingly. The baby had already experienced too much not enoughness (specifically, not enough milk or firm holding and connection with her mother) and, overwhelmed by unthinkable anxieties (Winnicott, 1965/1990) or presymbolic dread (Mollon, 1998), had given up. One of the striking features of this interaction was that Anne appeared to have no concern or awareness for the baby's needs and I (along with my colleagues) held all the worry. At this time, she was not able to approach awareness of her own failure to thrive as a mother, nor her own early deprivation. She could not let herself imagine her baby's state of mind as this would have put her dangerously in touch with her own experiences. Having already lost two children, she was terrified of connecting to another.

Cate concludes with a discussion of how through work with an Aboriginal artist, many of these women found a way to begin to narrate their experiences and thereby experience release from what she calls "the deadened space of trauma."

In Chapter 11, Annie Stopford offers a psychosocial perspective on trauma in African American neighborhoods in the United States, reporting on field work with community workers in Baltimore, Oakland and Philadelphia. Annie is clear that symptoms of trauma are quite prevalent in distressed neighborhoods, and that these symptoms need to be understood and responded to not in terms of individual pathology, but in terms of the ways in which U.S. society has constructed life in ghetto communities, and in which traumatic response represent an "enactment of national historical and contemporary relational trauma." Annie uses the word ghetto advisedly, following Loic Wacquant in defining a ghetto as an enclosed space "geared to the twin mission of isolating and exploiting a dishonored category." While Annie is a psychoanalyst, she is critical of the "racist, essentialist, and colonialist discourse underpinning psychoanalytic responses to interraciality and intercultural and postcolonial contact zones," and so she offers a carefully contextualized and self-reflexive analysis of what might be called life in urban ghetto communities in the United States She is critical, too, of the almost complete absence of interest within the academic community in the workings of intergenerational trauma among African Americans. Kirkland Vaughan's chapter in this volume is one exception to that trend. In a section of Annie's chapter entitled "American apartheid," she describes the systemic effort made by American institutions to marginalize African American communities, and she goes on to document the disproportionate levels of gun violence and incarceration among young Black men in the United States today. Although Annie is careful to recognize pockets of resilience, her conversations with community workers leave no doubt about the extent of the problem:

> When I went back to working with kids 15 years ago, I'd never seen kids make a will. I'd never seen kids talk about how they wanted their funeral. I'd never seen kids go to a cemetery to visit 10, 15 graves of their friends. This is a new normality where their mortality is part of their identity. (Millie Burns)

> You see sometimes the hopelessness in young people's eyes, people who are 14, 15, 13, 16, who seem to have lost all hope. (Rob Reed)

> We've had conversations like where do you think you're going to be in three years and when you look at them all they've got is a blank stare... in their neighborhood all they see is black people struggling, the addicts, the winos, the gratification they get from the now is all they're concerned about because they don't see a future. (Gardnel Carter)

Annie worries particularly about the segregation of ghetto communities, the normalization of death and injury in such communities, the indifference and othering of mainstream communities, and the complexity of the lives of young people, saturated in a material culture, yet living lives deprived of material accoutrements:

> There are a couple of things that I think the average American doesn't understand about the lived reality for young people in communities like East Oakland or disinvested communities any place in America. Poverty isn't just about not having; poverty is about the juxtaposition of not having to affluence. . . so the anger that people feel isn't because they don't have, it's because they see that other people have more than any one person can reasonably consume in a lifetime and that's where the rage comes from. (Olis Simmons)

In the concluding section of Annie's emotionally challenging argument she poses the possibility of urban violence as a public health issue and of pursuing a trauma-informed approach built around issues of empathy and understanding of the sociopolitical constitution of events, rather than on reactive punishment and incarceration:

> I think what trauma-informed care really teaches at its most basic is empathy. It is an understanding of how other people are living and suffering and I don't think people in the criminal justice system really focus on that because we generally focus on the victim rather than on the whole process, on the whole community, on the whole society. (Rob Reed)

As to what might be done, Annie's tale of the difficulty that emerged in the partnership between Johns Hopkins University and the ghetto communities of West Baltimore offers a clear indication that partnerships that are not built on respect, understanding, and allowing local community members the opportunity to chart their own futures are destined to fail. The tragedy is that when such approaches fail, all too often further blame is heaped on the local community for not playing the game on the master's terms.

People all over the world entrust their children to teachers and to schools for a significant portion of their lives. Though hardly trained for the emotional stresses of crisis, teachers often instinctively create holding environments for children, and sometimes they lay their lives on the line to protect children. This was evident in its most harrowing form during the school shooting in Sandy Hook, Connecticut, when teachers literally lay their bodies on top of children to try to shield them from bullets. We have seen it too in Nigeria, Uganda, Afghanistan, Pakistan etc., where teachers inisist on pursuing education for girls despite the threat of imminent annihilation. In Chapter 12, Richard Johnson and Michael Salzman raise important questions about the welfare and status of children in our world, and also question the degree to which we prepare teachers for the crisis roles that are, all too often, thrust upon them. Drawing on Rich's work in Afghanistan as an educational consultant, Rich and Michael begin with a reminder of the terrible risks to which children are exposed, though, indeed, these concerns are applicable to children in a multitude of conflict zones around the world:

> Over the course of the past 30 years, the war in Afghanistan has been the world's longest-running major armed conflict. In just 3 years' time (2009–2011), more than 1,000 Afghani children were killed or injured in conflict-related violence. Of these children, 128 were killed by armed opposition groups; 55 were killed and 199 injured in land-mine accidents and 131 children lost their lives in aerial bombings conducted by international military forces in 2009 (Child Victims of War, 2012). In 2010 alone, a total of 1,396 children were killed or maimed, an increase of 35% from 2009 (Child Victims of War, 2012). According to the United Nations, 2011 was the deadliest on record for civilians in the Afghan war, with 3,021 people killed, averaging 8.3 deaths per day. Although the number of Afghan civilians killed dropped 36 percent in the first four months of 2013, as compared with the year before. The violent acts

> continue, with physical, psychological, social, and emotional costs for children and adults alike.

The authors go on to note the profound effects childhood trauma has on future well-being. These effects are greatly exacerbated in countries where there are minimal mental health services. In Afghanistan, for example, in 2011, there were only two psychiatrists, neither of whom was engaged in clinical practice, and only a handful of other mental health professionals. Furthermore, in scrutinizing teacher preparation curricula in both the United States and in Afghanistan (which emulates Western technocratic teacher preparation), they found no address at all to understanding the emotional welfare of children, nor even a nod toward assisting teachers in preparing for the emotional consequences of mass trauma events, or for the kinds of individual traumas which children will invariably experience due to family conflict, school bullying, membership in subjugated or stigmatized groups, and so on. Even in affluent Western countries there will never be enough mental health workers to address all of the emotional needs of children. Preparing teachers to understand the developmental effects of trauma, the importance of holding and containing environments, and the critical importance of narrating painful experience would seem essential. How much more must this be so in countries where there are, at best, skeletal mental health services, and the only concerned and committed professionals to which many children are exposed are their teachers?

Judy Atkinson pioneered the development of an undergraduate training program on trauma and healing in Aboriginal communities at Gnibi College of Southern Cross University[1] and she also wrote the indispensable book *Trauma trails: Recreating song lines, addressing intergenerational trauma in Aboriginal communities.* In Chapter 13, Judy invites us into the complexity of trauma work that is informed by western understandings of trauma but that is finely modulated by Judy's immersion in Aboriginal worldviews, and particularly the notions of *Dadirri* and *The Dreaming,* key concepts in aboriginal epistemology. In her chapter Judy begins by locating the soul wounds in Aboriginal communities in terms of the ravages of colonialism, and the devastation caused particularly by the severance of social bonds, and the separation of Aboriginal people from the sources of sustenance provided by kinship with nature and communion with ancestors. Judy offers interview excerpts that reveal the depth of Aboriginal pain and suffering, including the transmutation of suffering into the body, and the intergenerational transmission of trauma. These excerpts also reveal the depth of Judy's work and the complex transferential issues that emerge in work with deep trauma, nowhere better illustrated, perhaps than in the following remarkable story:

> A young man I was working with entered a "dissociated" state, coming towards me as if he had been drinking (which I knew he had not). He

> had taken on the persona of a woman as he stumbled around the room. He appeared to be searching for something. This lasted for approximately 20 minutes. After a while, he entered another state in which it appeared that he was giving birth. Elders present at that time were upset until I told them to stay with what was happening, and just allow the story, whatever needed to emerge, to unfold. Again, after some time, he settled down to rest, and some hours later entered another state of "dissociation." This time, I could not understand what was happening, but he was extremely distressed. Over a period of eight hours, he acted out three separate and distinct stories. When the night ended, I was exhausted and in crisis. What was happening here? Was I responding in the right way to what was presenting? They told him that the stories he had felt and acted out belonged to his great grandmother: she had been raped on the frontier; she gave birth to a girl child; the child was taken from her by the state; and she spent the rest of her life wandering around that area, trying to find her child, and drinking to sustain her distress.

In *Beloved* (1987), Toni Morrison invites the reader to confront the awfulness of slavery by contemplating the mental state of a mother who would prefer to kill her children than see them returned to slavery. It is a difficult book to read because of Morrisons's insistence that we not avert our eyes. Kirkland Vaughans tells us in Chapter 14 that despite the enormity of slavery in American history, it is nonetheless the family secret of America, the skeleton in the closet. Kirkland notes that it is not a secret because it is erased or banned from memory, but rather because we have managed to keep slavery "on the periphery of the national imagination." His chapter offers an exploration of the collective memory of U.S. slavery, and its psychic consequences. Part of the difficulty with the slavery story, as with all histories, is that the stories that get told, are necessarily privileged, and Kirkland is seeking to tap into a collective memory that is too often unnamable and unspeakable. In the first paper of the chapter Kirkland offers some excerpts from published slave narratives to evoke the kinds of ruptures and losses that slavery entailed, but that are too often denied by contemporary society. For example, consider these vignettes from Harriet Jacobs and Fannie Moore:

> In her autobiography, Incidents in the life of a slave girl (1861/1987), Harriet Jacobs shares her personal thoughts on this issue after being threatened by her owner Dr. Flint, who stated, "These brats will bring me a handsome sum of money one of these days. . . I thought to myself that, God being my helper, they would never pass into his hands. It seemed to me I would rather see them killed than have them given up to his power" (p. 80). John Boggs, who was formerly enslaved, echoed similar views: "That is what our people dread the most. The idea is like this. When a man goes out in the morning, he may have a wife and a parcel of children, and maybe when he comes back at night, he will find nobody who will tell him anything about them. If a woman ask

> about her children that had been sold, she would be whipped or knocked and slashed about." (Blassingame 1977, p. 422)

> In recalling her childhood, Fannie Moore spoke of the love and protection displayed by her mother. She states, "I never see how my mammy stan sech had work. She stan up for her chillum tho. De ol overseeah he hate my mammy, case she fight him for beatin her chilun. Why she get more whippins for dat den anything else. She had twelfe chillum." (Berlin 1998, p. 133)

Kirkland goes on to document the hopes and disappointments of Reconstruction after the American Civil War, and shows that while African Americans relied on Black churches for support, they insisted that all reference to old Negro spirituals, the "Sorrow songs" referred to by W.E.B. DuBois, be removed from the hymnals, as African Americans attempted to purge slavery from the collective memory of the Black community. This inclination toward amnesia was more than abetted by white dominant society, which erected numerous memorials to the fallen dead on both sides of the Civil War, but failed to acknowledge the calamity of slavery, and indeed continued to perpetuate regimes of discrimination against African Americans. While Kirkland acknowledges the considerable successes African Americans have achieved in U.S. society, he remains convinced that the legacy of slavery has not been successfully redeemed. In the concluding section of the chapter Kirkland poignantly documents his own racial heritage, and the tragic split that occurred in his family between the light-skinned line and the dark-skinned line, and he shows how the ghost of slavery has colonized parts of his own mind:

> I recall sixty years ago my father's painful confrontation with the past when a picture of my White maternal great-grandfather arrived in the mail. He violently threw it in the garbage, saying that no picture of a White bastard that had preyed on Black women would ever hang in his house. My White great-grandfather had eighteen children by several different Black women, and their descendants are largely divided by color cleavage to this day. Those who pass as White, and those who are very light, go by his surname of Arbuthnot, and the others, including me, are known as Vaughans. It is only now that I am finally able to reach back into that garbage and reclaim that picture as a part of my heritage and as a part of my own identity. . . A confrontation with my own son challenged my own comforting illusion that I had worked through these issues in my multiple therapies and two personal analyses. The fact of the matter is that the topic of race and the trauma of slavery was never broached in any of those therapies. In chastising my young son David over some misdeed, I asked him "if he was out of his cotton-picking mind." He responded with the perplexed inquiry, "Dad, why would my mind have to be cotton picking?" I apologized to him and assured him that it was my mind that was still "cotton picking,"

> not his; that some injuries just take an awful long time to heal, especially when we are unaware of our wounds.

In the final section of the chapter Kirkland takes up clinical matters, and particularly the ways in which the clinical encounter, mirroring U.S. society, often maintains a taboo on matters to do with race, and the terrible legacy of slavery on both White and Black Americans.

In the concluding chapter, Michael O'Loughlin and Barbara Ann McLeod pose the question of pedagogy. In a world of health care delivery where definitions of suffering are increasingly operationalized, and clinical strategies are quantified and measured against pseudo-objective criteria, what are the prospects for creating in the next generation of clinicians a therapeutic sensibility that will increase their receptiveness to suffering and their valuing of not knowing over insight? In the first half to the chapter Michael describes a doctoral level clinical psychology course founded on principles of depth pedagogy, and inspired by the pioneering work of Shoshana Felman who articulated a Lacanian vision for depth pedagogy. A key principle of this pedagogical work is that if students are to develop a capacity to bear witness to trauma, the pedagogical address of the course muse be to the unconscious. Michael notes:

> My course began—as all of my courses do—with an autobiographical invitation. The students could not be expected to embark on the journey from any point other than their own starting points. To emphasize that that this was a journey where the only tools required were humility and a capacity for exploring their own vulnerability, I began by sharing with them some aspects of my own autobiography. I shared some writings (Appendix: Week #2, O'Loughlin, 2007b, 2009) that revealed my own struggles seeking to ward off—and ultimately to embrace cautiously—the nameless anxieties and formless dread that have been my constant companion probably at least since birth. I purposely chose for them writings by Marilyn Charles, Dori Laub, and Annie Rogers (Appendix: Week #3, Charles, 2003; Week #9, Laub, 1992, 1995; Weeks #11-#12, Rogers, 2006) because these writers model beautifully the necessity of inner work and an address to the unconscious as key to mutative depth-therapeutic work with people who have suffered greatly.

My hope was that witnessing this kind of inner journeying among seasoned therapists would give them permission, if they needed it, to view the learning experience I offered as primarily a space for internal work, rather than a place for intellectual understanding and omniscient interpretation. Students were invited to write to me weekly, and this became a private conversational space that many students used to begin working though the interaction between their own unconscious archive—the "tattered script" of the inheritances littering their archive (Fraiberg, Adelson & Shapiro, 1975)—and the evocative testimony to which we bore witness. The heart of the course, then, was extensive viewing of videotaped testimony in a wide variety of narrative styles—, each one chosen for its capacity to produce the kind of emotional impact that creates an address to the unconscious. A variety of formats was used in order to trouble the possibility of students either taking comfort in privileging a certain presentation as what should constitute trauma narrative, or in privileging any one type of narrative as representing a prototypical victim tale.

Barbara Ann was a student in Michael's class in Fall 2013, and because her final written meditation for the class appeared to resonate so well with the course objectives, Michael invited Barbara Ann to share her deeply personal and thoughtful final written reaction to illustrate the power of this invitation to depth work. Barbara Ann's reflection exemplifies the kind of working through that sophisticated therapists do as they engage with metaphors from the field, mull over clinical puzzles from their work with patients, and, especially, engage in thoughtful reflection on the place of suffering and loss in their own subjective formation. Barbara Ann's work deserves to be read as a whole, but these two excerpts convey the potential of depth pedagogical work in the hands of a thoughtful and introspective clinician:

> Several years ago, I made a collage in response to the story about my father losing me and as a response to his princess story. I called it *Smoke Signals*. This image is confounded with another beach memory of a family bonfire. In it, I was also around three. Apparently, we did not have a permit to have a beach fire, and the authorities came to tell my parents to extinguish it. I remember the confusion of adults buzzing around, our dogs running and barking, and horseflies swarming. My mother was trying to pour sand over the fire and a horsefly flew at me. I tried to run away from the fly, but instead I ran into the fire. As my mother screamed, I jumped over the embers. This work represents a habitual retreat from pain to an inner landscape free from other humans and the irony of running from danger but becoming more embroiled in it. This beach represents a space I have created within myself, both a longing for connection and the belief that it will not come.

> Analytic work requires we push past our clinical impasses through a continued circling back to our histories and sore spots. It demands the recognition that it will at times be more than we can bear. My efforts here to approximate a transformation have merely pointed toward a source, a potential narrative of subjectivity. That effort alone exceeded my capacity. These words are still frozen and my story stuck somewhere I cannot access. It is a pain that can make it hard to write, hard to work, hard to come close. It is a life's work and an imperative if I am to live it, if I am to learn to remember and not to forget.

If you have an appetite for more reading in this area we hope you will consider consulting the companion volume, *The Ethics of Remembering and the Consequences of Forgetting: Essays on Trauma, History and Memory, an interdisciplinary volume* edited by Michael O'Loughlin, and published simultaneously by Rowman & Littlefield.

NOTES

1. http://scu.edu.au/coursesin2014/?action=matrix&command=matrix_temp_load&spk_no=301090\

REFERENCES

Felman, S. (1995). Education and crisis, or the vicissitudes of teaching. In *Trauma: Explorations in memory*, ed. C. Caruth. Baltimore & London: Johns Hopkins University Press, pp. 13-60.

Fraiberg, S., Adelson, E., & Shapiro, V. (1975). 'Ghosts in the nursery, '*Journal of the American Academy of Child Psychiatry, 14,* 387-421.

Morrison. T. (1987). *Beloved*. New York: Vintage

Morrison. T. (1970). *The bluest eye*. New York: Vintage

ONE

Trauma, Fragmentation, Memory, and Identity

Marilyn Charles

Traumatic memory is often spoken through the gaps, the ellipses, through what is missing rather than what is present. This is the realm of the *memory shot through with holes* of which Raczymow (1994) writes so poignantly. We are born with a safety valve, a system through which we become numb to pain, inured to meanings that are unmanageable. This safety valve enables us to survive the unsurvivable. After my son was killed some years ago, a researcher who studies dog attacks came to speak with us. She told us that those who survive such attacks report having become detached from their bodies, which enables them to watch the occurrence without feeling it. That information was comforting to me, helping me to torture myself a bit less through the repetitive reliving of what I had imagined my child had suffered (Charles, 2008). For those who do survive such horrors, the challenge is to try to make sense of that which has not quite yet happened because we were not there to experience it (Winnicott, 1974).

Historically, psychoanalysis has provided a means by which the unknown can be encountered, by focusing its lens on hidden or unconscious aspects of experience that reveal themselves in subtle, displaced, or coded fashion, whether through dreams, enactments, or slips of the tongue. Through his willingness to look beyond the more comfortable readings of his experience, Freud provided a method by which one might peer beyond the veil of convenience or convention and discover more about one's history and motivations. Trauma, however, is particularly elusive because it is insufficiently encoded in memory and thus is often known primarily through the ellipses or gaps that mark a conspicuous absence (Charles, 2012). Lacan had a particular resonance to these missing elements of experience. Through concepts such as 'empty speech,' he helps to attune us to the missing affect or meaning that might hide behind something that has the appearance of conversation (Lacan, 1953/1977). In this way, he highlights our responsiveness to melodies that may be sufficiently familiar in form to speak to us if we can allow ourselves to be resonant with them.

Trauma poses particular difficulties for memory and identity. To the extent that we cannot tolerate the onslaught of experience in the moment, that experience remains to be encountered, an obstacle we would like to pass over rather than passing through. I know all too well the urge to move past the haunting melodies that feel too entangling, like the siren's call that tantalizes and terrifies. From a distance, these calls can have great allure but, as we move closer to the truths we resist, panic can ensue. Such are the tensions we encounter in relation to intolerable truths. At times, these truths are hidden in shallow graves, near the surface of our memories, as in the vignettes too tinged with shame that have been smoothed over and disguised. At other times, however, the memories have eluded encoding. They are "shot through with holes" because the scenes they represent have been caught only in fragments, in the harsh glare of a light that strobes and barely captures wisps of whatever was unfathomable. When we try to peer more closely, it is hard to distinguish between memory and confabulation. Is this truly our history or merely a story we are fabricating for some motive yet unclear?

When I encounter this type of memory shot through with holes in the consulting room, it is inevitably a difficult and perplexing experience, in part because it is rarely entirely clear whose memory it is that bears the holes. I may feel as though there has been some gap in my attention, because I thought I had been listening but suddenly find myself uncertain as to how to make meaning of whatever is being said. It is as though I have been caught napping, and I feel taken off guard and embarrassed by this gaffe. Over time, however, I have come to view that particular experience as a marker of a story that is being told and untold, a story that in itself contains gaps such that I stumble and have trouble locating myself in the moment. Increasingly, it is the teller's indifference to the gap that perplexes and engages me, the disinterest that presumes that I should be able to follow the story as it is being told. In such moments, if I can recover myself sufficiently, I inquire into the gap. I say that I think I missed something, could the teller please go back so that I can catch up? As we go back through the story, we can then both be more attentive to the story as it unfolds and disappears, and trace together its relative coherence. These joint efforts help us to notice where the gaps might be and to discover what our willingness to inquire into them might reveal.

If we think about the dilemma of the individual who is left to try to make sense of a story that does not make sense, we can understand why she might pass over the gaps and run toward something that has the appearance of coherence. Particularly when the family context has been one of intergenerational transmission of trauma, the need to construct a story in spite of having little solid ground becomes compelling. The solid ground of identity is built in the context of a relational engagement that is reliably attuned enough for the child to be able to find herself in the eyes and the mind of the parent. In the absence of the solid ground afforded by attuned parenting, the child must learn to survive in the world as she encounters it, and to negotiate the shifting terrain. Insufficient grounding complicates that challenge, and leaves fault lines in the self that result in greater vulnerability to stress across the life cycle (Parkes, Stevensen-Hinde, and Maris, 1991).

The attachment literature shows clearly the importance of parental coherence in the development of a secure self, and also ways in which trauma can disrupt coherence (Van Ijzendoorn, Schuengel, and Bakermans-Kranenburg, 1999). Disjunctive or frightening parental behaviors are experienced as especially traumatic to the young child who needs to be able to approach the parent as a secure base during times of distress. Even with otherwise caring and attentive parents, disjunctive behaviors of this sort can lead to the type of disorganized attachment described by Main and Hesse (1990), characterized by a breakdown in a more generally organized and consistent strategy of affective regulation. In such instances, we find that a self has developed that coheres sufficiently to function relatively effectively under normal conditions but is not sufficiently integrated to hold together under strain. Notably, these types of disjunctive and frightening parental behaviors have been linked to families who are struggling with unresolved trauma or loss. Pushing past mourning rather than facing it takes a toll. The parent who cannot face his or her own traumatic past turns that blind eye to the attendant difficulties faced by the child, as well. In turn, the child registers the difficulty but, without the words to speak about it, the unrecognized knowledge often lodges in the body itself, through the symptom (McDougall, 1989).

Davoine and Gaudillière (2004) have worked extensively with individuals for whom unresolved intergenerational trauma has manifested in disrupted life narratives and psychotic symptoms. These authors highlight ways in which trauma speaks across the generations in coded form, speaking whatever has become unspeakable within the family. Psychotic symptoms often capture in concrete terms the metaphors and family myths that are affecting family members without being overtly recognized. Unacknowledged and unresolved, traumatic truths haunt us, distorting and undermining development. Like a tree trying to survive under harsh, austere, or toxic conditions, our very adaptations can undermine our development. Our resilience enables our roots to grow, but the very roots that anchor us to the ground can become tangled, brittle, and vulnerable under harsh conditions with insufficient care.

Disorganized attachment is associated with lack of coherence in autobiographical memory, resulting in conflicting narratives that are difficult to integrate into a cogent whole (Main, 1991). As mentioned previously, these types of incoherent, conflicting memories are often the result of unresolved traumatic experience, fragments that have not yet been sufficiently integrated to become part of the story of one's life. Instead, these fragments tend to erupt in odd, incomprehensible ways, as gaps, intrusions, or symptoms that elude conscious understanding. Such discontinuity makes it difficult to recognize one's own strengths and weaknesses and, as such, to rely on and make use of internal resources with consistency. Adaptive development is thereby constrained and impeded. When families resist recognizing the extent of the trauma that has taken place, it is difficult for the child to be able to recognize the contexts within which the experience or symptom might be understandable. There is no Third perspective from which to evaluate truth claims in relation to one's own experience or values (Muller, 2011). It is that perspective that psychoanalytic psychotherapy can afford.

Inchoate, ineffable memories that have not been integrated tend to haunt us, often taking the form of the "ghosts" in the nursery, described so compellingly by Fraiberg and her colleagues (Fraiberg, Adelson, and Shapiro, 1975). Looking back, I can recognize that my history has been haunted by the unaspirated voices of my ancestors. I can see ways in which I pieced together fragments from the bits of stories I was told and also from the books that chronicled histories similar to my own. There was a hunger in me for these fragments that was difficult to make sense of until psychoanalysis and attachment theory afforded me ways of thinking about the adaptive purposes of being able to unlink the bits that are fundamental but seem too painful to put together (Bion, 1977), and also the importance of being able to establish those links in ways that could both be bearable and make sense. The price of turning a blind eye is very high.

I think that my family survived, in part, by keeping various bits separate. As such, there were peculiarities that seemed idiosyncratic and meaningless unless read through the lens of traumatic losses. Psychoanalysis has long held respect for ways in which idiosyncrasy can mark important meanings. Bion (1977), for example, noted the constant conjunctions, the ways in which meanings can be attributed to elements of experience that tend to co-occur. Much like Bion's (1977) conceptualization of the constant conjunction, Lacan (1974-75, 1975-76) used the term sinthome to mark the particular ways in which meanings are knotted together for an individual. By using this term, which he took from the Latin form of the French word for symptom, Lacan invites respect for the layers of meaning that can be embedded in a symptom if we can attend to the ways in which the meanings are knotted together for that individual. Through this term, Lacan designates an idiosyncratic solution to the problems of existence that then also becomes the key to the meanings displayed and implied by that solution. Rather than merely a symptom of pathology, the sinthome is an important puzzle waiting to be explored, a key to the individual's mystery, a key that may be essential if one is to approach any real understanding of the idiosyncratic reality of the other.

Through this conceptualization, Lacan invites us to consider the possibility of a disjunctive reality that is not necessarily deranged or maladaptive but rather can be a stabilized and adaptive resolution for the individual. He points to a place where the clinician can stand in relation to an individual who is clearly and firmly embedded in his own reality, one that does not easily coincide with that of the clinician. The idea of the sinthome potentially makes visible such meanings, or at least recognizes that there is a logic, a structuring at work that may be too idiosyncratic to be comprehensible outside the realm of that internal logic. From this perspective, there is no substitute for the willingness of the clinician to intuit and inhabit, as best we might, the universe of the other. This is also true of our relationships with our own lives and experience. Poet Adrienne Rich (1978) notes that we are perennially faced with the challenge of facing unpleasant truths or else denying essential aspects of our own reality or, as she puts it, to take ourselves more seriously or die.

Taking oneself seriously when the memory has been shot through with holes is no easy challenge, when the feeling of truth may be strikingly at odds with what can be known with any reliable certainty. Invalidated, implicit truths often have the feel of the uncanny, inviting a sense of certainty that may be at odds with what is otherwise known or accepted. When such implicit meanings cannot be verified, they may go underground, where they can remain safe from further assault. Meanings that cannot be validated within the family system as it stands are particularly problematic because they are likely to be actively opposed (Boszormenyi-Nagy and Framo, 1965; Bowen, 1978). Such disjunctions can be literally crazy-making.

Human beings are born into meaning structures that are utterly embodied, assimilated through our attempts at 'reading' the nonverbal communications that assail us through sound, image, touch, taste, and smell. The truths of the young child, therefore, are grounded in these primary meaning structures, without initially being conditioned or constrained by formal language or logic. Socialization processes impose upon us complex rules regarding what may or may not be recognized, acknowledged, or spoken about. Over time, we learn to turn a blind eye to the inconvenient truths that may not be known within the family, community, or other social structure. Survival hinges on being able to adapt to these conditions of social existence but the price can be high in terms of our ability to recognize and rely upon our own internal resources and, at the extreme, to put together a coherent narrative through which we can understand ourselves and others.

For those whose families have survived trauma, adaptation has often meant forgetting truths that have become inconvenient or at odds with whatever story needs to be told. Those truths, then, remain nascent and largely unrecognized, and yet they do tend to emerge in the hearts and minds of future generations. For example, I have a memory that is not my memory. It marks meanings that are compelling affectively, holding a truth that defies rational comprehension. I think I hold on to this memory in part as a way of trying to piece together fragments of a story to which I was exposed in various ways in childhood but that could not explicitly be told precisely because it could not be linked to my current experience. The exposure was to echoes of the past, the debris of wounds, slights, and losses that had not been passed along in the annals of our publicly acknowledged collective history. Such are the unaspirated lullabies that we croon unconsciously to our children through our own attempts at self-soothing. In some families, these melodies take the form of melancholic remembrances, transliterations of a dirge for a funeral that could not be attended. Likely, it was my intuitive recognition of the truth contained in these contours of meaning that made the issue of patterns so salient in my work and thought (Charles, 2002). The sense of a patterned order that might make inchoate meanings decipherable became a driving force in me (Charles, 2011a).

In this incorporated memory, my uncle is a young child standing at the doors of a synagogue, holding his father's hand and feeling as though those doors were locked to him forever (see Charles, 2001). This event, at which I certainly was not present, has a particular vividness in my mind because it seems to encapsulate affective tones that had always been present in my family but for which there had been no words. Much like myth, these types of vignette metaphors capture complex meanings that we intuitively recognize as important but cannot yet sufficiently unpack to discern their complexities. Metaphors enable us to hold the relationships among the elements in mind so that we can work at various threads without entirely losing sight of the whole. Psychoanalysis affords a logic and a method whereby we can make sense of these complex configurations over time and begin to locate them in relation to one another in narrative form. Having undergone this process herself, the psychoanalyst is thereby afforded a means for making use of her hard-won insights with others as they struggle to make sense of their own histories and prehistories (Charles, 1999a, 1999b).

Essential to this process is the presumption of the essential meaning underlying tenacious bits of affectively charged content that emerge in a symptom—or in the sinthome. That affirmation becomes an important counter to the denial of meaning that occurs by way of the intergenerational transmission of trauma, a denial that can be massive and pervasive. As pretense comes forward and the masks more effectively cover the pain, neglected family truths become less decipherable. And yet, like fingers rubbing old stones, we find ourselves captured, smoothing out the tangles of threads we are caught in and cannot escape. Paradoxically, it is only when we can relax from the struggle and embrace these truths that we can begin to decipher their meanings. Ambivalently, we sit on the laps of our ancestors, hungry for the stories that might, perhaps, hold a key to the mystery. Like the prized needlepoints buried by my family during World War II, we must have some sense of where the family truths are buried, and why, in order to begin to locate them and shake them loose from whatever has covered them over. These buried treasures have their own beauty, carrying traces of whatever has been lost in the annals of the collective unconscious.

At the Austen Riggs Center, we collect as much family history as possible because of our recognition that missing parts of an individual's narrative can be highlighted in their prehistory. Recognizing the contexts that have framed the story can help us to reintegrate bits that have been lost along the way, and thereby to introduce cogency into a story that has eluded telling. In these efforts, it is important to have a companion alongside—the type of witness afforded by psychoanalysis—who can both empathically enter the experience and also remain separate. The analyst is in the paradoxical positon of standing as a witness for an event that has not yet happened, in ways that can invite into being a person who has not yet cohered. In Felman's (1995) words, "The narrator herself does not know any longer who she was except through her testimony . . . In itself, the knowledge does not exist, it can only happen through the testimony: it cannot be separated from it" (p. 53). For the traumatized individual, finding sufficient space within which to encounter herself and bring together the bits and fragments that have remained unlinked is an essential precondition for narrativization to occur. It is through this process of narrativization that the subject emerges.

When the family narrative is shot through with holes, it can be difficult to keep faith with one's own experience. For me, it has been difficult, at times, to keep faith with my own sense of a reality that is opposed, in part, by patriarchal systems that valorize the rational realm (Charles, 2011b). As a result, theory that has affirmed the validity and value of learning from experience (Bion, 1977) and the truths gleaned from the nonverbal realm have been very important to me. Stern's (1985) work on the developing child, for example, shows the crucial role played by affect in structuring nonverbal meanings. Describing affect as "the supra-modal currency into which stimulation in any modality can be translated" (p. 53), he notes ways in which affect registers in us and is recognized directly and consistently, across modalities. Affect has its own prosody, melodies we recognize implicitly when we encounter their various manifestations, whether through changes in tone, touch, or gesture. These affective prosodies are highly patterned and are intuited directly, like music (Charles and Telis, 2009; Trevarthen, 2005), so that:

> the dimensions of experience such as shape, texture, and location in space, all come to carry meanings beyond any specific representation. We learn to 'read' nuances of line in works of art as in faces. The slope, the turn, the sweep, the rhythm: each in some important way seems to mirror the type of affective prosody described by . . . theorists. . . Although we may not be able to decode them in verbal terms, these types of meanings become reference points [that speak to us quite directly and evocatively]. (Charles, 2002, p. 111)

Tomkins's (1982) affect theory afforded me a way of making sense of these implicit truths and patterned meanings that seemed to have their own particular prosody. According to his conceptualization, each affect has its own clearly discernable melody that is directly evocative of the feeling it marks. Shame, for example, is evoked when our interest, concern, or curiosity is broken into suddenly. That nexus is the same place that Bion (1977) points to in highlighting the crucial choice between seeking knowledge or avoiding it. When our natural curiosity has been punished, it becomes easier to turn a blind eye. Shame not only casts down our eyes, it also amplifies emotion, leading to the magnification of particular scripts that carry meanings forward in ways that can preclude reflection or integration (Tomkins, 1979). In Bion's terms, meanings become 'saturated,' as though all is known and there is no point in inquiring further.

Because shame amplifies affect, it inhibits reflective function and also inhibits curiosity and engagement (Tomkins, 1982). This is the critical moment Bion (1977) refers to in terms of the constant choice between seeking knowledge or turning a blind eye. Shame not only impedes social interactions, it also makes it more difficult for the individual to sustain curiosity in the face of novelty and to take the types of risks required for new learning and the experiences of mastery that build positive self-regard and help to develop our metacognitive capacities (Fonagy, Gergely, Jurist, and Target, 2002; Lysaker et al., 2010, 2011). Metacognition involves the ability to obtain sufficient perspective to distance oneself from one's immediate experience and thereby to reflect on one's own thoughts and feelings in relation to the thoughts and feelings of others. Shame inhibits our ability to look outward and thereby closes down the perspective necessary in order to make sense of self in relation to others.

In many ways, the more traumatic the memory, the greater the inhibition against rational reflection. As Matte-Blanco (1975) notes, there is an optimal balance between thinking and feeling. As affective intensity increases, logic is driven, not by rational thought, but rather by the nonverbal, more highly associative system of meanings we term primary process. As distress increases, the nonverbal memory system is enhanced, leading to fight or flight responses and decreased reflective capacity. In interviews with individuals who dissociate under stress, we can see the types of cognitive slippage under strain that make it difficult to sustain a coherent narrative, particularly in relation to traumatic events.

Recurrent experiences of shame can result in scripts that are linked with the attendant affect and so tend to be triggered by that affect when it is present. Inherent in these scripts are expectations of humiliation, defeat, and victimization that are self-validating and therefore resist moderation or repair but rather can result in a tendency to ruminate over past and current failures (Tomkins, 1962, 1979, 1982). These expectations are, in part, self-validating because they inhibit reengagement with others in ways that might ease the distress or alter the expectation. Shame invites us to turn down our eyes, inhibiting our interest and enjoyment in relation to the "perceived barrier to positive affect with the other" (Tomkins, 1982, p. 378). In this way, shame breaks the interpersonal bond and initiates withdrawal and avoidance of the very interpersonal engagement that might prove reparative, and invites, instead, it invites an inhibition against knowing oneself that makes it difficult to learn from one's experience in ways that enhance adaptation and self-knowledge.

Such inhibitions often result in the pretense of certainty in ways that preclude inquiry, creating a disjunctive narrative that makes it difficult for the clinician to build a story in her own mind. In such circumstances, we can find ourselves reframing a story that is only partly told, trying to impose cogency on a narrative that may not yet have sufficient substance to cohere. Inquiring into the gaps helps to illuminate that which has been hidden, or at least the contexts in which these elusive facts lie. When truths are too difficult to encounter, working in the displacement can be useful, as a way of uncovering truths from sufficient distance that they might be easier to bear. Altering perspective can enable us to change the frame sufficiently that we might be able to catch a glimpse of whatever has become invisible (Parsons, 1986; Symington, 1983), those tangled threads of meaning that become easier to negotiate as they come more clearly into view. As Bion (1990) notes, at times we need to deepen the darkness sufficiently for hidden truths to reveal themselves.

For the child who has grown up in a family in which there are strong prohibitions against knowing, finding oneself can be severely impeded. Lack of acknowledgement is profoundly destabilizing. Studies show that when individuals are offered discrepant data, they can become confused even as to the contours and limits of their own bodies (Petkova and Ehrsson, 2008). In this way, the fundamental discriminations between self and other that are a precondition for self-knowledge are impeded. Such difficulties impede the child's ability to make adaptive use of the mirror neuron system through the type of embodied simulation through which emotional experience (and its avoidance or inhibition) is communicated directly from parent to child (Gallese, 2009).

The parent caught up in unmourned losses can be inaccessible to the child (Field, 1992). Because of the importance of both imitation and interaction in the early months and years, the failure to engage the parent has significant consequences for the child's social and emotional development (Tronick and Reck, 2009). The child who cannot elicit responsiveness from the parent tends to become preoccupied with self-soothing at the expense of interpersonal engagement (Tronick, 1989). The inability to find the mother one seeks is a terrible rupture for the young child, who is born unable to fend for herself and is even more dependent upon the parent as a secure base during times of stress.

In order to be able to come into being as a separate self, the infant must first be able to find himself in relation to the parent. Winnicott (1971) suggests that the important developmental challenge with which the infant is faced in making distinctions between himself and his environment depends on his ability to find himself in the mother's eyes. In his terms, what the baby see when he looks into the mother's face is, primarily, himself. "In other words the mother is looking at the baby and what she looks like is related to what she sees there" (p. 112). In this way, the attuned mother reflects back to the child a reflection that is also a recognition of the child's experience in a way that fits, that matches. The preoccupied parent, in contrast, may reflect "her own mood or, worse still, the rigidity of her own defences" (p. 112). In Winnicott's formulation, when the parent cannot reflect the child back to himself, the focus shifts and the child becomes preoccupied with getting something back from the environment. When the mother's face is not a mirror, "perception takes the place of apperception, perception takes the place of that which might have been the beginning of a significant exchange with the world, a two-way process in which self-enrichment alternates with the discovery of meanings in the world" (p. 113). Through this shift away from self and self-development, the child's creative capacities can begin to atrophy.

Developmental theory culled from infant observation, helps to make sense of some of the deficits that accrue through this lack of parental responsiveness. Studies show that infants are not merely responsive to and imitative of the gestures of others but that they also come to anticipate and invite a continued exchange. Nagy and Molnár (2004), for example, found that "newborns spontaneously produced previously imitated gestures while waiting for the experimenter's response" (p. 54). They termed this capacity *provocation*. Such observations underscore the importance in human development of being able to elicit responses from the parent in ongoing exchanges of intersubjective rhythmicity or musicality (Trevarthen, 2005). Trevarthen (2009) notes how profoundly and integrally knowledge of self and other is built through interpersonal engagements. "Meaning grows by confirming and 'cultivating' innate rhythms and values, in communication, and it is fabricated with aesthetic sensibility for harmony and beauty, in relationships that are regulated by moral—pride and shame, trust and mistrust, confidence and fear of failure to agree or cooperate" (p. 512). These threads of meaning become firmly integrated and entrenched in our awareness, much as Lacan depicts in his idea of the sinthome, the ways in which meanings become knotted together for us all. When the knots have holes, it is difficult to put together a story in ways that make sense and afford resilience.

Crucial to the development of resilience are the parental responses to misattunements, as depicted in what Beebe and Lachmann (1994) have termed moments of rupture and repair. When trauma has left holes in the parent's experience, however, there is a tendency to dissociate or become preoccupied in moments of high affective arousal that can leave the parent unavailable to the child. In this way, intergenerational transmission of trauma occurs through the holes by which traumatic experience is reenacted in the parent-child dyad. Notably, the dissociative response to trauma is particularly toxic in the parent-child relationship. Whereas the preoccupied parent shifts the focus away from the child's needs and experiences toward that of the parent, the dissociated parent presents the child with a terrible absence that cannot be penetrated and is difficult to endure. "If the mother's face is unresponsive, then a mirror is a thing to be looked at but not to be looked into" (Winnicott, 1971, p. 113). This child does not so easily learn to attend to the parent to ensure his own survival but rather is pulled toward further emptying out when overloaded with emotion, making it even more difficult to develop and sustain consistent and organized strategies for affective self-regulation. In the absence of such strategies, environmental strains and pressures that otherwise might merely present bumps in the road can become calamities.

In such instances, what we can see is a lack of contingency, the failure of the child to have an impact upon the other, and so to be able to find himself in the engagement. "The infant's perception of contingencies, in conjunction with an optimally contingent environment, organizes the infant's expectation that he can affect, and be affected by, the partner, a crucial origin of the experience of effectance" (Beebe, Rustin, Sorter, and Knoblauch, 2003, p. 826). Holes in the family story that lead to moments of nonrecognition can have far-reaching effects because disruptions in the experience of contingency is so profoundly disorganizing for both parent and child in ways that echo back and forth between them (Murray and Trevarthen, 1985).

When working with individuals whose parents were neither available nor emotionally present during times of stress, there is a hole not only in terms of factual memory but also in terms of the self as the subject of the story told in autobiographical memory. Lacan notes ways in which we are inevitably in search of the lost subject, trying to find the self that can be both authentic and valued. This situation is complicated when the locus of self-experience has not been firmly established. Beyond affective or cognitive instability, there is evidence that unresolved mourning can be passed along even more directly, that this type of "traumatic dislocation" can register directly in the infant's body (Goldsmith and Cowen, 2011). For the young child, direct contact with the parent's attuned touch, whether through literal body contact or through the acknowledgement and expression of feelings of sadness that have been repressed or inhibited can help to diminish symptoms and repair relational difficulties (Goldsmith and Cowen, 2011).

The parent's ability to acknowledge his or her own affect makes an important delineation for the child regarding the locus of the bad feeling. To perceive difference as well as similarity is a crucial precondition for self-development, grounded in the early attunements between child and parent (Beebe, Rustin, Sorter, and Knoblauch, 2003). Both cognitive development and neurological functioning depend on "the capacity to perceive what is familiar, what repeats, and what is invariant" (p. 809). That knowledge helps the child to abstract common properties and form generalizations, cornerstones of language use and abstract thinking. Tronick and his colleagues (1998) suggest that the affective quality of these engagements are also important, noting the dejection and disorganization observed in the child who cannot invite the mother's responsiveness in contrast to what they term a "dyadic expansion of consciousness" (p. 295) observed in responsive and engaged mother and infant pairs. In contrast to the toxic effects on social, emotional, and cognitive functions in infants of depressed mothers (Tronick, 1989; Weinberg and Tronick, 1998), the child with a responsive mother is able to learn through his engagements with her because of what can be created between them.

We are born with the capacity to recognize and respond to these primary forms of behavior that have meaning beyond the particular modality in which they occur. Stern's (1985) work, in particular, shows the ways in which our capacities for cross-modal matching provide a language of nonverbal meaning and metaphor through which the capacities for analogy, distinction, generalization, and abstraction can evolve. These capacities are essential for self-development, as we come to recognize our commonalities with others and also whatever makes us particular and unique. Notably, Stern highlights affect as the locus for these nonverbal meanings, through the forms of feeling that are exchanged. When all goes well, the playfulness of these exchanges afford not only the basis for self-development but also enhance our natural curiosity and interest in further exploring the world in which we live. In positively toned engagements, disjunctions tend to increase the duration of the behavior, whereas in negatively toned disjunctions, there is a tightening of the exchange (Jaffe et al., 2001). In effect, in positively toned exchanges, room is left for further playfulness, whereas when the exchange begins to go awry, there is a pull back toward homeostasis that also invites greater inhibition and rigidity.

Research into early nonverbal prelinguistic communications between parent and child shows us the power of these nonlinguistic forms of communication that we draw on when language fails. Trevarthen's (2009) work shows the melodic, amodal nature of these more primary communications in ways that help us understand the intuitions we rely on without necessarily understanding the mechanisms by which these meanings are transmitted. Bion (1977) was prescient in this regard, noting the ways in which common sense is culled from the confluence of data gleaned from the various senses taken together. He also recognized the importance of passion in terms of the emphatic validation that is at times afforded by our intuitive senses. While it is important to be able to reflect on these sense impressions when they occur, rather than merely reacting, it is also important to take them seriously, to make use of these countertransference reactions so that we might discern what our less conscious registers are trying to tell us. The ability to take our experience seriously, to reflect on it and make use of it, is built upon those early engagements through which our knowledge of self, other, and categorical distinctions has been built (Blum, 2005).

When working with individuals whose memory has been shot through with holes, knowledge of ways in which these holes develop can be crucial. Such individuals often come to an impasse at the threshold of adulthood, when the child is taxed with the challenge of consolidating a self without sufficient internal resources to be able to negotiate this difficult transition. The need to move beyond imposed desires, to discover one's own desire, is at the core of Lacan's ideas about the psychoanalytic process. For the child who cannot locate the parent sufficiently to both identify and deidentify, it can be difficult to find his or her own way. Much like Winnicott's (1971) observations about the 'use of the object,' the adolescent must be able to kill off the parent and find him still standing. The parent who cannot recognize the particularity of his or her child impedes this process of separation and individuation.

Complicating this issue, for those for whom trauma has impeded the process of meaning-making, perception may override the possibility of apperception. For such individuals, there is a move toward the concrete such that words are no longer layered and meanings cannot be investigated (Charles, in press). Although language can be clarifying, it can also be eviscerative, glossing over, excessively simplifying, or eradicating meanings. The longed for "answer" can preclude any possibility of finding answers, in the plural, to the complex and layered questions hidden behind the holes in memory and in speech.

In my work with individuals waylaid by trauma, I have learned to have a deep respect for what is at stake in relation to Lacan's idea of the Subject caught by the desire of the other. Because our parents' ideas about us precede our entry into the world, we internalize that world as it is given, accommodating to these demands even while also rebelling against them. For the child who cannot ask fundamental questions that are relevant to who he is in relation to the family in which he has been born, it can be difficult to determine "what I want." That conversation, then, tends to be subverted into "what I have learned to want," a position that the psychoanalyst opposes through her efforts to try to locate each patient in relation to his desires and values, rather than her own. With those who have become lost in relation to themselves, whose memories have become shot through with holes, this is the salient challenge, how to locate the subject in relation to the internal and external chaos that could override him at any turn. Particularly difficult is the opposition invited by the challenge to the family myths that can feel as though greater self-knowledge can only be attained at the price of losing one's place in one's family.

From a Lacanian perspective, at the heart of the psychoanalytic process is the seeking of the lost Subject. Because we become lost in relation to that Desire of the Other that holds the possibility of an unlimited Jouissance, the challenge is to accept the inevitability of lack—of limit—and to recognize and articulate our own particular desire. The analyst, too, must face that challenge and try to avoid being caricatured as the One who Knows, so that she might invite the patient to become the Subject of the inquiry. From that place, the work can focus around locating a desire that is truly one's own, without filling in or glossing over the holes, but rather leaving room for the person to discover himself as best he might. From this perspective, learning to be respectful of the holes and all they represent, both in terms of terrible losses carried forward and also in terms of the pragmatic difficulties of trying to build a life and identity in spite of them, becomes a worthy challenge in its own right, as the clinician struggles to contain the pain such work inevitably entails.

When working with someone who is struggling to make sense of the fragments that have not yet been put together, it is particularly important to be able to recognize the sinthome—the problem in context—so that we can respect what is being offered while also breaking into what are often concrete and universal presumptions of meaning. If we think of Bion's (1967) admonition to abjure both memory and desire, we can, at times, come to a relative quiet place with the patient through which we can accept the gaps sufficiently to be able to hear their echoes and recognize their speech. Psychoanalysis affords the individual the opportunity to construct a more coherent narrative from the fragments that had resisted integration. This type of autobiographical construction provides the individual with an opportunity to restructure events in ways that add coherence and stability to the sense of self in relation to the external world (Sommer, Baumeister, and Stillman, 2012). For example, I worked with a young man who had become severely waylaid in his development. When I met him, he was in his early thirties and had been unable, in spite of stellar academic achievement, to consolidate a professional career or satisfying interpersonal relationships. Rather, his increasingly desperate attempts to keep his mind focused on achievement had resulted in an amphetamine-induced psychosis that had left him unable to sustain independent living.

When I met him, "Greg" reported having little interest in feelings or relationships. He described himself almost like a robot or automaton. One might have given him a diagnosis of Asperger's Syndrome and thought little more about it except for bits from his life narrative that invited further inquiry. Notably, Greg's only sibling had died shortly after birth. Greg had been conceived soon after that event. Remarkably, the mother reported having no feelings of either sadness at the loss of her first child or anxiety during her pregnancy with her second. That curious lack of affective engagement brought up questions regarding unmourned losses with the family. In taking the family history, we could recognize those unmourned losses, even though they seemed insignificant to family members. My work with Greg therefore initially focused around my interest in the feelings he purported not to have and in putting together a chronology in which his symptoms might make sense. He had a keen intellect and, in spite of the intense and debilitating shame he experienced when someone knew something he did not, he was able to be interested in the various developmental challenges that had not been met in his early years.

As I tracked for Greg his experiences so that they made sense in a developmental context, I became a new object who did possibly have his needs and feelings in mind. In spite of his wariness, he could find me in this place of reflective interest. Much of our preliminary work involved my conjectures about what it must have been like for him at various stages of his early life, given the context and characters he described. As we began to build a narrative in which we could locate a child with needs that were not being recognized, and developmental milestones that were not being achieved, Greg began to have a sense of himself as in need of further maturation and development rather than feeling impossibly flawed. From this perspective, he was better able to tolerate the shame and narcissistic injury he experienced when learning something from another person. He was able to recognize that our work together also carried the potential for growth and perhaps even pride, though we could recognize that real learning for Greg only occurred when he could take in some bit of information and make use of it himself.

In spite of his determination, it was difficult for Greg to imagine that our work might have any benefit for him. Our conversations seemed so remote from his reality that it was difficult for him to find a link. That remoteness was difficult for us to break through. Particularly important, then, was the moment when I tracked for him the experience of shame, as a cut breaking into a moment of pleasure or interest. That conceptualization related directly to his own experience, inviting him to be curious about shame as an experience-near phenomena, an interest he was able to bring into his conversations with peers. Engaging in conversations that mattered to him, that he felt implicated in, helped to reconstitute the interpersonal bonds that had been broken so long before, helping to attenuate the shame while also inviting greater connection and understanding with those peers. If we think of the child's relationship to learning described earlier, we can recognize that it is precisely this experience-near learning that includes both affect and reason on which self-development rests, and we can also recognize the importance of breaking through the shame so that real moments of meeting can occur.

Also crucial in our work together was Greg's ability to recognize the potential value of understanding his dreams, and to bring the dreams into the consulting room. The extent to which the other's mind becomes suspect is a particular hazard when working with schizoid or paranoid patients, making the dream an important opportunity to enter together into a more reflective space. Much as analysts from GIFRIC in Quebec (Apollon, Bergeron, and Cantin, 2002) describe, a dream can be a pivotal point in working with patients who struggle with psychosis because the dream can be recognized as one's own production in ways that the symptom cannot, particularly for those who are profoundly paranoid.

Greg's dreams helped us to locate him in relation to his fears and to his desires. His initial dreams were cloaked and hidden, first an intricate and elaborate desk with important papers in it that belonged to his father, and then a dream of a girl who was "not my Mom" and people in costumes. As the months went by, he began to bring in dreams that brought to life his paranoid anxieties, including a dream about me in which I was characterized as well-intentioned but misguided, highlighting the very real dangers he experienced with me in relation to his awareness that I might believe I knew something but could, in fact, be wrong. Two minds were needed in order for Greg to be able to provide his own corrections to my inevitably limited perspective.

Greg was excited about that dream about me, seeming to sense its importance. In his associations to the dream, we could see his difficulty in even considering relying on me, and we could also see him grappling with his awareness that he cannot necessarily rely on the products of his own mind. Bion (1977) talks about the importance of bi-nocular perspective, much as Lacan (1977) refers to the importance of the 'Third' that brings us out of an autistic or symbiotic relationship with self and other into a confrontation that includes the constraints of culture and the social order. For Greg, this perspective could only be found by allowing himself to think about my perspective as not only different than his own but also as potentially useful or reliable and fallible. He had hoped that by not letting people in, he could keep himself safe but he increasingly recognized that his isolation fed his persecution. And yet, how to live in a world with other people remained a dilemma, particularly in relation to his terrible dependence on his mother.

Greg's inability to know himself in relation to his mother left him feeling as though closeness with another person would utterly submerge and annihilate him. His mother—and individuals who reminded him of his mother—were experienced as dangerous objects to avoid or pacify. He first avoided his mother entirely but then learned to manage her by keeping the telephone at arm's distance when he could not tolerate her speech. This experience became an important vignette metaphor regarding his need for connection with the other while also needing to be able to control what is taken in, how much, and when. That metaphor began to figure prominently in our work, helping us to work through the difficult moments when even my acknowledgement of his success could take away the very vitality he had managed to build. The ease and speed with which pleasure could be banished was remarkable, enabling us to recognize that this was a far more pervasive pattern for him. Similar in form to the prosody of his experience of shame, in terms of the disruption of his own curiosity or pleasure when faced with another's mind or feelings, we learned to recognize that even positive recognition imposed the other upon him in ways that could destroy his fragile connection with his own inner pride or pleasure. In that process, I had to be able to recognize myself as the well-intentioned but dangerous other of his dream in order to have any idea at all about the terrain in which he needed to learn to navigate.

The capacity to recognize a problem in context has been crucial to breaking into Greg's concrete and universal presumptions of meaning. His ability to look inside himself and recognize aspects of his own inner world, in terms of the feelings and the ideas and experiences to which those feelings are connected, has helped Greg to build the metacognitive capacities so crucial to building a solid self and making his way in the world. Critical in this process was his ability to engage sufficiently with another person who had him in mind to be able to repair some of the damage that had been done in those early years when his parents had been too preoccupied and likely damaged by their own troubles to truly hold him in mind in the moment-by-moment ways so critical to the development of a healthy and resilient self.

This is the extraordinary opportunity afforded by psychoanalysis, to encounter an individual whose experience has been shot through with holes and to help that person to sustain engagement sufficiently to make sense of the gaps and look beyond the barriers and inhibitions that have been erected. In the encounter between one mind and another, there is the possibility of two minds meeting, and recognizing both sameness and difference. This recognition is the ground on which reflective function and resilience are built.

REFERENCES

Apollon, W., Bergeron, D., and Cantin, L. (2002). *After Lacan: Clinical practice and the subject of the unconscious*. Albany: SUNY Press.

Beebe, B., and Lachmann, F. M. (1994). Representations and internalizations in infancy: Three principles of salience. *Psychoanalytic Psychology, 11*, 127–165.

Beebe, B., Rustin, J., Sorter, D., and Knoblauch, S. (2003). An expanded view of intersubjectivity in infancy and its application to psychoanalysis. *Psychoanalytic Dialogues, 13*, 805–841.

Bion, W. R. (1967). Notes on memory and desire. *Psychoanalytic Forum, 2*, 3.

Bion, W. R. (1977). *Seven servants*. New York: Jason Aronson.

Bion, W. R. (1990). *Brazilian lectures*. London and New York: Karnac.

Blum, H. (2005). Language of affect. In S. Akhtar and H. Blum (Eds.), *The language of emotions: Development, psychopathology, and technique* (pp. 1–18). Lanham, MD: Jason Aronson.

Boszormenyi-Nagy, I., and Framo, J.L. (1965). *Intensive family therapy: Theoretical and practical aspects*. New York: Harper and Row.

Bowen, M. (1978). *Family therapy in clinical practice*. New York: Jason Aronson.

Charles, M. (1999a). The Piggle: Confrontations with non-existence in childhood. *International Journal of Psycho-Analysis, 80*(4), 783–795.

Charles, M. (1999b). Sibling mysteries: Enactments of unconscious fears and fantasies. *Psychoanalytic Review, 86*(6), 927–951.

Charles, M. (2001). The outsider. *Free Associations, 8*(4:48), 625–652.

Charles, M. (2002). *Patterns: Building blocks of experience*. Hillsdale, NJ: The Analytic Press.

Charles, M. (2008). Grief in the family: A mother's view. *Clio's Psyche, 15*, 106-112.

Charles, M. (2011a). Remembering, repeating, and working through: Collage: Piecing together the fragments of traumatic memory. In L. DellaPietra (Ed.), *Perspectives on creativity: Vol: 4* (pp. 145–175). Newcastle upon Tyne: Cambridge Scholars Publishing.

Charles, M. (2011b). What does a woman want? *Psychoanalysis, Culture, and Society, 16*(4), 337–353.

Charles, M (2012). *Working with trauma: Lessons from Bion and Lacan*. New York: Jason Aronson.

Charles, M. (in press). Working at the edge: Meaning, identity, and idiosyncracy. *Contemporary Psychoanalysis* Special Issue: *More Simply Human*.

Charles, M. and Telis, K. (2009). Pattern as inspiration and mode of communication in the works of Van Gogh. *American Journal of Psychoanalysis, 69*, 238–262.

Davoine, F., and Gaudillière, J. M. (2004). *History beyond trauma: Whereof one cannot speak, thereof one cannot stay silent*. New York: Other Press.

Felman, S. (1995). Education and crisis, or the vicissitudes of teaching. In *Trauma: Explorations in memory*, ed. C. Caruth. Baltimore and London: Johns Hopkins University Press, pp. 13–60.

Field, T. (1992). Infants of depressed mothers. *Development and Psychopathology, 4*, 49–66.

Fonagy, P., Gergely, G., Jurist, E.L., and Target, M. (2002). *Affect regulation, mentalization, and the development of the self*. New York: Other Press.

Fraiberg, S., Adelson, E., Shapiro, V. (1975). Ghosts in the nursery: A psychoanalytic approach to the problems of impaired infant-mother relationships. *Journal of the American Academy of Child Psychiatry, 14*, 387–421.

Gallese, V. (2009). Mirror neurons, embodied simulation, and the neural basis of social identification. *Psychoanalytic Dialogues, 19*, 519–536.

Goldsmith, J. and Cowen, H. (2011). The inheritance of loss. *Journal of Child Psychotherapy, 37*, 179–193.

Jaffe, J., Beebe, B., Feldstein, S., Crown, C., and Jasnow, M. (2001). Rhythms of dialogue in infancy. *Monographs of the Society for Research in Child Development, 66* (2 Serial No. 264).

Lacan, J. (1974–75). *Seminar XII: RSI.* C. Gallagher (Trans.). http://www.lacaninireland.com/web/published-works/seminars.

Lacan, J. (1975–76). *Seminar XII: Joyce and the Sinthome.* C. Gallagher (Trans.). http://www.lacaninireland.com/web/published-works/seminars.

Lacan, J. (1977a). *The four fundamentals of psycho-analysis.* New York: W. W Norton.

Lacan, J. (1977b). The function and field of speech and language in psychoanalysis. In A. Sheridan (Trans.), *Écrits: A selection* (pp. 30-113). New York: W. W Norton.

Lysaker, P.H., Erickson, M., Buck, K. D., Procacci, M., Nicolò. G., and Dimaggio, G. (2010). Metacognition in schizophrenia spectrum disorders: Methods of assessment and associations with neurocognition and function. *European Journal of Psychiatry, 24*, 220–226.

Lysaker, P.H., Erickson, M., Ringer, J., Buck, K.D., Semerari, A., Carcione, A., and Dimaggio, G. (2011). Metacognition in schizophrenia: The relationship of mastery to coping, insight, self-esteem, social anxiety, and various facets of neurocognition. *British Journal of Clinical Psychology, 50*, 412–424.

Main, M. (1991). Metacognitive knowledge, metacognitive monitoring, and singular (coherent) vs. multiple (incoherent) model of attachment. In C.M. Parkes, J. Stevensen-Hinde, and P. Maris (Eds.), *Attachment across the life cycle* (pp. 127–159). London and New York: Routledge.

Main, M. and Hesse, E. (1990). Parent's unresolved traumatic experiences are related to infant disorganized/disoriented attachment status: Is frightened and/or frightening parental behavior the linking mechanism? In M. Greenberg, D. Cicchetti, and E. M. Cummings (Eds.), *Attachment in the preschool years: Theory, research, and intervention* (pp. 161–182). Chicago: University of Chicago Press.

Matte-Blanco, I. (1975). *The unconscious as infinite sets: An essay in bi-logic.* London: Duckworth.

McDougall, J. (1989). *Theatres of the body: A psychoanalytical approach to psychosomatic illness.* London: Free Associations.

Muller, J. (2011). Why the pair needs the third. In E.M. Plakun (Ed.), *Treatment resistance and patient authority: The Austen Riggs reader* (pp. 97–120). New York: W. W. Norton.

Murray, L., and Trebarthen, C. (1985). Emotional regulation of interactions between two-month-olds and their mothers. In T. Field and N. Fox (Eds.), *Social perspectives in infants* (pp. 177–197). Norwood, NJ: Alex.

Nagy, E., and Molnár, P. (2004). Homo imitans or Homo provocans? Human imprinting model of neonatal imitation. *Infant behavior and Development, 27*, 54–63.

Parsons, M. (1986). Suddenly finding it really matters. The paradox of the analyst's non-attachment. *International Journal of Psychoanalysis, 67*, 475–488.

Parkes, C.M., Stevensen-Hinde, J., and Maris, P. (1991). *Attachment across the life cycle.* London and New York: Routledge.

Petkova, V.I., and Ehrsson, H.H. (2008, December 3). If I were you: Perceptual illusion of body swapping. *PLoS ONE 3(12).* Retrieved from http://www.plosone.org/article/info%3Adoi%2F10.1371%2Fjournal.pone.0003832

Rich, A. (1978). *The dream of a common language: Poems, 1974–1977.* New York: W.W. Norton.

Raczymow, H. (1994). Memory shot through with holes. *Yale French Studies, 85*, 98–104.

Sommer, K.L., Baumeister, R.F., and Stillman, T.F. (2012). The construction of meaning from life events: Empirical studies of personal narratives. In P.T.P. Wong (Ed.), *The human quest for meaning: Theories, research, and applications* (pp. 297–313). New York: Routledge.

Stern, D.N. (1985). *The interpersonal world of the infant: A view from psychoanalysis and developmental psychology.* New York: Basic Books.

Symington, N. (1983). The analyst's act of freedom as an agent of therapeutic change. *International Journal of Psychoanalysis, 10,* 283–291.

Tomkins. S.S. (1962). *Affect, imagery, consciousness: Vol. 1.* New York: Springer Publishing Co.

Tomkins. S.S. (1979). Script theory: Differential magnification of affects. In H.E. Howe, Jr., and R.A. Dienstbier (Eds.), *Nebraska symposium on motivation: Vol. 26* (pp. 201–236). Lincoln: University of Nebraska Press.

Tomkins. S.S. (1982). Affect theory. In P. Ekman, W.V. Friesen. and P. Ellsworth (Eds.). *Emotion in the human face* (2nd ed.) (pp. 353–305). Cambridge: Cambridge University Press.

Trevarthen, C. (2005). First things first: Infants make good use of the sympathetic rhythm of imitation, without reason or language. *Journal of Child Psychotherapy, 31,* 91–113.

Trevarthen, C. (2009). The intersubjective psychobiology of human meaning: Learning of culture depends on interest for co-operative practical—affection for the joyful art of good company. *Psychoanalytic Dialogues, 19,* 507-518.

Tronick, E. (1989). Emotions and emotional communication in infants. *American Psychologist, 44,* 112–119.

Tronick, E.Z., Bruschweiler-Stern, N., Harrison, A.M., Lyons-Ruth, K., Morgan, A.C., Nahum, J.P., Sander, L., and Stern, D.N. (1998). Dyadically expanded states of consciousness and the process of therapeutic change. *Infant Mental Health Journal, 19,* 290–299.

Tronick. E. and Reck, C. (2009). Infants of depressed mothers. *Harvard Review of Psychiatry, 17,* 147–156.

van Ijzendoorn, M.H., Schuengel, C., and Bakermans-Kranenburg, M.J. (1999). Disorganized attachment in early childhood: Meta-analysis of precursors, concomitants, and sequelae. *Development and Psychopathology, 11,* 225–249.

Weinberg, K., and Tronick, E.Z. (1998). The impact of maternal psychiatric illness on infant development. *Journal of Clinical Psychiatry, 59,* 53–61.

Winnicott, D.W. (1971). *Playing and reality.* London and New York: Routledge.

Winnicott, D.W. (1974). Fear of breakdown. *International Review of Psychoanalysis, 1,* 103–107.

TWO

Healing Transgressions of Tapu

Re-Membering the Body Sacred

Ingo Lambrecht

INTRODUCING THE CULTURAL CLINICAL INTERFACE

Trauma is never a simple construct. It is not only comprised of neurobiological and psychological determinants but it is also determined by other factors, such as cultural and political contexts over intergenerational meanderings (Danieli, 1998). As Foucault (1973) has noted, history has revealed shifting relations between reason and madness over time. In this chapter, I will explore working within a Māori[1] mental health service in regards to trauma. Besides setting out the preliminary historical and political dynamics of trauma (Davoine and Gaudillière, 2004), it needs to be held in mind that working with trauma is itself culturally constituted.

Working along the cultural-clinical interface holds complexities and depth that Western dominant mainstream mental health thinking, training and services often ignore or deny. It requires integrative thinking that reaches beyond the clinical taxonomies and formulations toward systems that involve political, historical and cultural processes. Of course all comprehensive and insightful clinical practice, even in Western mental health systems, should include an awareness of cultural-political processes. In this text, the aim is to highlight some of these processes. In New Zealand, the general mental health services are not experienced by the indigenous people of New Zealand as serving the needs of many Māori. There is a recognition that Māori require their own culturally appropriate services.[2] However, in this regard, working at Manawanui Oranga Hinengaro

Mental Health Services for Māori in Auckland, New Zealand as a clinical psychologist raises questions about the cultural-clinical interface.

In this brief overview I cannot do justice to the full Māori history of mental health. It is worth mentioning that the Māori mental health services in New Zealand emerged in the mid-1980s as a response to the increased referral of Māori to acute mental health services and inpatient units where they were not receiving adequate care. This was the result of many cultural factors being ignored, overlooked, or misdiagnosed as psychiatric phenomena. Importantly, in the 1940s and 1950s, White psychologists noticed that Māori were absent from the psychiatric asylums. They assumed this was because of their healthy life style and strong *whanau* or extended family orientation, as well as the supportive community involvement. Thus, significant cultural systems and processes provided a protective factor against clinical referrals to hospitals. Then, in the 1960s and 1970s more Māori moved into cities and towns due to economic pressures and poverty, and this led to an increase in urbanization (Kingi, 2007).

Many Māori moved away from their rural community connections to a lonely and alienating city life to find work, losing the rich supportive connections of the whanau or families they left behind. A rapid increase in referrals of Māori to acute mental health services occurred. Although it is beyond the scope of this chapter to explore fully all contributing factors, suffice it to say that the political impact of economic pressures, largely due to colonization, cultural genocide, and debilitating poverty are all factors that have contributed to rising mental health referrals for Māori until the present time (Durie, 2001).

Despite current Māori mental services, Māori are still over-represented, in terms of population size, in psychiatric inpatient units (Oakley Browne, Wells and Scott, 2006). They receive a diagnosis of schizophrenia or severe mood disorder more frequently. Hence the entanglement of the personal and the political remains active, and the political past haunts the present mental health of some Māori, not dissimilar to many colonized indigenous peoples across the world. The integration of clinical care and cultural-political practices within mental health services is an important process across the world. Globalization continues to widen the cultural context in which clinicians have to perform their healing practices. It is evident from the research that indigenous service users all around the world prefer the integration of both cultural and clinical practices (Ivey, 2013; Lambrecht and Taitimu, 2012). This is true whether such service users belong to the majority as in countries like South Africa, where 70 percent to 80 percent of the people first visit a traditional healer before accessing mental health services (Robertson, 2006), or whether they belong to minority indigenous peoples such as the Sane people in Norway (Sexton and Sorlie, 2009), or the Inuit in Canada (RN Health Society, 2010), or Māori in New Zealand for that matter.

Although service users politically call for the integration of Western clinical and complementary cultural mental health care, it is not clear is how this integration is applied on the ground. It seems that every cultural context requires its own form of integration based on the situation on the ground, be it the specific clinical capacity of a mental health service and/or the needs of the specific indigenous people. Personal trauma is political trauma, and trauma fragments meaning, both personally and politically, and so there are "attacks on linking" (Bion, 1984a), to use Bion's phrase, of personal and political processes (Lambrecht, 2014a).

Clinical-cultural Entanglements in New Zealand

In New Zealand, the Treaty of Waitangi of 1840 is the central document that addresses the complex and fraught relationship between Māori people and the crown or the state. This is very relevant for the cultural-political context of mental health in New Zealand. Ultimately the broken promises of the Treaty of Waitangi, the promises of land, and cultural genocide need to be considered.[3]

In New Zealand, therefore, Māori mental health services are the result of an awareness of a cultural-political position, that is, support for Māori by Māori in the face of White cultural dominance. This approach to treating indigenous people clinically has received validated support in many other countries (Griner and Smith, 2006). This position is a form of political activity to protect Māori tradition, language and practices, which will ultimately benefit everyone in the country. However, at times this position also unfortunately functions much like a monolith in political discourse. The splits and paranoia of political correctness function like a "primitive superego" (Klein, 1975), freezing discursive forms suggesting early defenses and dualistic options without dialectical subtlety (Linehan, 1993). There is much silence and resentment around such a position, and it is at times used moralistically.

Māori mental health services seek to highlight, respect and re-establish long-lost connection to culture and the land. Here is a process that has both light and shadow. It is equally important not to idealize and glamorize the historical and cultural aspects. There is a shadow side to identity as a Māori, which is of course true for all cultural and political identities across the world. The Māori mental health services often pride themselves on cultural holding through the importance of whanau or extended family relations. Workers in such services often mention that we all belong to *whanau*, and in many cases it gives *tangata whai ite ora* (persons seeking well-being), our clients, a sense of belonging and connection within a wider web of relations.

Another central issue that needs to be addressed is the idealized cultural countertransference, particularly from white therapists, who may romanticise traditional healing and view it in an uncritical manner. One example is witchcraft, which I have addressed elsewhere (Lambrecht, 2014b). I have witnessed how the belief in witchcraft can function very destructively in a community for clients both in South Africa and in New Zealand, such as *ukuthakatha* (Zulu) or makutu (Māori) (Lambrecht, 2014b). People have been killed or their lives traumatically altered by such accusations. Witchcraft is an example of a complex indigenous process that has very destructive aspects which challenge any naïve and idealizing view of indigenous practices. If witchcraft is symbolically processed, it may be reflective of inner relational dynamics, as well as systemic dynamics. However, if it becomes concrete and acted upon, it is highly destructive.

To take another example, sometimes among Māori it feels as if whanau gets evoked too often. Whanaus can also be toxic. The Māori mental health services themselves have a history that is intertwined with political trauma, and verbal and institutional abuse. Clinical and managerial leaders have at times protected the mental health workers or members of this whanau from their own questionable practices. This has led to a lack of trust by other mental health professionals. Equally, at times Māori staff have been demoralized and delegated by psychiatrists and managers into positions of being mere taxi drivers and shoppers for *tangata whai ite ora* (clients), when they have so much more to offer.

Furthermore, in regards to culture, it sometimes can be difficult when some Māori staff claim the cultural high ground, resulting in even Māori staff being told they are not Māori enough. This has led to young capable Māori mental health professionals avoiding Māori dedicated mental health services. It has been important in my experience to address this darker aspect in the clinical review by being very clear that abusive interactions remain abusive no matter who speaks. It can be understood as an identification with the aggressor and, still, such behaviors need to be attended to. Acknowledging the darkness has helped, and zero tolerance for abusive interactions between team members or whanau has diminished some of these behaviors (Lambrecht, 2014a). So, in this service, I am curious about the intersubjective space (Stolorow, Brandchaft, and Atwood, 2000), and seek to focus on the alliances between us and listen to the relational eddies and knots, constantly negotiating and mirroring "mentalizing" (Bateman and Fonagy, 2004) as a good-enough therapist by addressing both personal and political histories that move beyond empty articulations (Charles, 2012). This holds true both within the whanau of the mental health service, as well as when being with the clients or tangata *whai ite ora*.

Thus, when considering Māori identity, Bion's ideal of moving beyond desire and memory is quite relevant (Bion, 1984b) in clinical practice. All the politically correct issues could be cited, but the person in front of me may not identify with Māori culture in a straight-forward manner. Identity is often fluid, seldom fixed, shifting, and reconstituted.

Some Māori, for example, identify strongly with Christianity, others are rooted in deep historical *tikanga* or cultural practices. Some Māori identify more strongly with aspects of Western cultures and life styles, whilst others feel they are excluded from Western cultural practices, as well as having lost their own indigenous cultural heritage. Music and gang culture become spaces for establishing an identity. Some hold various positions in different social circles. Others again may identify strongly with Māori culture. However they may not want to see a Māori professional due to difficult experiences in the past around confidentiality. I am more curious as a therapist to listen to where a person comes from, how identities and relationships are formed, what patterns occur in specific stories. Such stories quickly lead to cultural, political and economic entanglements. These are always in some way intertwined with the political and the traumatic histories of the land. Indigenous people are clear that they seek both indigenous and Western clinical healing modalities. In fact, not all cultural practices can be simply integrated with the clinical work. (Lambrecht and Taitimu, 2012).

A vignette may be helpful to illustrate this point. Working with a Māori man, aged 52, diagnosed with paranoid schizophrenia, led to the exploration of his personal family history as one part of this therapeutic work. He described his father dismissively as an alcoholic who was physically violent in his family. When exploring the historical links more carefully, it emerged that his father had lost land to the state at that time due to boundary conflicts that had not been addressed by his grandfather. Generations of his *whanau* or family struggled through the land wars, struggled with unclear land purchases due to broken agreements with white settlers, and struggled with epidemics that literally decimated the local population. His father turned silent, sullen. Instead of being angry with the state about his land loss, so central to Māori identity and *mana* (power, respect), his shame due to status loss and the shame of losing his land in the face of his ancestors drove the father to the false solace of alcohol. His powerlessness became expressed in a disinhibited manner in the form of family violence toward his wife and children. The sullen anguish of loss of land, identity, and power of his father remained an unspoken memory that hovered at the edges of awareness. Disavowed through shame, unconnected to any meaning of such loss, it began to twist and tear at the fabric of family connections between generations.

Intergenerational trauma has been well accepted as central in understanding the meaning of personal trauma (Davoine and Gaudillière, 2004). I agree with Garon (2004) that trauma across generations leads to dissociations or splitting in the intergenerational transmission across generations. The first generation may begin with negation and then proceed to denial and, by the third generation, the secrets may become foreclosed. In therapy, this is manifested in a progression from the unspeakable to the unnameable to the unthinkable (Garon, 2004). In my client's case the unthinkable always hovered beyond the horizon of insight and morphed into a paranoid psychosis in which the unnameable is never quite grasped in the symbolic, and the unspeakable is disavowed in the real. As soon as my client began to appreciate these subtle entanglements, he suddenly appreciated how this political history had affected him personally. It shifted his own formulation of himself from being a genetic or psychological failure, a "broken vessel," as he put it, to being defined differently as a Māori man who has a long painful history shared with his people. His suffering is not only his, but shared politically with others. It becomes a new cultural-political identity. This provides other ways of being and healing that incorporate Māori practices, such as *karakia* (prayer), *waiata* (song), *whakapapa* (genealogy), going to a *Marae* (cultural site).

Beyond the static and frozen sense of memory in post-traumatic flashbacks, supported by the more neurobiological model of van der Kolk (1987), I find it valuable to consider imagery not merely denotatively but also connotatively, wondering about the symbolic and inner connections, fragments, and webs. I consider it important in the face of all the political and cultural dynamics, not to allow them to become monolithic in the face of the inner world of an individual, the inwardness of the self, however intersubjective it may be. With this client, the symbol of boundaries re-emerged in his work on the boundary between Māori and *Pakeha* (Whites), between father and son, between hurt and rage, as well between the real and the unreal in addressing witchcraft (*makutu*).

He worked through his boundary issues with his deep woundedness and destructive rage, compensating for the loss of *mana* (respect and inner power) of his whanau (extended family) and himself. He began to appreciate the brittleness of his false self as a defense against being overwhelmed, and approached his real self with more openness. He worked through his introjects and we experienced the projective identifications in the therapy room, both in terms of person and race. His work accessed the defended unaccepted feelings about his abuse and neglect. Being vulnerable and dependent was terrifying for this proud, superior man, so successful years ago, now shattered through the terror of witchcraft, a persecutory world of terror and isolation. Boundary conflicts with the state, leading to the loss of his father's land, created rigid and fragmenting transgressions of inner spaces and intergenerational aftershocks. With a more flexible, playful and vulnerable self—the true self in a Winnicottian sense—culture and spirituality became a potential and transitional space between himself and the world, in contrast to the rigid persecutory cultural demands that set him off into a world of horror.

The re-telling of trauma is not only about repetition to readjust faulty memory processing, but rather provides opportunity for creating new meaning, establishing a new body of meaning. The identity of this client became reconstituted or re-membered through this clinical-cultural work into a new configuration of intersubjectivity and relationships. This work settled his own anguish and rage, as his new sense of identity became more grounded in the history of being Māori. By listening to the gaps, the ruptures, the impasses, the underlying dilemmas, the political, the cultural, and the personal pain, it is then possible to explore with the person what may be helpful (Lambrecht, 2014a). The cultural and clinical entanglements are complex, and determined by their own history. Nonetheless, and because of the complexities, certain possibilities emerge. One of them is a Māori dedicated lens to understand mental health, *te whare tapa wha* (the house of well-being).

TE WHARE TAPA WHA

The Manawanui Māori Mental Health Service of the Auckland District Health Board has adopted the Māori mental health model of *te whare tapa wha* (the house of well-being) as a holistic model of Māori health or well-being. It is made up of the four pillars or aspects of well-being, namely whanau or the family health, hinengaro or mental health, tinana or physcial health, and wairua or spiritual health (Durie, 2001). These four pillars hold the protective space of health and well-being for Māori and in fact, it could be argued, for most people. The translation into English needs to be taken with care. For example, *whanau* means "family," however the notion of *whanau* in fact embraces a greater net of family compared to the modern Anglo-Saxon nuclear family world. It entails, for example, connections to close family friends and even includes cousins of many degrees removed from the primary family.

All four aspects of Māori mental health are considered to work together, and all aspects are necessary to achieve well-being. In this manner, Māori mental health is more clinically sophisticated than the common psychiatric medical model. This clinical-cultural interface avoids reductionism and also enhances clinical depth and range. In fact, all excellent clinical practice entails cultural and political sensitivities. Equally, in-depth and sensitive cultural work would include clinical aspects. Schizophrenia or psychosis within a Māori mental health model is not merely addressed as a brain disease or an intrapsychic process but requires the addition of understanding the *whanau* (extended family), the body (*tinana*), and the spiritual (*wairua*), which leads to an integrated intervention to heal the mind (*hinengaro*).

This model gives me the opportunity to access thinking that Western psychology struggles with, such as body-mind issues, political-systemic processes, as well as to work with "anomalous" experiences that belong to the wairua or spirit aspect of the model (Randal, Geekie, Lambrecht and Taitimu, 2008). The wairua part can incorporate the findings of parapsychological research and spiritual practices, such as mindfulness and meditation. Māori mental health professionals and clients are often grateful that their worldview and "anomalous" experiences are not dismissed or considered to be "crazy." At times, such experiences are reduced to just being "cultural" (i.e., not real) within a post-modern academic Western psychological discourse. It is often necessary in my meetings with *tohungas*, the Māori shamans, to apologize because academic Western psychology has many unresolved taboos and resistances in this area, despite sufficient scientific evidence (Radin, 2006). This gap is embarrassing, given psychology's claim to be scientific.

As stated above, although deceptively simple in description, the model of *te whare tapa wha* is in fact a sophisticated and inclusive model. It is more holistic and provides more therapeutic options than many other psychological models, including allowing psychoanalytic thinking to occur. Cognitive behavioral Therapy (CBT) is the preferred model in clinical psychology in New Zealand. This Māori model has far more space for innovation and experimentation. Given the *whanau* or family aspect of the model, a "good-enough holding" (Winnicott, 2005), the *whanau* theme, needs to occur along personal, systemic, political, cultural and spiritual dimensions when working at a Māori mental health service. Equally, Winnicott always had a social approach to trauma without having to sacrifice the inner world. Working with trauma and Winnicott's notion of holding (Alford, 2013) is evidence of the systemic thinking that considers the community as contributing to healing the ruptures and taboos of the mind, emotions and spirit. Importantly, as O'Loughlin points out so rightly: "This is not to suggest that memory work is easy. Families are fractious. Tribal groups are fractious. Nation states are fractious" (O'Loughlin, 2013, p. 259). Cultural taboos (*tapu in Māori*) are fractures in politico-spiritual systems.

At a Māori mental health service, these dimensions are openly acknowledged. Also, there is more scope to work with long-term psychotherapy within the clinical-cultural interface, because the *hinengaro* or the mind is respected. This is so different from working within a more medical model of the general mental health system. As O'Loughlin notes, "Here I would like to conclude by focusing on the capacity for psychoanalytically informed therapists to not only work directly with persons who have suffered trauma, but to extend their influence in the social arena to address the severance of social links, the denial of memory, the erasure of generational and ancestral wisdom, and the rupture of genealogical continuity" (O'Loughlin, 2013, p. 262).

WAIRUA AND THE SACRED BODY

In focusing on the sacred, it is worth wondering what spiritual holding, the wairua aspect of the whare tapa wha, would entail. It is an important cultural and even political component of Māori life for most indigenous peoples across the world. Although the Māori mental health services acknowledge wairua, the spirit, as one of the four corner stones of the whare tapa wha as stated above, how to integrate this value into a psychotherapeutic practice is not always clear. Bidois (2012) is a matakite, a seer in the Māori tradition, who works in a Māori mental health service. He has himself had experiences that could be described as "psychotic." He states that the term wairua is made up of two parts, first *wai*, which means unique, special, unprecedented. The second part of the word *rua* refers to abyss or container.

Wai-rua then is that which is unique, special, which is contained within. Importantly, *wairua* is not to be understood in a religious, ritualistic, or intellectual manner. It is not *tikanga* or cultural rules even, it is utterly unique. In other words, it needs to be experienced to be present. To move cross-culturally for a moment, *wairua* as a unique container and abyss at the same time within us in some manner is closer to the complex mystical definitions of Advaita Vedanta, Buddhist nirvana and the negative path of Meister Eckhart, the Christian mystic, compared to the common definitions of spirituality among the main religious establishments.

In New Zealand, the *tohunga* (Māori shaman) considers mental health difficulties to be the result of intergenerational afflictions between the living and the *tipuna* or ancestors. This is not so different from genetic, psychoanalytic or attachment theories of mental health. With this in mind, it is worth mentioning an integrated mental health intervention by a *tohunga*, named Wiremu NiaNia with a mental health team when they worked with a family (NiaNia,Tere, Bush and Epston, 2013). Wiremu was able to see and become aware of another ancestral figure in the room, namely a deceased grandmother, and thus the healing included working with all persons present, the living and the *tipuna* or ancestors. The healing occurred as the relationships became healed. Healing meant that the ancestors, whether external or internalized, achieve a positive, engaging, empathic holding function.

In Western psychoanalytic discourse concerning the sacred, this type of holding has some precedence, such as in Jung's (1957) "transcendent function," or in Grotstein's (2000) "transcendent position." Importantly, spiritual or wairua holding requires acknowledgement not merely in terms of thoughts and religious rules about the spirit, which is closer to religious thinking, but rather a greater focus on lived experience, namely sacred and unusual or "anomalous" experiences. Spiritual holding often requires us to make space to talk about such "anomalous" experiences. My own clinical and cultural experiences from many other parts of the world have taught me that most indigenous people are very wary of some Western clinicians' outright rejection of such experiences as unreal, imagined, or hallucinatory. It is important to actively explore certain anomalous experiences and validate their reality, for many Māori don't trust *pakehas* (Whites) in this regard. Such exploration requires an active respect for the reality of their world.

In fact, in my experience, when anomalous experiences among clinicians or clients are raised among mainstream Western clinicians, some (not all) psychoanalysts and psychologists become very conservative and very White in this regard. For example, projective identification is a pretty weird and wonderful voodoo concept and process. Yet when "telepathy" is mentioned, an experience that has clear scientific evidence and has been far more successfully researched (Carter, 2012), suddenly many Western psychoanalysts struggle with this concept. In fact, projective identification could be considered a special case of telepathic processes (Lambrecht, 2014a).

Madness and the Sacred

Recently the literature on psychosis and spirituality has increased (Gale, Robson, Rapsomatioti, 2013) and it will not be possible to fully explore this rich topic. The connection between psychosis and spirituality, from the highest states of consciousness to the depth of madness, has received enormous support from the recovery movement as well as from the United Kingdom (UK) spiritual crisis support network (www.spiritualnetwork.com). In Clarke's (2010) view, this support has facilitated a paradigm shift that has begun to seep into mental health services. Although it may be a paradigm shift for the dominant Western discourse, spirituality has always been accepted as a necessary component for Māori health, as depicted in the *whare tapa wha* model described above (Durie, 2001).

Lukoff (1988), a psychiatrist with his own personal experiences of madness and spiritual transformation, notes that there are important overlaps when comparing psychosis, mania, and mystical states. Such spiritual trauma has been termed spiritual crisis (Lukoff, 2012). The distinction between madness and spiritual crisis is not always easily made. In indigenous cultures, the shamans usually determine how to distinguish between madness and spiritual crisis. Shamans in indigenous cultures make use of tests based on reliability and validity, just as psychologists do through testing. What this means is that, within indigenous cultures, often certain 'voices' will be tested (Lambrecht, 2009), as I will explore below. Also, in other cultures, not all psychotic symptoms are by definition signs of a debilitating illness.

When unusual experiences are considered indicative of a shamanic initiation illness, bizarre behaviors are often explained in terms of the ancestors attempting to shift a talented but resisting person into the healing profession of a shaman. During my own apprenticeship, I was told by my teacher that as a *thwasa* (an apprentice to a South African sangoma or shaman), the pain would lessen as the relationship between the ancestral voices and the thwasa improved over time during the training. I recall asking my teacher: "How would I know whether the voices I heard are the ancestors or just me simply going mad?" "Ah that's easy," my teacher replied, "we test them" (Randal, Geekie, Lambrecht and Taitimu, 2008, 337). The 'true ancestral voices' would be those that in the eyes of the community are accurate, for example, in helping to find herbs and lost cattle, or in diagnosing and healing illnesses. Here voices or visions are the result of ancestor contact, validated and made reliable through training and testing the voices against reality.

Importantly, shamanic initiation illnesses can be terrifyingly mad. A *sangoma* I interviewed stated that when "you get like that, you don't know that you get very sick. Where other people get put away in Sterkfontein [mental institution], these people are not sick, they just need to go to school [*sangoma* training]. . . . They said I was crazy, some of the people told me I knocked people out." Another *sangoma* noted that during his *ukuthwasa* (initiation crisis), "I think I was nearly mentally disturbed. "Sangoma Nomsa described her *ukuthwasa* as beginning in "1986 after Easter that headache came back again, and it was serious because I throw my baby out of the bed, I was mad. So I decided that I must take the work, I must train, for I will kill the baby" (Lambrecht, 1998, p. 426).

Lukoff (2011) rightly points out that certain visionary spiritual experiences, if misdiagnosed as psychotic disorders, can lead to personal growth being interrupted by being pharmaceutically repressed through psychiatric medication and, even worse, through hospitalization. Pasricha (2011) is an Indian psychiatrist. He is open to the relevance of parapsychology in psychiatry, suggesting to be mindful of differential diagnosis, and to be discerning by checking statements of anomalous experiences against empirical reality. Thus, any voices would need to be tested against reality to check whether they are able to be an act of precognition or simply an expression of psychosis, no matter what the claims of truth may be (Johnson and Friedman, 2008).

During an initiation crisis, a person stating that she is being persecuted by spirits would, within the positivistic normative framework, be considered to be making utterances that reflect psychosis (Laubscher, 1937). *Sangomas* (South African shamans) on the other hand, are able to make a differential diagnosis between an initiation crisis, psychosis, or prodromal schizophrenia (Ngubane, 1977). Among indigenous people, shamanic behavior during initiation has been described and analyzed by past Western psychiatrists as acute psychosis (Silverman, 1967). When the South African shaman apprentices experience the spiritual crisis or the ukuthwasa as distressing, individuals in this state could be exposed to psychiatric diagnoses. It could then also be argued that the *ukuthwasa* represents an example of hysteria or a dissociative trance disorder (300.15 - DSM 5).[4] However, for example, South African sangomas themselves distinguish and differentially diagnose psychosis from the initiation crisis (Ngubane, 1977). Furthermore, not all shamans experience a severe initiation crisis that includes psychotic elements. When psychotic symptoms are present, it is short-lived, and seems unlikely to re-appear (Walsh, 2007).

In this regard, the psychologist Noll states that "devoid of personal experiences of ASCs (altered states of consciousness), yet quite familiar with altered states of the diagnostic manual, the incredible sagas of the shamans must indeed seem psychotic to an interpreter who only considers experiences in an ordinary state of consciousness to be valid, mentally healthy phenomena" (Noll, 1983, p. 444). So, "Western psychiatry has a long history of viewing mystics as madmen, saints as psychotics, and sages as schizophrenics" (Walsh, 1990, p. 75). Ecstatic, mystical, aesthetic and meditative states have been conceptualized within the psychodynamic framework as regressions in the service of the ego (Kris, 1952).

This equation of altered states of consciousness with pathological states of consciousness has been refuted in several hundred studies (Levey and Levey, 1991). It must, however, be pointed out that constructive and integrated psychoanalytic writings on mysticism (Merkur, 2010), on meditation (Shaffi, 1973), on spiritual emergencies (Perry, 2005), on shamanism (Smith, 1997), and specifically on Xhosa *sangomas* (Bührmann and Gqomfa, 1982) have provided invaluable contributions to this area of research.

However, certain spiritual practices are not without their mental health issues and risks (Engler, 1984), a fact also openly acknowledged among shamans. On a psychodynamic level, problems appear to arise particularly with those individuals who have a vulnerability and disturbance around identity and self-esteem, as well as intersubjectivity (Epstein, 1990; Stolorow, Brandchaft and Atwood, 2000). This would explain the high attraction of such meditative or spiritual practices to late adolescents and people undergoing a mid-life crisis. At the earliest developmental level, such difficulties could be explained by the pathologies of the self within Kohut's understanding (Kohut, 1971). In fact, an insecure or disorganized attachment in childhood produced by the trauma of neglect or sexual and physical abuse, leading to a failure of good-enough holding (Winnicott, 2005), will result in difficulties in self-regulation (Schore, 2003) that in turn leads to a propensity to dissociation (Granqvist, Reijman and Cardeña, 2011), a form of altered state of consciousness to escape the terror of the brutal moment. Trauma due to abuse and early neglect can lead to experiences of psychosis, as a traumagenic neurodevelopmental approach to psychosis has highlighted. (Read, Perry, Moskowitz and Connolly, 2001). All of this begins to emerge during spiritual practices. Also, in the attachment as well as transferences to spiritual teachers, such as gurus or shamans, much earlier unconscious processes are played out, at times intensely painfully and pathologically.

Sangomas work similarly to the tohungas or Māori shamans, namely by recognizing that supportive and therapeutic family life has effective healing capacities for psychosis or madness. Treatment for such mental distress and illness requires at times that the unwell person lives with the *sangoma* and becomes part of the *sangoma* homestead. This provided a certain degree of containment, holding, as well as safety. It also allowed the *sangoma* to speak to the person on a regular daily basis. It is a form of counseling. The ritual cleansing of the client and the family from evil spirits by the calling of the ancestors for protection leads to the client becoming embedded in the healed family relations both of the living and those that have passed on.

Secure containment and therapeutic care with *muthi* (traditional medicine) and counseling is provided in the *sangoma*'s home for the client. This includes an integration back into everyday life. By being involved in family life and chores, therefore the client increases a sense of value and everyday functioning through active participation. This is close to the psychotherapeutic work with psychosis and trauma described by Charles (2012), in which a more modern psychodynamic therapy allows for respectful depth and cultural sensitivity, addressing the traumatic distress carefully, thereby a move away from simplistic models. This respectful containment is equally true for other shamanic traditions.

The *sangoma* home treatment is similar to a form of treatment I have witnessed in Gothenburg, Sweden at the Family Care Foundation (www.familjevardsstiftelsen.se/en). Their work for over 25 years has become well known as an effective therapeutic alternative to the usual medical model approach to schizophrenia and psychosis. They work with people with complex mental health issues, such as severe psychotic disorders. In addition to intensive weekly psychotherapy, the distressed person is placed into a family that receives fortnightly support and supervision. In a certain manner, the therapy room becomes extended (Håkansson, 2014). This approach has consistently achieved notably positive outcomes, allowing people to come off their psychiatric medication and to achieve fulfilling lives, despite apparently hopeless prognoses.

It is not always easy to distinguish between madness and the sacred. I have worked with some who have had intense *kundalini* emergencies, *qigong* psychosis, *matakite*, a Māori term for hearing voices and seeing visions, as well as the *ukuthwasa* (shamanic initiation illness) and amafufunyana (possession and psychotic states). These distinctions are not always clear. Such devastating experiences in a cultural context can relate to the overstepping of taboos or tapu (Māori).

THE RE-MEMBERING OF THE BODY SACRED

The breaking of tapu or taboo, the sacred versus the mundane (*noa*), means that spiritual holding of the ancestors is lost and requires healing. One vignette that may address this is the *tapu* around old battlegrounds, where blood has been shed. Wiremu NiaNia, as a *tohunga*, shared a story of how a young adolescent became mad and terrified (personal communication, 2011). A home visit revealed that the home of this young man was on land that had been the site of a brutal battlefield. The land needed cleansing before personal healing could continue. The *tapu* of bloodshed needed to be removed and healed before other mental health healing methods could be applied. The sacred body needed to be resettled, remoulded and remembered in its relation to the land.

One of the *tangata whai ite ora* or clients I saw some years ago was diagnosed with schizophrenia and psychosis. A woman of few words, she wanted to see me for sessions at a Māori mental health service. She had been hearing voices since the age of thirteen, and was prescribed clozapine, an anti-psychotic medication. Her *whanau* or family was very supportive, and they have a deep and valued attachment to Māori customs (*tikanga*), the land (*tangata whenua*) and the language (*te reo*). Despite many different efforts by psychiatrists and spiritual healers, there was no significant shift in the critical and vicious voices that she would hear. I was not sure how effective I would be. Nonetheless, we began to meet weekly and, over time, shifts did occur. My focus was on helping her to relate to her voices differently, wondering about various possible traumas. She emphatically denied any abuse or neglect, and her mother confirmed this. The voices seemed to have emerged out of the blue, and then she began to smoke cannabis to manage the barrage of incessant negative commentary. She stopped smoking cannabis in her twenties. Her voices continued to criticize her mercilessly for more than three decades.

Working with her meant establishing a different relationship with the voices. The aim was to listen carefully to the history and meaning of the voices, the triggers and consequences. We began to explore her relationship with her voices in minute detail. She has a long history of silence and few words. Slowly, through finding a few words, symbols and links to different aspects of her life, she began to find her own words and her own past. It was after nine months that she suddenly spoke of the first time her voices arose. It was only then that the cultural trauma emerged. At the age of twelve, she was playing with a friend when she stepped over a boundary into an old small cemetery or *urupa*. It is *tapu* to transgress the boundaries of a urupa or to step on graves. She was aware of the *tapu* that had been transgressed. During that evening, she began seeing two men talking in the corner. The next day, she began to hear the voices of the men in her head. It was captivating how she suddenly found words, and spoke fluently and fully. These voices evolved into many other critical and horrifying voices, which began to haunt her for the next three decades. In other words, her diagnosis of schizophrenia or psychosis was in fact set off by a cultural trauma of a transgressed *tapu*.

In the following sessions, it emerged that she wished to heal the tapu. Both she and her *whanau* or family agreed that this was culturally appropriate and desirable. She would take us back to the site and, with *karakia* or prayer, the tapu would be healed and the sacred wairua body would be re-membered and re-moulded. This site of the small cemetery or *urupa* was about three to four hours drive. As Auckland was left behind, rain began to pour down strongly. A silent concern was rising in the car about enacting the ceremony in this downpour. As we drove down the washed out sand track toward the cemetery at the coast, no more than a few minutes away from the site, the rain stopped. We arrived and she buried a crystal at the point of transgression, and then *karakias* or prayers were recited by her mother. Energy or *mauri* work was performed by myself, and *waiata* or songs were sung by all. All of these actions were aimed at healing the transgressed *tapu*, and appeasing the *tipuna* or ancestors of this site. This all took place in fifteen minutes.

As we returned to the motor vehicle, another vehicle came down the track and the rain began to pour down again. In our vehicle, the *whanau* or family were in no doubt that the anomalous stoppage of the rain was a sign that the *tipuna* or ancestors, as well as mother earth and father sky, were in agreement with the ceremony. Asking my client how she was feeling after the ceremony whilst sitting in the car, she stated, "everything is brighter, and my head is clearer." She repeated this when we arrived many hours later in Auckland in the pouring rain. Weekly therapy ended shortly thereafter, as she had found employment for the first time in her life. Her *whanau* or family reported that she now was using makeup, buying new clothes more appropriate for her age, and speaking more. She is still very shy, yet more involved in her family's life. It is her own as well as her family's understanding that the healing of the tapu through the ceremony was important in shifting her into new levels of functioning, not denying the months of psychotherapy. She is now holding down a job, an accomplishment that had not been possible for the last thirty years.

In this chapter, my focus has been on the rich interactions in therapy between the personal and the sacred-political. Therapeutic vignettes with Māori clients at a Māori Mental Health Service in New Zealand were outlined. For many cultures the notion of the sacred is central in making sense of both personal and political traumatic experiences. Healing such ruptures of meaning requires healing transgressions of tapu or taboo. This means working through personal, political, and ecological connections with other beings, such as ancestors and the land. The body sacred has to be remembered and newly reconstituted, in other words, re-membered. In this chapter, such essential healing and political acts were highlighted in this cross-cultural work.

Therapeutic work with indigenous persons in general and Māori clients in particular was understood in terms of psychoanalytic considerations together with relevant political, cultural and spiritual factors. Although psychoanalytic thinking is not lost in this integration, it may, however, have to move beyond its own resistances and denials, already evident in Freud's time, when the ambivalent history between psychoanalysis and the sacred began to emerge. That ambivalence is still at times acted out in psychoanalytic circles today.

NOTES

1. Māori are the indigenous people of New Zealand, who first arrived in *Aotearoa,* the Māori name for this land in their *waka* or canoes from East Polynesia possibly between 800 and 900 AD. Waves of Māori canoe migrants followed before the arrival of *Tauiwi* or foreigners, first in the 17th century with Abel Tasman, and then in the 19th century, with Captain James Cook representing the British Empire. The gradual colonization and conflicts lead to a treaty between some Māori and thr British Crown in 1840, called the Treaty of Waitangi (Walker, 2004).

2. Māori mental health services, were the result of the principles of the treaty of Waitangi being applied to the New Zealand department of health's delivery of service. This occurred in 1986. As the Māori health commission of 1997 noted, components of a Māori dedicated health service would include an assessment that takes into account cultural values, *whanau* (extended family) participation, the use of Māori language and custom, outcome measures that are relevant to Māori understanding, and a Māori workforce with both cultural and professional competencies (Durie, 2001).

3. It is beyond the scope of this chapter to address these central issues (e.g., the translation errors, such as the questions of "sovereignty" versus "governance"), however, mental health professionals are bound by the treaty to protect the health, rights and *tikanga* or culture of the Māori. In New Zealand, the Treaty of Waitangi was first applied to the mental health system in 2000. The Treaty of Waitangi in relation to Māori health is understood in terms of the three "P". Briefly, the Treaty of Waitangi gives Māori the right to "Participation" in the health system both in terms of access and service, "Partnership" in terms of power relations, and "Protection" in terms of health and culture (Tapsell and Mellsop, 2007).

4. Dissociative trance disorder, as defined by the DSM 5, could also be referred to as a possession disorder. A possession trance state is an altered state of consciousness in which the person's usual identity is replaced by a new identity, be it a deity, a spirit, a demon, or an ancestor. A dissociative trance disorder is only diagnosed and applied to individuals who are suffering from distress or dysfunction. Not all possession states are pathological, as some are experienced positively and serve a social function within a religious context (APA, 2013).

REFERENCES

Alford, C.F. (2013). Winnicott and trauma. *Psychoanalysis, Culture and Society, 18*(3), 259–276.

American Psychiatric Association. (2013). *Diagnostic and statistical manual of mental disorders* (5th ed.). Washington, DC: American Psychiatric Association.

Bateman, A., and Fonagy P. (2004). *Psychotherapy for borderline personality disorder: Mentalization-based treatment*. Oxford: Oxford University Press.

Bidois, E. (2012). A cultural and personal perspective of psychosis. In J. Geekie, P. Randal, and D. Lampshire (Eds.), *Experiencing psychosis: Person and professional perspectives* (pp. 35–43). London: Routledge.

Bion, W.R. (1984a). Attacks on linking. In W. Bion (Ed.), *Second thoughts: Selected papers on psychoanalysis* (pp. 93–109). London: Karnac Books.

Bion, W.R. (1984b). *Attention and interpretation*. London: Karnac Books.

Bührmann, M.V., and Gqomfa, J.N. (1982). The Xhosa healers of southern Africa: 3. A family therapy session with a dream as central content. *Journal of Analytical Psychology, 27*, 41–57.

Carter, C.D. (2012). *Science and psychic phenomena: The fall of the house of skeptics*. Rochester: Inner Traditions.

Charles, M. (2012). *Working with trauma: Lessons from Bion and Lacan*. New York: Jason Aaronson.

Clarke, I. (2010). Psychosis and spirituality revisited: The frontier is opening up. In I. Clarke (Ed.) *Psychosis and spirituality: Consolidating the new paradigm* (pp.1–7). Chichester: John Wiley and Sons Ltd.

Danieli, Y. (1998). *International handbook of intergenerational trauma transmission*. New York: Plenum.

Davoine, F., and Gaudillière, J. (2004). *History beyond trauma*. New York: Other Press.

Durie, M. (2001). *Mauri Ora: The dynamics of Māori health*. Auckland: Oxford University Press.

Engler, J. (1984). Therapeutic aims in psychotherapy and meditation: Developmental stages in the representation of self. *The Journal of Transpersonal Psychology. 16*, 25–62.

Epstein, M. (1990). Psychodynamics of meditation: Pitfalls on the spiritual path. *The Journal of Transpersonal Psychology. 22*, 17–34.

Foucault, M. (1973). *Madness and Civilisation*. London: Random House.

Gale, J., Robson , M., and Rapsomatioti, G. (2013). *Insanity and divinity: Studies in psychosis and spirituality*. London: Routledge.

Garon, J. (2004). Skeletons in the closet. *International Forum of Psychoanalysis, 13*, 84–92.

Griner, D., and Smith, T. (2006) Culturally adapted mental health intervention: A meta-analytic review. *Psychotherapy: Theory, Research, Practice, Training, 43*(4), 531–548.

Granqvist, P., Reijman, S., and Cardeña, E (2011). Altered consciousness and human development. In E. Cardeña and M. Winkelman (Eds.), *Altering consciousness: Multidisciplinary perspectives. Volume 2: Biological and psychological perspectives* (pp. 211–236). Oxford: Praeger.

Grotstein, J.S. (2000). *Who is the dreamer, Who dreams the dream?* London: Routledge.

Håkansson, C. (2014). *The extended therapy room*. Doctoral thesis, University of Jyväskylä-Finland.

Ivey, G. (2013). Unconscious meaning and magic: Comparing psychoanalysis and African indigenous healing. In C. Smith, G. Lobban, and M. O'Loughlin (Eds.), *Psychodynamic psychotherapy in contemporary South Africa: Contexts, theories and applications* (pp. 141–168). Johannesburg: Wits University Press.

Johnson, C.V., and Friedman, H.L. (2008). Enlightened or delusional? Differentiating religious, spiritual and transpersonal experiences from psychopathology. *Journal of Humanistic Psychology. 48*, 505–527.

Jung, C.G. (1957). The transcendent function. *The Collected Works of C.G. Jung*: *Vol. 8*. Princeton, NJ: Princeton University Press. (Original work published 1916)

Kingi, T. (2007). Māori mental health: Past trends, current issues, and Māori responsiveness. *Matariki, 1*(1), 51–80.

Klein, M. (1975). Notes on some schizoid mechanisms. In R.E. Money-Kyrle (Ed.), *The Writings of Melanie Klein*: *Vol. 3* (pp. 1–24). London: Hogarth Press. (Original work published 1946)

Kohut, H. (1971). *The analysis of the self.* New York: International Universities Press.

Kris, E. (1952). *Psychoanalytic explorations in art*. New York, NY: International Universities Press.

Lambrecht, I. (1998). *A psychological study of shamanic trance states in South African shamanism*. Johannesburg: University of the Witwatersrand.

Lambrecht, I. (2009). Shaman as expert voice hearer. Retrieved May 27, 2013, from http://www.hearingvoices.org.nz/attachments/article/14/Shamans%20as%20Expert%20Voice%20Hearers%20By%20Ingo%20Lambrecht.pdf.

Lambrecht, I., and Taitimu, M. (2012). Exploring culture, subjectivity, and psychosis. In J. Geekie, P., Randal and D. Lampshire (Eds.), *Experiencing psychosis: First-person and research perspectives* (pp. 44–54). London: Routledge.

Lambrecht, I. (2014a). *Identity among differences: A personal account of a Pakeha psychologist working in a New Zealand Maori mental health service.* .

Lambrecht, I. (2014b). *Sangoma trance states: Exploring indigenous consciousness disciplines in South Africa.* Auckland: AM Publishing

Laubscher, B.J.F. (1937). *Sex, custom and psychopathology*. London: Routledge and Kegan Paul.

Levey, J., and Levey, M. (1991). *The fine arts of relaxation, concentration and meditation.* Boston, MA: Wisdom Publications.

Linehan, M. 1993. *Cognitive behavioral therapy for borderline personality disorder*. New York: The Guilford Press.

Lukoff, D. (1988). Transpersonal perspectives on manic psychosis: Creative, visionary and mystical states. *The Journal of Transpersonal Psychology. 20*, 131–160.

Lukoff, D. (2011). Visionary spirituality and mental disorders. In E. Cardeña, and M. Winkelman (Eds.), *Altering consciousness: Multidisciplinary perspectives: Vol 2, Biological and psychological perspectives* (pp. 301–326). Oxford: Praeger.

Merkur, D. (2010). *Explorations of the psychoanalytic mystics*. Amsterdam: Rodopi.

Ngubane, H. (1977). *Body and mind in Zulu medicine.* London: Academic Press.

NiaNia, W., Tere, Bush, A., and Epston, D. (2013). I will not leave my baby behind: A Cook Island Māori family's experience of New Zealand Māori traditional healing. *Australian and New Zealand Journal of Family Therapy, 34*, 3–17.

Noll, R. (1983). Shamanism and schizophrenia: A state-specific approach to the "schizophrenia metaphor" of Shamanic states. *American Ethnologist, 10*, 444.

Oakley Browne, M.A, Wells, J.E., and Scott, K.M (Eds.). (2006). *Te rau hinengaro: The New Zealand mental health survey.* Wellington: Ministry of Health.

O'Loughlin, M. (2013). Reclaiming genealogy, memory and history: The psychodynamic potential for reparative therapy in contemporary South Africa. In C. Smith, G. Lobban, and M. O'Loughlin (Eds.), *Psychodynamic psychotherapy in contemporary South Africa: Contexts, theories and applications* (pp. 242–271). Johannesburg: Wits University.

Pasricha, S.K. (2011). Relevance of parapsychology in psychiatric practice. *Indian Journal of Psychiatry, 53*(1), 4–8.

Perry, J.W. (2005). *Far side of madness*: Los Angeles, CA: Spring Publications.

Radin, D. (2006). *Entangled minds: Extrasensory experiences in a quantum field.* New York, NY: Paraview.

Randal, P., Geekie, J., Lambrecht, I., and Taitimu, M. (2008). Dissociation, psychosis, and spirituality: Whose voices are we hearing? In A. Moskowitz, I. Schafer, and J. Dorahy (Eds.), *Psychosis, trauma and dissociation: Emerging perspectives on severe psychopathology* (pp. 333–345). London: John Wiley and Sons Ltd.

Read, J., Perry, B., Moskowitz, A., and Connolly J. (2001). The contributions of early traumatic events to schizophrenia in some patients: A traumagenic neurodevelopmental model. *Psychiatry: Interpersonal and Biological Processes, 63*, 319–345.

Roberston, B.H. (2006). Does the evidence support collaboration between psychiatry and traditional healers? Findings from three South African studies. *South African Psychiatry Review, 9*, 87–90.

RN Health Society. (2010). First nations' traditional models of wellness. Environmental scan in British Columbia. Retrieved August 29, 2013, from http://www.fnhc.ca/pdf/Traditional_Models_of_Wellness_Report_FIN-_2010.pdf

Sexton, R., and Sorlie, T. (2009). Should traditional healing be integrated within the mental health services in Sami areas of northern Norway? Patient views and related factors. *International Journal of Circumpolar Health, 68*(5), 488–497.

Schore, A.N. (2003). *Affect dysregulation and the disorders of the self.* New York, NY: Guilford Press.

Shaffi, M. (1973). Silence in the service of ego: Psychoanalytic study of meditation. *International Journal of Psycho-Analysis, 54,* 431–443.

Silverman, J. (1967). Shamans and acute schizophrenia. *American Anthropologist, 69,* 21–31.

Silverman, J. (1975). ASCs: Positive and negative outcomes. *Journal of Altered States of Consciousness. 2,* 295–317.

Smith, C.M. (1997). *Jung and shamanism in dialogue.* New York: Pallis Press.

Stolorow, R.D., Brandchaft, B., and Atwood, G.E. (2000). *Psychoanalytic treatment: An inter-subjective approach.* London: Routledge.

Tapsell, R., and Mellsop, G. (2007). The contributions of culture and ethnicity to New Zealand mental health research findings. *International Journal of Social Psychiatry, 53,* 317–324.

Van der Kolk, B.A. (1987). *Psychological trauma.* Washington DC: American Psychiatric Press.

Walker, R. (2004). *Ka Whaiwhai Tonu Matou: Struggle without end.* Auckland: Pengiun Books.

Walsh, R.N. (1990). *The spirit of shamanism.* New York: Jeremy Tarcher Publications.

Walsh, R.N. (2007). *The world of shamanism: New views of an ancient tradition.* Woodbury: Llewellyn Publications.

Winnicott, D.W. (2005). *Playing and reality.* London: Routledge.

THREE

Black Maids-White Madams and the Ghosts in the Nurseries of Post-Apartheid South Africa

Cora Smith

"Niemand is skuldig aan onskuld nie." —No one is guilty of innocence. (Breyten Breytenbach, 1985, p. 158)

Much has been written on the political discourse between black domestic workers and white employers in apartheid South Africa (Cock, 1980, 2011; Goldman, 2003; Hook, 2012; King, 2007; Nyamnjoh, 2005; Shefer, 2012; Straker, 2012). Following the democratic dispensation of 1994 a trend emerged wherein many black domestic workers who live on the residential premises of their white employers are permitted to keep their children on the premises and rear them alongside their white counterparts. Many of these black children have been incorporated into the families of the white employers with varying outcomes. Some of these families have presented at the Child, Adolescent and Family Unit (CAFU), Charlotte Maxeke Johannesburg Academic Hospital as emotional and behavioral difficulties emerged. This chapter will focus on the blurring of boundaries between employer-employee and the power differentials that interplay in the co-parenting role of these children as old ghosts of power, white superiority and black submission re-surface between "black maids and white madams."

In a conscious effort to repair old wounds and right past wrongs, the white employers discussed in this chapter, often themselves reared by black domestic workers under apartheid rule, unconsciously undermine their domestic workers' parental authority, devalue their attachment roles and appropriate their children by offering these offspring a "superior white identity." These black domestic workers often feel dependent on their employers who provide their children with private education and material opportunities that they are unable to offer. Most report that they feel disempowered in their parental role in the process. Some express a sense of entitlement to compensation but find that this too comes with a cost. This chapter will focus on the psychotherapeutic interventions with these families who present with difficulties at the CAFU using a psychoanalytically orientated framework. The central debates that will be addressed include how toxic social discourses that are repeated unconsciously through a failure to deal with collective trauma, defensive disavowal, lack of reflective function and unacknowledged shame, contribute to re-enactments of racism. The process of re-constructing a sense of self that is palatable in post-apartheid South Africa as bound up in the politics of memory and forgetting will be discussed. It is essential to deal with both individual and collective accounts of memory and suffering, as without reflective thought and understanding these easily slip into serving various political agendas (de Kok, 1998; Nuttall, 1998; Robins, 1998). The consequences of forgetting and the recuperation of memory in order to set the ghosts of apartheid to rest will be explored in the psychotherapy of these families. In this chapter, I will argue that societal and individual healing is contingent upon reclaimed memory, integration of painful truths and recognizing the subjectivities of the other.

BLACK MAIDS AND WHITE MADAMS

The institution of domestic work is regarded as a key area of exploitation and racial inequality in apartheid South Africa (Ally 2009; Cock, 1980, 2011; Du Toit, 2010; Shefer, 2012). In what has been regarded as a classic study of power relations between domestic workers and their employers, Cock's (1980) study of "maids and madams" in South Africa under the era of apartheid, noted that due to a lack of educational opportunities, employment alternatives and influx control legislation restricting the mobility of black workers these women were trapped, powerless, and at the mercy of their white employers (Du Toit, 2010; Nyamnjoh, 2005). Russell (2002) reports that between 1966 and 1988 during the heyday of apartheid rule, approximately half of white urban households employed full time domestic help while between 35–40 percent employed no domestic help at all. Surveys have indicated that there has been a steady decline in domestic workers in South Africa over the past decade (Alexander, 2013), which may be due to white political anxieties but also economic difficulties and improved labor laws (Du Toit, 2010; Russell, 2002). In post-apartheid South Africa, significant steps have been taken to improve the working conditions and labor rights of domestic workers including: a set minimum wage, specific working conditions such as hours of work, overtime pay, salary increases, deductions, annual and sick leave, unemployment insurance as well as access to representation through trade union membership (Domestic Workers Sector, Sectoral Determination 7 of the Basic Conditions of Employment Act, No. 75 of 1997). However, despite these improvements the high levels of poverty, an unemployment rate of 25.6% and failure of uniform education delivery mean that an estimated 1 to 1.5 million individuals in South Africa work as domestic workers, gardeners, and child minders, as other employment opportunities remain limited (StatsSA, 2013). Concerns over the persistence of racist ideologies and exploitative practices, regardless of improved labor legislation, have been raised as it is noted that class inequalities begin to replace race inequalities in domestic service (Cock, 2011; Du Preez et al., 2010; King, 2007). More recently, a small number of publications have begun to address the role of black employers and their relationship with their domestic workers as well (Ally, 2009; Du Preez et al., 2010; Du Toit, 2010; Russell, 2002). Interestingly, in these households domestic workers are referred to as "helpers" or "auntie" (Ally, 2009).

As many black domestic workers currently live on the premises of their white employers properties, they rear their children alongside their white employer's offspring. It is here that some employers have become involved with the children of their black domestic workers, from offering emotional and financial support, or sponsoring education at expensive private schools, to direct engagement with child rearing and allowing these children to live in their homes, be included on their holidays and be part of their families. It is at this interface that difficulties have emerged. In many instances, the biological mother/domestic worker has retained her status as employee while her son/daughter has transformed to "family member" of the employer's family, leaving a dangerous power differential between child and parent mirrored in the power dynamics between employee and employer. Although she is the biological mother, as domestic worker, she may be instructed to take orders, clean up after family members, and generally be in a subservient role in the presence of her own biological child. Her attempts at parenting can be undermined by the employer who has greater power and status in this context, leaving her child confused about his or her mother's role as parent and authority as well as his or her own role and position in this family context. In one of the few papers which has describe this phenomenon, Burkhalter and Manala (2001) have noted that this informal fostering process can result in the biological mother relinquishing her role as mother as her maternal function becomes compromised and her fear of jeopardizing her employment renders her helpless and silent. While I agree with their observation of the destructive impact of this process on the role and authority of the biological mother, I do not agree that this phenomenon is analogous to one of fostering or adoption, albeit informal. What makes this practice unique is that the white employer usurps the maternal function of her black domestic worker, and does so in her presence. In both adoption and fostering situations, there are separate dwelling and living arrangements and contact with the biological/legal caretaker ranges from frequent to none at all. However, the role and maternal function of the birth mother in such instances is not continuously undermined in the presence of her child. In many cases, fostered or adopted children have to mourn the birth mother as they are incorporated into the adoptive or foster family (Eng and Han, 2006). In the context under question, the birth mother is present but her presence is absent. In her work on the experiences of domestic workers in South Africa, King (2007) has eloquently described the feelings of disdain concealed behind the façade of deference, in many of these women.

The children in these situations are often disappointed at the realization that their birth mother lacks power and status in their eyes and that their idealization of the "employer mother," ultimately becomes disappointed as she emerges as fallible and unable to fulfil their expectations. Their sense of betrayal by the perceived disinvestment of their biological mother, and their growing alienation from their materially privileged white "employer mother," as they begin to perceive her difference, leave many of these children with disaffected rage and a deep sense of deprivation. The realization that they are not really part of the white family, only honorary members, and that they are not accorded the same attachment and investment as the employer's own biological children, is deeply painful. Having distanced themselves from their African racial, ethnic and cultural identifications, their embrace of a "white" identity comes at a price of partial recognition and loss.

The employers also emerge as disappointed and frustrated as their well-intentioned endeavors and financial sacrifices are not rewarded with the recognition and gratitude they had felt their due. Burkhalter and Manala (2001) comment that the tragic irony is that the hope to provide better opportunities for these children is so often replaced by disappointment on all sides. It is also important to acknowledge that not all families supporting their domestic workers and their children fall into these difficulties with destructive outcomes. Families with positive outcomes do not present at clinics and are less likely to be reported or described. It is therefore, likely that the families described in this chapter reflect a skewed sample of those families who develop difficulties and may not be representative of all households involved in attempting to assist the children of their domestic workers.

Quite understandably, these cases raise a number of complex clinical and ethical dilemmas. In managing these cases at a clinical level, the determination of the best interests of the child is no easy matter. Should the biological mother who feels undermined and disempowered leave her place of employment, and seek alternative work elsewhere? Given the high rates of unemployment, will she find work? In addition, if she lives on her employer's property, this coupled with her financial constraints and an acute housing shortage, raises questions about where she will live. Should the young child be encouraged to leave the home, school and environment he or she has known since birth? Should he or she be removed from the "employer mother" he or she has become attached to? What are the implications for the child's attachment and psychological well-being in the face of such losses? Should he or she be removed from a private standard of education that offers hope and opportunities otherwise beyond his or her financial grasp? Can the mother reclaim her maternal function and parental authority while employed as a domestic worker? Is the mother able to put the ghosts of her apartheid past to rest and assert herself as a subject in the presence of her white employer? Can the child develop a healthy gender, racial, ethnic and cultural identity in this context? Can the employer offer support and financial assistance without colonizing the rearing of her domestic worker's child? Is the employer able to address her rescue fantasies and attempts at racial reconciliation without unconscious enactment? Can the employer move beyond a paternalistic relationship with her domestic worker? How does the psychoanalytic psychotherapist address these issues within the context of post-apartheid South Africa with its history of racism, traumatic interpellation of inferiority and superiority into the ordinary citizenship of its people and the need for reconciliation, recognition and racial healing? These are but a few of the clinical and ethical dilemmas facing these families and the professionals who see them.

While it is clear that the boundaries between parent/employee and parent/employer, their respective roles, functions and power relations need to be addressed and clarified, the forces at play are complex, historical and often unconscious. Didactic counselling and well-intentioned advice are notoriously overrated. Instead, it is suggested in this chapter, that through addressing the ghosts of their personal histories (Cavelli, 2012; Fraiberg et al., 1975; O'Loughlin, 2007; 2013) within their particular socio-political contexts that we have found ways to assist and bring healing to these families. The challenge has been to address these issues within the historical socio-political context of post-apartheid South Africa and offer a treatment that is clinically relevant and meaningful. A greater challenge has been to address issues of reconciliation and repair without unconsciously repeating or re-enacting trauma through our failures to process, recognize and deal with unpalatable truths and neglect of painful unwanted memories.

DISSOCIATION, RECOGNITION AND OTHERING

There has been a shift in contemporary psychoanalytic discourse from a focus on intrapsychic conflict and fantasy back to the impact of "real" trauma and a re-emergence of interest in the role of dissociative mechanisms in response to trauma over mechanisms of repression (Benjamin, 2009, 2011; Bromberg, 1998, 2003; Guralnik and Simeon, 2010; Stern, 1997; 2003). With this shift has come a renewed appreciation of the role of memory and forgetting in trauma and the need to address these issues in psychotherapy to avoid repetition, enactment and transgenerational transmission of such trauma (Bohleber, 2007; Cavelli, 2012; Charles, 2012; Coles, 2011; Connolly, 2011; Gerson, 2009; O'Loughlin, 2007; 2012; 2013; Silber, 2012). However a consistent criticism of psychoanalysis has been its tendency to address socio-political influences primarily through intrapsychic explanations and its failure to address the real effects of oppressive political and socioeconomic ideologies, practices and trauma that impact on our subjectivities as individuals (Altman, 1995, 2000; 2011; Benjamin, 2011; Gentile, 2013; Gobodo-Madikizela, 2009; Layton, 2010; Straker, 2002, 2004 Suchet, 2007; Ullman, 2006). While a great deal is written about the need to be cognizant of socio-political influences on the individual and the consequences of power differentials, little is said about how this might be achieved in the therapeutic context. The difficulty is how to address these issues within the therapeutic space in ways that are relevant to our history, cognizant of the intersubjectivity between therapist and patient, and meaningful with regard to the patient's intrapsychic world and subjective sense of self.

Central to the process of dealing with the painful issues that arise in these families is the role of recognition by the therapist of the subjectivities, feelings and experiences of the other. This draws directly on the work of Benjamin (1988, 1995, 2004, 2009), who refers to recognition as the ability to sustain connectedness to the other while accepting his or her separateness and difference. The other must be recognized as another subject in order for the self to fully experience his or her subjectivity in the other's presence (Benjamin, 1995, 2004). This recognition is the response from the therapist that makes meaningful the feelings, intentions and agency of the self. This recognition of the mind by another allows the self to realize its agency. Benjamin (1988, 2009) maintains that the capacity for mutual recognition has its roots in childhood and is essentially predicated on the capacity to attain secure attachment. When this process is disrupted and the complementary form of the relationship not balanced by mutual activity, the reverse of complementarity becomes entrenched and the relationship becomes a power struggle. A preoccupation with domination and submission is the result of a breakdown in the capacity for mutual recognition. In this instance, she argues, it is essential for the therapist to extricate him/herself from the reciprocal lock of complementary relations that characterize ruptures. In split complementarity, which forms the structure of these ruptures, a person is experienced as one's opposite pole, as in the relation of "doer and done to" (Benjamin, 2004), accuser and accused, victimizer and victim, good and bad, or right and wrong (Benjamin, 2009). This deadlock can be broken by the capacity to recognize multiple perspectives which opens the therapeutic space for the ability to think and reflect (Cavelli, 2012; Connolly, 2011; Gerson, 2009).

There is an on-going debate in the psychoanalysis of witnessing about whether subject and object can be reconciled (Boulanger, 2012; Gerson, 2009; Poland, 2000; Ullman, 2006). In addressing the issue of achieving mutuality in the oppressor group, Ullman (2006) suggests that witnessing, defined in relational terms, encompasses the constitution of knowledge about disavowed, dissociated reality of suffering and evil via the encounter with an other who is willing to be there. While the survivor may experience memories as traumatic, dangerous or shameful, the analyst as emotionally available witness, thinks together with the subject to allow memory to become transformed into an integrated cohesive self. This therapeutic function of witnessing in psychoanalytically orientated psychotherapy has been described by Orange (2011) as analogous to mirroring, as the therapist functions as a self-object for the patient. This view is challenged by Ullman (2007) who considers that the therapist must remain an other who enables the testimony, rather than be a self-object merged with the survivor. Witnessing as a therapeutic function is characterized by the struggle to know the other while still recognizing the other's difference and unknowability (Benjamin, 1998, 2004).

The function of therapist as witness is particularly sensitive when the patient is an aggressor or member of the oppressor group who has inflicted suffering on himself/herself as well as on others. When it has become possible for a painful truth about the bad parts of a patient to emerge there is an acknowledgement by the self of the suffering he or she has inflicted on others. This holding and witnessing of a painful internal truth requires an assumption of otherness in the therapeutic function. The therapist accepts and respects the reality of difference (Poland, 2000; Ullman, 2007). Witnessing is part of the struggle against destructive repetition compulsion and the defensive disavowal that enables dehumanization. It is this psychoanalytic function of witnessing that is crucial to the work with the employers of these families.

The current chapter will focus particularly on the role of unconscious enactment and ghosts of our apartheid past as manifest in the role of the employer. This is because it is difficult to work therapeutically with those identified as part of the oppressor or dominant group, and much of the literature on trauma tends to focus on work with victims of trauma and those generally identified with the oppressed groups in their societies. The question of when and how to name difference and confront otherness without evoking trauma, so that the dynamic of submission and domination may be replaced by those of recognition and mutuality, is central to the debate in this context (Guralnik and Simeon, 2010; Swartz, 2013). This debate immediately raises issues of the impact of apartheid on the oppressor group, who may be identified as perpetrators, bystanders, beneficiaries or victims.

There is an interesting debate in the literature regarding the experience of whiteness in post-apartheid South Africa. As whiteness has been interrogated notions of loss, shame, guilt, disavowal, accountability, culpability and racial melancholy have been discussed (Ally, 2011; Altman, 2004; Eng and Han, 2000; Jansen, 2008, 2009; Nicholls, 2006; Nuttall, 2001; Orange, 2011; Shefer, 2012; Steyn; 2004; Straker, 2004; 2011b; 2012; Suchet, 2007; Swartz, 2013).

Jansen (2009) describes his experience as the first black dean at a historically white university observing the racist ideology in post-apartheid children in which their beliefs and behaviors mirrored those of their parents, who had supported white domination before they were born. This received knowledge, the absolute truths received from infallible authorities, such as their parents, schools, churches and educational institutions, Jansen (2008, 2009) referred to as "bitter knowledge." His reference to this bitter knowledge as transmitted to subsequent generations is described as "knowledge in the blood" (Jansen, 2009). A central premise of psychoanalysis is that unprocessed trauma will inevitably return in some form and can be highly destructive for both individuals and societies (Charles, 2012; O'Loughlin, 2007, 2013). Therefore, it would seem imperative that the aim of post-apartheid psychoanalytic practice should be to engage in psychotherapies that would release both patient and therapist from the oppression of traumatic memories of the past that have a toxic effect on the present and contaminate our future (Boulanger, 2012; Gentile, 2013; Gobodo-Madikizela, 2009; Parish, 2012; Straker, 2011a; Walker, 2006). The transmission of such toxic knowledge often takes place not only in conscious form but unconsciously through pathological accommodation (Brandchaft, 2007, 2010, Orange, 2011) and unprocessed trauma (Charles, 2012; O'Loughlin, 2007, 2013). This is in no way to collude with a justification or apology for apartheid ideology but rather to understand how certain forms of racism become repeated in subsequent generations and the processes involved in unintentional enactments of subtle racism, so that they can be addressed meaningfully in therapeutic spaces.

While sections of the white community in post-apartheid South Africa grapple with their loss of status, their accountability, guilt, shame or sense of betrayal at receiving such "bitter knowledge" from their parents' generation, or having been interpolated by a coercive, oppressive state, others engage in a range of defensive processes such as disavowal, denial or blatant dishonesty, including historical editing, memory sanitation, and personal reinvention. Those whites who opposed apartheid were faced with the choice of joining the armed struggle or taking up various positions of a liberal political persuasion, one often regarded with great contempt by members of the oppressed group. I agree with Straker (2011b) that, while it is essential to understand the socio-political context in which South Africans variously occupied the position of victim/survivor or beneficiary/bystander/perpetrator under apartheid's pernicious rule, it is also essential to understand the psychological mechanisms that underlie racism and other forms of marginalization and exclusion of otherness.

The case material described below will demonstrate processes of naming, interpellation, shaming and othering as each member of this triangle struggles to deal with enactments of unprocessed and unremembered trauma from the past.

THE CHILD: KARABO/BRIAN

Karabo, a thirteen-year-old boy, was referred to the CAFU, because he had been fighting at school, bullying younger boys, defiant toward his teachers and refusing to do his homework. This had impacted negatively on his grades. At home, he had been rude and disrespectful toward his biological mother, whom we shall name Mavis, and he had recently stolen a second mobile phone from his mother's employer, whom we shall name Emma. The child was referred by the school but it was the employer who phoned the clinic. It is the policy of the unit to insist that the biological or legal parent/caretaker contact the unit and the employer Emma was informed of this at first contact. This policy often evokes hostility in some of the employers who personally refer the children of their domestic workers as they regard themselves as the de facto parent or ultimate authority. In this instance Emma accepted this requirement and Mavis duly phoned in later to refer her son. The usual outcome with these families is that each "mother" and the child are allocated their own individual psychotherapists who attempt to reinforce healthy boundaries and, respect for separate roles, re-instate maternal function in the birth mother, and deal with their individual psychodynamics as they play out in this complex process. Family therapy approaches are deemed inappropriate as these are not legitimate families, so that such an approach only serves to collude with blurred boundaries and solidify the power imbalances that erode the parent child relationship and undermine the biological mother's maternal function and parental authority. In this particular case, the biological mother was allocated a black psychotherapist who shared her ethnic background and the therapy was conducted in the language of Setswana. Karabo, who attends a private English language school, was allocated a white psychotherapist and I, a white South African psychologist, was allocated the employer as patient. The CAFU does not have a policy of matching race, ethnicity, culture or religion. However, where there may be communication difficulties, an effort is made to accommodate patients in their primary language.

On first meeting, Karabo, his mother and her employer, were in the waiting room with Karabo who appeared angry and sullen. He was seated alone, separate from them. Parents and caregivers are required to complete routine forms and sign consent forms. Mavis immediately handed the documentation to her employer, Emma, who completed the forms. The case managers who take the initial psychosocial histories of all patients in the unit pointed out that only Mavis could sign consent. It is clear from these initial meetings how Mavis, as a domestic worker, immediately deferred to her employer and how her employer assumed the mantle of superior authority. Karabo was referred to as "Brian" even though his official name was listed as Karabo. It emerged that Karabo chose this name and preferred to be called "Brian" and is known as "Brian" at his school.

Karabo was born to his mother while she was in the employ of Emma and has lived with this family constellation all his life. He has no contact with his father, who has shown him no interest and who does not contribute to his maintenance. As noted by Burkhalter and Manala (2001), the biological fathers, and indeed the fathers from the employer families, are usually absent, as was the case in this instance. Karabo's mother lived in a two bedroom cottage on the employer's property and Karabo had a bedroom in the employer's house. When he was born, it was the employer who changed his nappies and fed him while his mother continued her domestic duties. He initially slept with his mother in her bed but later slept with Emma and eventually, from the age of 6 years, was given his own bedroom in the employer's house. He attended a private school and took part in a number of sporting activities all funded by the employer, Emma. He called Emma "Mom," and his mother "Mamma."

In therapy, Karabo was initially very guarded and his seething anger quite apparent. However, he reported that he loved both his "mothers" and that he hated his school. He indicated that he became angry when adults shouted at him. He expressed a wish to own his own house and said that he felt life was so unfair. His greatest fear was that he would fail at school and let both his "mothers" down. He felt ashamed about his poor grades. Karabo also felt guilty that he attended a private school, had nice clothes and went away on exciting holidays, while his siblings, who lived with his grandmother, did not have access to the same privileged lifestyle. He said that he loved his grandmother and missed his siblings but he was anxious about visits and often felt alienated and different from his family. He had a best friend at school, who was a white boy from a particularly wealthy family whom he visited regularly on weekends. As his therapy progressed, Karabo softened and cried when he admitted he wanted to be a good boy but felt he was always in trouble.

He felt different from his peers at school who teased him for having a "white mother." It soon emerged that he preferred his white friends as they were more "fun" to be with and he disliked being teased by his black peers who regarded him as "spoilt." It appeared that he had rejected his black racial identity and preferred to adopt a "white" identity with an English name rather than a Setswana one. He revealed that he loved his biological mother a great deal but that she did not understand the problems he faced nor the world in which he lived. He felt a growing distance from his mother as their worlds seem to have drifted apart. She was unable to help him with his homework and his "employer mother" Emma assisted him in this regard. He was quite idealizing of his "mom," Emma, whom he perceived as better educated and more resourceful. Despite this he had become angry and resentful toward her but was unable to understand or make sense of these feelings. He felt that he did not really belong in his "white" mother's family, feeling marginalized or even an intruder at times. He was very ashamed of having stolen two mobile phones from Emma and admitted that he had also taken money from her purse. Karabo struggled between a wish to make a claim on his "white" mother and felt his claim was not entirely legitimate. He alternated between feelings of entitlement and feeling deprived and resentful. He stated a wish to be more independent, perhaps as a way to avoid this untenable ambivalent dependence.

Many of the children in these family situations, torn between their biological mothers and employer mothers, present with feelings of relative deprivation. Despite access to private schooling, sponsored holidays and living in materially wealthy conditions, their sense of exclusion and deprivation appears enhanced by their proximity to privilege. Burkhalter and Manala (2001) report that it is not uncommon for these children to be referred for stealing, an antisocial tendency seen by Winnicott (1975) as a sign of the deprived child's hope that his or her environment might recognize their need and meet their demand.

Karabo's struggle with his racial identity and cultural history is immediately apparent. It is clear that he is receiving mixed messages from his mother who has internalized an apartheid racist ideology and, due to this unprocessed trauma of her denigration under this destructive system repeats a communication of black racial inferiority to her son. Consciously she is angry that he has changed his Setswana name and that he mixes mostly with white peers but she is proud of his command of English and she does not facilitate his access to his cultural and ethnic heritage. She speaks to him mostly in English unless she wishes to reprimand him. She does so in Setswana, partly to conceal her communication from her employer and partly to assert some modicum of parental authority that cannot be challenged. The result is that Karabo associates his mother tongue with discipline, correction and criticism. Karabo's sense of alienation from his employer mother and his betrayal at being offered a hollow identity, alongside the realization that he is a visitor to the trappings of privilege and whiteness result in defiance. Karabo is trapped as an outsider as his claim to a black racial identity with a Setswana cultural heritage has been diluted and devalued. His response is to reject the privilege he has been offered, disinvest in his private schooling and turn on those smaller and weaker than him at school and bully them.

THE MOTHER: MAVIS

Mavis came from a rural area and was the youngest of six children. Mavis described her childhood as good and said that they were a poor but close family. Later in her therapy, she admitted that she was physically abused by her father and by her older siblings. She reported quite unemotionally that her one brother was murdered quite recently by a cousin and it slowly emerged that her childhood was marred by excessive levels of family violence. She reported that she had her first child at sixteen years. Karabo was her third child and the one she had kept. Her first and second born children had been sent to live with her mother and she saw them monthly. Mavis reported that she had left school in grade 8 as she was pregnant. She had always worked as a domestic worker and she had been in the employ of Emma for seventeen years. Mavis was polite and deferential in her therapy and avoided any critical remarks about her living circumstances. She referred to her employer as her 'mother' although she was older and repeatedly mentioned all the help that she had received from Emma. Mavis was very guarded and simply assumed that the details of her therapy were discussed with her employer. It was a focus of the therapy to ensure that Mavis claimed her right as an independent adult with her own rights to confidentiality and autonomy but this proved a very slow process and her trust in her therapist was tenuous. The first issue that challenged her trust was that she was HIV+ and frightened that the therapist would tell her employer. Her confidentiality was assured and, as this was confirmed over time in her experience of the therapy, Mavis became more open.

Mavis reported that she was worried about her son Karabo, who was very sensitive and angered easily. She said he used to be a shy, quiet person and now had become rude, disrespectful and defiant. She admitted that she had been hitting him with a belt to get him to listen but this appeared to have made matters worse. She was worried that he would fail at school and that her employer would stop paying for him to attend a private school. Her fear was that he would then have to attend a "township" school and she felt that his future would be compromised. She was angry that he was jeopardizing his private education, and placing her employment at risk. Mavis felt resentful that he did not appreciate having the opportunities that she never had. She felt he was spoilt and ungrateful.

Mavis felt that her son would have a better future and improved quality of life if he were to mix with successful affluent whites but at the same time was ambivalent that he seemed to be losing his cultural roots. While she was angry that he preferred to speak English and spent so much time visiting his white friends, she did not facilitate visits to his grandparents, siblings and cousins, or friendships with his black peers at school. Initially, she appeared very deferential toward her employer and only much later in the therapy was she able to tentatively confide her resentment that Karabo shows more respect toward her employer than he does toward her. However, she was quick to blame this on her son's defiant and ungracious attitude.

To do justice to the full complexities of Mavis's issues is beyond the scope of this chapter but certain issues will be highlighted. Mavis was clearly trapped in the power differentials that face most domestic workers in their relationships with their employers. She was dependent on her employer for her job, her home, and indeed for the education and lifestyle of her son. She has paid a terrible price for this as she has lost her parental authority and watches helplessly as he defers to his employer mother's authority and accords her more respect. As she defends against the uninvited guests of her own unremembered past she re-enacts her own personal experiences of abuse at the hands of her father, and her sense of lack of agency and autonomy are repeated with "terrible and exacting detail" (Fraiberg et al., 1975, p. 388).

Mavis has also been a victim of apartheid oppression interpellated by a racist ideology that conferred an inferior identity on her as a black disenfranchised woman. She continues to function without a voice and defer to her white employer, allowing her to colonize her child and appropriate his identity. The failure of adequate containment of the vulnerable child, disturbances of agency and dependency and incapacity to tolerate difference can be experienced hierarchically denoting an inferior versus superior polarity (Benjamin, 1988, 2009; Layton, 2010). This dynamic is apparent as Mavis' subjective narrative continues to be one of inferiority. Mavis also mimicked the feelings and perceptions of her employer in her perception of her son as ungrateful and entitled. Her ambivalence and envy at her son's perceived privilege has manifest in her physical beatings of him. She is trapped in this triangle by her sense of helplessness, and lack of autonomy and agency, which she perpetuates by being passive in her therapy. She expects that her therapist will advise her and act on her behalf. The price she has paid for her Karabo's "better future" is the loss of her child and the on-going loss of herself as subject.

THE EMPLOYER: EMMA

Emma came from a very wealthy family in which she was the eldest of two children of her father's second marriage. Her mother was much younger than her father and described as his attractive trophy wife. Her mother appears to have been very ambitious and this was transferred to her children who were required to achieve and perform to meet her narcissistic need for perfection and deliver on her obligation as the wife of a wealthy magnate. Emma was raised by a black nanny in a household of several domestic workers. Her mother, who did not work but devoted most of her time to social activities, delegated her mothering role to Emma's black nanny, "Ivy." Emma was abandoned by her black nanny when she was 3 years old and reported this loss in a matter of fact manner without affect. As an adult she later learnt that her mother terminated her nanny's services as she felt that Ivy was getting "too close" to the children. Emma recalled a series of domestic workers being employed over the years but none stayed for a period of more than 2 years. She was often anxious that she would not please her parents and that she would evoke her mother's criticism if she was not good and did not achieve. She felt that her vulnerability would not be tolerated and felt considerable shame when she was unable to contain her anxiety and fears. Although her father was busy and somewhat absent, she was aware that his approval also depended on her achievement both academically and in sport.

When Emma first came to therapy, she reported that as a student she was crippled by anxiety and unable to complete her final exams for fear of failure. She felt she had to pass with distinction or else she would regard herself as an utter failure and be ashamed at the thought of her inferior intellectual ability. She felt that she was a fraud and that she had been a disappointment to her parents. She had a very conflict ridden and competitive relationship with her younger sister who regarded her as the favored child. Emma did not feel favored and was constantly bewildered by her sister's endless envious attacks. Despite some ambivalence, she married a young man from a successful family as her parents approved and felt that he would be suitable. The marriage was considered more a merger of fortunes than an act of loving commitment by the media at the time. Soon Emma found that she was unable to please her husband, or meet his expectations, and she again felt she was a disappointment. She worked in a very demanding job but was expected to drop her commitments whenever her husband demanded, as his career and needs were deemed superior. She had two boys, and proceeded to exact the same demand for achievement and success from her children as had been demanded of her. Emma always felt that she was not good enough either in her career, or as a wife and mother. As adults, both her sons had emigrated, and her marriage felt empty, lonely and hollow. She came to therapy when her second mobile phone had been stolen by "Brian" (Karabo).

Emma felt angry, resentful, and depressed. She had spent an inordinate amount of time and energy trying to offer Karabo opportunities, stimulation, enrichment and "a better future." She had taken responsibility for his health, been involved in driving him to his various extramural activities, supervised his homework, taken him on holidays both local and overseas and she had funded these personally. Her husband was critical of her relationship with Karabo and irritated that the boy impinged on his time with, and demands of, his wife. He regarded his wife as a "bleeding heart" and denigrated her efforts to support and assist Mavis and Karabo. Emma felt betrayed by Karabo's defiance and stealing and his deteriorating school performance. She felt unappreciated and helpless. Interestingly, her domestic worker, Mavis did not really feature in her therapy initially, as her disappointment and anger tended to focus on Karabo, to whom she felt she had given a large part of her life.

GHOSTS OF THE PAST

It is clear that each member of this tragic triangle is faced with unconscious enactments and demands as they grapple with their own pain at lack of recognition, feeling devalued, confused about their roles and identities. Each is struggling to establish him or herself as a subject, different but validated and worthy. I wish to focus particularly on the work with Emma the employer who was my patient in this instance. I shall confine my focus on three pivotal factors in the history of Emma's identity, her constitution as white South African employer in post-apartheid South Africa, her abandonment by her black nanny at the age of three years, and her developmental sense of self as inadequate, unworthy, fraudulent and shameful.

Emma felt inadequate, inferior and was prone to shame affects from as far back as she could remember. She has been required to fulfill her mother's narcissistic ambitions and bring credit to her role as mother without making any claims for nurturance, affirmation and recognition in return. She repeated this relationship in her marriage. She understood, as very young children do, that her needs and vulnerabilities were unwelcome and shameful. She learned to dissociate from these as she pursued her parents' affirmation and validation through academic achievement. Achievement and success became her defining narrative. The work of Brandchaft (2007, 2010) is very helpful in trying to understand how certain structures of subjectivity are laid down in the developmental processes of pathological accommodation. He argues that these emerge when a child is required pre-emptively to adhere to the needs of his or her primary objects at the expense of his or her own psychological distinctness. These systems of pathological accommodation are the child's response to the trauma of dis-recognition (Chefetz, 2010) and fear of object loss. Through repetitive patterning, the child's first reality emerges as a form of fixed belief systems in which authoritative first truths remain absolute and the child's self is defined and appraised by alien referents. In such instances, Brandchaft (2007) suggests the emerging sense of self is usurped, spontaneous experience marginalized, and capacity for self-reflection curtailed. In essence the child gives up his or her own perceptions and sense of self to maintain desperately needed attachment ties. This was certainly Emma's experience of her first reality. Her intense investment in the achievement and success of her own children and similar investment in Karabo has led to her failure to recognize him as a young boy with other subjectivities and feeling states. She has struggled to deal with her own lack of recognition from her parents and their failure to allow her different and independent subjectivities. Bromberg (2003) has described shame as a disturbance of recognition, due to the early failure of responsiveness by a parent to a genuine aspect of the self, resulting in dissociation. Emma's dis-recognition at the hands of her own parenting experiences has led to the type of adult dissociation so frequently described in the maltreatment literature (Chefetz, 2010; Lyons-Ruth et al., 2006). Emma's attempts to rescue Karabo from his poverty and lack of opportunity by offering the promise of success and achievement, repeats her own history of failure, rejection and inferiority.

Her history, however, is further shadowed by the abrupt abandonment and loss of her black nanny at the age of three years. She holds both the memory of a safe, warm nurturing figure who she loved and the perception of her black nanny as lesser, inferior and her love forbidden. Her love for her nanny was punished and her black nanny banished along with Emma's needs for dependency and secure attachment. Not only are her worst fears of object loss realized but her trauma is constituted in racial terms. Emma's failure to recognize her domestic worker Mavis as an autonomous, independent adult with her own views, racial identity and cultural affiliation and values results in the reappearance of a most noxious ghost of racist superiority in the guise of good intentions but with the dis-recognition of paternalism. Such paternalism also serves defensively to disavow her membership of the oppressor group (Straker, 2011a).

The hope, in treatment, is to address the issue of otherness in the relationship between Emma and Mavis as part of the process of restoring maternal function and parental authority to Mavis while retaining the employer's support of Karabo's education and Mavis' employment security. Moving beyond her distress and disappointment to recognize that her efforts to help Karabo were in part a re-enactment aimed at rescuing her abandoned and traumatized self in Karabo, helped Emma to hear other perspectives. She was readily able to understand that Karabo was torn between two mother figures, two identities and two worlds, resulting in his alienation, resentment and defiance. She could understand the need to affirm Karabo's racial, ethnic and cultural identities and was able to help facilitate his access and exposure to his extended family.

The greater struggle came in recognizing the voice of Mavis, who remained a faded object in the background, and who Emma did not really regard as a fit and capable mother. Emma retained a somewhat paternalistic attitude toward Mavis and, when asked how she thought it might be for Mavis to accept her help, and what costs this might involve, she became rather angry and accused me of questioning her efforts of support and assistance and devaluing her as a responsible, sensitive white South African. After all, she, unlike her friends, was making a concrete effort to "make up for apartheid" in her generous sponsorship of Karabo's education and his mother's lifestyle. She did not appreciate the lack of gratitude she felt from Karabo, nor the passive entitlement from Mavis. And, since she never supported apartheid, she felt that her efforts were particularly noteworthy and my failure to recognize her efforts was "strange." This disavowal of the damage of apartheid racism robs us of reflective function (Swartz, 2012, 2013) and, through dissociation Emma is able to avoid recognising the suffering imposed on those othered. Throughout this therapeutic encounter, I was acutely aware that as a white South African, I too am a member of the oppressor/dominant group, having lived under and after apartheid, with my own subjectivities, personal narratives and unearned socio-political benefits that also play out intersubjectively.

At this moment in her therapy, although I could have made a transference interpretation about being an unappreciative, critical parent, instead I commented to Emma that, while some white South Africans did not support apartheid, the painful truth we all have to face is that we are all beneficiaries. The disclosure of my view that we are beneficiaries of apartheid by virtue of our designated white privilege did stop her angry barrage but left Emma somewhat disarmed and confused. By including myself in this act of naming our culpability as members of the oppressor group, I was hoping to open a space for mutuality that we shared a shameful history that needed to be acknowledged. As long as she remained the innocent bystander and rescuing white benefactor, Mavis could only remain other, her pain would remain disavowed and unacknowledged.

While Emma's good intentions did translate into a form of rescue rather than repair, they also served to protect her from recognizing that her current paternalistic behavior was in fact a racist re-enactment, taking the position of the superior white, and knowing what is best for her inferior black domestic worker. What began to emerge with more clarity for Emma was how this stance undermined Mavis as a mother, became a form of dis-recognition of her as an equal subject deserving of respect and autonomy and also was an enactment of a previous ghost in the form of the devalued and replaceable black nanny of her own past. This recognition was extremely painful for Emma to come to terms with, and her immediate response was to weep inconsolably and be consumed with shame as her feelings of inner badness were once again confirmed. At this time, I was left feeling much like a murderer of small babies and cuddly puppies, as I realized that my own interpellative gaze as therapist had caused this pain. I shared these feelings with Emma who was surprised at my admission, which appeared to restore some sense of mutuality between us.

Most important, however, it was through recognizing the loss of her beloved black nanny, and empathizing with the unacknowledged pain of the abandoned three year old Emma, that the adult Emma could reclaim her vulnerability and begin to consider the disregarded pain, suffering and loss endured by Ivy, her discarded nanny, and Mavis, her domestic worker. Emma could only become open to other perspectives and subjectivities when her own unprocessed trauma was addressed.

Validating her immense loss of Ivy, her black nanny, was pivotal in recognizing her pain and abandonment as a little girl and also in affirming the subjectivity of Ivy as an equal in her history of attachment figures. Emma was deeply relieved to realize that Ivy had not abandoned her but was acutely ashamed that her parents had banished her from the family home. Here, Emma was able to incorporate a sense of self that was not rejected or abandoned by Ivy, but she now had to deal with the dismissive, dis-recognition of her parents, not only of her attachment to her black nanny but their non-recognition and devaluation of Ivy herself. Layton's (2010) thoughtful work is helpful here in suggesting that it is more useful to address the shame and helplessness as an initial focus and not the complicity. The generational transmission of racist ideology from her parents, as they dismissed and terminated the services of multiple domestic workers, was painful to acknowledge. Emma had to come to terms with the implications of this heritage on her defensive disavowal and a sense of self no longer as bystander but as beneficiary and now as unwitting perpetrator.

PRE-DISSOCIATED CHILD

Citing their experience with their black nannies as example, Straker (2011a) has argued that white children began by dissociating racial experiences, during apartheid rule, but that these racial experiences later became disavowed. Because dissociation allowed whites to not recognize the effects of apartheid on its victims, leaving these experiences unformulated, the inferior status accorded black South Africans, enshrined by law, was taken over by whites and enacted and transmitted down the generations. Straker's view is extended by Orange (2011), who suggests that this process is likely to be far more complex. Orange (2011) proposes that the pre-dissociated child within a coercive system might be further understood through the types of systems of pathological accommodation described by Brandchaft (2007, 2010). Because pathological accommodation requires that children learn that they must sacrifice their own perception, Orange argues, such sacrifice could include their perceptiveness of the humanness of their early caregivers. Subjective perceptions of superior and inferior that become enforced by parents, schools, religious institutions and the law could easily be accepted by school age as the unconsciously negotiated price of desperately needed attachment ties. She argues further that a child torn between a deeply embodied attachment to a black caregiver and his or her parents might dissociate in order to preserve a sense of attachment as a basic attempt at survival at the cost of loss of the relational/emotional self-experience. Orange then predicts, quite accurately, that such a child might exact a similar price from the next generation in some form. I believe this explication further elucidates our understanding of the transmission of trauma and repeated enactments of racism permitted by unclaimed memory and unprocessed dissociation described in these families.

WITNESSING AS THERAPEUTIC FUNCTION

While I agree that psychoanalytically orientated psychotherapists in post-apartheid South Africa have an ethical obligation to listen for what our culture-political discourse disavows and abjects (Boulanger, 2012; Swartz, 2013), we do need to "tread softly" (Hartman, 2010, p. 433). Because psychoanalysis is not superior in its ability to interpret the interpellations of coercive ideology (Hoffman, 1998) and is equally capable of being an agent of interpellation or vehicle of shame (Guralnik and Simeon, 2010), we need to recognize our capacity to foreclose recognition of the other's subjectivities through our own unformulated experience and inevitable re-enactments.

One difficulty in trying to deal with the socio-political impact of oppressive histories as they permeate the personal and private spaces of individual subjectivities is the tension between the therapeutic function of witnessing and re-traumatizing the patient. With the emergence of the bad parts of the self in the therapeutic dyad, there is potential for rupture and split complementarity, where one part of the dyad is experienced as the other's opposite pole as in "doer and done to" (Benjamin, 2004) or, in this case potentially as accuser and accused. While Margalit (2002) described the moral witness as needing to take a risk, Benjamin (2011) comments that the risk taken by the witness need not be that of being in the same danger as the victim, rather the risk may lie in naming an uncomfortable truth the other wishes to deny. Not only may this elicit condemnation, it also forces the witness to bear the anxiety and anger that may incur through lifting of such dissociation. Without confronting our own dissociation, we run the risk of returning the condemnation back to the other and replacing it with a self-justifying stance in a blaming and blamed complementarity (Benjamin, 2011). While witnessing creates crisis, defensiveness and renewed attempts at disavowal as it challenges the denial or disavowal of a reality of suffering, it is the persistent presence and gaze of the other who is willing to listen and be present that allows both parties, opposite and other, to achieve mutual recognition and become more fully human (Altman, 2011; Poland, 2000; Ullman, 2006).

It is through the process of mutual recognition and the capacity to be both witness and other in bearing the emergence of unprocessed trauma, disavowal and disassociated memory that we are able to constructively engage the re-enactments of racism in these families. By being able to open up therapeutic spaces to hear other voices and consider multiple subjectivities we are able to restore maternal function and authority, and respect for roles, boundaries and cultural tradition in these families.

Unlike other countries with histories of gross human rights violations, in South Africa, victims and perpetrators continue to live alongside each other so that talking about trauma, forgiveness and reconciliation becomes imperative (Gobodo-Madikizela, 2008; Jansen, 2008, 2009).

A fuller understanding of our patients and ourselves requires recognition of the interplay between personal history, the socio-political context in which we live and the heritage of uninvited guests that each of these bring to our personhood. Through addressing the effects of apartheid on our memory, identity, and subjectivities, psychoanalysis can be a transformative clinical process (Hook and Long, 2011). Intersubjective approaches to psychoanalytic psychotherapy, with the emphasis on mutual recognition and an acceptance of theoretical plurality, have much to offer the process of building bridges in post-apartheid society (Altman, 2004; Benjamin, 2009, 2011; Layton 2010; Swartz, 2012, 2013). Globally, the need to consider the role of moral witnessing and socio-political context in psychoanalytic work has become germane as more individuals, forced by birth or citizenship, have to deal with human violations committed in their name. We only need to consider the controversial Guantanamo Bay prisoners, the legitimacy of the recent Iraqi war, suicide bombings committed in the name of Islam, restriction of Palestinian movement in Israeli occupied West Bank, or the rise of anti-gay legislation in Africa and Russia, to recognize the ubiquitous presence of difference and opportunities for othering. Our psychoanalytic work needs to pay more attention to the suffering generated by socio-political oppression and exploitation and, with it, our subjectivities as psychotherapists in these contexts (Altman, 2011; Benjamin, 2011).

Our capacity for humanity is dependent both on the learning we acquire through the transmission of personal, cultural and political values, beliefs and ideologies from one generation to the next, and our ability and courage to challenge the limits of such received knowledge.

A NOTE ON CONFIDENTIALITY

It is crucial that the privacy of all patients discussed in this chapter is protected. In each case the identifying details have been altered or disguised to protect the confidentiality of the individuals involved. As patients from an academic teaching hospital they are requested to give consent for their material to be used for teaching or publication in accordance with the Code of Ethics of the Profession of Psychology, Health Professionals Council of South Africa and the regulations of academic hospitals.

REFERENCES

Alexander, G. (2013). Disappearing domestic workers. South African Institute of Race Relations Annual South African Survey 2013. Retrieved January 15, 2014, from www.sairr.org.za/media-releases/Disappearing%20domestic%20workers.pdf.download/file

Ally, S. (2009). *From servants to workers: South African domestic workers and the democratic state.* Ithaca, NY: Cornell University Press.

Ally, S. (2011). Domestics, "dirty work" and the effects of domination. *South African Review of Sociology, 42*(2), 1–7.

Altman, N. (1995). *The analysis in the inner city: race, class and change through a psychoanalytic lens.* Hillsdale, NJ: The Analytic Press.

Altman, N. (2000). Black and White thinking: a psychoanalyst reconsiders race. *Psychoanalytic Dialogues, 10,* 589–606.

Altman, N. (2004). Whiteness uncovered: Commentary on papers by Melanie Suchet and Gillian Straker. *Psychoanalytic Dialogues, 14,* 439–446.

Altman, N. (2011). Response to Chana Ullman's paper: "Between denial and witnessing." *Psychoanalytic Perspectives, 8*(2), 201–206.

Basic Conditions of Employment Act, No. 75 of 1997 Gazette No. 18491, Notice No. 1631. Sectoral Determination 7: Domestic Worker Sector, South Africa. Published under Government Notice R437 in Government Gazette 29885, dated 15 May 2007.

Benjamin, J. (1988). *The bonds of love: Psychoanalysis, feminism and the problem of domination.* New York, NY: Pantheon.

Benjamin, J. (1995). Recognition and destruction: An outline of intersubjectivity. In J. Benjamin (Ed.), *Like subjects, love objects: Essays in recognition and sexual difference.* New Haven, CT: Yale University Press.

Benjamin, J. (2004). Beyond doer and done to: An intersubjective view of thirdness. *Psychoanalytic Quarterly, 73,* 5–46.

Benjamin, J. (2009). A relational psychoanalysis perspective on the necessity of acknowledging failure in order to restore the facilitating and containing features of the intersubjective relationship (the shared third). *International Journal of Psychoanalysis, 90,* 441–450.

Benjamin, J. (2011). Acknowledgement of collective trauma in light of dissociation and dehumanization. *Psychoanalytic Perspectives, 8*(2), 207–214.

Bohleber, W. (2007). Remembrance, trauma and collective memory: The battle for memory in psychoanalysis. *International Journal of Psychoanalysis, 88,* 329–352.

Boulanger, G. (2012). Psychoanalytic witnessing: Professional obligation or moral imperative? *Psychoanalytic Psychology, 29*(3), 318–324.

Brandchaft, B. (2007). Systems of pathological accommodation and change in analysis. *Psychoanalytic Psychology, 24*(66), 7–687.

Brandchaft, B. (2010). Toward an emancipatory psychoanalysis. In B. Brandchaft, S. Doctors and D. Sorter (Eds.), *Toward an emancipatory psychoanalysis: Brandchaft's intersubjective vision*. New York: Routledge.

Breytenbach, B. (1983). *('YK'): die vierde bundle van die ongedanste dans.* Emmarentia: Tauris.

Bromberg, P.M. (1998). *Standing in the spaces: Essays on clinical process, trauma and dissociation.* Hillside, NJ: The Analytic Press.

Bromberg, P.M. (2003). Something wicked this way comes: Trauma, dissociation and conflict: The space where psychoanalysis, cognitive science and neuroscience overlap. *Psychoanalytic Psychology, 20,* 558–574.

Burkhalter, T. and Manala, J. (2001). Living in no-man's land: An exploration of difficulties arising in children of domestic workers fostered by their employers. *Psychoanalytic Psychotherapy in South Africa, 9*(2), 51–62.

Cavelli, A. (2012). Transgenerational transmission of indigestible facts: From trauma, deadly ghosts and mental voids to meaning machining interpretations. *Journal of Analytical Psychology, 57,* 597–614.

Charles, M. (2012). Haunted by history: Working with trauma. *Psychoanalysis, Culture and Society, 17*(1), 82–86.

Chefetz, R.A. (2010). "T" in interpellation stands for terror: Commentary on paper by Orna Guralnik and Daphne Simeon. *Psychoanalytic Dialogues, 20,* 417–427.

Cock, J. (1980). *Maids and madams: A study in the politics of exploitation.* South Africa: Raven Press.

Cock, J. (2011). Challenging the invisibility of domestic workers. *South African Review of Sociology, 42,* 132–133.

Coles, P. (2011). *The uninvited guests from the unremembered past: An exploration of the unconscious transmission of trauma across generations*. London: Karnac.

Connolly, A. (2011). Healing the wounds of our fathers: Intergenerational trauma, memory, symbolization and narrative. *Journal of Analytical Psychology, 56,* 607–626.

De Kok, I. (1998). Cracked heirlooms: Memory on exhibition. In S. Nuttall and C. Coetzee (Eds.), *Negotiating the past: The making of memory in South Africa.* Johannesburg: Oxford University Press.

Du Preez, J., Beswick, C., Whittaker, L., and Dickenson, D. (2010). The employment relationship in the domestic workspace in South Africa: Beyond the apartheid legacy. *Social Dynamics, 36*(2), 395–409.

Du Toit, D. (2010). Extending the frontiers of employment regulation: The case of the domestic employment in South Africa. *Law, Democracy and Development, 14, 204–229.* Retrieved January 12, 2014, from http://dx.doi.org/10.4314/ldd.v14i1.6

Eng, D.L. and Han, S. (2006). Desegregating love: Transnational adoption, racial reparation and racial transitional objects. *Studies in Gender and Sexuality, 7,* 141–172.

Eng, D.L. and Han, S. (2000). A dialogue on racial melancholia. *Psychoanalytic Dialogues, 10,* 667–700.

Fraiberg, S. H., Adelson, E., and Shapiro, V.B. (1975). Ghosts in the nursery: A psychoanalytic approach to the problem of infant/mother relationships. *Journal of the American Academy of Child Psychiatry, 14*(3), 386–422.

Gentile, K. (2013). Bearing the cultural in order to engage in a process of witnessing. *Psychoanalytic Psychology, 30*(3), 456–470.

Gerson, S. (2009). When the third is dead: Memory, mourning and witnessing in the aftermath of the Holocaust. *International Journal of Psychoanalysis, 90,* 1341–1357.

Gobodo-Madikizela, P. (2008). Trauma, forgiveness and the witnessing dance making public spaces intimate. *Journal of Analytic Psychology, 53,* 169–188.

Gobodo-Madikizela, P. (2009). Exploring the ethical principle of social responsibility and other ethical issues in the context of mental health professionals' response to xenophobic violence in Cape Town. *Psycho-analytic psychotherapy in South Africa, 17*(2), 73–95.

Goldman, S. (2003). And what about the nanny? An introduction review of psychoanalytic literature. *Psycho-analytic Psychotherapy in South Africa, 13*(2), 78–105.

Guralnik, O. and Simeon, D. (2010). Depersonalization: Standing in the spaces between recognition and interpellation. *Psychoanalytic Dialogues, 20,* 400–416.

Hartman, S. (2010). L'etat c' est moi- except when I am not: Commentary on paper by Orna Guralnik and Daphine Simeon. *Psychoanalytic Dialogues, 20,* 428–436.

Hoffman, I. Z. (1998). *Ritual and spontaneity in the psychoanalytic process: A dialectic and constructivist view.* Hillsdale, NJ: The Analytic Press.

Hook, D. (2012). Apartheids lost attachments (1): On psychoanalytic reading practice. *Psychology in Society, 43,* 40–53.

Hook, D. and Long, C. (2011). The Apartheid Archive Project: Heterogeneity and the psychoanalysis of racism. *Psychoanalysis, Culture and Society, 16,* 1–10.

Jansen, J.D. (2008). *Bearing whiteness: A pedagogy of compassion in a time of troubles.* Fifth Annual Han Brenninkmeijer Memorial Lecture, (University of Johannesburg South Africa). Retreived January 15, 2014, from http://hdl.handle.net/10210/1263

Jansen, J.D. (2009). *Knowledge in the blood: Confronting race and the apartheid past.*
Stanford, CA: Stanford University Press.

King, A.J. (2007). *Domestic service in post-apartheid South Africa: Deference and disdain.* Hampshire: Ashgate Publishing Limited.

Layton, L. (2010). Irrational exuberance: Neoliberal subjectivity and the perversion of truth. *Subjectivity, 3*(3), 303–322.

Lyons-Ruth, K., Dutra, L., Schuder, M.R., and Bianchi, I. (2006). From infant attachment disorganization to adult dissociation: Relational adaptations or traumatic experiences? In R.A. Chefetz (Ed.), *Dissociative disorders: An expanding window into the psychobiology of mind* (pp. 63–86). Philadelphia, PA: Saunders.

Margalit, A. (2002). *The ethics of memory.* Cambridge, MA: Harvard University press.

Nicholls, L. (2006). When faith eclipses hope: Forgiveness within reparation. *Organizational and Social Dynamics, 6,* 161–182.

Nuttall, S. (2001). Subjectivities of whiteness. *African Studies Review, 44*(2), 115-140.

Nuttall, S. and Coetzee, C. (1998). Introduction. In S. Nuttall and C. Coetzee (Eds.), *Negotiating the past: The making of memory in South Africa.* South Africa: Oxford University Press.

Nyamnjoh, F.B. (2005). Maids and madams in Southern Africa: Coping with uncertainties and the art of mutual zombification. *Afrika Spectrum, 40*(2), 181–196.

O'Loughlin, M. (2007). Bearing witness to troubled memory. *Psychoanalytic Review, 94,* 191–212.

O'Loughlin, M. (2012). Trauma trail's from Ireland's Great Hunger: A psychoanalytic inquiry. In B. Willock, R. Curtis and L. Bohm (Eds.), *Loneliness and longing: Psychoanalytic reflections* (pp. 233–250). New York: Routledge.

O'Loughlin, M. (2013). Reclaiming genealogy, memory and history: The psychodynamic potential for reparative therapy in contemporary South Africa. In C. Smith, G. Lobban and M. O'Loughlin (Eds.), *Psychodynamic psychotherapy in South Africa: Contexts, theories and applications.* Johannesburg: Wits University Press.

Orange, D. (2011). Remembering and responsibility: Commentary on paper by Gillian Straker. *Psychoanalytic Dialogues, 21,* 658–663.

Parish, M. (2012). From the couch to culture through therapeutic community. *Psychoanalytic Psychology, 29*(3), 330–345.

Poland, W.S. (2000). The analyst's witnessing and otherness. *Journal of American Psychoanalytic Association, 48,* 17–34.

Robins, S. (1998). Silence in my father's house: Memory, nationalism, and narratives of the body. In S. Nuttall and C. Coetzee (Eds.), *Negotiating the past: The making of memory in South Africa.* Johannesburg: Oxford University Press.

Russell, M. (2002). *The employment of domestic workers by black urban households*. CSSR Working Paper No. 26. Centre for Social Service Research: University of Cape Town. Retrieved January 15, 2014, from http://www.uct.ac.za/delt/cssr/pubs.html

Shefer, T. (2012). Fraught tenderness: Narratives on domestic workers in memories of apartheid. *Peace and Conflict: Journal of Peace Psychology, 18*(3), 307–317.

Silber, L.M. (2012). Ghostbusting transgenerational processes. *Psychoanalytic Dialogues, 22,* 106–122. StatsSA (2013). Key indicators. Statistics South Africa, Pretoria. Retrieved January 12, 2014, from www.statssa.gov.za/keyindicators/keyindicators.asp

Stern, D.B. (1997). *Unformulated experience: From dissociation to imagination in psychoanalysis*. Hillsdale, NJ: The Analytic Press.

Stern, D.B. (2003). The fusion of horizons: Dissociation, enactment and understanding. *Psychoanalytic Dialogues, 13,* 558–574.

Steyn, M (2004). Rehabilitating a whiteness disgraced: Afrikaner white talk in post-apartheid South Africa. *Communication Quarterly, 52*(2), 143–169.

Straker, G. (2004). Race for cover: Castrated whiteness, perverse consequences. *Psychoanalytic Dialogues, 14,* 405–422.

Straker, G. (2011a). Shaping subjectivities: Private memories, public archives. *Psychoanalytic Dialogues, 21,* 643–657.

Straker, G. (2011b). Beneficiaries for evermore: Reply to commentaries. *Psychoanalytic Dialogues, 21,* 670–675.

Straker, G. (2012). The racialization of the mind in intimate spaces: The "nanny" in the failure of recognition. *Studies in Gender and Sexuality, 13,* 1–13.

Suchet, M. (2007). Unravelling whiteness. *Psychoanalytic Dialogues, 17,* 867–886.

Swartz, (2012). The broken mirror: Difference and shame in South African psychotherapy. *International Journal of Psychoanalytic Self Psychology, 7,* 196–212.

Swartz, S. (2013). Naming and otherness: South African intersubejctive psychoanalytic psychotherapy and the negotiation of racialized histories. In C. Smith, G. Lobban and M. O'Loughlin (Eds.), *Psychodynamic Psychotherapy in South Africa: Contexts, theories and applications.* South Africa: Wits University Press.

Ullman, C. (2006). Bearing witness: Across the barriers in society and in the clinic. *Psychoanalytic Dialogues, 16*(2), 181–198.

Walker, S.C. (2006). Trauma in South Africa: Psycho-analytic psychotherapy in South Africa. *Psychoanalytic Quarterly, 75,* 657–684.

Winnicott, D.W. (1975). The antisocial tendency. In, *From Paediatrics to Psychoanalysis: Collected Papers (pp. 306–315).* London: Hogarth Press.

FOUR

The Lifelong Impact of Institutional Childhood Abuse

The Perspective of the Irish in Britain

Jeff Moore and Christine Thornton

> Loss is the most significant word in my life. I lost my mother . . . my childhood, my education and nothing will ever get them back
> (Witness to the Commission to Inquire into Child Abuse, 2009, Volume III, para. 11.83)

In recent years accounts of past and recent child abuse have been made in almost every type of institution serving children. Two apologies by Irish Heads of State (1999, 2013), alongside historical accounts and inquiries, have highlighted the suffering of children and young people in Irish industrial schools and reformatories. For the most part, these inquiries have documented the abuse and sought to examine the causes and consequences, with a view to establishing blame and ensuring the safeguarding of future generations. Apart from some notable exceptions (such as Carr et al., 2010) there have been fewer attempts to understand how institutional childhood abuse (ICA) affects former residents over time and how others might usefully understand these experiences, and the context within which they occurred, so as to be of help. In Ireland, perhaps as a result, many former residents feel that mainstream helping professionals do not understand their needs (Higgins, 2010).

To date, the majority of research on ICA has focused on experiences whilst in institutional care (Raferty et al., 1999) and the psychological adjustment of former residents (see Carr et al., 2010, Wolfe et al., 2006). However, some research has sought to understand this abuse in a wider context. For example, Wolfe et al., (2003) developed a framework for understanding the impact of child abuse in nonfamilial settings. In describing what they call the factors contributing to harm, Wolfe et al., (2003) highlight the significance of the institution and its role within society, the role of the perpetrator, the degree and nature of the child's involvement with the institution, the degree and longevity of abuse, and post abuse events, as critical factors when examining the impact of ICA. In this chapter, we use this framework to understand ICA in the Irish context.

In the second part of the chapter, we present composite case studies drawn from the work of Immigrant Counselling and Psychotherapy (icap), a UK-based Irish agency providing therapy for Irish emigrants. Approximately 40 percent of former residents left Ireland to spend their adult lives in the UK and icap is recognized as the leading provider of therapy for this group. icap also delivers training to non-specialist front-line practitioners who work with former residents of Irish industrial schools and reformatories. The training sets out to help participants understand the unique characteristics of ICA, and to give attendees an awareness of the complex and varied life histories of many former residents. We have a similar aim here. icap's Clinical Director, Christine Thornton, has written composite case studies which reflect the typically complex realities found in icap's consulting rooms rather than the experience of any individual; we also seek to reflect gendered and acculturated differences in experience. In order to provide context for readers, we begin by providing a short history of ICA in Ireland.

THE INDUSTRIAL AND REFORMATORY SCHOOL SYSTEM

The residential child-care system in Ireland has traditionally been dominated by the Catholic Church. From the mid-nineteenth century, a large network of institutions was developed to care for children whose parents were deemed incapable of looking after them. The three main categories of institutions were orphanages, reformatories and industrial schools. Orphanages were for children from more affluent backgrounds who were in need of state care. Reformatory schools were established by the Reformatory Schools (Ireland) Act, 1858 and housed children convicted of criminal offences. A decade later, industrial schools were introduced through the Industrial Schools (Ireland) Act, 1868. Industrial schools were intended for children who were neglected, abandoned or otherwise in need of care. They provided practical training and aimed to equip children with skills for employment rather than academic learning. By the end of the century, only seven of the 10 original reformatories survived. However, by 1875, there were 50 industrial schools.

The system housed large numbers of children. Raftery and O'Sullivan report that "a total of 105,000 children were committed to industrial schools by courts between 1868 and 1969" (1999, p. 20). Irish government figures state that "approximately 29,500 people, born since 1930, were committed by the courts to industrial and reform schools… up until the 1950s they contained over 6,000 children at any one time" (*Dail Debates*, 1 October 2003, vol. 571). Although it is difficult to establish accurate figures, it is clear that the industrial and reformatory school system had a massive scope in Ireland.

Some contributors have claimed that poverty was a core reasons for the establishment and continuance of industrial schools. The institutionalisation of poverty in Ireland was historically a feature of the British occupation, from the enactment of the penal laws in the eighteenth century onwards. Kee (1976) quotes General Gordon in a letter to the Times (1880) describing the Irish peasantry as "patient beyond belief, loyal, but at the same time broken-spirited and desperate, living on the verge of starvation in places where we would not keep our cattle" (p. 78). Poverty was equally endemic in Ireland in the late 1920s, 1930s and 1940s. This is evidenced by high rates of tuberculosis, rickets, anemia, emigration, money-lending and unemployment, especially in Dublin, Cork, Waterford and Limerick (CICA, 2009). Although poverty did play a part, it is important to be aware of the considerable complexity in social circumstances which resulted in admission to industrial schools and reformatories.

ADMISSION AND INSTITUTIONAL LIFE

The Commission to Inquire into Child Abuse (hereafter referred to as CICA), a body established in 1999 to investigate ICA in Ireland, found that 80 percent of children were committed to the industrial schools for "lack of proper guardianship." This, some suggest, was a catch-all heading that included children of unmarried mothers; children who had lost parents, or whose parents were debilitated through illness, or whose families were unable to look after them due to poverty; children who were homeless, or whose families had broken up due to desertion by a spouse or partner (Ferguson, 2007).

Work was a feature of daily life in the schools. The types of work included both indoor and outdoor work in weaving, shoemaking, tailoring, and carpentry workshops, kitchens, staff residences, farmyards, fields and bogs, as well as day laboring for local farmers and businesses (CICA, 2009). Many former residents have described engaging in heavy, manual work as children for or on behalf of the schools. Industrial schools for girls provided a narrower range of training than those housing boys, focusing on domestic service, laundry, and sewing (CICA, 2009).

INSTITUTIONAL ABUSE

Writing before the publication of the Commission to Inquire into Child Abuse, Brennan commented that "there is little dispute now that these institutes were at best austere places, at worst some were scenes of extreme suffering" (2007 p. 257). We now know that many thousands of children and young people experienced suffering that some suggest amounts to crimes against humanity (Groome, 2011). Upon the publication of the CICA (2009), the Irish Times called it "a map of an Irish hell" (21 May, 2009). The commission found that "physical and emotional abuse and neglect were features of the institutions. Sexual abuse occurred in many of them, particularly boys' institutions. Schools were run in a severe, regimented manner that imposed unreasonable and oppressive discipline on children and even on staff" (CICA, 2009, para. 6.01). Carr et al., (2010) working with a sample of 247 former residents, found that more than 90% of cases were classified as having experienced physical and emotional abuse or neglect and 47% as having experienced sexual abuse within the schools. As well as physical and sexual abuse, evidence shows that residents of these schools were neglected or maltreated in a range of other ways. Children were frequently hungry and food was inadequate and badly prepared in many schools. Some survivors have spoken of scavenging for food from waste bins and animal feed (CICA, 2009).

The CICA heard testimony of emotional abuse relating to deprivation of family contact, personal identity, secure relationships, affection, approval, and a lack of protection. The commission observed that "witnesses reported a daily existence in the schools that was dominated by fear, humiliation, loneliness, and the absence of affection. Fear was strongly associated with the daily threat of being physically and otherwise abused, and seeing co-residents being abused. Constant apprehension about the next abuse to which they would be subjected was also a feature" (CICA, 2009, Volume 3, para. 7.221).

SIGNIFICANCE AND ROLE WITHIN SOCIETY

To understand the context of CICA in Ireland, it is important to understand the Catholic Church's influence and power over Irish politics and society. While opinion polls were not conducted in the 1950s, a detailed sociological study of Irish Catholicism was undertaken in Dublin in the early 1960s by Bruce Biever, an American Jesuit. Clerical influence was generally viewed in a positive light and 88 percent of respondents agreed that the Catholic Church was "the greatest force for good in Ireland today" (Girvin, 2008, p. 76).

According to CICA,

> It seemed natural that churches should take responsibility for providing assistance to the poor. In Ireland, Catholic emancipation in 1829 made the Church a central institution. It was powerful both at the level of the Hierarchy and, even more so, at grassroots where, in the absence of a trusted landowner class, educated and nationalistic priests were regarded as community leaders. Apart from religion, the main focus of the Church's influence lay in education. (2009, Volume II, para. 2.16)

This heritage is of immense importance in a historical context where, under English rule, the freedoms and rights of Irish Catholics to own land, pursue a profession or an education were severely restricted. Thus, the church's perceived role contributed to its immense standing after independence. Its special status meant that during the twentieth century in Ireland it was difficult to speak out about the Catholic Church, and even politicians who openly challenged the Catholic Church were exposed to a hostile public counterattack. Complaints and commissioned reports which detailed the conditions and abuse in the industrial schools and reformatories (such as the Kennedy report, 1970) were commonly dismissed or ignored. Subsequent reports have found that Irish government bodies did not apply the standards in their rules and guidelines when investigating complaints, but sought to protect the religious congregations running the schools (CICA, 2009).

When confronted with evidence of sexual abuse, the response of the religious authorities was often to transfer the offender to another location and in some instances the perpetrator re-offended in the new setting. The welfare of children was frequently secondary to protecting the Church. As a result of the Church's standing, it was not uncommon for disclosures of abuse to be met with skepticism or disbelief. Understanding the context of previous responses to disclosures is important when thinking about ICA across the lifespan, and how former residents may feel now about future help seeking.

ROLE OF THE PERPETRATOR WITHIN THE SETTING

The majority of abuse was perpetrated not by volunteers or peers, but by priests, brothers and nuns employed in the schools. Within wider Irish society, the religious were considered "something special," a status given practical expression through their involvement in a range of influential spheres (Girvin, 2008). Some reports give examples of care, kindness, attention and support provided by individual religious in the institutions, but this was not the norm. We know that the role of most brothers, priests or nuns was to enforce a regime of punishment and to maintain a system of abuse. Many also had an educational remit. However, most former residents describe their time in the classroom as being dominated by fear and the anticipation of being abused. The classroom was a frightening place, not in any way conducive to learning. Below is evidence given to the CICA describing the type of abuse experienced in a classroom setting.

> If he asked a question and you put the hand up, you got a beating if you could not . . .(give the right answer). . . . If you were too slow with the answer you got beaten. . . . I got to the stage that I didn't answer because I would get a beating. Everything operated on fear. There was one Br . . . X . . . if you done it too slow he hit you, he had 2 leathers, if he appeared on the scene there was fear. No matter what you done, you would always get it wrong. (CICA, 2009, Volume III, para. 7.46)

Understanding the status and role of perpetrators within the institutions is imperative when considering the potential impact and consequences of ICA. As Wolfe et al., explain, "when a child feels that an adult has a great deal of power in his or her life, that child may feel unable to prevent, stop, or disclose abuse by that individual for fear of retaliation" (2001, p. 10). Reports show that children were acutely aware of the power the religious had over them and were unmistakably conscious of their powerlessness to prevent the abuse or disclose it to others.

According to Wolfe et al.,

> . . . coupled with the degree of involvement is the influence and power some organizations have on the child or on his or her family. A perpetrator may use his or her position within the organization to obtain the child's compliance; alternatively, the perpetrator may use coercion by telling children that such acts are "the will of God" or that God will punish them if they do not do what they are told. (2003, p. 14)

Some have suggested that children in these settings experienced a particular form of spiritual entrapment, differentiating clerical ICA from abuse in other institutions (Rossetti, 1995). Victimized Catholic children learnt that perpetrators were God's representatives on earth and so, for some, submitting to the abuse was somehow "God's will." As a result, some suggest, clerical abuse may create a special "trauma bond" associated with the victim's faith (Kennedy, 2000).

DEGREE AND NATURE OF CHILD INVOLVEMENT WITH THE INSTITUTION

Children who are highly involved with an institution may have more difficulty avoiding or stopping abuse. In these cases, perpetrators have more opportunity to overcome the child's resistance and children have less opportunity to disclose to other trusting adults (Wolfe et al., 2003). Observing that care homes, prisons and military encampments are very similar in that they influence the lives of residents completely, Erving Goffman (1961) coined the concept of total institutions. Industrial schools and reformatories might be understood as total institutions, as they exerted total control over all aspects of residents' lives. Although some children did leave to visit family, most were there continuously and short-term leave or escape was impossible. The following is evidence given to the CICA describing the consequence of trying to run away from an industrial school.

> I ran away when I was 12, I was caught and 2 of them . . . (Br X and Br Y) . . . would lay into you and not only the Brothers but the lads as well, especially the monitors. They were told they could not see their film because of me, I got the head shaved, a scissors and the hand clip. (CICA, 2009, Volume III, para. 7.41)

POST-ABUSE EVENTS

We have known for some time that men and women who were abused during childhood experience a high incidence of PTSD and other mental health disorders. Following a number of landmark studies (Carr et al., 2010, Wolfe et al., 2006), we know that ICA is associated with poor psychological adjustment across the lifespan. Carr et al., (2010) examined the psychological impact of ICA, finding that "the prevalence of psychological disorders among adult survivors of institutional abuse was over 80% and far higher than in the normal population, with anxiety, mood and substance use disorders being the most prevalent diagnoses. Survivors also had high rates of trauma symptoms and insecure adult attachment styles" (p. 477). Other studies on ICA in Ireland (O'Riordan et al., 2007) suggest an association between ICA and adult suicidal ideation. This squares with the high degree of suicidality found among icap's patients (Fonagy, 2012).

It is important to understand the post abuse environment in Ireland and how abuse and subsequent vulnerability were understood for those leaving institutional care. At the time, children were not thought of in terms of what they were (survivors of ICA) but what they were going to be. Mahood and Littlewood suggest that "they were seen as future threats to social order as much as victims. The child in danger would in time become the dangerous child. The challenge then was to catch these children early and channel them into an appropriate regime of moral rehabilitation" (1994, p. 225). Children, whom we might expect to be most in need of a different kind of response, were viewed as the most "contaminated." As Louise Jackson explains, while the act of sexual abuse was regarded as the most atrocious crime,

> . . . it was viewed as having corrupted the girl and effecting her "fall" from innocence. Within a Christian moral economy, the sexually abused child was given a special status as a "fallen" girl/woman and seen as a threat as well as victim. The associations between delinquency, corruption and sexual knowledge had a significant impact on the treatment of the victim of sexual abuse. (Jackson, 2000, p. 6)

For most of the twentieth-century history of child welfare, the effect of abuse on children was seen as moral damage rather than psychological trauma. The assumed deviancy of abused children was used to justify not treating them as victims of child abuse, and to provide a rationale for further marginalization. This position had disastrous implications for abused children and meant that in Irish society as a whole their true vulnerability was not understood or responded to and was hidden behind a veil of secrecy.

After being discharged from these schools, many former residents chose to emigrate. In the CICA, 37% of respondents were living in the UK (2009). Casual labor, factory and domestic work were commonly reported occupations in the lives of former residents after leaving the schools. Although some suggest migration was the result of dire economic conditions, an unfortunate reality for many Irish people at the time, contemporary Irish therapists also identify migration as an attempt to escape scenes of past suffering, to the relatively benign anonymity of England. Anecdotal evidence from former residents affirms this view.

> I left here. . . (Ireland). . . because of. . . (discrimination). . . I was frustrated with Ireland. I said "to hell with this, I'm getting out of this country". I went to . . . (university abroad). . . I have never been unemployed. . . I put Ireland behind. (CICA, 2009, Volume III, para. 11.56).

> In England there was no one watching you, no one knows anything about me. . . . (I was). . . always told by nuns "you are the rubbish of Ireland". . . . In England nobody knows me. (CICA, 2009, Volume III, para. 11.54)

THE REAL-LIFE CONTEXT OF INSTITUTIONAL CHILDHOOD ABUSE

Beyond historical accounts, understanding ICA requires us to pay attention to the individual, and to the social, political and cultural context of the lives of former residents. Case studies can facilitate this type of multi contextual understanding. In this section, we provide two composite case studies illustrating typical real life issues icap encounters when working with former residents of the industrial schools and reformatories.

Case Study 1

Bernadette first appeared as a skimpily dressed, waif-like figure who came to the London therapy service after going home with a man she met in a pub, who had then raped her. She rarely met my eyes and her sentences would fade away, as though the energy to speak had run out. The details of what happened were hazy, as though behind a screen. The man was still around in the pub and she was scared to go there now. She had no wish to go to the police but would be wakened from sleep by vivid flashbacks. Although she expressed anger at moments, when I acknowledged her anger it would evaporate, like water on a pavement. I found it hard to understand what she wanted from me or how things could be better for her.

Her life story also had many vague spots . . . she had grown up in an institution, but did not know which one. She had been there from an early age and did not know her true name, or place or date of birth. There was no real schooling in the "school," but plenty of hard work, and punishment if you didn't work fast or hard enough. There was never enough to eat. She remembered eating grass, and wheat grains when she was working in the fields. "I didn't stop even when I got shocking bellyache." Profound neglect was completely normal.

She could not recall what part of Ireland the school was in, but she had been sent to Dublin to work as a maid in a doctor's family when she was 16. The doctor was watching her and often brushing against her, and after a few weeks followed her into her bedroom one evening and pushed her onto the bed. She had fought and called out, and luckily the woman of the house had come back unexpectedly, so he left her alone. She then told the woman what had happened, but was not believed. "She wouldn't entertain me and my lies, she said, and she threw me out of the house. I was that ashamed I didn't know what to do." With the little money she had, Bernadette bought a ticket for the ferry to England.

The first part of her time in London was also behind a veil, but she had then moved in with an African man and borne him a child. He later brought his wife to England, and the woman beat her and expected her to do all the work, abused her, and treated her as a servant. She did not know how to leave, but eventually when she saw the woman strike her son, she took him and fled, begging on the street. It did not occur to her to seek help from the authorities, but a soup kitchen worker directed her to a mother and baby refuge. She was rehoused, but did not know how to look after herself or her son, and he was taken into care. She had then 'gone off the rails' by which she meant drinking a great deal and sleeping with any man who asked. This had gone on for some years and she had borne another child who was also taken into care.

When Bernadette told me this, I felt that we had made a breakthrough in building a fragile trust between us. She missed the next three sessions.

I knew that she could not read well so, rather than writing, I telephoned her to express my concern and my hope to see her again. She did come back in the fifth week, but once again was so gripped by shame that she could not meet my eyes or hear anything that challenged her self-disgust. I was not surprised when she did not return after this session. I was left with feelings of being useless and worthless, very much as Bernadette herself felt.

About five years later, Bernadette again contacted the service and I was half-surprised to hear that she wanted to see me. Once again, her clothing was thin and revealing, inappropriate for a brisk November day. After a brief spell in prison, she had been through rehabilitation and had recognized that she kept making the same mistakes. She did not tell me what her offence had been, but her fear of the prison guards and the police was palpable in the room. She had been unable to speak in court and, in prison, locked in at night, had started having flashbacks of her childhood in the school.

"You had to get up in the night to pee so you didn't wet the bed, and when you were older you had to get the smaller ones up. You would be beaten if they wet the bed. Sometimes you weren't allowed to go to the toilet till you wet yourself and then you would be beaten raw, shamefully, with your bottom exposed as the other girls watched." At night, Bernadette would go to sleep with her fingers in her ears to block out the sounds of hopeless crying, the crying of desolate children.

Over the next six years, progress for Bernadette was never a straight line. As she became able to trust me enough to reveal her "shameful" secrets and to cry for herself, she would often miss the next couple of sessions or more, but she did keep coming back. The relief of being seen for herself at last was finely balanced with the risk that I, too, might turn on her and abuse her when she needed me most.

My Irishness was important to Bernadette, but she had no desire to go "back to Ireland." At her AA meetings, she made some new friends but avoided the other Irish people. It was as though her past could be "buried" with me. As the therapy went on, her anger grew at the way she had been treated in the School. She would sometimes come in spitting with rage at some news story, and when Enda Kenny, the Irish Prime Minister, made his apology[1] to the Magdalene[2] women, her sobbing was deep and heartfelt. In his acknowledgement of the state's responsibility and the wrong done to those women, she felt an acknowledgement of the wrong done to her in the school; the Irish state had apologised to her too. Her dominant feeling at the idea of her story being written was pride and the hope that it might help others. She became a careful critic of what I had written.[3]

Bernadette's wariness of authority had led her to miss the deadline to apply for compensation under the Redress Scheme,[4] but she conceived a strong desire to study and give herself the education she was never offered. She had completed a literacy course, then some GCSEs, and now is doing an access course to study for a degree. She is determined to be single at the moment, but takes care of her appearance. An important step for her has been to establish a legal identity; she has a national insurance number and has chosen a date of birth which is now used in all documents. She tried to get information from Ireland about her people, but the trail had long gone cold. She is still racked with guilt at how she failed her children, and longs to see them "but maybe I would do them more harm than good. I see now that I had completely zoned out, I wasn't there for them at all." Her story is ongoing and will no doubt have further twists and turns.

Case study 2

Aidan appears as a handsome if well-worn man in his mid-forties. He is very well presented and it is hard to believe that he currently resides in a halfway hostel for homeless men. Aidan was given up by his mother and sent to a school when he was four years old. His mother had twin younger children, a boy and a girl, whom she kept with her. He went home from the school for a couple of brief visits when he was very young but was always sent back again. "I remember hanging onto my mother and begging her not to make me go" but he was sent back and stayed in the school until he was 16. He then ran away and went to his mother's house, but she was not there and the neighbors said she had gone away with the other children.

The school was grim "in the usual ways," said Aidan, who "put a brave face" on the retelling of his story. It was cold and desolate with inadequate clothing and food, and hard work. "You got the strap for anything at all, you were afraid all the time." Many of the boys were sexually abused and Aidan was no exception, "but I was lucky," he said. "It was Father X and he was alright, he would just sit me on his lap and. . ." (voice trailed off). The sexual contact had not included penetration and he had been the special "property" of this senior religious for some years, which protected him from the brutal rapes inflicted on many of his peers. "The worst thing was hearing what was happening to the others, the screaming and crying." Aidan and three other boys had formed a small "society" to help each other out covertly. "You couldn't let them see you were doing it, they would have singled one out." When Aidan was 10, a boy singled out for special punishment took his own life by hanging.

When he could not find his mother, Aidan went to Dublin and charmed his way into a job in the music scene. The availability of drink and drugs suited him because he wanted to block out his feelings when he was not working. However, he worked hard and was soon offered a job in London. By 28, he was a successful businessman and had even married and had two small children. However, he was deeply troubled by feelings of worthlessness and hopelessness, and a sense that he wasn't good enough for his children—though no one would have known it to look at him.

He had managed to trace his mother, brother, and sister, and re-establish some contact with them. His mother had re-married, but when Aidan was 35 she contracted cancer. He visited her several times, hoping that she would at last tell him that she loved him. "But on her deathbed she turned her face away from me, she asked for Kevin and Maeve" [his brother and sister]. This final painful rejection led him to cut off all ties with his brother and sister. He did not attend their mother's funeral, and they made no attempt to contact him.

The gap between Aidan's apparently successful life and the feelings of self-hatred became too great for him. Leaving his wife and children and his job, he bought a van and travelled through Europe for a year, but still he found no peace. When the money he had taken from the joint account ran out, he came back to London. Though homeless, he again found work through his personal charm but did not re-join his family.

It was at this point that I met him, as his trip had not resolved the issues that led him to flee. In the room, I struggle to stay with both parts of the paradox Aidan represents—the apparently competent and attractive man who cannot believe in his own success or happiness. He has survived, but at the cost of any ability to trust another or to allow them to rely on him since he fundamentally does not trust himself. His survival compelled him to re-enact the rejection he experienced from his mother on his wife and children. He treats me politely but keeps me at a distance. My experience tells me, it will take many years of work for Aidan to be able to rely upon another person, if he ever can.

INSTITUTIONAL CHILDHOOD ABUSE: A CRITICAL UNDERSTANDING

As with other forms of childhood abuse, wider society is often prone to focusing on the perpetrator, and on the sickening abusive act itself, whilst neglecting wider analysis. For example, in our experience those with only a cursory understanding of ICA often automatically associate institutional abuse with sexual abuse. While the evidence shows us that as many as half of those who were in industrial schools or reformatories in Ireland may have experienced sexual abuse, we also know there were many who did not experience this form of abuse (CICA, 2009). We believe the framework developed by Wolfe et al. (2003) can help us to understand the impact of ICA in Ireland in the widest sense and, so, fully understand the effects of the abuse across the life course. In our work, former residents often tell us that they want to work with someone who understands their childhood, someone who will not be shocked or "gob smacked" by accounts of horrifying childhood maltreatment. As Wolfe's framework highlights, it is also important that those working with former residents consider factors beyond the initial childhood abuse in order to understand the wider and continuing impact of this abuse.

A theme evident in Bernadette's case study is that of re-institutionalization. After a childhood immersed in a total institution, the new-found freedom, or lack of structure, can be frightening. We know that many males joined either the Irish Defence Forces or overseas armies at some time during their lives. Some described the Army as providing security, shelter and a structured regime. Evidence suggests that many females sought other forms of institutionalized life in the UK, such as nursing or domestic service. Some managed to spend their whole lives working in one institution after another, often the only places familiar enough to be comfortable. As former residents of the schools age, some will again require institutional care. How these "homes" are constituted and managed will require careful thought by the Irish state, while those who have emigrated are likely to be cared for by people with little understanding of their past or its legacy.

Irish people in the UK have poorer physical and mental health than the general population, and some have suggested that this is because of pre-migration experiences, such as childhood abuse (Delaney et al., 2013). Furthermore, evidence indicates that this community is less likely to seek help than the general population (Tilki et al., 2009). Our work tells us that these trends can be reversed through appropriately tailored services. Fonagy et al. (2012) found that icap's work is particularly effective with Irish people who are marginalized and normally unable to access mainstream services. The key to this seems to be an organizational willingness to accommodate the individual and tailor the service to their needs in a variety of ways. For example, it may be necessary to accept that weekly attendance at therapy, normally a given for effective treatment, is a developmental target for some clients. Through culturally sensitive long-term work, many people gradually become able to access services.

The case studies highlight the serious problems adult survivors of ICA can have in sustaining meaningful adult relationships. As well as affecting former residents' ability to form relationships with helping professionals, these attachment issues may affect survivors' parenting skills, despite the heartfelt need to offer their children a better experience than their own. Recognition of the inter-generational impact of the childhood trauma perpetrated in the schools has led the Irish state to fund icap's therapeutic work with the children and grandchildren of former residents in the UK.

An important theme for Bernadette is education. The systematic denial of education was a particularly cruel aspect of the deprivation in the schools, in a country where education has been seen historically as the route out of poverty and hardship. Depriving children of education keeps them "in their place." As Bernadette begins to face and move on from the trauma which has ruled her past, she chooses to seek an education. It is a concrete way of expressing to herself that she is worth something, a person of value. This is a theme we see repeatedly in icap's work. Aidan had found a role which did not require a formal education, but we could speculate how far his obvious talents might have taken him with a better start in life.

Both case studies indicate the continued issues many survivors face in relation to identity. Identity is the totality of one's perception of self, how we as individuals view ourselves as unique from others. In Bernadette's case, she was deprived the most fundamental aspects of her individual identity, her name and her birth place. Record keeping in institutional care in Ireland was virtually non-existent (CICA, 2009). Upon discharge, many survivors were unable to find any record of their parents or family; others were unable to find records of the circumstance surrounding their entry into institutional care. Sibling relationships were strongly discouraged, with siblings either being kept apart or placed in different institutions. Some children grew up in Institutions in which their siblings were also resident, without ever being aware that they were brothers or sisters.

This deprivation would be harmful anywhere but it is particularly so in Ireland, where the sense of place and "who your people are" runs especially deep. Perhaps the "ethnic tent" (Volkan, 1997) aspect of identity is tight because of the occupation by another state. One of the subtler injuries of a childhood in the industrial schools is the loss of a geographically-located identity. Bernadette's story pinpoints this deprivation. "We were robbed of Ireland in the schools," said one survivor, meaning that the ubiquitous sense of Ireland was absent there. Bernadette cannot participate in the socially mandated Irish idealization of "home" nor identify her home town or village. Like many survivors, she is tormented by that universal question "Where are you from?"

We have already noted that disbelief following a disclosure can be devastating for survivors of ICA, offering them a choice between loyalty to their own experience and a sense of belonging in the wider community. This tension seems to be an important motivator for migration for many former residents, and the desperation of Bernadette's flight to England is a story we have heard many times. Alongside this desperation is the anonymity England offers, where not only does no one know you, and you are less likely to be asked "where are you from?" since you are clearly from "Ireland," but few will know of the Institutions themselves or of their significance. The extent to which the abuse and neglect in the schools was known in Ireland seems an important source of the contemporary societal guilt and responsibility. The institutions were used to scare children: "if you are bold you will be sent to. . ." and so, at some level, the misfortune of those children housed there was the "unthought known" (Bollas, 1987), justified because those "other" children were "bold." Nevertheless, the revelation of the scale and extent of abuse has been a shock to the roots of Irish society, in Ireland and beyond.

These case studies illustrate the long-term disadvantages experienced by many former residents of industrial schools and reformatories. In research conducted in Ireland, a quarter of survivors described chaotic work lives (CICA, 2009). Reports of long-term unemployment among males were associated with time spent in prison (CICA, 2009). However, at the same time, both case studies illustrate the extraordinary resilience of survivors of ICA. Although for many, the consequences of ICA are a lifetime of trauma, some manage and even thrive despite this trauma. In studies conducted in Ireland, 18% of a sample of 247 showed no signs of mental health disorders despite having suffered ICA (Fitzpatrick et al., 2010). Both case studies highlight the non-linear healing pathways experienced by many survivors of ICA. Unlike survivors of less severe trauma, even the most resilient survivors of ICA vividly remember their childhood, and vivid memories and flashbacks can be triggered by a wide range of apparently innocuous stimuli, such as seeing a collar reminiscent of a clerical collar, or the smell of a particular floor polish which evoked memories of the institution.

In conclusion, the impact of ICA can be traced in the lives of former residents through several spheres, relational and emotional, educational, in employment and financially, and in accessing public services when needed. These categories describe the ways in which former residents of industrial schools and reformatories face additional obstacles to a satisfying and fulfilled life as a result of the terrible world they occupied in childhood. The categories should never obscure the reality of their suffering, nor prevent us celebrating the remarkable resilience of those who managed, nevertheless, to survive.

NOTES

1. On February 19, 2013 Taoiseach [Prime Minister] Enda Kenny apologised unreservedly on behalf of the State to the survivors of the Magdalene Laundries. The full transcript of the apology is available at http://liveblog.irishtimes.com/a4936be25b/LIVE-Magdalene-Laundries-Report/
2. Ireland's Magdalene Laundries were residential, commercial and for-profit laundries operated by four Irish orders of nuns where between the foundation of the Irish Free State in 1922 and 1996, when the last institution closed, a number of girls and women, estimated in the tens of thousands were imprisoned, forced to carry out unpaid labor and subjected to severe psychological and physical maltreatment. For more information see http://www.magdalenelaundries.com/jfm_comm_on_torture_210411.pdf
3. This case study is composite but we have observed this reaction in several former residents.

4. The Redress Board was set up under the Residential Institutions Redress Act, 2002 to make fair and reasonable awards to persons who, as children, were abused while resident in industrial schools, reformatories and other institutions subject to state regulation or inspection.

REFERENCES

Bollas, C. (1987). *The shadow of the object, psychoanalysis of the unthought known*. New York: Columbia University Press.

Brennan, C. (2007). Facing what cannot be changed: The Irish experience of confronting institutional child abuse. *Journal of Social Welfare and Family Law, 29*, 3–4, 245–263.

Carr, A., Dooley, B., Fitzpatrick, M, Flanagan, E., Flanagan-Howard, R., Tierney, K., White, M., Daly, M. and Egan, J. (2010). Adult adjustment of survivors of institutional child abuse in Ireland. *Child Abuse and Neglect, 34*, 477-489.

Commission to Inquire into Child Abuse. (2009). Commission to Inquire into Child Abuse Report. Dublin, Ireland: Stationery Office.

Delaney, L., Fernihough, L., and Smith P. J. (2013). Exporting the poor health: The Irish in England. *Demography, 50*(6), 2013-2035.

Ferguson, H. (2007). Abused and looked after children as moral dirt? *Journal of Social Policy, 36*(1), 123–39.

Fitzpatrick, M., Carr, A., Dooley, B., Flanagan-Howard, R., Flanagan, E., Shevlin, K., Tierney, K., White, M., Daly, M. and Egan J. (2010). Profiles of adult survivors of severe sexual, physical and emotional institutional abuse in Ireland. *Child Abuse Review, 19*, 387-404.

Fonagy, P., Jennings-Hobbs, R., and Speed, M. (2012). Coming Home to Ourselves. London: icap.

Girvin, B. (2008). Church, state, and society in Ireland since 1960. *Aspire-Ireland, 43*(1and 2), 74-98.

Goffman, E. (1961). *Asylums: Essays on the social situation of mental patients and other inmates*. New York: Doubleday Anchor.

Groome, D. (2011). The church abuse scandal: Were crimes against humanity committed? Retrieved from http://elibrary.law.psu.edu/fac_works/6

Higgins, M. (2010). Developing a profile of survivors of abuse in Irish religious institutions. Retrieved from http://www.ssgt.ie/files/developing_a_socio_economic_profile_of_survivors_o.pdf

Jackson, L. (2000). Child sexual abuse in Victorian England. London: Routledge.

Kee, R. (1976). *The bold Fenian*. Dublin: Penguin.

Commission of Inquiry into the Reformatory and Industrial School System (1970) Report

of the Commission of Inquiry into the Reformatory and Industrial School System

(Kennedy Report), Dublin, Government Publications Office.

Kennedy, M. (2000). Christianity and child sexual abuse: The survivors voice leading to change. *Child Abuse Review, 9*, 124-141.

Mahood, L., and Littlewood B. (1994). The vicious girl and the street-corner boy: Sexuality and the gendered delinquent in the Scottish child-saving movement, 1850-1940. *Journal of the History of Sexuality, 4*, 549-78.

O' Toole, F. (2009, May 21). The savage reality of our darkest days. *The Irish Times,*

O'Riordan, M., and Arensman, E. (2007). *Institutional child sexual abuse and suicidal behaviour: Outcomes of a literature review, consultation meetings and a qualitative study.* Dublin, National Suicide Research Foundation.

Raftery, M., and O'Sullivan, E. (1999). *Suffer the little children*. Dublin: New Island.

Rossetti, S. J. (1995). The impact of child sexual abuse on attitudes toward God and the Catholic Church. *Child Abuse and Neglect, 19*, 1469-1481

Tilki, M., Ryan, L., D'Angelo A., and Sales R. (2009). The Forgotten Irish; a report of a research project commissioned by the Ireland Fund of Great Britain.

Twomey, L. (2003). Dail Debates, 1 October 2003, vol. 571.

Volkan, V. D. (1997). *Bloodlines: From ethnic pride to ethnic terrorism.* New York: Farrar, Straus and Giroux.

Wolfe, D. A., Francis, K. J., and Straatman, A. L. (2006). Child abuse in religiously-affiliated institutions: Long-term impact on men's mental health. *Child Abuse and Neglect, 30,* 205–212.

Wolfe, D. A., Jaffe, P. G., Jette, J. L., and Poisson, S. E. (2001). Child abuse in community institutions and organisations: Improving public and professional understanding. (Law Commission of Canada), York: Anchor/Doubleday.

Wolfe, D. A., Jaffe, P. G., Jett´e, J. L., and Poisson, S. E. (2003). The impact of child abuse in community institutions and organizations: Advancing professional and scientific understanding. *Clinical Psychology: Science and Practice, 10,* 179–191.

FIVE

Django Unchanged

Identifications with the Oppressor and Intergenerational Cycles of Traumatic Hauntings and Reenactment

Claude Barbre

When the philosopher Martin Heidegger wrote about our being-in-the-world in order to explore the nature of ethical relationships and how we occupy the sites of our lives, he quotes a story that Aristotle reports about the Greek philosopher Heraclitus:

> The story is told of something Heraclitus said to some strangers who wanted to come visit him. Having arrived, they saw him warming himself at a stove. Surprised, they stood there in consternation—above all because he encouraged them, the astounded ones, and called for them to come in with the words, "For here too the gods come to presence (Auch hier namlich wesen Gotter an). " (1977, p. 233)

We see in this story how Heraclitus's visitors find the location of their meeting to be at odds with what they expected. David Krell points out that the meaning of the Greek word for "stove " suggests an indoors oven used for heating water for a bath, which might explain the strangers' discomfort. Krell also suggests a further meaning of the word as a "dung-hill or privy, " another reason that the strangers could be hesitant to enter the space, expressing surprise, astonishment, and embarrassment. In any event, Heraclitus responds with a simple utterance that the gods are present too in the site where they meet in the moment. About the story, Heidegger states:

> Heraclitus himself says *ethos anthropoid* daimon. This is usually translated "A man's character is his daimon." Ethos means abode, dwelling place. The word names the open region in which man dwells...the abode of man contains and preserves the advent of what belongs to man in his essence. . . The fragment says: Man dwells, insofar as he is man, in the nearness of god. (1977, p. 233)

As James Hans notes about this passage, "The gods are present wherever the openness of a dwelling invites them in, whenever a site allows their disclosure to take place," adding that "the *essence* of the individual is not an otherworldly *daimon,* to use Heraclitus's word, but rather some thing that manifests itself in relation to that through which one conjures one's context in the world" (1995, p. 223). For Heidegger, this dwelling place, this ethos, is the site through which the mystery and flow of Being is disclosed. Hans suggests that Heidegger conveys in this disclosure that "one must be willing to give up the essential sense of autonomy in order to makes a place for the autonomy that is based on the openness of the dwelling one's site in the world is" (1995, p. 222). This is to say:

> Our site in the world—that which we have made familiar by inhabiting it for years and living through the necessities it imposes on us and discerning the capabilities that are to be found within it—is also a function of a crucial relation to the unfamiliar, to our daimon, to that which always remains—yet remains concealed—within the openness of the context we establish in life. (Ibid, p. 233)

Even if we question Heidegger's ontological framework, his use of Heraclitus's story draws us into a meditation about the presence and naming of the unfamiliar in our particular abodes, the nearness of the gods or spiritual energies in unexpected contexts, and the way discourse about our dwelling in the world conjures the daimones that appear in our everyday life.

Keeping in mind that the daimon is part of our sitedness in the world, as Heidegger attests, can we wonder if there may be other unnamed and unfamiliar forces conjured unexpectedly around Heraclitus's stove? Rollo May drew from the classical Greek idea of the daimon to suggest that the daimonic,

> Is any natural function which has the power to take over the whole person. . . The daimonic can be either creative or destructive and is normally both. When the power goes awry, and one element usurps control over the total personality, we have "daimon possession," a traditional name through history for psychosis. (May, 1969, p. 123)

As Stephen Diamond points out, we must distinguish the term daimon as a classical synonym from the word theos, or god:

> The term daimon referred to something indeterminate, invisible, incorporeal, amorphous and unknown, whereas, "theos " was the personification of a god, such as Zeus or Apollo. The daimon was that divine, mediating spiritual power that impelled one's action and determined one's destiny. . . Indeed, one's daimon manifested as a sort of fateful "soul " which spurred one on toward good or evil. (Diamond, 1996, p. 66)

C.G. Jung suggests that "the Greek words *daimon* and *daimonion* express a determining power which comes upon man from outside, like providence, or fate, though the ethical decision is left to man" (Jung, 1968, p. 27). However, the meaning of the word shifts when in the Septuagint translation of the Hebrew Bible into Greek, the term daimonion was understood to denote the presence of evil spirits. In contrast, Diamond points out, the word "devil" is a diminutive from the root div and from it we get the word divine; devil merely means "little god," and not the evil we usually associate solely with the term. (Diamond, p. 74) Underscoring the distorted meanings of daimones that have been transformed into evil demons and devils, Jungian analyst James Hillman says succinctly that "the denial of daimones and their exorcism has been part and parcel of Christian psychology, leaving the Western psyche few means but the hallucinations of insanity for recognizing daimonic reality." (Hillman, 1983, p. 65). In short, despite the profound influence of the Enlightenment to eradicate the history of the daimones as spiritual energies, they cannot be erased from human ethos and dwelling. As Diamond says well, rather than dispelling the diamon influences from their various meanings in historical discourses, "a more psychologically or spiritually sound solution may be achieved only by confronting and meaningfully assimilating what these daimones symbolize for us today into our selves and our daily lives" (Diamond, p. 74). We will explore the daimonic nature of intergenerational transmissions of trauma with a particular reevaluation of how identifications with the aggressor/oppressor inhabit the individual psyche and cultural discourse.

In *The Subject of Childhood* (2009), Michael O'Loughlin points out a resonance between psychoanalysis and the related field of hauntology where,

> Ghostly memories are thought of as those memories of traumatic events that were denied symbolization and pass on from generation to generation unless somebody brings them to the light of day and exposes them to the possibilities of being spoken and therefore symbolized and ultimately worked through. . . Judy Atkinson (2002) describes these kinds of unconscious memories as trauma trails that can be traced across generations. (2009, p. 52)

Indeed, we might think of these trauma trails as aligned with the Heraclitian gods who come to presence in an abode that Stephen Frosh characterizes as "an amalgam of issues around otherness (the secret of the other), abjection and spectral truth" (2013, p. 43). In the face of traumatic daimones that dwell in unfamiliar places and unexpected moments, we can explore how each subject can be inhabited by social otherness and the transmission of historical contexts. For example, Avery Gordon (1997) suggests that:

> The ghost is not simply a dead or a missing person, but a social figure and investigating it can lead to the dense site where history and subjectivity make social life. The ghost or the apparition is one form by which something lost, or barely visible, or seemingly not there to our supposedly well-trained eyes, makes itself known or apparent to us, in its own way, of course. The way of the ghost is haunting, and haunting is a very particular way of knowing what has happened or is happening. (Gordon, 1997, p. 8; quoted in Frosh 2013, p. 44)

Gordon underscores that hauntings can be understood as "an animated state in which a repressed or unresolved social violence is making itself known, sometimes very directly, sometimes more obliquely (2013, p. xvi). Frosh adds to Gordon's perspective by suggesting that repressed and unresolved social violence, prevalent in political oppression, can manifest as "representations of the kinds of living death associated with ghosts" (2013, p. 44). Frosh summarizes the traumatic, daimon presence:

> In each case, what is left unresolved in history works its way into the present as a traumatic haunting that is profoundly social, yet is lived out in the deepest recesses of individuals' lives. This stance also fuels the idea that ghosts have to be thought of as real: they actually exist, because what haunts us is the denied reality of oppressed lives, lives demoralized or cut short, lives marginalized and written out of history, precarious lives treated as dispensable but impossible fully to forget precisely because their effects linger on. (2013, p. 44)

Gordon and Frosh remind us that traumatic hauntings are not simply located within the individual's psyche; rather they are found in the unfamiliar dwellings of our shared lives, deeply attached to the symbolic structures of society that "maintain the liveliness of some memories whilst marginalizing others" (Frosh, p. 44). This emphasis on social representation is reminiscent of how Michael O'Loughlin reevaluates the assumptions of an essential self in development, suggesting that we "avoid the binary that much of psychology and psychoanalysis poses between the interior subject and the material environment, and look instead at ways in which a human being, through immersion in material culture, becomes the ongoing person that they are" (O'Loughlin, 2009, p. 12). But this immersion into material culture may include the traumatic social origins of the modes of haunting that are housed by our particular idiom and personal history. There are invisible threads connecting us to family and cultural alliances. Recalling Augustine's statement, "The dead are invisible, but not absent," we can say that the unconscious, spectral presences of trauma can set the traps of unconscious transgenerational repetitions and actions. As Julia Kristeva notes, "the existence of an unconscious 'inside' each one of us means the haunting of the individual human subject by something else, strange, foreign, and yet real"(Kristeva, p. 181, quoted in Frosh, p. 46). Yet, unlike Heraclitus' welcoming invitation to join him where the gods are present even in the unexpected places of an earthy abode, we are often hesitant to acknowledge the daimon spirit of trauma in our dwelling, in turn becoming divided and foreign to ourselves. We will see that this haunting of the individual subject also arises from social identifications, and can constitute the hallmark of traumatic induction, creating complex links to the realms of unspeakable, unthinkable, unvoiced secrets—unassimilated experiences that are often at the heart of traumatic repetitions and cycles of reenactments. We will see that such repetitions are made stronger by the disavowal of what Boszormenyi-Nagy calls "invisible loyalties" (Boszormenyi-Nagy and Spark, 1973, p. 14), especially illustrated by individual and social identification with the aggressor/oppressor and traumatic events. Before exploring the powerful dynamic of identification with the aggressor/oppressor, let us look at the phenomena of transgenerational linkages in regard to traumatic transmissions.

A personal example of such hauntings comes to mind. My mother's family were farmers since the 18th century near the eastern marshlands of South Carolina. When I was a child in the late 1950s, our family would drive from North Carolina several times a year to visit my grandparents' farm. I recall an ancient water mill not far from the county farmstead that dated back to the 1700s, and flecked among the edges of corn and tobacco fields, broken-planked shacks, their porches left to chance, half-listed into heavy seas of hedge and hyacinth. These dilapidated structures seemed to float from afar in the heavy air and dense humidity like swamped rafts on a tide of green shadows. Many of these fallen-down structures were at the end of overgrown dirt roads that bent into the distance beyond the field ponds and forest pines. My grandmother always told us not to stray down those old roads, saying there was "Nothin' there but snakes and bees and rusty nails—so stay away!" Of course, after playing stick ball in the late day shade of the barn with the local African-American kids just home from school, we would escape the eyes of the murmuring grown-ups, and flushed with transgression, fly down the dirt road that stretched into the woods behind the packhouse. Most of the local teens would swim in the pond at the end of the road, but I often preferred to explore the ruins of the vine-wrapped, roofless houses and wander among the faint indications of lost gardens and stone walls.

I recall one particular homestead that frightened me. It was surrounded by several moss-strewn oaks that seemed out of place in the broken pines, and although its front porch had retained frame enough to stand on, the doorless yawn of the dark entrance felt foreboding, forbidden, and uncanny. I remember a felt sense of unnamable presences there that the skin could see what the eyes could not. Each time I turned to run back to the pond and company, I would look over my shoulder expecting to see someone or some others watching me recede down the road. When I asked Hennigan, an African-American local minister and sharecropper who oversaw the farm, about the place, he simply said "Maybe ghosts, maybe your own fear. Anyway, it's not surprising that there might be hauntings where people lived and died. You feel what you feel." In contrast, when I asked my grandmother about the house at the end of the dirt road, she would say sternly that I was not to go there, and that it was only the skeletal remains of an empty farmhouse of no use to us, to the world, to anyone anymore.

Years later I visited my great aunt in a nearby town, and as we talked we eventually came around to stories and memories about the farm. I asked her about the far house at the end of the road by the two live oaks, telling her that it had always frightened me as a child, and that the ruins had always left me feeling uneasy.

She looked at me hard. "I am surprised your grandmamma let you play there considering. All those ruins were old slave quarters, and in decay" she said curtly, "and I'm not surprised you were frightened of that particular house—you should have been frightened of that house." She paused, looking beyond me like someone was approaching but was not.

"A lot of people died in that house" she said softly. She mopped her brow and rocked slowly. "My, My," she said in rhythm with the rocking. I could see her eyes brimming. "That was the birthing house used by the slaves long before I was born," she said, "and later some people lived in it, but mostly it fell empty. Many births and deaths were there. Other unspeakable things happened there as well, things not to be talked about. Now it is gone, gone, torn down, the planks used for the barn furnace to cure tobacco."

My great-aunts' words verified what I knew but did not know—the felt awareness of something real yet denied by my family; a history unacknowledged, unspeakable, and torn down, but very much alive and embodied in the family and cultural psyche—the dead invisible but not absent. Even there the gods would come to presence. My grandmother's contempt and dismissal of social otherness and the historical flow of being contrasted strongly with Hennigan's sense of tragic forces in the dwelling of our shared worlds. As Frosh notes, the traumatic eruption and lineage,

> Is often hidden away, as explosive and damaging to all concerned; yet without facing it, without giving it its proper name—the damage caused by the perpetrator generation continues. The problem is that the

> repressed and the disavowed never go away; it is precisely the fact that they always come back that lies at the heart of haunting. The worst of it is when what is passed down from generation to generation is something unspeakable, pinned to a hidden word so that we are burdened by the secret of those who have come before, unacknowledged victims or perpetrators leaving their unworked-through heritage to their children and children's children. (p. 48)

The perpetrator generation continued in my grandmother's denial of the slave houses, and the historical trauma and tragedy; and though disavowed and denied the history of the terrible desecration of human life would be palpable as the felt haunting of intergenerational trauma and transmission.

I thought of the hauntings in the deep pines when I was watching a scene in the film *12 Years A Slave* (McQueen, 2013), an historical drama and adaptation of the 1853 memoir of the same name by Solomon Northup. Northup was a New-York African American who lost his freedom when he was kidnapped in Washington DC and sold into slavery. In the film that reflects the historical story, Northup was given the name "Platt" so that he would be identified as a runaway slave from Georgia. For twelve years he worked on the William Ford and Edwin Epps plantations in Louisiana before being restored to freedom and his family in New York. The film is a story of enduring will and survival in the haunts of cumulative, horrific trauma.

In a particular moment in the film's narrative, John Tibeats (Paul Dano), a carpenter on the plantation—filled with resentment against Northup (Chiwetel Ejiofor) because he is receiving constant approval for his engineering skills by the plantation owner William Ford (Benedict Cumberbatch)—attacks Northup with a whip. Northup fights back, taking the lash from him and fighting back. Tibeats runs away and returns with his friends to lynch Northup for his retaliation. A field overseer stops them from hanging him, but even though Tibeats and his cohort run away vowing revenge, the foreman rides away as well, leaving Northup struggling in the noose. All day he must balance on his toes to prevent the full weight of his body from strangling him. As he struggles for life through the heat of the day and the heavy sound of cicadas, the slave community goes about their daily routines, walking eyes down around Northup in his interminable ordeal, unable to help him without the threat and fear of severe punishment or death. At day's end Northup is finally cut down from the live oak branch by Ford upon his return to the farm.

Cinematographer Sean Bobbitt, working with director Steve McQueen, creates a widescreen approach to this particular scene, pulling the visual focus to a distance while softening and blurring faintly the background characters of the slave community. By doing so, the figures in the background that circle Northup in his agony appear spectral and timeless in the rising heat, yet real and visceral at the same time. McQueen would say about his visual approach that he is painting the scene in film like Goya who painted grotesque and arabesque paintings of violence with such beauty and power that one could not look away from the remarkable moment, instead saying "Look—look at this " (Goodsell, 2013, p. 2). The presentation of this scene in the film flooded me with a feeling that was painfully familiar. I knew the place of the narrative ordeal. It was my grandparents' farm; it was the wandering presences in the ruins of vines, unseen yet palpable, moving around the live oak porch; it was the tortured lives that still inhabit the generational psyche and family matrix, the traumatic phenomena that I could not assimilate or understand as a child. The film's figures circling a man who struggles to survive the onus of his own weight evoked the ineffable terror of not looking away even as we wish to avert our eyes, even as the full gravitas of what took place remains in many respects disowned and denied by the perpetrator generation, yet transmitted to the dwellings of its children's children.

Psychoanalysts Francoise Dolto (1985), Nicholas Abraham, and Maria Torok (1994) suggest the hypothesis of a "preservative repression,"

> Where what matters is the preservation of a shut-up or excluded reality. For the children who carry the unmentioned and therefore "encrypted" secret, a chain connecting one generation to the next around an unspoken event becomes a suffering they can represent but not speak (mentioning it is forbidden), and which becomes registered, or encrypted, in the unconscious like an internal structure. At the third generation, the unspoken secret, the unspeakable, becomes unthinkable, because it can no longer be represented (a genealogical inconceivable event); it becomes a "ghost" that haunts a person who shows unexplainable symptoms, hinting at a secret a parent unknowingly projected on to him. . . In transactional analysis, the psychoanalyst Fania English goes as far as saying that one passes a "hot potato" from one generation to another to be rid of it, like a closed system. (Schutzenberger, 1998, p. 144)

We can see in this description of generational repression that a traumatic event can initiate a psychical, modulating transaction of sorts, culminating into transmitted experiences that cannot be assimilated or represented in the next generation. Whereas an early response to traumatic events—in a cultural sense the response of a perpetrator generation—may employ the defense operation of identification with the aggressor/oppressor; and where the victim of a trauma identifies with the power of the victimizer in order to defend and deny the terror of being powerless, the transmission of this ongoing defensive encryption leads to unexplainable symptoms, the genealogy of a traumatic energy that affects the daimon spirit of the psyche. Identifications to traumatic events can become transgenerational. For instance, Dolto (1985) suggests that the parent's and the child's unconscious are linked, "and the child knows, guesses, and feels family events over two or three generations" (1985, p. 145). In fact, as Abraham and Torok point out, "The phantom is a formation of the unconscious that has never been conscious—for good reason. It passes—in a way yet to be determined—from the parent's unconscious to the child's (1994, p. 145). These family transmissions reflect cultural linkages as well. In addition to the notion of unconscious generational linkages, Samuel Gerson (2004) posits the presence of a "relational unconscious" which stems from "reciprocal and mutual influences of unconscious minds upon one another, " suggesting that

> The uniqueness of each relationship is in large part due to its singular mix of the permitted and the prohibited, a mix that is formed from, yet transcends, the individual conscious and unconscious elements of each partner. (Gerson, p. 71)

As we have discussed, this mix of relational unconscious forces in a family context may contain trauma transmission that deeply affect the developing personalities of subsequent generations and communities.

In *The Interpretation of Dreams*, Freud talks about "ghosts" or "revenants"—meaning one who returns from the dead or from a long absence. As Freud wrote about naming his children: "I had insisted on their names being chosen, not according to the fashion of the moment, but in memory of people I had been fond of. Their names made the children into revenants (Freud, 1900, 1953, p. 487). In *Totem and Taboo* (Freud, 1913; 1953, pp. 157–158) the phenomena of family and cultural lineages are explored in Freud's notion of the collective mind, and we see the idea of generational influences on the psyche as well in C.G. Jung's theories of the collective unconscious. In comparison, Jacob Levy Moreno, a founder of psychodrama and group psychotherapy, postulated the existence of family and group *co-conscious* and *co-unconscious*, describing "a conscious and unconscious shared by several individuals joined by intimate bonds, as in a family, a surgical team, or a squadron on a dangerous mission " (Schutzenberger, 1998, p. 7). Echoing the phenomena of past experience that remains as revenants, Freud, speaking of the lingering horrors of World War I, will later define the uncanny, as:

> The unexpected return of elements that should have been surmounted long ago—remains of primitive beliefs, a return of the archaic—or elements that should have been repressed and are once more revived by some impression. . . The uncanny is what is frightening—what arouses dread, and horror. . . which as may easily be guessed, lie in the times in which we live. (1917/1953, p. 217)

We can see in Freud's thinking about the uncanny the haunting effects of family and cultural secrets, and the unexpected return of the repressed trauma.

Keeping in mind the perspectives of transgenerational communication models, the psychoanalyst Boszormenyi-Nagy returns us to the importance of relational bonds in families, in particular the pull of loyalty, justice and fairness in family dynamics that can be passed down the generations. As Schutzenberger says about this point of view:

> Loyalty is composed of a social unit which depends on and expects loyalty from its members as an individual. Thus the concept of justice and "family justice." When justice is not accomplished, there is injustice, unfairness, and exploitation among family members, which sometimes translates into fleeing, revenge or vengeance, or even illnesses or repetitive accidents. . . Otherwise, there is affection and reciprocal consideration balancing the family ledger. So we can talk about "balancing family accounts" and the extended "family balance sheet" on which you can see if you have credit or debit, if you have debts, obligations or merits. If the ledgers are not balanced, problems can be passed on from generation to generation. (Schutzenberger, 1998, p. 19)

Hence, Boszormenyi-Nagy speaks of "debts" and "family loyalties" that are communicated to children from parents. The generational links to merits and debts in the family ledger are often discerned in the way future generations remember the dead, rely on retrospective information that informs what they know about their families and themselves, "even if they do not consciously know what they know" (Schutzenberger, 1998, p. 19). In short, every family, through a kind of family code, communicates what each member needs to contribute to the family accounts. As Schutzenberger says, summarizing Boszormenyi-Nagy's writing on the implicit family book-keeping and its intergenerational impact, "The family code determines the scale of merits, advantages, obligations and responsibilities, which are learned reactions, grounded in the family history, in the family's genetic and historic relatedness, and which we can uncover (Schutzenberger, 1998, p. 20). Boszormenyi-Nagy speaks about how such family accountings create suffering in the unfolding family legacies, saying "we have to keep in mind that the individual's needs contain the condensations of the unsettled relational accounts of a persons' family of origin, in addition to the re-enactments of his [or her] own early psychic processes." (1973, p. 14)

When we see repetitions of values and attitudes that appear inured from change or an observing ego—an example being my grandmother's defensive erasure of the farm's history—then the coded roles can become fossilized and buried, which means that "the fixity of their roles serves the requirements of the total family obligations network." (Boszormenyi-Nagy and Spark, 1973, p. 14) These roles are often sustained by an identification with the family obligations by the next generations, and these networks in turn drive individuals to cycles of reenacted sufferings and complementary, generational predicaments and distress. To understand the nature of family networks and their impact on cultural legacies, let us look at the powerful daimon of identification.

The phenomenon of identification as described in psychoanalysis was first used by Sigmund Freud in order to explain certain transformations of the parent-child relationship. In his later work, Freud would utilize the term to discuss the ego aspects of relationships within organized groups. Freud himself was aware of how the dynamic of identification was insufficiently conceptualized and often difficult to describe. He speaks of identification not only as an original form of emotional tie with the other, but also in a regressive way when it becomes a substitute for a libidinal connection to the other by means of introjection. Freud also talks broadly of identification as "a shared common quality" (Freud, 1922, p. 65) with another person. When identification instills an affective relationship between two people, it serves as a modeling of a person's own sense of identity in the form of that taken from the mold of a previous emotional bond. As we grow and assimilate characteristics of others for our own personality, then identification is an organizing function and essential process of that development. Otto Fenichel (1945, p. 83) broadened the dynamic of identification to include the incorporation of the external world, and S.H. Fuchs (1937) says succinctly that "Each identification is a monument of an object-relations, and our character, being itself in-part composed of identifications, contains the history of our object-relations" (1937, p. 271). Hence, identification was originally discussed as "a modification of the ego in which a person acquires qualities which have first been those of another object or person" (Axelrad and Maury, 1951, p. 175).

Freud (1917) also thought that identification emerges as a solution to conflicts. The desired object is relinquished and replaced by an identification or, as in *Mourning and Melancholia*, the loss of a loved object can be survived and lived through by an identification with it (1917, pp. 237–258). In addition, Freud wrote about identification in regard to primary, narcissistic and empathic identifications, suggesting a variety of structures and functions of the dynamic. He often explored the diverse expression of identification in such varieties that focus on the nature of the internalized content, and the reason for the identification in terms of its function. In essence, a broad view of identification suggests two particular functions that shed light on trauma transmissions—one that is discernable in terms of general development and common quality, and the second as a defense against danger, and a means of coping with the danger. Sandor Ferenczi (1933) and Anna Freud (1947) are known for exploring the latter. For example, Anna Freud wrote of how the patient sometimes placed the analyst in the role of victim while the patient acted out an identification with an aggressor toward the therapist.

In 1933, Sándor Ferenczi presented the *Confusion of Tongues* [COT] paper seven years after he had actually written it. Freud had encouraged the suppression and censorship of the paper because it provided an alternative version of the oedipal theory, and he desired to protect the oedipal explanation of neurosis as the cornerstone of psychoanalytic therapy. Writing about Ferenczi's contribution to understanding identification, Arnold Rachman suggests that the COT theory proposes three basic areas of human functioning as an extension to the earlier views of identification: 1) the parent-child experience, especially where seduction and trauma have intruded into the relationship 2) the analyst-analysand encounter which has the potentiality for retraumatization and 3) the experience in any relationship where issues of seduction, power, status, and control predominate (Rachman, 2000 pp. 35–36). Ferenczi returned the focus on neurosis to actual trauma and not only oedipal wishes. He discerned in his clinical work that when the parent, usually the father, "under the pressure of his/her own unhealthy narcissistic and inappropriate needs, distorts the total motivation of the child who seeks tenderness, reducing it to a predominately sexual, erotic one, the stage is set for pathological, incestuous, acting out with the child" (Rachman, 2000, p. 37). The child's reality is seriously altered in such an interaction as the parent exerts status, power, and control over the child. The child becomes confused about the reality of his or her experience, often leading to a denial of his or her subjective experience while adapting to the parent's distorted reality. On this point of distorted reality, Rachman underscores Ferenczi's point that the child is developmentally inclined to believe the parent's representation of reality "because acceptance of parental authority is associated with love, protection, and object attachment" (Rachman, 2003, p. 63). The child's reality itself is thus betrayed. Adapting the parent's distorted control, the child cannot speak of the sense of confusion. In short, the defenses that Ferenczi described that enable the child to cope with the actual sexual seduction are: splitting, dissociation, denial, detachment, blunted affect, confusion and identification with the aggressor.

Ferenczi's attempt to understand the psychology of victimization is an important contribution to the study of intergenerational trauma transmission, especially in terms of defenses activated by trauma triggers, confusions of identity, and the struggle to make sense of distorted realities. The term was originally defined as a fearful identification with and introjection of the threatening or attacking person (1933). As Rachman points out, "The defense mechanism compels traumatized children to subordinate themselves like automata to the will of the aggressor, to divine each one of his desires, and to gratify these while completely oblivious of themselves" (Rachman, 2000, p. 36). Ferenczi himself felt that this identification with the aggressor is a complicated mechanism, but helps explain the masochistic bond that develops in an abusive, traumatic situation. The child, instead of rebelling or rejecting the abuser and perpetrator, psychologically attaches him or herself to the parental seducer. It is a desperate attempt to gain and continue an affectionate tie to the parent, while holding on to the lie that the seduction is an act of tenderness. By introjecting the bad object, the child attempts to master the trauma, by becoming like the oppressor. This dynamic is also underscored in regard to children acting out abuse or trauma with someone else—a wish of the victim to be powerful, inflict harm on others, or master anxiety. Treatment of the abused child and adult must include a relational dynamic. Further, the abused individual wants his or her distress to be understood and ameliorated by a significant other, underscoring the need for any clinical interaction to rest on an empathic presence and communication. The writer Barry Lopez captured this hope of being understood when he said of his own childhood abuse, "what I needed more than anything was to be believed " (Lopez, 2013, p. 48)—a major component of healing, he points out, in his therapeutic treatment.

Ferenczi's analysis of how the victim attaches to the oppressor is taken up by Bailey Jackson and Rita Hardiman (1997) in regard to social identity development models. They note that attempts to fully comprehend oppression and to design effective strategies to prevent or eradicate oppression have been limited by the ways that the problem is conceptualized. There is often a failure to recognize that oppression is learned by both the oppressor and the oppressed, and that this unlearning process or disidentification does not happen in one step. This perspective reflects the insights of Brazilian educator and philosopher Paulo Freire, whose work centers on helping others learn and unlearn the processes of oppression. As Freire says, "Every act of conquest implies a conqueror and someone or something which is conquered. The conqueror imposes his objects on the vanquished, and makes of them his possession. He imposes his own contours on the vanquished, who internalize this shape and become ambiguous beings 'housing' another" (Freire, 1993, p. 41). As Miguel Morin (2010) notes, echoing Freire, "When a traumatized and oppressed person adopts the traits of the oppressor through a process of psychological internalization, they are bound as long as they continue to house the oppressor, and actually may reach a point of accepting themselves as oppressors who are only aspiring to attain their rightful place upon the throne of oppression" (Morin, 2010, p. 4). Hence, the oppressed individual may possess a fear of freedom. As Morin explains, "because of a traumatized person's inability to clearly objectivize the oppressor, due to his or her own adhesion to him, the oppressed individual will desire the oppressor's freedom to oppress—a tragic dilemma" (Morin, 2010, p. 2). Signals of this tragedy are often manifested in the way oppressed individuals inflict violence on their peers and themselves—an indirect or displaced attack on the oppressor. There is a tendency to buy into the myth of their condition—why their plight is an inevitable outcome of forces— a myth that includes the so-called cultures of the poor and ignorance of the people. Their self-depreciation comes from their internalizing the oppressor's opinion of them. Ferenczi's early definition of the identification with the aggressor holds true to many of these outstanding characteristic mindsets.

We can think of many examples of cultural oppression and identification with the oppressor. A fascinating study is the case of Willie Bosket who in the 1980s was called "the most dangerous man in American" due to his sudden and vicious attacks on anyone at any given time. However, when one examined the intergenerational trauma that affected Mr. Bosket, we see that his family legacy matriculated from one of the most violent and savage counties in the south, Edgefield County, South Carolina—called "bloody Edgefield" because of the violence of white southerners, perpetrated against other white communities. Mr. Bosket's ancestors were slaves in this county. Biographical research into the history of Willie Bosket reveals a powerful identification with the oppressor that materialized as one of the most violent legacies of American citizens from one area of the country. Indeed, we can see that a portion of the history of violence in our country stems from such tragic identifications and masochistic bonds between oppressor and oppressed.

Robert Jay Lifton's term, *the death imprint*, the impression left by traumatic encounters, is reminiscent of Atkinson's trauma trails, and is illustrated in the case of Willie Bosket. The death imprint is part of the encounter with trauma and death—a death that has been survived. Noel Walsh notes that trauma survival often requires a coming to terms with the experience of helplessness and powerlessness and an acceptance of the inner psychological change from anxiety, where the threat of death is anticipated, to a giving up or surrender, where the self is no longer able to hold itself together and the feeling state changes to one of passivity or rage and progressive inhibitions of mental function (Walsh, 1996). Added to these feelings are those of guilt and self-condemnation for somehow failing to prevent the traumatic situation. We see this trauma imprint in the film *12 Years A Slave,* when Samuel Northup, rescued from the horrors of Louisiana slavery, arrives home at last to his family in New York. Upon entering the room to reunite with his family, he bows his head in shame and asks for forgiveness, stricken with a kind of survivor guilt that is endemic to trauma imprints. Lifton writes of the importance of bearing witness to the pain and suffering of the victim which "requires a coming to terms with some kind of meaning that one needs to give to that trauma…so that finding meaning in the death encounters helps the person find meaning in life in general" (Lifton. 2013, p. 211). In addition, Lifton points out how often survivors of trauma retain indelible images of the trauma imprint, leading to psychic numbing or a diminished capacity or inclination to feel. Unnamed and unassimilated, trauma imprints can be passed down to the child's unconscious and to subsequent generations.

Another example, in film, of the trauma imprint, is found in Lee Daniels's *The Butler* (Daniels, 2013), loosely based on the real life of Eugene Allen—in the film portrayed as Cecil Gaines (Forest Whitaker), an

African-American who recounts his life story beginning with his life as a child of sharecroppers in Georgia and culminating in a 34-year tenure as White House butler. A traumatic event occurs when Cecil is a child. While he is working with his family in the cotton fields, the farm's owner, Thomas Westfall (Alex Petty), walks into the field and drags his mother away to a nearby house where he rapes her. When Cecil's father silently confronts Westfall on his return by eclipsing his path, the owner shoots him. Later we learn that Cecil's mother has collapsed from the cumulative trauma, and must be cared for by others. The estate caretaker, Annabeth Westfall (Vanessa Redgrave), takes Cecil in and trains him as a house servant—skills he will later employ as he moves from work at a Washington DC hotel to the White House staff.

Although the film reviews the generational history of civil rights, as seen through the eyes of Cecil Gaines, another level of the story reveals and dramatizes the way that trauma can "remain attached to a family in the forms of a ghost or revenant, hidden or poorly buried in a crypt in the heart of a descendant" (Schutzenberger, 1998, p. 20). We see the phantom of the trauma expressing itself in the way that Cecil becomes highly agitated when his son participates in civil rights protests—how Cecil is wedded to a predictable routine, and cannot challenge the unequal pay of the White House staff until much later in his life. We can see that for Cecil to protest is to die like his father, the danger of death triggered by the trauma imprint of his father's murder when he protested against Westfall. It is a kind of death that Cecil survives. For him, the identification with this experience of the oppressor's destructiveness means that Cecil's son Louis will also die if he protests—indeed a reality in many civil rights causes, but extensively imbued with the projection of the past trauma onto the current circumstances. The effect of Cecil's trauma phantom may even account for the life struggles of his wife, Gloria (Oprah Winfrey), whose alcoholism and despair suggests a kind of psychic numbing. The film is actually a story of traumatic transmission and identification with the oppressor, rather than simply a historical overview seen through the lived experiences of Cecil's family and culture.

We began our exploration of intergenerational, traumatic cycles and reenactments with a discussion of how daimon energies, inherited from individual and cultural trauma transmissions, can be manifest in both destructive and creative ways depending on the difference between the integration of past ordeal into meaning, opposed to the repetition of the daimon forces reflective of the oppressor's power. Let us conclude our overview of defensive identifications and intergenerational trauma with final examples from the films of Quentin Tarantino where the medium is the message—film examples that illustrate the daimonic force of identifications with the aggressor/ oppressor when they are activated in service of defenses against overwhelming victimization and unspeakable suffering.

In a scene from the film *Inglorious Basterds* (Tarantino, 2009), First Lieutenant Albo Raines (Brad Pitt) barks at a group of recent recruits: "We are going to kill Nazis. When we see a Nazi we are going to kill him. Anybody have a problem with that?" Everyone shakes their heads. No problem. And indeed, Quentin Tarantino has no problem with killing in any and all in his corpus of revenge sagas. As the filmmaker says, "If I made it a little easier for artists to work in violence, great. I've accomplished something" (Tarantino, 2011, p. 1). But what Tarantino has accomplished is more than what he attests to achieving. He says that:

> Violence is just one of many things you can do in movies. People ask me 'Where does all this violence come from in you movies?' I say 'Where does all this dancing come from in Stanley Donen movies? If you ask me how I feel about violence in real life, well, I have a lot of feelings about it. It's one of the worst aspects of America. In movies, violence is cool. I like it. (Tarantino, 2013, p. 2)

When pressed about the killing in his films, Tarantino once said, "To say I get a big kick out of violence in movies and can enjoy violence in movies but find it totally abhorrent in real life—I can feel totally justified and totally comfortable with the statement. I do not think one is a contradiction of the other" (Tarantino, 2013, p. 3) Tarantino does not take stock in the notion that movie violence creates actual violence—rather, they exist in separate realms.

Considering our exploration of trauma legacies, one can argue that Tarantino's films actually create in the audience powerful identifications with cultural traumas that often masquerade as separate cinematic phenomena, especially in terms of the filmmaker's view of separate realms of violence. This is to say that many of Tarantino's films both depict and infer examples of this defensive strategy of identification with the oppressor in his characters, as well as seducing us into experiencing in real time an accommodation with the pull and undertow of the dynamic itself.

Objective examples of trauma imprints and identifications with the oppressor abound in Tarantino's revenge stories. In *Django Unchained* (Tarantino, 2012) we see clearly the house servant Stephen's (Samuel L. Jackson) own self-image as at once self-deprecating and sadistic, calculating and envious of the Plantation owner, Calvin J. Candie (Leonardo DiCaprio), and his powerful, abusive world. Django's (Jamie Foxx) striving for freedom as he seeks to recover his lost wife is introduced as a heroic foil to the characteristic flaws we see in Stephen's identification with the oppressor. Django appears to not internalize the opinions of his oppressor, nor self-deprecate. He is not resigned to the oppressor, though in chains. But as the film unfolds into the odyssey of revenge, we see Django learning how to kill as a bounty hunter, trained by Dr. King Schultz (Christopher Waltz) who employs Django to help him identify a wanted bounty. "He's a natural!!" Schultz exclaims at one point, when Django kills a man for money they now share. Is Django's bounty violence a housing of the oppressor? The same kind of question appears throughout Tarantino's films as a whole. For instance, in *Inglorious Basterds*, Shosanna Dreyfus (Melanie Laurent) and Aldo Raines justify their killing because of the murderousness of the Nazi oppressors, but when Lieutenant Raines carves a swastika into the forehead of the SS officer Col. Hans Landa (Christopher Waltz), and says he thinks it is his "best work to date," the separation of oppressor and oppressed becomes muddled. The same can be said about *Black Mamba* or the *Bride* (Uma Thurman) in the *Kill Bill* series as we see her learn from a martial arts master only to turn her skills to revenge and carnage.

In addition to these examples, what is significant in Tarantino is not simply the dramatization of the identification with the oppressor phenomenon. It is the way that the audience is pulled into a mystification with the defensive tragedy of the identification cycle. When Schultz in *Django Unchained* suddenly shoots Calvin Candie, while he is insisting that they eat white cake in the parlor, he turns with a comic flair to the room, and seemingly to us as well, and says "I just could not help myself," even as Candie's henchmen shotgun him to death. This scene pulls us in to identifying with Schultz's impulse, for how long can one bear the oppressor's distorted logic without reprisal? But the fact is that Tarantino is drawing us into an experience of liking murder—in short inculcating a forced empathy to the power of revenge where we can viscerally share in the undeniable undertow of the identification process—and, if we can acknowledge this cinematic manipulation, we can also marvel at how potent a force it is when we feel a kindred identification with not only the victims, but also with the power to right the injustice by exulting in the retribution. It may be just a movie, as Tarantino says, but the identification with the aggressor is not just in the characters' portrayals—we too experience that defensive pull to accompany the aggressor—perhaps an unintended characteristic of Tarantino films in general. As film critic Roger Ebert said about why he loved films—"they give us a chance to be someone else for a few hours" (Ebert, 2014) and that is the greatest opportunity to experience empathy by being part of a person you are not. The same might be said of the surprising affinities in Tarantino's revenge sagas to the uncanny impulses to identify with the oppressor and to cheer when the plantation blows up, the movie theater burns Nazis to the ground, and the martial arts heroine destroys her adversaries in the name of retributive justice. What more of an introduction to understand and experience the powerful defense dynamic of the identification with the aggressor than in Tarantino's cinematic world?

About our identifications with the ghosts of traumatic events, oppressive suffering, and intergenerational cycles of reenactment that imbue our individual and cultural lives, affecting the nature of our daimon spirits and our shared worlds, Stephen Frosh notes that "we should avoid trying to bring history to a close. . . History does not end because everything is in the process of return" (p. 170). Instead, Frosh underscores the need to:

> Seek out ceremonies of reparation, rituals of recovery . . . We must understand that if a ghost keeps troubling us, it may mean that we have missed the point; but it may also mean that we are the only hope the ghost has left. We must recognize that we are ghosts too. There is little distinction between the haunted and the one who haunts; the former turns into the latter soon enough. Perhaps our capacity to recognize ghosts is what determines the likelihood that we too will be recognized in our struggle to be heard and seen. It is not obvious that there is any other way to do it. (Frosh, 2013, p. 170)

Indeed, in contrast to the way characters identify with the oppressor's violence, as depicted in Tarantino's films, we can see examples of disidentification from intergenerational traumatic hauntings by the way we participate in rituals of recovery and recognition. For example, when Myrlie Evers-Williams was once asked why she did not speak angry invectives against the murderers of her husband, Medgar Evers—an African-American civil rights activist from Mississippi who was assassinated by members of the White Citizen's Council—she responded that to hate means that she would be the same as the men who killed her husband (West, 2014). We can see in this remarkable and courageous wisdom, that to bring into the forefront of our awareness the links and repetitions associated with generational violence and atrocities is to give meaning to the events where the context of identifications with the aggressor can be transformed. As Schutzenberger says about acknowledging the daimon of intergenerational hauntings and reenactments, when the trauma transmission can be revealed from its encryption and spectral reality,

> Meaning emerges, a context is transformed, another form emerges from the depths and things change. The subject can breathe, gets rid of the weight of the past, often his body changes, his life changes. He becomes another person. . . and (sometimes), in addition he is cured of a serious or even life-threatening illness. (Schutzenberger, 1998, p. 129)

This meaning-making, this healing transformation of the trauma context and imprint, is what is possible in the therapeutic process. There is now a Samuel Northup trail from Washington to Louisiana that maps the legacy of his journey to slavery and home again. There are plans for the descendants of the Epps family to meet with the descendants of Northup on the Louisiana plantation in the near future. Even there the gods may come to presence.

REFERENCES

Abraham, N., and Torok, M. (1994). L'Ecorce et le noyau. In N. Rank (Ed. and Trans.), *The shell and the kernel*: Vol. 1. Chicago and London: Chicago University Press.

Atkinson, J. (2002). *Trauma trails: Recreating song lines: The transgenerational effects of trauma in indigenous Australia*. North Melbourne, Australia: Spinfex Press.

Axelrad, S., and Maury, L.M. (1951).Identification as a mechanism of adaptation. In G. Wilbur, and W. Muensterberger (Eds.), *Psychoanalysis and culture*. New York: John Wiley and Sons.

Boszormenyi-Nagy, Spark, I., and Spark, G.M. (1973). *Invisible loyalties*. New York: Harper and Row.

Daniels, L. (Director). (2013). *Lee Daniels'* The butler. [Motion picture]. United States: Weinstein Company.

Diamond, S.A. (1996). *Anger, madness, and the daimonic*. Albany: State University of New York Press.

Dolto, F. (1985). *La Cause des enfants*. Paris: Laffont.

Fenichel. O. (1945). *The psychoanalytic theory of neurosis*. New York: Norton.

Ferenczi, S. (1933). Confusion of tongues between adults and children: The language of tenderness and passion. In *Final contributions to the problems and methods of psychoanalysis* (pp. 156–167). London: Hogarth Press, 1955.

Freud, A. (1947). *The ego and the mechanism of defense*. New York: International University Press.

Freud, S. (1900). The interpretation of dreams. In *The standard edition of the complete psychological works of Sigmund Freud*: Vols. 4 and 5. Ed. James Strachey. London: Hogarth Press, 1953–1974.

Freud, S. (1913). Totem and taboo. In *The standard edition of the complete psychological works of Sigmund Freud*: Vol. 13 and 17. Ed. James Strachey (pp. 217–252). London: Hogarth Press, 1953–1974.

Freud, S. (1917). In Mourning and melancholia. In *The standard edition of the complete psychological works of Sigmund Freud*: Vol. 14. Ed. James Strachey. (pp. 237-258). London: Hogarth Press, 1953–1974.

Freud, S. (1922), *Group psychology and analysis of the ego*. London: Hogarth Press.

Friere, P. (1993). *Pedagogy of the oppressed*. New York: Contiuum Books.

Frosh, S. (2013). *Hauntings: Psychoanalysis and ghostly transmissions*. New York: Palgrave Macmillan.

Fuchs, S. H. (1937). On introjection. *International Journal of Psychoanalysis*, 18, 271.

Gerson, S. (2004). The relational unconscious: A core element of intersubjectivity, thirdness, and clinical process. *The Psychoanalytic Quarterly* 73(1), 63-98.

Goodsell, L. (2013). Interview: Steve McQueen and Chiwetel Ejiofor talk about *12 Years A Slave*. Rotten Tomatoes, Flixster.

Gorden, A. (1997). *Ghostly matters: Haunting and the socialogical imagination*. Minneaoplolis: University of Minnesota Press.

Goren, E. and Alpert, J. (2013). The analyst as witness, historian, and activist: A conversation with Robert Jay Lifton. *Psychoanalysis, Culture, and Society*, 18(2).

Hans, J. (1995). *The site of our lives: The self and the subject from Emerson to Foucault*. Albany, NY: State University of New York Press.

Heidegger, M. (1977). Basic writings (A. Frank, J. Capuzzi, G. Gray, and D. F. Krell, Trans.). *Letter on humanism*. New York: Harper Books.

Hillman, J. (1983). *Healing fictions*. New York: Station Hill.

Jackson, B., and Hardiman, R. (1997). Conceptual foundations for social justice courses. In M. Adams, L. A. Bell, and P. Griffin (Eds.), *Teaching for diversity and social justice*. New York: Routledge.

James, S. (Director). (2014). *Life itself: A memoir* [Motion Picture]. United States: Kartemquin Films.

Jung, C.G. (1968). Aion: Researches into the phenomenology of the self. In H. Read, M. Fordham, G. Adler, and W. McGuire (Eds.), *The collected works* of C.G. Jung, (2nd ed., Vol. 9, part 2) (R.F.C. Hull, Trans.). Princeton, NJ: Princeton University Press.

Krell, D. F. (1992). *Daimon life: Heidegger and life-philosophy.* Bloomington: Indiana University Press.

Kristeva, J. (1988). *Strangers to ourselves.* London: Harvester Wheatsheaf.

Lopez, B. (2013, January). Sliver of sky. *Harper's Magazine,* 41-48.

May, R. (1969). *Love and will.* New York: W.W. Norton.

McQueen, S. (Director). (2013). *12 years a slave.* [Motion picture]. United States: Universal Pictures.

Morin, M. (2010). *Examining the internalized oppressor complex.* Retrieved February 21, 2014 from http://4strugglemag.org/2010/07/23.

O'Loughlin, M. (2009). *The subject of childhood.* New York: Peter Lang.

Rachman, A. (2000). Ferenczi's "Confusion of Tongues" theory and the analysis of incest trauma. *In Psychoanalytic Social Work,* vol. 7: pp. 27–53.

Rachman, A. (2003). Freud's analysis of his daughter Anna: A confusion of tongues. In C. Barbre, B. Ulanov, and A. Roland (Eds.) *Creative dissent: Psychoanalysis in evolution.* Westport, CT and London: Praeger Press.

Schutzenberger, A.A. (1998). *The ancestor syndrome: Transgenerational psychology and the hidden links in the family tree.* London and New York: Routledge Books.

Tarantino, Q. (Director). (2012). *Django unchained.* [Motion picture]. United States: Weinstein Company.

Tarantino, Q. (Director). (2009). *Inglorious bastards.* [Motion Picture]. United States: Weinstein Company. Tarantino, Q. (Director). (2003/2004). Kill Bill: Volumes 1 and 2. [Motion Picture] United States: Miramax Films.

Tarantino, Q. (2011). Quentin Tarantino quotes: Top ten best quotations and sayings. Retrieved January 31, 2014 from http://voices,yahoo.com.

Tarantino, Q. (2013). Everything Quentin Tarantino really thinks about violence and the movies. Retrieved February 1, 2014 from http://www.theatlanticwire.com/2013/01/quentin-tarantino

Walsh, N. (1996). Trauma and death. In C.B. Strozier and M. Flynn (Eds.), *Trauma and self* (pp. 245-254). Lantham, MD: Rowman and Littlefield Publishers.

West, C. (2014). On being a Chekovian Christian and a blues man. Wheaton Colleage. Retrieved March 20, 2014 from http://www.wheaton.Edu/WETN/All media/Lectures-and-conferences.CACE

Wilbur, G., and Muensterberger, W. (1951). *Psychoanalysis and culture.* New York: John Wiley and Sons.

SIX

Trauma and Resilience among a Stolen Generation of Indigenous People

Janice A. Walters

In this chapter I will focus on the ways in which trauma and race have impacted the lives of Australia's Indigenous people. The unconscious transmission of trauma through generations has been highlighted by the work of Fraiberg, Adelson and Shapiro (1975) who suggest that trauma experienced in one generation has profound effects on the emotional lives not only of the children of the next generation, but even on the lives of descendants six or ten generations hence. Aboriginal family members who were taken and placed in white institutions as children live with the daily consequences of trauma, which is being passed down through the generations. These individuals are referred to as the Stolen Generations, as I explain below. Resilience is also present in members of the Aboriginal community and it is important to understand the ways in which this resilience develops and can be utilized to circumvent intergenerational trauma.

I began my journey into the world of the Stolen Generations when I spent several months conducting ethnographic research within a community where Aboriginal families live side-by-side with non-Aboriginal families. The Indigenous name for this area is Dharruk, which is derived from the name of the Darug people, an Aboriginal tribe associated with the area west of Sydney. The 2011 Census found that over 5% of the population who live in this community are Indigenous Australians (Australian Bureau of Statistics, 2012). Public housing was built in this area during the 1960 and 1970s and many Aboriginal families relocated to these homes. Over time, extended family members followed. Those who are not family by blood are welcomed into the larger family often referred to as "The Mob." This strong allegiance is important within the Aboriginal culture and provides a supportive network for residents. The older generations, referred to as the Elders are respected and their role is to pass on the cultural traditions. They are commonly referred to as Aunty or Uncle. *Kanyini* is the principle of connectedness through caring and responsibility that underpins Aboriginal life, and Kanyini is nurtured through caring and practicing responsibility for all things. This principle facilitates strong family connections within this community.

When I left Australia in 1981, I was a university student involved with the struggle for land rights and the Aboriginal people's quest to reclaim their cultural heritage. I was unaware of any national conversation about the children who were forcibly removed from their families. This was an unspoken trauma that silently haunted the Aboriginal people and deliberately was placed outside of the conscious awareness of non-Aboriginal people. I was aware that white society didn't see Aboriginal people because they either lived in remote areas on missions or they were living in poverty on the outskirts of urban areas.

I left with the goal of returning to record and engage in the Aboriginal people's quest to regain their cultural heritage. When I returned to begin this project in 2010, I realized that while awareness, acknowledgement and acceptance of Aboriginal cultural heritage is essential, it is idealistic to believe that current generations can go back to their traditional culture. Addressing everyday needs is imperative to the future well-being of the Aboriginal people. With this realization, I focused my interest on the issues that have been unspoken for too long and these are the ways in which race and culture have divided the nation and its people, and the role that intergenerational trauma is playing in the problems that the Aboriginal people confront on a day-to-day basis.

I was introduced into the Dharruk community by anthropologist Gillian Cowlishaw, whose work with Aboriginal families is well documented (Cowlishaw, 2009). The day we drove to the suburb where we hoped to find families who would be willing to meet me, I felt trepidation because even though I am Australian I was far from both my New York and Australian homes. I was also aware that I was not only an intruder into the lives of these residents, but I am a descendant of the white colonizers who continue to impose their paternalism and cultural ideologies on Aboriginal people. I left that day with an invitation to return to meet with two women. I continued to visit as often as I could and I embraced any opportunity to participate that came my way. It took two months for me to build trust and to find my place within this community. Unfortunately, when I was beginning to feel confident in my place, and more families were willing to participate, I had to return to New York. I didn't know what would happen when I returned. However, despite the physical distance and long intervals between visits my relationships have expanded and become very fulfilling. A limitation of working from the other side of the world is that I often have to leave when new opportunities are presenting themselves.

THE IMPACT OF COLONIZATION

Raphael, Swan and Martinek (1998) suggest that the foundations for intergenerational trauma began with the proclamation of the doctrine of *Terra Nullius,* land belonging to no one, by British colonial authorities. This stripped the Aboriginal people of their home and their humanity. The loss of land that was theirs for 60,000 years prior to settlement continues to impact the Aboriginal community. Family, kinship structures and communities were destroyed and attempts at eradication took the form of massacres, poisoning of food and water supplies, and virtual annihilation.

The subjugation of survivors led to a breakdown of traditional ways of family life that were essential to passing on Aboriginal worldviews, languages, cultural practices and ways of life. Raphael, Swan and Martinek (1998) suggest that the active discrimination, denigration, breakdown of culture, racism, and denial of the most basic rights, added a second level of ongoing trauma stating "the psychological impact of the experience of dispossession, racism, exclusion, extermination, denigration and degradation are beyond description and they strike at the very core of our sense of being and identity"[1] (p. 328).

The policy of removing Aboriginal children was enacted with the goal of blending them within the white population, assimilating and civilizing them, and training them for the lower orders of society. Half-caste children were targeted because it was believed they would expedite the bleaching of the races. Justification came from the appalling conditions that Aboriginal families were living in, but the role of the colonists in forcing them to live in these conditions was denied. Further, their rich cultural and community life, which placed a strong emphasis on kinship, family and the care of children, was denied. Thus, the forced movement of Aboriginal people to life in fringe camps or on white properties was used to invalidate their competence and capacities. Today, most Aboriginal families live on the urban fringes of society. They are caught between two worlds that they struggle to reconcile. They cannot return to the homes they were taken from nor can they regain the culture they lost. In a paper presented at the NSW Aboriginal Mental Health Conference in Sydney in 1999, Lola, an Aboriginal woman, spoke about the Aboriginal peoples being an invisible people within their own country. She suggested that not only are they invisible, living on the fringes of country towns, but they are also invisible in the minds of the majority of people (Kabaila, 2012). This national denial has had devastating consequences.

IDEALIZATION OF ABORIGINAL CULTURE BY WHITE SOCIETY

Following the nation's 1967 acknowledgement of Aboriginal rights, there has been a national interest in revitalizing Aboriginal traditions. This often takes an idealized form. Aboriginal artwork and cultural demonstrations are tourist attractions and promoting these images has become a lucrative industry. Australia's portrayal of Indigenous people serves as a mask for the real issues, as well as the underlying racism that continues to divide the country. Cowlishaw (2010) points out that cultural revival programs serve as blinders for those who participate in the acknowledgement of Aboriginal rights. She argues that the real needs and complexities that suburban Aboriginal people are confronted with daily need to be addressed. I embraced this ideal until I participated with and saw the everyday issues and challenges that Aboriginal people face.

While, the families from the Dharruk community value their Aboriginal identity, many of the Elders were deprived of their traditions because they grew up in white institutions. They speak of their sadness that their languages and traditions were lost to them. When I met with Bertha she described the day that she returned to her family. She said that her initial response was "Wow! These are my people; people I have been ashamed of all my life." She told me that when she lived within white society they portrayed the Aboriginal people as living in tents and humpies. She said she was made to feel ashamed of her family. When her Aunties came to greet her, she questioned being ashamed of her family for so many years and said she began to cry. I agree with Kendall (1994) who found that Aboriginal people experience problems with identity, especially the children who moved back into Aboriginal society after being reared as non-Aboriginal. Bertha identifies with her Aboriginal identity but seems to have some conflict related to her childhood internalization of white society.

The Stolen Generations of Dharruk struggle with poverty and racism as well as the devastating effects of intergenerational trauma. Tara, an Elder who lives in a government subsidized house, waits for her pension check. By the time it arrives, she is often without the food essential for a woman of her aging years. She has a comfortable home but she struggles with poverty as well as the emotional traumas of her past, and her children's present. Tara is secure in her Aboriginal identity, but her day-to-day needs are not met. Cowlishaw (2010) states, "if the Aboriginal people do not know who they are they would be merely a racialised segment of the poor" (p. 19). Reclaiming their historic identity is of great importance to their status within the nation.

THE ESTABLISHMENT OF RACIAL AND CULTURAL DIVISIONS

As a child, I was introduced to the racial and cultural divide that exists between Aboriginal and non-Aboriginal people. The first settlers colonized what became Australia in 1788. While the purpose of colonization was economic gain, the men who were sent to the shores of Australia were mostly prisoners who were deemed inferior citizens in Britain and Ireland. When the prison system could no longer accommodate them, they were outcast from their homeland and sent to establish a penal colony. This became their opportunity to claim both economic and personal superiority. They landed with great anxiety, together with feelings of abandonment, persecution and dehumanization. They perceived an uncivilized land inhabited by an uncivilized people. This led to intolerable anxiety and caused their flight to an idealized, internal object in order to keep their ideal and persecutory objects separated and under control (Klein, 1946). Both real and perceived fears of persecution and annihilation led hatred and destruction to govern their relationships. Alford (1989), drawing on Melanie Klein's theories, states that paranoid-schizoid and depressive positions represent not merely our archaic heritage, but also our way of relating to others and ourselves. When paranoid-schizoid anxiety is given an objective focus, groups legitimate and reinforce paranoid-schizoid defenses, such as splitting and idealization. This resulted in the formation of an idealized white culture and an Aboriginal culture that was deemed inferior (Walters, 2012). The previously persecuted colonizers became the persecutors, and the Aboriginal people were the recipients of their projected hatred and destruction.

The capacity for ego splitting and projection plays an important role in our perception of and feelings about others. According to Byles (2003), the process of projective identification is responsible for how we make others feel about themselves and ourselves. Through projective identification the hateful, bad parts of ourselves are placed onto and into others, and the introjection of our hatred makes others feel hateful toward themselves. For decades, the Aboriginal people have introjected messages of hatred and inferiority. These messages, and ensuing dehumanization, has resulted in the internalization of shame and rejection in relation to Aboriginal identity. Kwok (2012) suggests that shame represents the painful embodiment of a social order premised on the subjection and exclusion of a minority group. However, it also serves as a measure and guardian of Aboriginal cultural autonomy. Working with the Aboriginal people, you become aware of the subtle and not so subtle ways in which shame impacts their daily lives and often silences them.

The greed of the colonizers necessitated their need to claim the land. The resistance of the Aboriginal people to giving up their lands, or participating in cultivation fueled the colonists' hatred and aggression. They drew upon the ideas of Darwin (1984) that cultivation represented higher order intelligence and found justification in their belief that the Aboriginal people were inferior in the chain of evolution making them undeserving of survival. This contributed to their decision to implement policies of annihilation (Roberts, 1978).

Freud (1918) proposed that war provides a perfect channel for repressed impulses. He suggested that in order to control and protect the self from anxiety, an individual channels integrated anxieties into real external dangers. He further suggested that when a person is unable to bear the painful reality of rejection, hurt or abandonment, he or she identifies with the one who brought this about, causing the individual to become full of self-reproach. If we see the colonists through this lens, they were abandoned by their country, which led to feelings of rejection and hurt as well as self-hatred. According to Freud (1917), the person becomes responsible for the action of the loved one and instead of anger and frustration being directed toward the loved object, aggression is turned on the self. Thus, self-reproaches are reproaches against a loved object that are shifted away and integrated into the person's own ego. To preserve the attachment to the absent loved one, the attack is redirected and idealization of the object can be retained and preserved from the hatred and rage provoked by the narcissistic wounding of the initial abandonment (Freud, 1917). The colonists' homeland became the idealized love object and their individual need to channel internal psychotic anxieties and protect themselves from anxiety resulted in the need for an outlet through which these anxieties could be externalized and projected onto an enemy. The Aboriginal people became that enemy.

In *Civilization and its Discontents* (1930), Freud suggested that the cultural superego harbors the risk of death instinct aggression being released at any favorable opportunity, under the pretext of idealism and patriotism. Volkan (1988) suggests that the individual, idealized superego may merge with the cultural superego and justify a nation's implementation of systematic acts of physical and cultural genocide. Fornari (1975) proposed that, "war can be seen as an attempt at therapy carried out by a social institution, which by institutionalizing war increases to gigantic proportions what is initially an elementary defensive mechanism of the ego in the schizo-paranoid phase" (pp. xvii–xviii). The psychological conditions for war and genocide were established with the splitting of the nation through biological and cultural justifications, and through the need for an outlet for the colonists' internalized anxieties, aggression and economic greed.

STEREOTYPES AND SHAME

Cultural and racial divisions facilitated stereotypes and the internalization of shame. Dalziell (1998) suggests that shame developed in response to the proliferation and application of colonial myths about Aboriginality. He states that the Aboriginal people who interact with these myths are painfully subjected to the premises contained within them, and these have often been accepted and internalized. Kwok (2012) reports that for Aboriginal people shame is a feeling of acute self-consciousness and often painful inadequacy which arises when they leave the comfort of their communities and are exposed to the critical gaze of others. The anticipation of being exposed to those who live outside of their communities also elicits these feelings. She also suggests that while life in an Aboriginal community provides a familiar security and fond sentimentality that can be taken for granted, it can also bring desperate confinement and hopelessness in which the social burdens of their position as a dispossessed minority play out in lives marked with trouble, conflict, impoverishment and personal trauma. In addition, while the Aboriginal people maintain a sphere of life they call their own, they are incorporated within and dependent upon the institutions of dominant Australian society (Kwok, 2012). Despite this, many continue to question and resist the stereotypes imposed on them by mainstream society. Mary told me that her father and the other men always worked. She said that she really disagrees when white people claim that the Aboriginal people are all "bludgers" who are no good. This is a commonly held belief within white society.

The negative stereotyping of the Aboriginal people has had psychological consequences. They have been portrayed as an inferior people who should be avoided. The stolen children were led to believe the Aboriginal people are inferior and that they were removed from their homes because their people didn't want them. To accomplish the goal of eliminating the race through marriages to white men, the women were told that they should avoid Aboriginal men because they would be bad for them. Bertha told me that when she was freed from the home she was afraid to cross the street if there was an Aboriginal man on the other side. The children were expected to be white and they were told that white people would care for them. However, they found themselves rejected by white society. They were lost within their Aboriginal communities and confronted daily with the negative stereotypes associated with their Aboriginality. This led to lost and traumatized generations.

THE STOLEN GENERATIONS

Growing up in Australia, I listened to the conversations between non-Aboriginal people who accepted the commonly held belief that Aboriginal children needed to be saved by white Australia. Even at a very young age, I felt that something was inherently wrong. I found myself identifying with these children and being fearful that I might be taken from my mother and lose the attachment bond that linked us so tightly together.

However, I did not put meaning to these conversations because I was too young to realize the impact of what was happening around me.

Between the years 1883 and 1969, Aboriginal children were forcibly removed from their families. Many residents of the Dharruk Community were taken to either Cootamundra Girls Home or Kinchela Boys Home, where they were often subjected to not only the trauma of abrupt separation and loss of a mother, family and culture, but to unspeakable physical and sexual abuse. These children are the Elders whose skeletons in the closet (Garon, 2004) are being passed down as ancestral ghosts (Fraiberg, Adelson and Shapiro, 1975). Carol's story is documented in a book titled *The Stolen Children and their Stories* (Bird, 1998). In telling her story, she speaks about the impact that being taken has had on five generations of her families ability to mother. "Four generations of my family went without parently love, without mother or father. I myself found it very hard to show my love to my children because I wasn't given that, so was my mother and grandmother" (Bird, 1998, pp. 59–60). Carol is aware that the inability to give love is a consequence of the deprivation imposed on her grandmother, mother and herself. She also speaks about the mistreatment she experienced during her childhood. "I was abused by the missionaries from all angles—sexual, physical and mental. I am a strong person myself. I had to be strong. I had no-one to turn to, no-one to guide me through life" (Bird, 1998; pp. 59–60).

THE STOLEN CHILDREN'S VULNERABILITY TO ABUSE

The Stolen Children were vulnerable to abuse. The boys who were taken to Kinchela were forced to place all of their belongings in a fire. They were then taken to a room where their hair was shaved off and they were given clothes with a number stamped on them. From that day on they were referred to by a number and they remained nameless. This dehumanization and the messages that they were unwanted children, together with the severe rules and punishments caused many children to disconnect emotionally (Kabaila, 2012). They projected the emotional state of nothingness that they were forced to live with onto their caretakers, who in turn, sensed their vulnerability making them the recipients of their own psychotic anxieties. Those who rebelled against the rigid rules experienced brutal retaliation. The women of Cootamundra describe being locked in either a morgue or a box room for days. They not only experienced the terror of their isolation but they also feared the goundjas (ghosts) who they were told would get them (Kabaila, 2012). When I met with Dave he told me that in Kinchela, if you answered an attendant back you were sent up the line where the other boys would line up to punch you, even your brothers and cousins. If they didn't participate they would themselves be sent up the line. Even when the children had broken ribs or noses, the other children had to pick them up and carry them through to the end of the line. He said that this happened every day.

Bill, who is Lila and Bertha's brother, was sent to Kinchela at age four. He said that ex-soldiers took care of the children and they thought that all Aboriginal kids were "scum" and they treated them this way. They were not allowed to speak with Aboriginal people and were led to believe that they were a class above them. Bill said that these boys were made to grow up in a world where they did not belong and this had severe effects on them later in life. He said many "went crazy" after they were freed and those who went to jail described it as a summer camp compared to Kinchela. Bill said:

> It was hate, hate, hate for 10 and half years, that's a lot of hate to fit into one little system; into one little mind. And you'r walking around and where can you get? Even if you go and sit underneath a tree, even then you think the tree is prejudiced against you, and won't give you the shade to sit under. (Cowlishaw, 2012, p. 63)

Bill described Kinchela as a jail for children who were referred to as uneducated or uncontrollable. The boys learned to support each other and when one was beaten the other brothers would say, "Don't cry. Don't give him the satisfaction that he's hurting ya" (Cowlishaw, 2012, p. 63). Bill said "They thought you were animals. You know it was like a place where they go around and kick us like a dog . . . it was just like a prison" (Cowlishaw, 2012, p. 63).

Lila, Bertha and their deceased sister were taken to Cootamundra as infants. They were told that their mother did not want them. Bertha told me that it was very difficult for them in the home. She said they were punished with the cane and forced to miss meals for things they did that were not really bad. The sisters believe they were spared some of the atrocities experienced by the other children because of their unspoken, emotional support. It seems that this made them less likely to project vulnerability onto their caretakers. I observed their need for protection from the white world when they unexpectedly changed the arrangements of my first visit. During our initial conversation, we agreed that I would drive to Bertha's house and then together we would drive to meet with Lila. However, when I arrived at Bertha's house, I was greeted by ten people who I assumed were present in case I should become an unwelcome intruder and there might be a need to preserve their unspoken trauma.

THE IMPACT OF TRAUMA

The impact of these experiences on the Stolen Children has and continues to have serious consequences for these families and Aboriginal communities. Swan (1998) states:

> The devastating experiences of Aboriginal parents and families brought on by the removal of their children, the loss of control over their lives, powerlessness, prejudice, and hopelessness, have left many problems for us to deal with today. The theft of Aboriginal children . . . has produced the background for many years of horrific memories, distress, and mental health problems that still need to be addressed. (pp. 15–16)

Atkinson (2002) suggests that, "the unnamed and unmetabolised violence becomes internalized and can lead to an escalation of self-destructive violent acts as well as to an increase in domestic and societal violence" (p. 72).

Clinical outcomes of immense trauma have been documented and these outcomes are commonly experienced among Aboriginal communities. Herman (1992) described complex PTSD, which includes a wide range of general psychological and somatic symptoms, an impact on personality and identity, vulnerability to self-harm, suicide, substance abuse, re-victimization and further abuse. In their study of First Nation Citizens in Canada, Manson, et al. (1996) reported increased rates of suicide, sexual abuse, alcoholism and family violence as recognized effects of trauma. Other outcomes for Aboriginal people include depression, anxiety, phobias, crime, homicide and the abandonment of children. Gagné (1994) makes an important point in suggesting that the original trauma leads to outcomes in the form of behaviors and consequences that become traumatic events in themselves, and these events bring additional trauma to the originally traumatized individual. This vicious cycle only serves to increase the impact of intergenerational trauma as these re-traumatizing experiences are passed down through families.

A major issue that has impacted Aboriginal communities is emotional availability of parents for children. Many of the stolen children are emotionally unavailable due to their inability to bond with their children, or due to their physical and psychological removal resulting from conditions such as depression, alcohol and drug abuse and incarceration. Based on her work with Holocaust survivors, Kaplan (1995) notes that most survivors could not remember or speak of what they experienced, but their psychological absences and tortured silences transmitted to their children events these survivors were unable to witness. Children of survivors from the Stolen Generations are left to wonder why their parent(s) are physically and psychologically unavailable.

Children of the Stolen Generation were subjected to conditions under which survival took priority. Kinchela boys describe daily physical and sexual abuse from their caretakers. In addition, they tolerated abuse from siblings and peers who were forced to participate in the sadistic practice of dealing out physical punishments (Kabaila, 2012). Dave told me, "if you wet your bed, they got every boy to go and punch them—even if you were their brother." These children lived in an environment of continued, silent vigilance and many took this with them to their new lives. This is evident in Bill's statement that even the tree was prejudiced against him. Kaplan (1995) suggests that those who survived did so because psychologically they were not fully present during their experiences. Under conditions of threat to survival, showing signs of humanness can lead to one's demise. The Holocaust survivors reduced their emotions and the needs that defined their humanity to the simple need of survival. Not only did the stolen generations live with survival as their priority, when they left they were confronted with a hostile social and cultural environment that further challenged their capacity for survival. According to Kaplan (1995), a level of anxiety is required to signal and evaluate threat levels, but not enough so as to be overwhelmed by the traumatic events. Emotions such as shame, guilt, attachment, terror and panic had to be hidden; therefore, survivors built a shell around their ego and emotions, which reduced the self to a non-thinking, non-feeling machine. Many of the stolen children continue to maintain this shell and this has impacted their lives and their children's lives.

When they left the institutions, the stolen children were lost. These children were taken from their families and denied access to their parents and communities. They found that they did not belong within either cultural group. They were indoctrinated into accepting the perception that the Aboriginal people were an inadequate group and that they belonged within white society. However, they soon learned that they were rejected by white society. But they no longer fit into their Aboriginal communities either. This left a generation without a place to belong. Lola in her address to the NSW Aboriginal Mental Health Conference held in Sydney in 1999, said:

> Is it any wonder that some of us: can't bond with our children; are over protective of our children; won't let our children or grandchildren out of our sight; can't share our deepest hurt and sorrow; try to buy affection; camouflage our real feelings suppress our memories; and are reluctant to trust. (Kabaila, 2012, p. vii)

Byles (2003) suggests that to understand genocide we need to understand how the individual is placed in the social, and the social in the individual. Davoine and Gaudillière (2004) speak to this in their statement "whereof one cannot speak thereof one cannot stay silent" (front flap). They also warn of the grave consequences of what they refer to as social linkages wherein, repressed memories find expression in both individual symptoms and potentially in the character that an entire group of people or a nation assumes. The repressed memories of the nation can be seen in the denial of the racial and cultural divide that exists, as well as the failure to recognize the needs of Aboriginal people and the impact of intergenerational trauma.

TRANSMISSION OF INTERGENERATIONAL TRAUMA

Kaplan (1995) found that survivors of trauma experience guilt for submitting to humiliations and degradations and for abandoning the values and ideals of virtue that make life worth living. She suggests that events that are so horrible that they cannot be witnessed at the time are transmitted long after their occurrence in the form of silence. She further suggests that this silence causes their children to wonder what is the truth that must not be spoken. Thus, children of survivors often live out their parent's nightmare. For Kaplan (1995), this happens through the process of transposition, which becomes the mechanism for the transmission of trauma. In this process, the past reality of the parent intrudes into the present reality of the child. The temporal positions of parent and child are exchanged and the parent's past occupies the psychological space that would ordinarily belong to the life of the child. Therefore, the child must give up the right to exist in his or her own present. The transposition of trauma, which originates in the parents' unconscious needs and wishes, must rely on and exploit the child's happier susceptibilities to be at one with and to be close to the parent, to partake of the parent's power, to be like the parent, to be loved and admired by the parent and to maintain a dialogue with the parent. However, what the child absorbs is the parent's reactions to the trauma as the parent unconsciously positions his or her trauma within the child. The child then sets out to cure the parent and undo his or her trauma by placing him or herself in the parent's position. The process of transposition can be observed among children of the Stolen Generations.

Trauma also reduces the mother's availability. Green (1986) suggests that the dead mother of infancy, resulting from either neglect or absence, remains as an empty or dead space within the psyche instead of a space where love and desire once held life and potential. When the mother is unavailable and fails to be empathic over an extended period, the child begins to sense that he or she must protect him or herself. The child also senses that something more drastic and imperiling than his or her own immediate survival is at stake and that, in addition to protecting him or herself, he or she must also protect the parent. In order to survive, the child must attempt to empathize and care for the mother. Thus, the child must become the parent's bridge to life.

TARA'S EXPERIENCE[2]

I met Tara on my first visit to the community. She is an elderly woman who lives alone in a house in the suburbs of Sydney. At that time, her daughter was living with her. Tara agreed to tell me her story and I visited her and sometimes her daughters during the months I spent in Sydney. Since then I continue to visit her and follow her family. Tara grew up on a mission where she lived with both of her parents. She was one of eight children. She describes her childhood as happy because she was with her mother and father. Tara's father worked hard and her mother suffered from tuberculosis. At 13, she left school to help the family and then left at 17 to work as a nurse's aide. She married her non-Aboriginal husband and was pregnant at age 21. He was a boxer and they moved around a lot. He drank excessively, abused her and often deserted the family. When the house Tara lived in was condemned, because of lack of electricity or water, she had to move. When she questioned her husband about taking the children's money, he broke her leg and abandoned her and their four children. She was about to give birth to their fifth child. She said that three couples who were white Christian people, ministers and some other people from a church group came to her house. They offered to take her children and assured her it was only for a little while until she found work and was able to get a home for them. Three of the children went with one family and one was with another family. Tara said that she thought the people from the church were trying to help her. When they took the children, they told Tara she could see them at any time and have them back when she found housing. When she went to see the children they sent her away and told her that she was no good for them. This devastated her. After her son was born, a woman came to where she was staying and took him from her arms, telling her that the authorities had someone to give him to. She was homeless, had no money and was deserted by her husband. Despite his mistreatment of her, Tara reunited with him and they had three more children. He again deserted her. She thought that because he was white he could help her to get the children back. He agreed but before this could happen he passed away.

Tara lived with the unspeakable trauma of the loss of her children. She was a recipient of racial discrimination and subjected to abuse. Her emotions were severely compromised when she learned that her taken, firstborn son drowned. She also held a skeleton in her closet (Garon, 2004) that was released when a government worker revealed it to her daughter. This opened up previous trauma and shame. Thirty years prior, Tara had been sexually assaulted by a non-Aboriginal man, left unconscious and awoke in a hospital. She later found out she was pregnant. For years, Tara had been settled in the Dharruk community where she lived with her four youngest children until the stolen children were returned as teenagers. She said "I was drinking then: I think because I was traumatized from all that had happened to me. Through it all, the drinking took over my life and I wasn't able to cope with it anymore. I was angry at everybody." Tara was also severely depressed. She described herself as "feeling crazy" when she believed that violent intruders were plotting to break into her home. It seems that she experienced a disintegration of the ego (Winnicott, 1971) and a movement to a paranoid-schizoid state (Klein, 1946). She was terrified and boarded her windows locking herself inside. She was ultimately taken out to receive help by one of her sons, who took on the role of the bridge to his mother's life.

Intergenerational trauma exists within this family. There is the trauma of being a stolen child, the guilt of being the child that remained and the burden of living with an emotionally unavailable mother. For Alice, Tara's youngest daughter, the process of transposition (Kaplan, 1995) has occupied her personal space and the need to be her mother's protector has impacted her identity. Alice married her non-Aboriginal childhood sweetheart and they have three children. Tara and Alice were bound by unspeakable terror when the skeleton that was locked tightly in the closet was revealed. Alice left her children with her husband, believing they were better without her. She escaped to drugs and was full of anger, rage, and shame. As she acted out these emotions, she was constantly re-traumatized and this ultimately led her to turn her anger and rage inward and to succumb to self-hatred and severe depression. The outside world became the enemy and she was unable to leave her mother's side. She became the unavailable, dead mother (Green, 1986) for her children. The ancestral ghosts (Fraiberg, Adelson and Shapiro, 1975) are now impacting a third generation.

Tara's son, Ben, who was taken as an infant, is addicted to drugs. He, his wife and children are often homeless and his children are suffering the direct consequences of his traumatized past and their trauma laden present. On occasion, he and his family moved in with Tara. He brought drugs with him and this caused Tara and the other children to become distressed by his behavior, especially her sons who had given up drugs. She feels guilty and questions her competence as a mother, because the last time he asked she would not allow him stay with her. She no longer has contact with him and continues to worry about his well-being, wishing she had not lost him as an infant. He appears to be suffering the consequences of his childhood trauma and is passing this down to his children.

Tara's two sons, who remained with her, live close by and have established their own families. While, they have had problems with alcohol and drug abuse, they are resilient. They became good fathers to their children who are currently very successful. Tara is happy that they are looking after their children.

Tara's other daughter, Leslie, who remained with her, married a non-Aboriginal man and they have two children. They are currently separated. Leslie suffers from intermittent but severe episodes of depression, which impede her ability to be available for her children. Her daughter Jessica has engaged in the process of transposition referred to by Kaplan (1995) and has taken on the role of caretaker for her mother and brother.

Tara's stolen children have experienced the consequences of the trauma of being taken. Those who remained had to cope with the guilt of being survivors, as well as coping with their mother's trauma and inability to be available for them. The ancestral ghosts (Fraiberg, Adelson and Shapiro, 1975) are silently doing damage to three generations of this family.

GENDER DIFFERENCES IN THE RESPONSE TO TRAUMA

The Stolen Children were subjected to physical, sexual and psychological abuse. However, opportunities for peer bonding within the homes differed for males and females. For the Cootamundra girls, even though discouraged, there were opportunities for bonding with each other, which reduced their emotional disengagement. Today these women think of each other as family. They speak of the resilience they found within the boundaries they created and the importance of this to their survival. In telling her story in a book titled *Home Girls* (Kabaila, 2012), Tibby said "we were very lonely and frightened at first. We stuck close together in the playground and at night. We used to hop into bed together, especially when the nights got real cold. There were always groups of us who stayed together" (Kabaila, 2012, p. 56). It seems that the attachment bonds that developed between the girls allowed them to compensate for the loss of their mothers. However, these bonds were often broken because the children, including sisters, were fostered, adopted or sent to serve white families.

Kinchela men committed atrocities against each other and this prevented emotional bonding. Hunter (1994) found that Aboriginal male children were particularly affected by their fathers' traumas. The traumatized fathers were lost both through separations and through the criminal justice system leaving their children without models for male initiation into mature manhood. Drawing on the experience of Holocaust survivors, Danieli (1985) suggests that because the experience of total helplessness was inconsistent with the male self-image, men were more adversely affected by trauma than were women. Many Stolen Generation men relinquished their role within the family and culture and this has impacted their children. Alan, the son of a Stolen Generation parent was distraught when he told me "my generation of males is a lost generation and I am concerned for the next generation."

MOTHERLESS CHILDREN

The loss of parenting skills for the Stolen Generations has had an impact on their children. The traumatic effects of separations and loss as well as the loss of parenting role models has had profound psychological effects, disrupting attachment and creating vulnerabilities to anxiety and depression, among other problems (Swan and Raphael, 1995).

The stolen children's abrupt separation from their mothers left them with the internalization of a dead mother (Green, 1986) and a memory either real or imagined of their mother as an unloving, abandoning mother to be ashamed of. Winnicott (1971) suggested that the prolonged absence of the mother brings a break in life's continuity. He argued that this occurs when the individual's defense system cannot survive intact, and feelings of terror and persecutory anxiety develop. Traumatic experiences break through a defense system established to cope with normal life and to manage more primitive aggressive feelings and early fears. According to Alcock (2003), anxiety reawakens early fears and fantasies previously managed by our defenses. These early feelings of terror and persecutory anxiety add to new experiences of trauma and it builds up to the point of being unbearable. When external events confirm these deep anxieties, meaning collapses and the experiences become too much to cope with. Winnicott (1971) referred to this as a break in the continuity of being. Primitive defenses become organized to defend the baby against a repetition of unthinkable anxiety, and fear of annihilation from being left alone beyond what is bearable, or a return of the acute state of confusion that belongs to the disintegration of ego. Winnicott (1971) stated that the baby experiences a break up in the continuity of existence that he calls the experience of having been mad. For Klein (1946), this leads to paranoid-schizoid defenses, idealization and splitting.

Raphael, Swan and Martinek (1998) suggest that, for the Stolen Generations, the inability of many women to care for their own children has led to these children being passed on to other family members or institutions. They further suggest that this cycle will continue throughout the generations if satisfactory parenting is not achieved. Grandmothers, Aunts, and women in traditional roles of support for childbirth and child rearing are frequently left to provide care. This is common practice in the Dharruk community and there is a need to provide support for young mothers who have been deprived of mothering.

Bertha gave birth to two children from Aboriginal men, but ultimately married a non-Aboriginal man and together they had six children. He abused her, and her children grew up being her protector. They not only felt the responsibility of her unspoken childhood trauma, but they were confronted with the trauma of having to protect their mother from abuse at the hands of their father. She and her husband separated and he later passed away. Bertha said, "I always knew what the kids needed. I made them fend for themselves like I did. I didn't spoil them. I just gave them what they needed and that was it." It seems that Bertha believed she knew what her children needed based on the deprivation of her childhood. While she was physically present, she lacked the ability to be emotionally available. Her children have been the recipients of her unspoken trauma and lack of parenting skills. This has led to problems including the abandonment of their own children, whom Bertha is currently parenting.

RESILIENCE AND THE FUTURE

The question of resilience is important. While some individuals within Aboriginal communities exhibit great resilience, others have little and succumb to alcohol and drug abuse among other disorders. Resilience is also an important determinant of the extent to which trauma is passed down through the generations. Where do we find resilience in the face of severe trauma? It seems that for the Stolen Children this depends on the severity of abuse and the availability of others to provide a feeling of not being alone. The origins of resilience begin in a mother-infant relationship in which the psychological bonds and linkages can be established and strengthened within a containing and secure relationship (Bowlby, 1979; Klein, 1946; Winnicott, 1971). When I last saw Tara I asked her how she saw the future of the Aboriginal people. She spoke about the importance of children having parents at an early age and being able to find their roots. For many among the stolen generations there are no records available for them to trace their families. Tara believes that forgiveness is essential. She expressed her concern that many young people are taking drugs and wandering the streets. She said "They are lost, they are hurting so they can't do it and everything is forgiveness. If they haven't got that in life, how can kids get on with their life?" Tara said that she had to shake herself up because of her children and that she grew up with forgiveness in her home, a lesson she learned from her mother. Her mother told her "that this bloke murdered her sister's daughter." She said that her mother prayed that God would forgive him for what he did:

> I had a wonderful mother, very wise. I didn't understand it at the time but I learned forgiveness from her. My dad was a good dad to. When I was on the grog because of the loss of my children, dad came and said Tara, 'me and mum didn't bring you up to be like this' and it turned things around and made me think differently. I loved my mum and dad. I miss them.

It seems that while Tara experienced unspeakable trauma and has passed this on to her children, she was ultimately able to draw on the resilience she developed during her childhood to turn her life around.

Mary told me that she grew up by the riverbank. She remembers her parents being there for her. Her father worked hard and she often helped him putting up fences. Even though her mother passed away when she was young, she remembers her presence as an infant. She was embarrassed in school because she did not have the materials that the white children in the classroom had, and they made cruel remarks to her. She believes that her father took her and her sister to the bush because he wanted to make sure they would not be taken. She was unaware of that happening until she met her husband, who had been taken as a child. While she was able to minimize the impact of his trauma on the family through her own resilience, her daughters struggle with addiction and Mary now parents their children.

Mary appears to have developed resilience from her childhood with her parents. She is one of a group of women who work tirelessly to provide volunteer services for the Aboriginal people who live within their community. Among other activities, these women have developed a center to provide parenting skills for young, single mothers who were deprived of mothering. The women are the source of resilience within the community where many of the men have been unable to fulfill their traditional roles. They are also the transmitters of Aboriginal cultural heritage, self-worth, purpose and pride.

On my last visit, I participated with the Elder women in an overnight retreat in the Blue Mountains, a location that contains Aboriginal sacred land and is steeped in Aboriginal cultural history. This workshop was skillfully led by a male Aboriginal leader who in two days was able to break the silence of the trauma that some of the women had held within them for decades. With the emotional support of the group, these women were able to grieve their losses and walk away with renewed energy and investment in their lives and community.

I was quickly swept up in the amazing positive energy and support that I felt within the boundaries of this Aboriginal family. For two days, we ate, listened, shared emotions and thoughts, and weathered the bitter cold in quarters that lacked heat. The feelings of belonging and safety I experienced are difficult to put into words but I imagine they may be close to what it might have felt like to be part of the tradition of Kanyini. It is these relationships and my desire to support and facilitate such efforts that brings me back across the world as often as I can.

The resilience of these women is fueled by their close attachments and the boundary they have successfully created around their group. Kwok (2012) points out how this can be a positive aspect of Aboriginal life because it provides feelings of safety and security as well as a protection against shame. However, it can also be an obstacle to confronting their poor treatment by and dependency on the institutions of the dominant society. It could be that shame stands as a barrier to permeating the boundaries that have been established between Aboriginal and non-Aboriginal Australians.

The future of Aboriginal people in Australia lies with Aboriginal led groups and not with the many programs developed by those who hold the postcolonial belief that they know the Aboriginal people's needs and how they should be addressed. As a psychoanalyst, my approach to this work has been influenced by psychoanalytic perspectives. There are many layers that exist at the individual, community and national level that need to be peeled away for the status of the Aboriginal people within Australia to change. In addition, their needs cannot be successfully addressed without consideration of the socio-historic, racial, cultural and political context within which intergenerational trauma exists.

In the Aboriginal culture, *Dadirri* is a deep contemplative process of listening to one another in reciprocal relationships (Ungunmerr, 1993). When an individual is vulnerable, a space is provided within a circle of support where he or she can open up and reveal the depth of pain. This process allowed each of the women I spoke about above to recreate their story. In the analytic relationship, the process of listening and expressing within the analytic space is not unlike the experience of Dadirri. It is through this process that freedom to confront the unspeakable, repressed memories of the past and to recognize the role of trauma in creating problems that lead to new trauma can take place for the Aboriginal people.

Dobson (1994) contends that Aboriginal people have a right to transmit their culture and should be encouraged to do so. He suggests that many underlying processes as well as direct intervention and more indirect effects of the social environment and the dominant non-indigenous culture have severely interfered with the ability of indigenous cultures to transmit their culture. He also suggests that the dismantling of the family has had profound effects for Aboriginal children and that this has contributed to the disproportional levels of problems such as social problems, addictions and extraordinarily disproportionate rates of incarceration. Helping the Aboriginal people became aware of self and other within the social-cultural environment that creates and maintains barriers, especially the role that dependency and shame play in silencing them is essential to their finding their voice. Without a voice, the ghosts of the past will continue to haunt them and facilitate new traumas.

Those who work with the Aboriginal people can play a role in helping them to find the freedom to choose their individual and collective future. To do this, we need to participate with them and utilize resilient Elders to break the cycle of intergenerational trauma through the development and implementation of programs that will reach those in most need. I agree with Atkinson (2002), who states that putting Dadirri into practice involves the process of learning to stay with the flow of the community in which need and sharing is sometimes slow and deep, while at other times it can be fast and turbulent. The role of the participant is to listen and to stay in the place where the Aboriginal people need to go as their experiences are defined and redefined. This will lead to their recreating their own stories and participating in their own healing.

At the national level, there is a need to confront the racial and cultural divisions that exist. Knowledge of the ways in which we internalize what we understand about divisions that began with colonization may liberate the nation from its collective traumatic past and the continued racial and cultural divisions imposed upon its people. Byles (2003) suggests that through the substitution of the libidinal object ties that are involved in projective identification, and the re-introjection of the object into the ego, it is possible to reach a common feeling of sharing, of being part of the other, of empathy. The reciprocity of the container and the contained relationship (Bion, 1986) through both positive projective identification in the form of empathy, and introjection or re-introjection can result in a positive allowance of difference in other worlds, and a healthy acceptance of and adaptation to the other within the self and the self within the other (Byles, 2003).

The challenge for both Aboriginal and non-Aboriginal people, is to question preexisting myths and stereotypes. Further, there is a need to permeate the tightly structured racial and cultural boundaries that exist within Australia and to find ways to share and respect cultural beliefs and traditions across boundaries, while developing mutually reciprocal, empathic relationships that can lead to change.

NOTES

1. *Terra nullius* is a Latin expression deriving from Roman law meaning land belonging to no one, which is used in international law to describe territory which has never been subject to the sovereignty of any state, or over which any prior sovereign has expressly or implicitly relinquished sovereignty. Sovereignty over territory which is terra nullius may be acquired through occupation, though in some cases doing so would violate an international law or treaty.

2. The names of all those who have participated in this project have been changed to protect their identity.

REFERENCES

Alcock, M. (2003). Refugee trauma: The assault on meaning. *Psychodynamic Practice, 9* (3), 290–306.

Alford, F. C. (1989). *Melanie Klein and critical social theory: An account of political, art, and reason based on her psychoanalytic theory.* New Haven, CT: Yale University Press.

Atkinson, J. (2002). *Trauma trails: Recreating song lines: The transgenerational effects of trauma in Indigenous Australia.* North Melbourne, Australia: Spinifex Press.

Australian Bureau of Statistics (2012, October 31). *Dharruk (State Suburb).* 2011 Census Quick Stats. Retrieved May 1, 2013.

Bion, W. (1986). *Second thoughts.* London: Karnac Books.

Bird, C. (Ed.). (1998). *The stolen children their stories*. Sydney: Random House Australia.
Bowlby, J. (1979). *The making and breaking of affectional bonds*. London: Tavistock.
Byles, J.M. (2003). Psychoanalysis and war: The superego and projective identification. *Journal for the Psychoanalyses of Culture and Society*, 8, 208-13.
Cowlishaw, G. (2009). *The city's outback*. Sydney: UNSW Press.
Cowlishaw, G. (2010). Mythologising culture part 1: Desiring Aboriginality in the suburbs. *The International Journal of Anthropology* , *21* (2), 208–227.
Cowlishaw, G. (Ed.). (2012). *Mt. Druitt life story series. Women and men tell stories of how I got here.* Fremantle, WA: Vivid Publishing.
Danieli, Y. (1985). The treatment and prevention of long-term effects and intergenerational transmission of victimization: A lesson from Holocaust survivors and their children. In C. R. Figley (Ed.), *Trauma and its wake.* (pp. 295–313). New York: Brunner/Mazel.
Dalziell, R. (1998). *Shameful Autobiographies: Shame in contemporary Australian autobiographies and culture.* Melbourne: University Press.
Darwin, C. (1984). *The descent of man* (2nd ed,). New York: A.L. Burt Co.
Davoine, F. and Gaudillière, J. M. (2004). *History beyond trauma*. NY: Other Press.
Dobson, M. (1994). The rights of indigenous people in the international year of the family. *Family Matter, 37*, 34–41.
Foronari, F. (1975). *The psychoanalysis of war*. Indiana: Indiana UP.
Fraiberg, E., Adelson and Shapiro, V. (1975). *Journal of the American Academy of Child Psychiatry*, *14*, 387–421.
Freud, S. (1917). Mourning and melancholia. *The Complete Works of Sigmund Freud, 14*, 237-258. London: Hogarth Press.
Freud, S. (1918). *Reflections on war and death* (A. A. Brill and A. B. Kutiner, Trans.). New York: Moffat, Yard and Co.
Freud, S. (1930). Civilisation and its discontents. *The Complete Works of Sigmund Freud, 21*, 64–145. London: Hogarth Press.
Gagné, M. A. (1994). *A nation within a nation: Dependency and the Cree*. Montreal: Black Rose Books.
Garon, J. (2004). Skeletons in the closet. *International Forum of Psychoanalysis, 13*, 84–92.
Green, A. (1986). *The dead mother. On private madness*. London: Hogarth Press.
Herman, J. L. (1992). Complex PTSD: A syndrome in survivors of prolonged and repeated trauma. *Journal of Traumatic Stress, 5*, 377-393.
Hunter, E. (1994, April 12). *Freedom's just another word: Aboriginal youth and mental health*. The Bill Robinson Memorial Lecture, Perth, Australia.
Kabaila, P. (2012). *Home girls*. Canberra: Canprint Publishing.
Kaplan, L. J. (1995). *No voice is ever wholly lost* . New York: Touchstone.
Kendall, C. (1994). The history: Present and future issues affecting Aboriginal adults who were removed as children. *Aboriginal and Islander Health Worker Journal, 18*, 18–19.
Klein, M. (1946). Notes on some schizoid mechanisms. *International Journal of Psychoanalysis*, 99–110.
Kwok, N. (2012). Shame and the embodiment of boundaries. *Oceana*, *82* (1), 28–44.
Manson, S. M., Beals, J., O'Nell, T., Piaseki, J., Bechtold, D., Keane, E. and Jones, M. (1996). Wounded spirits, ailing hearts: PTSD and related disorders among American Indians. In A. J. Marsella, M. J. Friedman, E.T. Gerrity and R. M. Scurfield (Eds.), *Ethnocultural aspects of posttraumatic stress disorder: Issues, research and clinical applications*. (pp. 225-284). Washington, DC: American Psychological Association.
Raphael, B., Swan, P., and Martinek, N. (1998). Intergenerational aspects of trauma for Australian Aboriginal people. In Y. Danieli (Ed.), *The international handbook of multigenerational legacies of trauma* (pp. 327–339). NY: Plenum Press.
Roberts, J. (1978). *From massacres to mining: The colonization of Aboriginal Australia.* Great Britain: Camra.

Swan, P. (1998). *200 years of unfinished business.* Paper presented at the Australian National Association for Mental Health Conference. Aboriginal Medical Service Newsletter, 12–17.

Swan, P. and Raphael, B. (1995). *Ways forward: National and Torres Strait Islander mental health policy.* Report prepared for Office of Aboriginal and Torres Strait Islander Health Services, Commonwealth Department of Human Services and Health. Canberra: Australian Government Printing Office.

Ungunmerr. (1993). Dadirri: Listening to one another. In J. Hendricks and G. Hefferan (Eds.), *A spirituality of Catholic Aborigines and the struggle for justice* (pp. 34–37). Brisbane: Aboriginal and Torres Strait Islander Apostolate, Catholic Archdiocese of Brisbane.

Volkan, V. D. (1988). *The need to have enemies and allies.* NY: Jason Aronson.

Walters, J. (2012). The psychological and social consequences of trauma and race relations on the Australian Indigenous people. *The International Journal of the Humanities, 9* (8), 149–164.

Winnicott, D.W. (1971). *Playing and reality.* Great Britain: Tavistock Publications Ltd.

SEVEN

The Subtle Trauma

Premenstrual Syndrome, Language, and Subjectivity

Marie C. Hansen

In this chapter I investigate the relationship between trauma, subjectivity, and premenstrual syndrome. In keeping with the theme of "Fragments of Trauma and the Social Production of Suffering," PMS is contextualized as existing within a phallogocentric[1] culture that associates the female reproductive body with original primary trauma. I begin by problematizing premenstrual syndrome as an exclusively biomedical event, thus allowing for a more nuanced psycho-social approach to the phenomenon. The experience of menstruation and menarche is then located within contemporary North American menstrual discourses, particularly through acknowledging the social absence thereof. This absence is then tied to a particular form of shame, the complicated nature of which is posited to include elements that are both socially produced, that is, in terms of inadequate menarche "rites," and intrapsychically rooted. The social existence of menstrual shame is considered as a fragment of the original trauma of separation-individuation that is, leaving behind a corporeal language for a verbal one.

I draw from Kristeva (1986a) to illuminate the movement from a body-ego to emergence within language as it relates to the maternal (feminine) body. I also reference Irigaray's (1980) concept of *corps-á-corps* to further explore the possibility of a "language before language" that exists by way of the mother/infant union. The concept of "original trauma" is explored through the inevitable rejection of this primary corporeal language in the movement toward becoming a singular, speaking subject.

This rejection, in turn, can be seen as a rejection of an aspect of the feminine. Here, menstruation is posited to relate to the original preverbal language of the mother/infant union, particularly in terms of premenstrual symptoms, which occur at the boundary of the semiotic and the symbolic, or what Kristeva (1986a) calls the *thetic*. The "subtle trauma" of rejecting *corps-á-corps* during separation-individuation is considered to be played out intrapsychically by way of the tension existing between the masculine and feminine aspects of the psyche, and is expressed in the social realm through Western culture's attempts to understand women's experiences via phallogocentric means. I examine the intrapsychic tension between the masculine and feminine functions through Irigaray's (1985) discussion of the structure of female sex organs, before bringing together the intrapsychic and the social realms by way of Charles (2000, 2002) to situate women's bodies and the feminine within a Western culture that unavoidably fails us. The Lacanian concept of sexuation will be adopted in order to distance masculinity and femininity from typical notions of gender and sex, allowing this discussion to be inclusive of the fragments of trauma located in all forms of sex and gender classification. That is, my concern is not with the overt and systematic oppression of women by men, but with the inherent conflicts of masculinity and femininity as defined by Lacan (Fink, 2002), and with the ways in which this conflict is related to our original separation from the mother/infant union.

PMS: LIVED EXPERIENCE

There is an image I once saw on the Internet of a woman, drawn in the style of a Sunday paper comic. Her eyes are wide and stricken with terror. Beads of sweat drip from her forehead as she anxiously brings her hand toward her temple. A thought-bubble near her states, *"I'm fine. I hate you. I love you. Come here. Get away. Oranges?"* Above her head are three bold all-capital red letters: PMS. Premenstrual syndrome, broadly described, is a heterogeneous group of symptoms, consisting of affective, behavioral, and physical changes that occur in women before the onset of menses. It is a phenomenon that has remained ill defined, with confusion in respect to everything from causality and duration, to the specifics of symptomatology. To date, approximately 200 different symptoms have been linked to the disorder with the predominant symptoms in the West being depressed mood, anxiety, irritability, feelings of "loss of control," erratic mood changes, bloating, breast tenderness, abdominal discomfort, headaches, and fatigue (Gise, Kase, and Berkowitz, 1988). While estimates vary widely, it is commonly stated that as many as 85% of menstruating women experience at least one symptom of PMS (Dickerson, Mazyck, and Hunter, 2003). If we are to assume this is a relatively accurate figure, this is a very high number of women who feel they experience an emotional and physical shift that corresponds to their reproductive cycle. Furthermore, in one woman's lifetime, she will experience this shifting state of emotions over 400 times (Walker, 1997).

Despite decades of scientific research, no conclusive evidence has ever been found regarding the precise biological etiology for the symptoms of PMS. In fact, scientific discourse has investigated such diverse biological factors as sleep-cycles, progesterone, estrogen, serotonin, vitamin deficiencies, thyroid hormones, and melatonin as contributing factors (Gise, Kase, Berkowitz, 1988; Ussher, 2006). There are no known laboratory tests or specific biological markers to date that can absolutely confirm a diagnosis of PMS (Matsumoto, Asakura, and Hayashi, 2013). In addition, controlled trials have shown no consistent or identifiable pattern that can physiologically differentiate women with PMS from control subjects (Richardson, 1995). Adding to this confusion is the time frame for defining the "premenstrual period." Women report the emergence of symptoms anywhere from 3 to 10 days before the onset of menstruation (Nelson, 2011). Subjective reports of the experience of PMS are striking for the way in which women often seem unable to put into words the exact feelings they experience. Many women report feeling a generalized sense of upset and anger, but are unable to locate or determine a root-cause of this upset. Many Western women, when discussing the subjective experience of PMS, describe a "nameless discontent" seemingly connected to their immediate personal lives or relationships and yet also to the wider world. For example, de Beauvoir writes:

> . . .nervous and irritable, the woman frequently undergoes a state of semi-alienation each month; central control over the nervous and sympathetic systems is no longer assured; circulation problems and some autointoxications turn the body into a screen between the woman and the world, a burning fog that weights on her, stifling her and separating her: experienced through this suffering and passive flesh, the entire universe is a burden too heavy to bear. Oppressed and submerged, she becomes a stranger to herself because she is a stranger to the rest of the world. (2011, p. 342)

Western women often describe the experience of themselves during PMS as greatly contrasted to the way they experience themselves post-menstruation. Ussher (2006) interviewed 36 British women about their subjective experience of premenstrual syndrome. An analysis of these narratives found several descriptions of contrasted identities. Women described the following juxtapositions:

> Bad versus good; introversion versus extroversion; out of control versus in control; irresponsible versus responsible; failing versus coping; angry versus calm; anxious versus relaxed; depressed versus happy;

> irrational versus rational; intolerant versus tolerant; vulnerable versus strong; irritable versus placid; [and] frustrated versus accepting. (p. 48)

Similarly, Kolod (2010) describes PMS through the psychoanalytic concept of "self-states." She sees cyclical hormonal experiences as allowing for the manifestation of multiple states each with "its own narrative, memory configuration, and perceptual reality" (p. 79). Each of these symptoms speaks to a break or rupture in women's subjectivity, and to a confusion regarding which moods, emotions, affective and intersubjective states compose her being. That is, she at once opens herself to all modes of being and simultaneously rejects them as "other."

Although not widely acknowledged by scientific discourse, cross-cultural comparisons of PMS symptomology have found large variation between cultures. Adewuya, Loto, and Adewumi (2009) studied the self-reports of PMS symptomology in 409 Nigerian university students. Given a checklist of premenstrual symptoms, Nigerian women rated breast tenderness, sleeplessness, decreased interest in usual activities, lethargy/easy fatigability, and changes in appetite as the most prevalent symptoms experienced during PMS. Western women were more likely to report affective symptoms including irritability, anxiety, depression, and mood liability, while placing somatic complaints such as fatigue and headaches low on the list of commonly experienced symptoms. Johnson (1987) argues that PMS should be considered a *culture-bound syndrome*. In the *Diagnostic and Statistical Manual of Mental Disorders* (DSM-IV-TR), culture-bound syndromes are those disorders defined as "recurrent, locality-specific patterns of aberrant behavior and troubling experience" (American Psychiatric Association, 2000, p. 898). Culture-bound syndromes involve constellations of symptoms that a given culture categorizes as indicative of disease. The etiology of these diseases can be understood to symbolize core meanings and reflect the preoccupations of a given culture. In addition, the diagnosis and treatment are dependent upon culture-specific technology and ideology (Johnson, 1987). The symptom clusters of culture-bound syndromes may exist across cultures, but the ways in which they are associated with notions of disease vary. These factors are important in problematizing theories of PMS as a purely biological phenomenon and allow us to locate this type of suffering within a historical, cultural, and psychological framework.

LEARNING MENSTRUATION, TEACHING SHAME: FAMILIAL AND CULTURAL TRANSMISSIONS

Growing up, I was given the message that menstruation is an unspoken secret, a bodily function that must remain profoundly concealed. Great lengths were taken to insure it remained hidden from view—from learning how to secretly carry menstrual products to school, to attempts to silently rip open tampons while in a public restroom. Not even other girls could be alerted to its presence. Used menstrual products were not casually disposed of like other garbage, but wrapped tightly in wads of toilet paper before being tossed into the can. No sign of blood was allowed to show, even in the trash. Although my mother never explicitly taught me this, it was a message that I received nonetheless. *We do not speak of menstruation; we do whatever we can to keep it hidden.* This is the same message that millions of Western girls receive each year, making this rite of passage a silent one. This silence is perpetuated not only by the wider culture, but also within the home, in the strange silences of our mothers as they usher us quickly from the bathroom cupboard into a lineage of female shame.

Costos, Ackerman, and Paradis (2002) studied the menarche narratives of 138 women and found that 58% of their mothers had not openly discussed menstruation with them. A common theme of these narratives was the nonverbal messages of secrecy and concealment communicated to them. McKeever (1984) claims this secrecy and lack of communication stems from the extreme discomfort mothers feel when teaching their daughters about menstruation. In *My Little Red Book*, a collection of women's menarche narratives, Maynard (2009) talks of hiding evidence of her first menstrual periods by storing used pads in her bedroom closet. She describes feeling an unbearable sense of shame about her menstruating body and a sense that if her mother found out, she would not approve. This shame was so extreme that Maynard felt compelled to store six months, worth of used pads in her closet, fearful of throwing them into the trash and exposing her secret. She states:

> The bag had been large enough, and my periods were short enough in duration, that the same one bag continued to hold sanitary napkins from as much as a half-year's worth of periods. I still hadn't told my mother I menstruated. She didn't ask. The fact that she did not confirmed for me the belief that what went on in my body now was truly, deeply, horribly shameful. (p. 122)

When mothers do have "the talk" with their daughters, they often find support in materials such as pamphlets, created by the femcare industry in order to facilitate the conversation. Costos, Ackerman, and Paradis (2002) note that these pamphlets completely omit any psychosocial information about menstruation and do not make room for young girls and their mothers to discuss the large array of feelings and emotions that occur with menarche. Similarly, these pamphlets often contribute to the shame and secrecy of menstruation by presenting menstruation as a 'hygiene crisis' rather than a sign of healthy female development (cf., *sanitary* napkin). Garmisa (2009) illustrates this point through a story about receiving a box from Kotex in the mail: "The day I got my period, my mom was away. I called her to ask what I should do, and she said, 'Well, there is this box. . .' Periods were never discussed before and have never been discussed since. My entire support system was a box" (p. 101).

In writing about intergenerational trauma, O'Loughlin (2010) states, "What appears to be universal in all theories of phantomic experience is silence, secretiveness, or some form of unspeakability as precipitant for transgenerational effects" (p. 60). In this light, it is possible for us to consider contemporary menstrual practices as containing an element of "phantomic experience," of ghostly reenactments passed down through the generations from mother to daughter. Fraiberg, Adelson, and Shapiro (1975) explain how unresolved childhood feelings within parents are condemned to be repeated as they interact with and relate to their children. In thinking of menstrual practices, we can see how generations of mothers have suffered the unresolved wound of menstrual shame. A "silent lesson" given by one's mother is in this way passed down to her daughter. O'Loughlin (2009) writes, "A child does not necessarily need to be exposed to a concrete traumatic event in order to be left with the silent burden of unsymbolized experience. All it takes is for the parents to pass on their own unconscious, unmetabolized psychic pain to the child" (p. 87).

These phantomic experiences are seen in the larger culture as well. Historically, a shift occurred from mothers teaching menstrual practices at home to classroom education. By the 1940s, most menstrual education was taught in the classroom, often with educational materials produced by the femcare industry (Houppert, 2000). The shift may be explained in part by women's own reluctance to teach their daughters about menstruation. Allowing "the talk" to happen in a school environment saves the mothers from embarrassment, and perhaps from reopening the wound of their own menstrual shame. That the femcare industry has succeeded in breaking a fundamental aspect of the social link between mothers and daughters is disturbing. Solely concerned with selling menstrual products, the lessons provided by the femcare industry teach girls early on that menstruation is an inconvenient, unsanitary, and disgusting bodily act that needs to be concealed, hidden, and regulated through the use of their products. Vostral (2008) applies the concept of "passing" to menstruating women. *Passing* is a term often used when discussing identity shifts, particularly in regard to race, gender, and sexuality, for example, a light-skinned black "passing" as white, or a person "passing" as a certain sex within drag or transgender communities. Vostral (2008) sees menstrual technology as focused on allowing women to "pass" as non-bleeders, speaking to the sense of the female body as dysfunctional, problematic, and "out of control."

Contemporary classroom practices reinforce a sense of shame about menstruation not only in their reliance on femcare materials, but also in the fashion that this information is distributed. I can remember fragments of my own experience learning about menstruation in school. At the end of class one day, we were given permission slips that we needed our parents to sign allowing us to attend a special health class only for girls. I remember the embarrassment I felt asking my mother to sign the permission slip, which she did without saying a word. However, I do not recall much about the actual lesson. I do remember that it consisted of watching a VHS tape but I do not remember what exactly the film told us about menstruation, including what causes it, what to expect, or what is "normal." The only thing I definitely remember is the feeling of being horribly ashamed and embarrassed, first, when I had to ask my mother to sign the permission slip and later, when the teacher asked only the girls to get up and leave the room. I can remember the giggles and stares of the boys in their seats as we filed past them into the hallway. The practice of separating girls and boys for the lesson on menstruation is very common in schools in the United States, and further contributes to the feelings of shame and "otherness" of the menstruating body. It removes the opposite sex from the conversation, further polarizing girls from boys. Girls are seen as having "unruly, leaking bodies, whereas boys" (Ussher, 2006) bodies are healthy and "controlled." In addition, the practice of allocating one isolated lesson to menstruation distinguishes it from other bodily systems. In health education, many weeks are devoted to the study of, for example, digestion. Yet, the female reproductive cycle is a mere footnote in the education of the body.

The strange silences regarding menstruation continue into adulthood. Within everyday discourse, menstruation is rarely spoken of directly, but rather hinted at through metaphor. Ernster (1975) found over 128 American expressions used to refer to menstruation. Often these expressions are negative, for example "The Curse," "under the weather," and "on the rag." In addition, however, there are also many terms used that are not necessarily pejorative, but are curiously vague. For example, perhaps the most commonly used term for menstruation is "period." The adoption of this word is particularly striking, since it implies both an indeterminate passage of time, and the finality of the punctuation mark with which it shares its name—the silence that follows the end of speech. This use of metaphor is indicative of the *unspeakability* of menstruation. This same type of redacting can be seen in femcare commercials where blue liquid is used to depict menstrual blood. A signifier is used as a holding place for the unspeakable. These social and cultural practices give the message that there is something so horrific and terrifying about menstruation that it can only be spoken about indirectly, through metaphor and symbol.

In the English-speaking world, a strange relationship exists between language and the menstrual cycle. The signifier *girl* is used until menarche, at which time she is said to have *become a woman*. De Beauvoir infamously stated, "One is not born, but rather becomes, a woman" (2011, p. 301). In Western culture, we are said to *become a woman* through a corporeal act that is seen as disgusting, shameful, and problematic. This shift in social identity allows us to reflect on the cultural meanings of womanhood, femininity, and the reproductive body. In cases of trauma, memories are often held by the body. O'Loughlin (2013) writes, "We either speak of our symptoms or we are spoken by them in the elegant but disguised communication of the messages from our body; in the eccentricities of our ways of being; and in the preoccupations that constitute our neuroses, compulsions, obsessions, even psychosis" (p. 29). These "unspeakable traumas" travel down through the generations, producing what Atkinson (2002) refers to as "trauma trails." Considered as a strange set of emotional and physical symptoms that appear to travel from mother to daughter, what could PMS be signifying? In discourses surrounding the intergenerational transmission of trauma, there is always the underlying question of memory. The following section examines the intrapsychic roots of menstrual shame and the relationship between premenstrual syndrome, femininity, and the developmental process of separation-individuation.

FEMININITY AND THE DEVELOPMENT OF A PERSON

In psychoanalytic theory, the experience of the body is important in the development of subjectivity. Freud (1923/1961a) stated, "The ego is first and foremost a bodily ego; it is not merely a surface entity, but is itself the projection of the surface" (p. 26). Bodily sensations gradually come to form a cohesive whole through the recognition of patterns. It is through smell, movement, and touch, that we leave the stage of primary narcissism and can begin to experience ourselves as individuals. Winnicott (1960) uses the expression, "the psyche indwelling in the soma" (p. 590) to describe how sensory and motor sensations become patterns from which the infant's state of personhood arises. For Lacan, this is taken further with the development of language. For him, language is the means by which we separate from the maternal realm and emerge into the world as a subject. This coming into language is associated with entry into the symbolic order. Becoming a subject inevitably entails alienation as the body comes to be overwritten by language, thus taking on socially determined meanings (Fink, 1997). Additionally, the body is regulated, primarily by the mother, through practices such as toilet training and instruction about social and behavioral norms (Fink, 1997). This same regulation is seen in the Freudian stages of psychosexual development. In looking at both Winnicott and Freud/Lacan, we can see how the body is implicated in both *forming* the subject, and *providing form* for the subject.

Lacan's theory of sexual difference, *sexuation,* bases distinctions between masculine structure and feminine structure on *jouissance* (Fink, 2002). Jouissance is the pain that results from transgressing the pleasure principle (Evans, 1996). It is, paradoxically, the suffering inherent in satisfaction and the satisfaction inherent in suffering. For Lacan, there are two forms of jouissance that correspond to sexual difference: *phallic jouissance* and *Other jouissance*. These two forms of jouissance relate to modes of being within the world, as well as to modes of relationship with the other. Phallic jouissance is what Fink (2002) describes as "the jouissance that fails us, that disappoints us" (p. 37). This type of jouissance leads to disappointment because it sees the other as incomplete and a partial object. Phallic jouissance is closely connected to the symbolic order and the limitations of language. Phallic jouissance is part of both masculine and feminine structure, whereas feminine structure has an added form of jouissance that masculine structure lacks: "Other jouissance." The reason that women have this second form of jouissance, according to Lacan, is that they are not completely subject to the symbolic order—part of them remains outside of the signifying chain. This "Other jouissance" of women cannot be articulated, precisely because it is not part of the symbolic order, and therefore must by definition remain ineffable (Fink, 2002, p. 40). The question of inexpressibility is perhaps suggestive of the allusion that Freud (1926) makes to the "dark continent" of feminine sexuality (p. 212). It is important to note that although Lacan talks about women, his conceptualization of feminine and masculine structures does not correspond to typical gender and sex discourse, but rather are explained as "a function of one's position with respect to the Other" (Barnard, 2002, p. 9).

Kristeva (1986a) adds nuance to Lacanian theories of the development of subjectivity and the relationship of that subjectivity to the maternal. She uses the word *chora* to describe the state of the infant prior to differentiation, even prior to what Winnicott (1960) describes as "the psyche indwelling in the soma" (p. 590). She states, "The *chora* is not yet a position that is representing something for someone (i.e., it is not a sign); nor is it a *position* that represents someone for another position (i.e., it is not yet a signifier either); it is however, generated in order to attain to this signifying position" (p. 94). *Chora* is seen as a process that is connected to pre-verbal experiences of the body as it learns to recognize the physical and affective patterns that will eventually come to construct the body proper. Kristeva (1986a) uses the term *semiotic* to describe that which "precedes the establishment of the sign" (p. 95).

The semiotic is the organizing function of the infant prior to language. Kristeva describes this as a "psychosomatic modality of the signifying process" (1986a, p. 96). Therefore, the *semiotic chora* is a place of tension. We are both *generated* by these organizing forms and *negated,* as our original state of primary narcissism is reworked, shifted, and evolved. This concept is very similar to the neuroscientific idea of *synaptic pruning,* whereby patterns of experience cause both the strengthening and severing of neuronal and synaptic connections. The development of a subject requires the loss of what came before. Kristeva describes the rupture and/

or boundary between the semiotic and the symbolic as the *thetic*, the threshold of language. Because of this rupture, Kristeva sees the semiotic as a threat to the symbolic order of things. The existence of the semiotic exposes the instability of the symbolic order.

Part of what is given up in the process of becoming a subject can be explored through Irigaray's (1980) concept of *corps-á-corps,* the original non-verbal, corporeal language of the mother-child bond. For Irigaray, *corps-á-corps* is particularly important in the mother-daughter relationship because they share similar bodies. Boys differentiate from the maternal bond through verbal (phallic) language, a function in keeping with their bodies and mode of *jouissance*. Girls, however, are never completely differentiated from the maternal bond because the female reproductive body is incompatible with the symbolic order. Therefore, mothers and daughters ultimately share bodies that are, at least in part, removed from language.

Irigaray (1985) uses the physical structure of women's reproductive organs to illustrate how the two modes of jouissance exist within women. Generally speaking, she equates clitoral pleasure with phallic jouissance, and vaginal pleasure with "Other jouissance." Irigaray (1985) is interested in how women's genitals are in constant contact with themselves, making distinction ambiguous. She states, "Thus, within herself, she is already two—but not divisible into one(s)—that caress each other" (Irigaray, 1985, p. 24). She views the autoerotic touching of the vaginal lips as being disrupted by the phallus' entry into the vagina. Her use of sexual imagery is interesting in that it seems to speak to an aspect of feminine subjectivity that is about connection, blending, and blurred boundaries. Whereas the phallus is about singularity, femininity is about multiplicity. Irigaray's contributions to the question of feminine subjectivity are important in that they reconstitute feminine desire back to women themselves, and achieve this without need of "othering" the feminine by defining it in contrast to the masculine. Whereas prior psychoanalytic theories have revolved around the phallus, Irigaray sees the vagina/vulva as important in its own right. The vagina is no longer seen as an empty space to be used and shaped by the phallic order, but contains its own distinguished subjectivity. However, due to the ineffability of the feminine, the vaginal function is seen only in opposition or contrast to the phallus. Irigaray describes this lost subjectivity of women in the following way:

> As Freud admits, the beginnings of the sexual life of a girl child are so "obscure" so "faded with time," that one would have to dig down very deep indeed to discover beneath the traces of this civilization, this history, the vestiges of a more archaic civilization that might give some clue to woman's sexuality. That extremely ancient civilization would undoubtedly have a different alphabet, a different language. . . Woman's desire would not be expected to speak the same language as

> man's; woman's desire has doubtless been submerged by the logic that has dominated the West since the time of the Greeks. (1985, p. 25)

With emergence into the symbolic order, the feminine (fragments of which I have explored here through the concepts of *Other jouissance*, *corps-á-corps*, and the *chora*) by default needs to be disavowed. Within Western culture, this disavowal is often experienced as sexism. However, if sexism is seen as a symptom, then perhaps it can be understood as a cultural attempt to 'speak' this original trauma. Much like in psychoanalytic practice, this symptom then can be viewed as an opening to the possibility of working through our relationship to the feminine.

MENSTRUATION AND CULTURAL EXPERIENCES OF THE FEMININE

Charles (2002) describes the tendency in Western culture to obfuscate women's corporeality, pushing women to live outside of their bodily-felt awareness by holding the immature child/woman's body as the ideal. Recall that it is at menarche that we "become a woman." What is it that is feared about women's bodies? And what is the relationship between that fear and menstruation? Perhaps this cultural phenomenon can be related back to the original trauma of becoming a subject: women's bodies represent melding, blending, and union. The mother's pregnant body might be seen as representing symbiosis, provoking questions about where her body ends and her child's body begins. In non-collectivist cultures such as in the west, these aspects of the body are terrifying, representing enmeshment, engulfment, and annihilation. In speaking from the perspective of a Western culture that is unable to conceive of a self so completely entwined with an Other, perhaps women's bodies cause us to fear for our egos and individuality. The preverbal union with the mother may not be an idealized place, but a place of terror we are desperately seeking to avoid. Therefore, perhaps menstruation is a reminder of the connection to the semiotic and capacity for fusion. It is at menarche that females gain the ability to become mothers and to perform the act of ultimate union. Possibly here lies the root of the menstrual taboo. It reminds us of the tenuous nature of our own identity. Kristeva (1982) in her theory of *abjection* states: "It is thus not lack of cleanliness or health that causes abjection but what disturbs identity, system, order. What does not respect borders, positions, rules. The in-between, the ambiguous, the composite" (p. 4).

Returning to Irigaray (1985), it is within the phallic/symbolic order that we exist as one, while within the vaginal/semiotic we are at least two. The masculine function does not allow for a more nuanced understanding of feminine sexuality. Terrified by multiplicity, the feminine is therefore only understood in relationship to the phallus. Charles (2000) describes women's psychosomatic experience as revolving around metaphors of emptiness and voids, potential and meaningfulness. These metaphors are representative of the greater tension between the masculine and feminine function. Women could be seen as vapid and empty space that needs to be filled, or as embodying a place of possibility and integration. Because our cultural values are dominated by the phallic function, the *possibility* of the feminine becomes obscured. This same tension appears in the English language. Lacan and Freud were very much concerned with the particularities of speech. For them, words and phrases point to unconscious conflicts. Rogers (2007) states, "Ironically, you can only hear the unsayable through what is said" (p. 61). Linguistically, women are entwined with men (e.g., wo/man, s/he, fe/male). This entanglement is an interesting one. At once, it speaks to our unconscious knowledge that s/he is *at least two*, yet at the same time, it essentially negates woman's subjectivity by causing her to exist only in relationship to the masculine. The feminine becomes "that which lacks the not-male." Perhaps this element of "not-male" is what causes women to feel the emptiness described by Charles who writes: "Days are spent filling in spaces in between, in fear that one might not be filled. Or, conversely, that one might be filled with something alien, leaving no room for oneself any longer" (Charles, 2000, p. 10).

In many ways, Western culture appears to be obsessed with women's bodies. Could it be an attempt to unconsciously rediscover the lost feminine within? If so, an embeddedness within the symbolic order may preclude this. Women's bodies are prominent on the covers of Western magazines, subway advertisements, television screens, and Facebook pages. These idealized forms do seem to approach the semiotic, touching on the non-verbal experiences of the feminine, but are not the *corps-á-corps* that speaks directly to feminine experience. There is something here of the quality of "safe sex," in that it approaches the mystery of the feminine without the threat of becoming pregnant. We search these images for meaning, but come up empty handed or worse—filled with "something alien" (Charles, 2000). This is what Kristeva (1998) means when she talks of the "maladies of the soul," so elegantly described by Anne-Marie Smith (1998) in the following passage:

> We are all submitted to the facile absorption of images and information but those images bear no relation to the subjective work of the imagination, and that information does not bear the mark of experience. In the virtual time and space of global networks and information systems there are few limits, there is no time and space for subjectivity to define itself, that is, to seek expression, encounter obstacles, imagine ways round them, to resign itself to the inevitable and revolt against the impossible. (p. 56)

So where does this leave the question of PMS? This eclectic group of symptoms might be considered as an expression of *corps-á-corps* and a remnant of women's lost corporeal language. Through pre-menstruation, our bodies speak to us, and communicate via non-verbal means, information about our health and well-being. In *Women's Time*, Kristeva (1986b) links female subjectivity to two forms of time derived from Nietzsche, *cyclical time* and *monumental time*. Kristeva sees these forms of time as linked to women through motherhood and reproduction. In addition to cyclical and monumental time, she also identifies *linear time*, characterized as sequential, historical, teleological, and masculine. It is within this form of time that language resides. Menstruation, like cyclical time, is about repetition and return, a departure from linearity. Similar to the analyst's office, premenstruation provides a recursive place of reflection, allowing us to reconnect with our bodies and unrecognized emotional experiences. When this somatic dwelling place is cast as shameful and its meaning obscured by phallogocentric culture, a rupture is caused. It is at this rupture that the affective states of premenstrual syndrome exist, located at the edge of language, an experience of the *thetic*. We can never fully grasp the lost language of the maternal bond through the symbolic order. It will always fall short. Kristeva (1998) says that all psychosomatic conditions share a common denominator—*the inability to represent* (p. 9). How then, do we reconnect with a time before the beginning, before the Biblical word with which creation began? Perhaps we ought to listen to what we refuse to hear.

SILENCING SYMPTOMS

The latest edition of the *Diagnostic and Statistical Manual of Mental Disorders* (DSM-V) (American Psychiatric Association, 2013) released on May 27, 2013 included a new diagnosis: Premenstrual Dysphoric Disorder (PMDD). Prior to this edition, premenstrual disorders were only included under various appendices, and were not given full diagnostic criteria. The movement of PMDD into a full-fledged diagnosis marks the first time in recent history that women's reproductive cycles have officially been noted as leading to mental illness.

PMDD is described as an extreme version of PMS. For a diagnosis of PMDD to be made, symptoms typical of PMS must be 'clinically significant' or cause interferences with work, school, or relationships. The inclusion of PMDD in the DSM-V reifies PMS as a biological disorder with current research seeking to prove PMDD is a brain disease (e.g., Epperson, 2013). The establishment of PMDD as a diagnosis, by definition, situates PMS within the same biomedical framework. The inclusion of PMDD in the DSM-V brings what is a normal, common, and healthy experience of women's psychology into the realm of psychiatric illness and registers it as a condition to be eradicated.

Ussher (2006) states, "If women see themselves as being at the mercy of their raging hormones, they position themselves as being attacked from within. The body thus becomes objectified, alien to the woman, something that is acting against her in an out of control manner" (p. 54). This recapitulates the original trauma of corporeal alienation and further obstructs women from finding meaning and purpose in their symptoms. Women will be encouraged to "treat" (i.e., eradicate) premenstrual symptoms by biomedical means, rather than embrace their experience through supportive therapy, psychoanalysis, and other exploratory practices. Already, the suggested first line of treatment for PMDD is psychotropic medication, with companies such as Eli Lilly "feminizing" the packaging of their medications to meet this new market (Ussher, 2011). Hormone treatment is another mode of therapy suggested by the mainstream psychiatric community as worthy of consideration. Women now have the option to completely eliminate menstruation through cycle-stopping contraception, a practice with potential health risks (Society for Menstrual Cycle Research, 2007). Even more disturbing, is the suggested use of procedures such as hysterectomy and bilateral salpingo-oophorectromy to surgically remove the interior sex organs altogether (e.g., Mishell, 2007).

CONCLUSION

Jung (1961) describes secrets as having a powerful formative influence (p. 22). In his biography, Jung tells a story from his childhood about a little manikin that he crafted. He carved the manikin into the end of a ruler and then placed it into a yellow pencil case. He provided the little figure with a bed made of a piece of wool and hid the pencil case in the "forbidden" attic of his family's home, tucked away under a roof beam where no one could ever find it. This little man became an important secret for Jung, a secret that he would visit in times of adversity. After a particularly difficult day at school or an argument with his father, he would sneak up to the attic and look at the manikin. Jung saw this secret as being the "essential factor" of his boyhood. The secret gave him a sense of security, something that was purely his own, that no one could ever get at or destroy. In her diary, Anne Frank (2003) describes a similar notion:

> Each time I have a period—and that has only been three times—I have the feeling that in spite of all the pain, unpleasantness and nastiness, I have a sweet secret, that is why, although it is nothing but a nuisance to me in a way, I shall always long for the time that I shall feel that secret within me again. (p. 492)

The idea of a secret might allow menstruation to be moved from a *shameful* experience to a *formative* one. Globally, menarche and menstrual rituals have often included aspects that speak to a "formative secret." For example, in orthodox Jewish communities women have rituals that correspond to *niddah* (menstruation), including ritual bathing (*mikveh*) and checking for blood using a special cloth called an *eid*. Similarly, in Indian traditions there is the celebration of *Ruthu Sadangu* at menarche, which also consists of ritual bathing. In biblical times, menstruating and birthing women would often gather communally in tents. These practices have created communities built around secrets. Here, the act of separation between men and women is founded in a principle of participation in the life of the community, and not in shame. Eliade (1958), in discussing puberty rights states: ". . .the initiation is not the concern only of the young novices. The ceremony involves the tribe as a whole. A new generation is instructed, is made fit to be integrated into the community of adults. And on occasion, through repetition, the *reactualization*, of the traditional rites, the entire community is regenerated" (p. 4). In practices such as these, menstruation is given a proper setting to be acknowledged. Distinguishing menstruation in this way is contrary to the Western notion of "passing," it recognizes menstruation as both a secret *and* an important recursive rite.

While premenstrual syndrome speaks to inherent conflicts within subjectivity that are necessarily painful, the acknowledging of this phenomenon is essential if we are to mend our broken social links. Current educational practices destroy these links by casting shame on the menstruating body, polarizing men and women, and causing women to disavow their own bodies. Much like the systematic erasure of indigenous languages, memories, and communities, reliance on profit-driven corporations to provide us with menarche 'rituals' does a disservice to the mother-daughter bond, not to mention our perceptions of the feminine itself.

NOTES

1. Phallogocentrism is a Derridean concept pertaining to the privileging of the masculine in the Western construction of meaning, language, and logic.

REFERENCES

Adewuya, A.O., Loto, O.M., and Adewumi, T.A. (2009). Pattern and correlates of premenstrual symptomatology amongst Nigerian university students. *Journal of Psychosomatic Obstetrics and Gynecology, 30*(2), 127–132.

American Psychiatric Association. (2000). *Diagnostic and statistical manual of mental disorders* (4th ed.). Washington, DC: Author.

American Psychiatric Association. (2013). *Diagnostic and statistical manual of mental disorders* (5th ed.). Arlington, VA: American Psychiatric Publishing.

Atkinson, J. (2002). *Trauma trails: Recreating song lines: The transgenerational effects of trauma in Indigenous Australia.* North Melbourne, Australia: Spinifex Press.

Barnard, S. (2002). Introduction. In S. Barnard and B. Fink (Eds.), *Reading Seminar XX: Lacan's major work on love, knowledge, and feminine sexuality*. Albany: State University of New York Press.

Charles, M. (2000). Convex and concave, part I: Images of emptiness in women. *The American Journal of Psychoanalysis, 80*(1), 5–27.

Charles, M. (2002). *Patterns: Building blocks of experience*. Hillsdale, NJ: Analytic Press.

Costos, D., Ackerman, R., and Paradis, L. (2002). Recollections of menarche: Communication between mothers and daughters regarding menstruation. *Sex Roles, 42*(1/2), 49–59.

De Beauvoir, S. (2011). *The second sex*. (C. Borde, and S. Malovany-Chevallier, Trans.). New York: Vintage. (Original work published 1953)

Dickerson, L.M., Mazyck, P.J., and Hunter, M.H. (2003). Premenstrual syndrome. *American Family Physician, 67*(8), 1743–1752.

Eliade, M. (1958). *Birth and rebirth: The religious meanings of initiation in human culture*. New York: Harper and Brothers.

Epperson, C.N. (2013). Premenstrual dysphoric disorder and the brain. *American Journal of Psychiatry, 170*, 248–252.

Ernster, V. (1975). American menstrual expressions. *Sex Roles, I*, 3–13.

Evans, D. (1996). *An introductory dictionary of Lacanian psychoanalysis*. London: Routledge.

Fink, B. (1997). *The Lacanian subject: Between language and jouissance*. Princeton, NJ: Princeton University Press.

Fink, B. (2002). Knowledge and jouissance. In S. Barnard and B. Fink (Eds.), *Reading Seminar XX: Lacan's major work on love, knowledge, and feminine sexuality*. Albany, NY: State University of New York Press.

Fraiberg, S., Adelson, E., and Shapiro, V. (1975). Ghosts in the nursery. *Journal of the American Academy of Child Psychiatry, 14*, 387–421.

Frank, A. (1952). *The diary of Anne Frank: The revisited critical edition*. New York: Doubleday.

Freud, S. (1961a). The ego and the id. In J. Strachey (Ed. and Trans.), *The standard edition of the complete psychological works of Sigmund Freud: Vol. 19*. (pp. 3–68). London: Hogarth Press. (Original work published 1923)

Freud, S. (1961b). The question of lay analysis. In J. Strachey (Ed. and Trans.), *The standard edition of the complete psychological works of Sigmund Freud: Vol. 20*. (pp. 183–250). London: Hogarth Press. (Original work published 1926)

Garmisa, B. (2009). My support system was a box. In R. K. Nalebuff (Ed.), *My little red book* (pp. 101–104). New York: Twelve.

Gise, L.H., Kase, N.G., and Berkowitz, R. (1988). *Contemporary issues in obstetrics and gynecology: The premenstrual syndromes*. New York: Churchill Livingstone.

Houppert, K. (2000). *The curse: Confronting the last unmentionable taboo: Menstruation*. New York: Farrar, Straus and Giroux.

Irigaray, L. (1980). Body against body: In relation to the mother. In Irigaray, L., *Sexes and Genealogies* (pp. 9–21). New York: Columbia University Press.

Irigaray, L. (1985). *This sex which is not one*. Ithaca, NY: Cornell University Press.

Johnson, T.M. (1987). Premenstrual syndrome as a western culture-specific disorder. *Culture, Medicine, and Psychiatry, 11*, 337–356.

Jung, C.G. and Jaffé, A. (1961). *Memories, dreams, reflections*. New York: Random House.

Kolod, S. (2010). The menstrual cycle as a subject of psychoanalytic inquiry. *Journal of the American Academy of Psychoanalysis and Dynamic Psychiatry, 38*(1), 77–98.

Kristeva, J. (1982). *Powers of horror: An essay on abjection* (L.S. Roudiez, Trans.). New York: Columbia University Press.

Kristeva, J. (1986a). Revolution in a poetic language. In T. Moi (Ed.), *The Julia Kristeva Reader* (pp. 89–136). Oxford, UK: Blackwell Publishing. (Original work published 1974)

Kristeva, J. (1986b). Women's time. In T. Moi (Ed.), *The Julia Kristeva Reader* (pp. 187–213). Oxford, UK: Blackwell Publishing.
Kristeva, J., (1998). *New maladies of the soul* (L. D. Kritzman, and R. Guberman, Trans.). New York: Columbia University Press.
Matsumoto, T., Asakura, H., and Hayashi, T. (2013). Biopsychosocial aspects of premenstrual syndrome and premenstrual dysphoric disorder. *Gynecological Endocrinology, 29*(1), 67–73.
Maynard, J. (2009). Out of the closet. In R. K. Nalebuff (Ed.), *My little red book* (pp. 119-125). New York, NY: Twelve.
McKeever, P. (1984). The perpetuation of menstrual shame: Implications and directions. *Women and Health, 9*, 33–45.
Mishell, D. (2007). Premenstrual dysphoric disorder: A new treatment paradigm. Retrieved February 11, 2014, from http://www.medscape.org/viewarticle/557445_9
Nelson, R.J. (2011). *An introduction to behavioral endocrinology.* Sunderland, MA: Sinauer.
O'Loughlin, M. (2009). *The subject of childhood.* New York: Peter Lang.
O'Loughlin, M. (2010). Ghostly presences in children's lives. In. M. O'Loughlin, and R.T. Johnson (Eds.), *Imagining children otherwise: Theoretical and critical perspectives on childhood subjectivity* (pp. 49–74). New York: Peter Lang.
O'Loughlin, M. (2013). The uses of psychoanalysis. In O'Loughlin, M. (Ed.), *The uses of psychoanalysis in working with children's emotional lives* (pp. 27–45). Lanham, MD: Jason Aronson.
Richardson, J.T.E. (1995). The premenstrual syndrome: A brief history. *Social Science Medicine, 41* (6), 761–767.
Rogers, A.G. (2007). *The unsayable: The hidden language of trauma.* New York, NY: Ballantine Books.
Smith, A. (1998). *Julia Kristeva: Speaking the unspeakable.* London: Pluto Press.
Society for Menstrual Cycle Research. (2007, June 8). Society for Menstrual Cycle Research calls for more research on long-term effects of cycle-stopping contraception. Retrieved February 11, 2014, from http://menstruationresearch.org/position-statements/position-statement/menstrual-supression-2007/
Ussher, J.M. (2006). *Managing the monstrous feminine: Regulating the reproductive body.* London: Routledge.
Ussher, J.M. (2011). *The madness of women: Myth and experience.* London: Routledge.
Vostral, S.L. (2008). *Under wraps: A history of menstrual hygiene technology.* Lanham, MD: Lexington Books.
Walker, A.E. (1997). *The menstrual cycle.* London: Routledge.
Winnicott, D.W. (1960). The theory of the parent-infant relationship. *International Journal of Psycho-Analysis, 41*, 585–595.

II

Interventions in Social Spaces

EIGHT

Life after "Death"

An Empirical and Clinical Perspective on Trauma

INTRODUCTION

In this chapter we argue and offer empirical support for the belief that trauma is not the proscribed and narrowly defined experience often cited in diagnostic manuals and in the empirical literature, but rather a psychological phenomenon, based more on *how* something is experienced rather than *what* is experienced. Through the exploration of the subjective experience of traumatization, the intention is to come to an understanding of trauma which acknowledges internal psychological phenomena while also avoiding the pitfall of the inclusion of any experience as trauma simply because it is subjectively considered to be so. Trauma is more than a popular term for negative experience; it is also more than the concrete set of behavioral reactions to potential death as described in its most common clinical formulation.

Trauma studies first arose from the work of Janet (1889) in France and Breuer and Freud (1893–1895) in Vienna, each of whom studied hysterical symptoms in Victorian Europe. Janet's work on dissociation as a reaction to trauma remains relevant today. Subsequently, the subject of trauma was largely ignored until the return of shell shocked soldiers from the battlefields of World War I. As an officially classified diagnosis, posttraumatic stress disorder did not appear in the American Psychiatric Association's *Diagnostic and Statistical Manual* until the third edition in 1980.

For assumed etiological reasons, the hysteria of women and the shell shock of soldiers were not initially considered related to one another. The coincidence of the women's liberation movement and the anti-war movement in the 1970s provided the ground of connection, inaugurating contemporary trauma studies. The attempt to provide relief to traumatized soldiers returning from Viet Nam and the feminist focus on the plight of battered and sexually abused women provided a dual focus for a contemporary understanding of trauma. Current trauma studies have become an increasingly interdisciplinary field, ranging from the psychological to the neurobiological to the cultural. Debates about the singularity and personal nature of traumatic experience continue to be central to the discourse on trauma.

TRAUMA: PSYCHOANALYTIC ORIGINS

In a significant humanistic turn, early Freudian theory shifted the theory of the psychoneurosis of hysteria from a biological dysfunction to traumatic personal experience. Hysteria, from the Greek *hysterikos,*—"suffering in the womb"—, was traditionally regarded as a biological disorder. A women's dis-ease, the womb was thought to have become detached from its proper location; hysteria was a disorder of a "wandering womb." In a brilliant reversal, Breuer and Freud's *Studies in Hysteria* (1893-1895) presented five cases of women suffering from hysteria, and, taking into account the women's direct reports, attributed their symptoms to incestuous seduction and/or rape when they were children. The significance of these cases, compelling in their presentation of each woman's subjective experience, are now all but lost, as Freud later reversed his theory in favor of infantile fantasy tied to the Oedipus complex, repudiating actual human experience in light of his discovery of childhood fantasy. Others, most notably Ferenczi, retained the notion of actual trauma without losing the significance of childhood phantasy.[1]

At the same time that he abandoned the seduction theory, Freud remained troubled by the war neuroses, particularly during WWI, as men returned from the battle. Described as shell shock, among the symptoms these men evidenced were tinnitus, amnesia, headache, hypersensitivity to noise, touch, and other sensations. Originally attributed to brain injury from the effect of exploding bombs (hence shell shock), brain injury could not be determined in many of these cases. The additional presence of fugue states, mutism, and other symptoms of "neurasthenia" shifted causality from the merely physical to the emotional and psychological. In one of his earliest formulations, Freud (1920) argued that trauma arises from a breach of psychic boundaries. Freud considered as traumatic:

> Any excitations from outside which are powerful enough to break through the protective shield [of the psyche]. It seems to me that the concept of trauma necessarily implies a connection of this kind with a breach in an otherwise efficacious barrier against stimuli. (p. 33)

Freud's notion of trauma relied on the element of fright or shock, a confrontation with the unexpected. For Freud, traumatic symptoms arose in response to this confrontation with the fearful unexpected; prototypically, the confrontation with death. In *Beyond the Pleasure Principle* (1920), written as he grappled with the war neuroses of World War I, he proposed that it is not the encounter with death itself, but rather the shock of survival that disturbed; what remained was a constant expectation of a death that did not occur, leading to symptoms of anxiety and stress.

Freud (e.g., 1915–1917) made the distinction between actual neuroses (in this group, we may include the war neuroses, the hysterical neuroses of his early seduction theory, and those that attack the body, such as neurasthenia, hypochondria, and anxiety attacks) as provoked by actual occurrences, such as violence or persistent frustration, and the psychoneuroses proper, which he saw as a conflict between impulse or desire and defense against that desire. Others, contemporaneous with him or following him, do not make that differentiation. Notably, his contemporary Ferenczi (1932) spoke of the confusion of tongues between the adult and the child, where the child's language of play and tenderness are unexpectedly met by passion in the adult, reframing the seduction theory into a traumatic mis-meeting of the needs of the child for love with the erotic aggression of the adult through the violation of generational boundaries. Here, to place it on the most basic level, the need for love is met with the perversion of love into domination and hatred. The images Ferenczi evokes to describe the subjective experience of trauma include "splitting off of a dead part, killed by the violence of the shock. . .with part of the personality . . .out of reach, like a sort of cyst inside. . .which may go so far as atomization" (Dupont, 1998, p. 235). Winnicott (1974) uses similar language when he describes a list of primitive agonies arising from a failure of the interpersonal environment to facilitate personal growth: disintegration, falling forever, a loss of psychosomatic existence, a failure of indwelling, a loss of the sense of the real, a loss of the capacity to relate to objects. Here, Winnicott is speaking of the fear of breakdown; he maintains that a form of traumatic failure *has already* occurred, and is hidden away and carried in the unconscious. The thing that is feared has already been experienced. Winnicott is primarily speaking here of trauma occurring early in life, before the trauma can be personalized or symbolized. However, the same logic applies to traumatic events that are *too real* to be assimilated. Referring to Klein (1946/1963), whose focus is neither on the linearity of time nor on symptomatology, trauma exists in the timelessness and spatiality of the unconscious. Trauma may occur at any time, held as a mark in the unconscious, where the past and the present are one. Her theory, unlike Freud's (and sometimes Winnicott's), is not linear or hierarchical— traumatic wounds are experienced in a paranoid-schizoid mode, which contains unsymbolizable experience, no matter when the trauma occurs in the development of the individual in linear time. Similarly, with reference to Lacan's register of the Real (1966), traumatic experiences occur in that realm of experience which exists without language or signification.

CLOSE TO DEATH

Winnicott says that the fear of breakdown is closely related to death anxieties. But this fear of death is not necessarily literal; rather, he speaks of "phenomenal death," a death that has already happened, an annihilative psychic state that remains a mark on the psyche.

Trauma is, at its core, a rupture. It is a moment that tears into the course of normative living, altering the very bounds of identity. Trauma breaks the frame of contextual experience and the capacity to continue narrative accounts of personal history. A break, a rupture, a tear, a fracturing in the psyche, trauma atomizes one's sense of subjectivity, disturbing psychic boundaries, neurological encoding, and symbolic functioning. Language breaks down. Understanding breaks down. The body breaks down. This is what trauma does.

We caution here, that death anxieties do not necessarily arise from literal experience, although literal experience, such as being surrounded by death on the battleground or in the concentration camps, may be present. Here, regardless of whether our own lives are threatened, we hear what we are not meant to hear and see what we are not meant to see: screams of agony, body parts strewn about on the battlefield where there was once a person, the body starved into skeletal forms. Just as literal brushes with death force us to encounter that which we should never have to see or hear, other experiences may have the same effect. In those moments, we see a version of ourselves that is unbearable to us, leaving as profound a mark on the psyche as the threat of death to the body.

Both Winnicott's primitive agonies and Klein's persecutory experiences of the paranoid-schizoid position bring us close to psychic death: the fear of falling endlessly, falling into bits, atomization, all describes the fracturing of subjectivity that we propose as the sequelae of trauma. Winnicott stresses the failure to be held psychically, to feel the safety in the arms of another. Klein stresses the effect of hatred endemic to the persecutory experience of the paranoid-schizoid position, which is her phenomenological translation of the functioning of the death instinct. In each case, there is no space for one's own thoughts, no room for personal creativity. Subjectivity has been truncated; vistas that might once have been spacious and open are narrowed to a slit, or seemingly altogether closed up. Not just the psychic wounds of war or rape or incest, but traumatic separations (such as hospitalism in young children), beatings by parents or partners who are meant to cherish us, the cumulative trauma (Khan, 1963) of the caregiver's repeated failure to adapt to the needs of the child, to cite some instances, all lead to potential breakdowns in subjective personal existence.

SYMBOLIZATION AND THE UNCONSCIOUS TRANSMISSION OF TRAUMA

Closeness to death may be experienced in ways that do not involve assaults to bodily integrity. For some, the encounter with death is psychical rather than physical, a profound alteration of one's sense of self: "I am no longer who I was or who I thought I was." For others, there is closeness to death imposed from outside their own awareness or concrete experience. The early childhood trauma referred to by Ferenczi, Winnicott and Khan may never have been experienced consciously and therefore cannot be remembered or accessed through language. Death anxieties experienced in the parents, projected into the child, leave a mark on the child, regardless of whether the child is actually in danger. On a personal level, a parent who feels paralyzing fear about the survival of her child, who feels murderous rage, who feels dead inside, transmits these affects to the child. This intergenerational transmission of trauma has been referred to as ghosts in the nursery (Fraiberg, Adelson, and Shapiro, 1975), as haunting or ghostly signifiers (O'Loughlin, 2013), and as hauntology (Derrida, 1994). In speaking of his hospitalizations in the first two years of his life, O'Loughlin suggests that the trauma of those hospitalizations was multiplied by his parents' anxiety over his survival. Many years later, after a discussion with his mother about his hospital experience, "she casually mentioned that I got so upset when she and my dad visited me in the hospital that the nurses recommended that whenever possible my parents should stand by the window and peer through the glass so that they could visit with me without upsetting me." (p. 51) With this new knowledge, O'Loughlin was able to connect the photograph of a chalk statuette of a 1940s style woman peering with a downcast expression through a window, that had hung in his office for many years as a ghostly signifier, pointing to the longing and loss of the child and his mother. I (Karen) had similar hospitalization experiences (though apparently not life-threatening) at the ages of three and five, followed at ages 5 through 8 by frequent bouts of pavor nocturnus and sleepwalking. It was not until many years later, following a seemingly unrelated trauma, that I was able to connect the sequelae of anxiety following my hospitalizations with an event in my mother's life, in which I was helplessly entwined. Mine was a caesarean birth, and although my mother never complained about the condition of my birth, other relatives told me that my mother nearly died while giving birth to me. My mother's anxiety about my survival during my hospitalizations was unconsciously connected with the threat of my birth. Her anxiety about killing/losing me was equated with my unconscious anxiety about having almost killed her; this connection was a new perspective on the mutual multiplication of traumatic anxiety.

Symbolization may fail as a result of the horror of the actual trauma, an unthinkable attack on the subjectivity of the person (rape, repeated sadistic attacks, the torture of the concentration camp, and so on). Symbolization may also fail because the trauma remains unspoken, but is nevertheless unconsciously communicated. For example, the intergenerational transmission of trauma (parents' and grandparents' experience of the Holocaust, historical situations of starvation and displacement[2]) while not experienced directly by the subject, may nevertheless leave their mark through the shame, abjection, and feelings of helplessness of the previous generations which are affectively passed down to the following generations.

To return to Freud, we support the notion of actual neurosis as a condition for trauma; however, we question the conditions of the actuality of the actual. The original traumatic injury may reside on a personal level in the unconscious projections of the parent to the child, or on a cultural level, residing in the historical suffering of previous generations. In this sense, while the original trauma is an actual (not a phantasied) assault, the transmission of trauma may be passed unconsciously from parent to child, or from generation to generation. Similarly, actual assaults may not always be traumatic on the personal level; those who are able to fight back, or to seek revenge or justice, may in large part bypass the lingering mark of trauma. The ability to speak about trauma, to have trauma acknowledged, to actively engage and successfully oppose the traumatizer, all tend to mitigate its lasting effects. It is when trauma is hidden, unspeakable, and unopposable, when it remains within an encapsulated shell of experience, that it does most damage. To this end, our investigation centers on the subjective experience of trauma, and which subjective experiences contribute to lasting effects.

THE CULTURE OF TRAUMA: POLITICAL CONSIDERATIONS

Those who argue that traumatic reactions are rare, and that diagnosis based on high prevalence rates are suspect (e.g., Breslau, 2002; Yehuda and McFarlane, 1995), bring us to a consideration of the varying ways in which individuals experience and survive the culture of trauma. Prevalence rates are bound to be higher in cultures that inscribe trauma into the very fabric of their society; however, high prevalence rates do not in themselves mitigate the subjective experience of trauma. Communities are subject to trauma, just as are individuals. Communal traumatization can occur through the direct traumatization of all members of a community, as in a natural disaster, or through the repetitive traumatization of a community's members throughout history. In the latter case, individuals may come to experience the traumatogenic effects through membership in the community, even in the absence of direct attacks. Identification with the group posits a potential threat through the group's history of abuse, systematic exclusion, or terrorization. As examples, the historical persecution of African-Americans, homosexuals, or Jews does not require a particular individual to be subject to direct victimization in order to feel the effects of hatred which become bound up in his or her (threatened) identity.

Dave Eggers's (2006, 2009) novelistic biographies illustrate, with poignancy and amazing depth, ways in which trauma is structured within the culture, as well as trauma's personal effects, both in its terrible aspects and in the individual's wondrous ability to move through the trauma. *Zeitoun* (2009) narrates the journey of the Zeitoun family—Abdulrahman, Kathy, and their children—and their extraordinary circumstances in the aftermath of Hurricane Katrina. Abdulrahman, a Syrian immigrant, a man with a big heart who fully embraced American ideals, stayed behind to protect his properties while Kathy and the children drove inland to relatives in anticipation of Hurricane Katrina. Abdulrahman worked throughout the aftermath of Katrina, paddling around his neighborhood in a canoe, saving his neighbors and feeding the neighborhood dogs that were left behind, speaking to authorities in attempts to save endangered lives, all the while seeing dead bodies float by. The real trauma was yet to come. Six people in military garb, with bulletproof vests and M-16s, stormed into one of Zeitoun's properties and forced him into a boat without explanation, taking him to a temporary headquarters set up at the Union Passenger Terminal, now called Camp Greyhound. When Zeitoun asked passing soldiers for an explanation, he discovered he was suspected of being a terrorist, variously of al Qaeda or the Taliban. Strip searched and put in a cage, not charged with anything, not allowed calls, fed ham sandwiches which he could not eat; pepper sprayed through the fenced cages that held them, Zeitoun was eventually taken to the Hunt Correctional Center, still not charged with a crime. Imprisoned for nearly a month, shackled, with an illness that was refused attention, Kathy finally found out where her husband was being held and was able to post bail.

In the aftermath of this unassimilable trauma, it was Kathy, not Zeitoun, who suffered most from post-traumatic stress. Four days after his release on bail, Kathy persuaded Zeitoun to return to Camp Greyhound to retrieve his wallet, which contained the IDs that were necessary to prove his innocence. While speaking to a Dutch reporter on the grounds, they were confronted by a female officer. Anxious and angry that they were speaking to the reporter, the officer snapped at them and threatened Zeitoun with re-arrest. Kathy's anger flared: "Now you take away my freedom of speech? Really! You took away my husband, you wouldn't let me speak to or see my husband, and now you take away my ability to speak freely? I don't think so! You know anything about freedom of speech?"(p. 315). That was the last time Kathy was focused in her anger. Since then, she has had classic symptoms of post-traumatic stress: vagueness, lack of focus, fearfulness. Obsessively worried about her family's safety, she double locks the doors and doesn't like to let her children play in the neighborhood. She wakes in the night, checking on her children, and has trouble going back to sleep. Her memory has become shredded, as if it has snapped. When asked by doctors what the most traumatic part of Katrina was, Kathy realized that it was in the moment that, when trying to reach her husband at the Hunt Correctional Center, she was told that the location of his hearing was private information. The moment that she was denied all information of her husband, that she could not attend his hearing, that she confronted a government that had the power to simply make people disappear, was too much for her. It was at that moment that she describes herself as having been broken.

> Zeitoun, on the other hand, remains hopeful, even strengthened. "It was a test, Zeitoun thinks. Who among us could deny that we were tested? But look at us, he says. Every person is stronger now. Every person who was forgotten by God or country is now louder, more defiant, and more determined. They existed before, and they exist again, in the city of New Orleans and the United States of America. He can only have faith that he will never again be forgotten, denied, called by a name other than his own" (p. 324).

What Is the What (2006) reminds us of the power, and empowerment, of being able to speak through trauma, of the healing effects of narration. Valentino Achak Deng, a lost boy of Sudan, interlaces past and present trauma as he describes his journey through a war-torn nation from the perspective of narrated memory as he lays on the floor, tied up in his Atlanta apartment, a victim of robbery and mugging. Trauma, doubling on itself, exists here, in a literal sense, both on an organized politico-historical level and on a random personal level. Born into a fairly comfortable family in the village of Marial Bai, the Second Sudanese Civil War, between soldiers and rebels, ripped apart their village and many of the people in it. Escaping from his village, Deng runs as softly and quickly as he can, his thoughts running with him: "*Oh God of the sky, keep me safe tonight. Keep me hidden, keep me quiet...*Run now. *Oh God of rain, let me find water. Let me not die of thirst. . . Oh God of the soul, why are you doing this? I have done nothing to ask for this. I'm a boy. I'm a boy.*" (pp. 97–98). His boyhood ripped away from him, he finds people, some of them kind, some of them tormenters. Banding together with other young boys who must take charge of themselves, they trek to Ethiopia in hopes of escaping their war-torn land. On the way, he suffers terrible hunger, attacks by villagers, and the loss of many of his comrades through murder, starvation, collapse, and suicide. He speaks of the traumatic effects on the boys in his group, including the absence of narrative: boys who were so terrified they would not sleep, others who compulsively parceled out bits of food for fear of starvation, another who, like Hansel in the fairy tale, made a line in the dirt with a stick so that he could find his way home. But mostly, the boys walked on in silence, as there was nothing to say.

Reaching Ethiopia and the Pinyudo refugee camp was scarcely better than their trek. There were too many boys and not enough supplies, not nearly the comfort of home that the boys had imagined. The small measure of safety that the end of walking afforded also brought forward the collapse into post-traumatic stress. Deng describes the sounds of his first nights in the camp, hearing the once silent boys wail endlessly from all corners of the camp, the end of their trek marking a breakdown of their stoic silence, giving way to mourning and despair.

After several years and a further a displacement to Kakuma refugee camp in Kenya, Deng finally makes his way to the United States, settling in Atlanta, supported to some degree by refugee associations but largely making his own way while trying to secure a college education. It is here that his apartment is invaded by an African-American woman who knocks on his door, asking to use his phone because her car broke down. Before he knows it, he is beaten with the butt of a pistol and tied up by her black male companion, called "African" and "fucking Nigerian motherfucker!" a misnamed foreigner wherever he is. Surviving this attack, Deng decides to leave Atlanta (he eventually secures acceptance to Allegheny College in Pennsylvania). The novel ends with the following remarkable statement on the significance of narration and witnessing:

> Whatever I do, however I find a way to live, I will tell these stories I have spoken to every person I have encountered these last difficult days. . . because to do anything else would be something less than human. I speak to these people, I speak to you because I cannot help it. It gives me strength, almost unbelievable strength, to know that you are there. I covet your eyes, your ears, the collapsible space between us. How blessed are we to have each other? I am alive and you are alive so we must fill the air with our words. . . .I will tell stories to people who will listen and to people who don't want to listen, to people who seek me out and to those who run. All the while I will know that you are there. How can I pretend that you do not exist? It would be almost as impossible as you pretending that I do not exist (p. 535).

SUBJECTIVE EXPERIENCE OF TRAUMA

I (Avigail) recently completed an empirical study of subjective experience of trauma (Gordon, 2014). The study operated on the premise that subjective experience is a significant reference for the diagnosis of trauma. Clinicians and theoreticians generate notions of what defines trauma, but ultimately it is the patients who embody and speak through traumatic experience. To determine which of the existing definitions best capture traumatic experiences, I developed a self-report questionnaire to assess participants' trauma history. The questionnaire assessed subjective traumatization, concordance with various definitions, symptoms, and dissociation in response to a wide variety of negative events, allowing us to compare events that were traumatic with those that were judged to be merely negative.

The definitions in the questionnaire included those based on external and internal aspects of the experience. Some questions focused on emotional experience, some on the impact of the event on psychological constructs such as self and worldview, and others on the physical impact of the event (such as damage to the body). The current clinical definition of Post-Traumatic Stress Disorder in the *Diagnostic and Statistical Manual of Mental Disorders* (DSM-V; American Psychiatric Association, 2013) is based entirely on the last category—physical impact of event. Interestingly, in my findings, this was the only category unrelated to participants' subjective sense of traumatization.

The sample included 215 participants, recruited through a local university subject pool and online, through snowball sampling methods. After filling out a brief demographic questionnaire, participants completed a checklist in which they endorsed which of a set of negative experiences they had experienced themselves, which had been experienced by someone close to them, and which they had witnessed. They also had the opportunity to provide responses to open-ended questions about other traumas they had experienced. The list included events traditionally viewed as traumatic (e.g., sexual assault or war), events considered to be traumatic by some theorists and clinicians (e.g. foster care or divorce of parents), and events generally viewed as negative but not traumatic (e.g. breakup of a romantic relationship or losing a job). For each endorsed event, subjects filled out a Peritraumatic Dissociative Experience Questionnaire (Marmar, Weiss, and Metzler, 1997), and a symptom checklist which measured symptoms at five different timepoints (immediately after the event, one month after, three months after, six months after, and continuing at the time of the study). Participants were also asked to respond to the questions "Did you feel traumatized at the time of the experience?" and Do you feel traumatized now as a result of this experience?" to assess subjective traumatization, and the question "Did you process this experience while it happened?" and Have you processed this experience now?" Both subjective traumatization and processing of the event were measured on a seven point Likert scale.

Of these 215 participants, 150 indicated that they had experienced one of the listed events as traumatic. A total of 1,754 negative events were indicated, of which 510 were listed as traumatic. Participants reported a variety of definitions for what was considered subjectively traumatic at the time of an experience and what led to continuing feelings of traumatization. At the time of the event, subjective emotional experience was most salient, including helplessness, fear, and horror. Following, in order of salience, were "challenged my worldview", "challenged my sense of safety", and "challenged view of myself". Equally significant, but at lower levels of reporting, were threats to physical integrity ("threat to body", "threat to life", "certain I was about to die"). By contrast, the definitions most strongly correlated with continuing traumatization were "changed my view of myself", "I felt helpless, and 'changed my view of the world'". These results suggest that there is a distinction between what makes an experience traumatic in the moment and the longer term effects of trauma, which involve an altered sense of one's self in the world.

A related finding was that helplessness and altered views of the self and the world were most strongly correlated with symptom counts across the 4 time periods that were assessed. These definitions are most likely to cause symptoms following a traumatic event, as well as to best describe subjective feelings of traumatization.

Hierarchical regression analyses were conducted to determine which definitions accounted for the variance in subjective traumatization over time. Again, helplessness and change to self-view and worldview were the best fit, and models that included additional definitions were not found to be better predictors. These results taken together indicate that this constellation best reflects the internal experience of traumatization in this sample.

According to the results of this study, the internal picture of traumatic experience is one of helplessness leading to a changed view of self and world. While many theorists suggest that trauma relies on a confrontation with death (see, e.g., Boulanger, 2007), these results suggest that it is rather a metaphorical death. Subjective experiences of threats to life and to the body are significant, but less salient, at the time of trauma, and tend to fade out over time, while the subjective experiences of helplessness and a changed view of self and of the world are more salient at the time and have more lasting effects. A traumatic experience is one in which the subject's sense of self is altered. Whether or not there was a risk of physical death or bodily harm, traumatic experience causes a rupture within one's sense of subjectivity; some psychical part of the individual has been disturbed.

CLINICAL EXAMPLE: DON[3]

Don's history was so full of extreme traumatic events that at times it seemed his life followed the script of an exceptionally outlandish film. At age five he was forced to stand guard repeatedly as his older brother raped his sister—incidents that Don both watched and heard. Two years later, his brother began to sexually assault Don. The background to Don's sexual trauma is that throughout his childhood, he suffered physical, verbal, and emotional abuse at the hands of his sociopathic father. By the time he left home at seventeen, he had been subjected to multiple and repeated traumas within his family.

Leaving home at seventeen with no money or other resources, he made his way from California to New York, living by his wits, often encountering dangerous people and risky situations. In the 1980s, Don contracted AIDS, and has subsequently lost many peers in the gay community in New York to the disease over the past three decades.

More recently, upon the death of his wealthy partner and the loss of his own fortune due to poor investment decisions, Don's standard of living has been drastically reduced. He now survives with the aid of subsidized housing, food stamps, and a variety of other social service programs. Don feels deep shame about his financial situation, and works hard to hide his poverty from his friends, who are wealthy and largely unaware of his altered circumstances.

Much of my (Avigail's) work with Don centered on acknowledging parts of himself he had denied in the wake of his traumatic experiences, parts of himself that were too painful to acknowledge as he identified them with his victimizers. He strongly disavowed anger and aggression, even as he made subtly devaluing comments and displayed signs of deep-seated bigotry. To Don, open expression of anger and aggression would be tantamount to the personal admission of the sadism and psychopathy that he experienced at the hands of his father and brother. His carefully construed identity as "just a nice guy" who never got angry—and as a passive recipient of all manner of abuses—was firmly established by his early childhood experiences as the target of hatred and abuse. Don acted as if accepting traumatic experiences with a smile and a shrug were the only way to survive the repeated terrible experiences that made up his everyday life.

Don rarely identified his experiences as traumatic—accidents in which he was riding his bike and was hit by a car, incidents in which strangers pulled knives on him, his progressive illnesses as a result of AIDS. Arriving at one session, Don informed me with a wide smile that he almost had not made it to the session, "especially because I was almost killed two minutes ago when the brakes on my bike didn't work." When I remarked on the discrepancy between the content of his words and his emotional presentation, he laughed and brushed me off, saying "You have to laugh, right?" As the session progressed and I was able to tie further material to this same tendency to smile through any experience, he acknowledged that it would be a powerful change for him to be able to share these experiences without laughing. "You see", he said, sadly this time, "You have to laugh because what is the alternative?"

Don embraced the internalized helplessness of his repeated traumatic experiences in early childhood, unconsciously choosing repeated victimizations over confrontation with the horror of his traumas. We might see his risky behavior, which has led him to re-experience countless "little" victimizations, as a sort of repetition compulsion, an unconscious attempt to force a new resolution (see Freud, 1915–1917, 1920). However, the suppression of the full breadth of his emotional reactions to his multiple traumas is what was most present in my work with Don. As he began to allow and experience his anger, and then his fear, he has been able to develop a more balanced view of himself and the world around him, not seeing everything around him as a threat nor seeing himself as, inevitably, the victim, destined to be damaged. Along with the dissociation of powerful affects related to his traumatic experience, Don split his subjectivity into a conscious, passive, "nice guy" victim and an unconscious monstrous victimizer who would emerge if given the slightest chance. Central to our work was a lessening of the fear that beneath his victimization lay a cruel sadist—the father/brother who lay nestled in his unconscious identifications. His dissociation served multiple purposes, not only to keep painful affects at bay, but to preserve some sense of positive identification with the family who ruptured his sense of agency. Without a confrontation with the monstrosity of the father and brother who victimized him, he lived not only in the repetition of his identification with victimhood, but also in the fear that if he confronted those monsters it would release a monstrosity within him.

On the surface, it may appear that Don had been able to symbolize his traumatic experiences. He had full memory of his experiences, and was able to talk about them freely. However, he had dissociated all feeling connected to these experiences, acting out the traumatic scenarios over and over again rather than allowing a full engagement with the horrors he endured.

Don and I reenacted his trauma in the treatment. Although consciously disconnected from his emotions, I experienced them powerfully in my countertransference. As Don was provocative and at times demeaning, I often felt more of a determination not to let him beat me than a true desire to keep engaging with him. My focus on not being beaten mirrored his defenses against his victimization. I struggled to draw out his feelings into consciousness, at times holding them myself and using my visceral experience of the affects in the room as a bridge to help Don acknowledge them. My hope was that if I could acknowledge the feelings circulating in the room, that they would become less toxic and threatening to him.

After I had canceled a session with him, when we were discussing his difficulty embracing his own negative feelings of other people, I asked him if he had been angry with me for failing to show up, or for not communicating clearly enough to him that I could not be there. He categorically denied any anger felt toward me. I asked him what it would be like if he were angry, and as I did so my body began to shake uncontrollably, visibly and intensely. I spoke of my reaction, and he said "That's what I would feel like." I see this countertransferential moment as a melding of my fear and his own—his fear of losing a relationship if he were not passively all-accepting, his fear of acknowledging the imperfections in others, especially as a parental container and protective force, so absent in his early life, fears of his repressed and potentially demolishing anger and my possibly inadequate resources in the face of that fury.

As Don became increasingly fluent with his own emotions, acknowledging feelings of anger, fear, and sadness, he was increasingly able to connect those feelings to his early experiences with his father and brother. He began to speak of the need to cut off his emotional experience, as they appeared to him at the time to threaten his survival in the family. Don, having read his traumatic experience into his life going forward, was now beginning to loosen the effects of his trauma, and to see other possibilities than the repetition of his victimization.

In my work with Don, I actively challenged his tendency to split himself, and others, into good and bad terms, with little room for some space in between. His insistence on seeing himself as 'just a nice guy' kept not only his rage at bay, but also his sense of agency. My active challenges were taken up by Don, and he began to challenge these assumptions himself. He began to make links between his self-destructive and dangerous behaviors and his early traumas. Recognizing that he put himself in dangerous situations was a powerful realization for Don. He began to appreciate that he had created for himself a destiny of destruction and pain; when we were able to link that awareness with his traumatic experiences, Don began to shift his sense of his own subjectivity. From seeing himself as always about to be destroyed (and defined by that "fact," and deserving that fate), he shifted to a sense of the possibility of a future beyond trauma.

My role with Don was as a witness, not just to his traumas but to the powerful and unacknowledged emotions that continued to haunt him. Part of the work was in linking his traumatic past, his dissociated emotions, and the passive good-guy stance he had adapted as a way to get by. But perhaps most importantly, I was unfailingly impressed by the strength and resilience of the man sitting across from me. Shaped by experiences that would make many people give up in despair, he kept fighting for a better future, even when he was unwittingly replicating his traumas with every attempt to overcome them. Don chose a line of flight at the age of seventeen, leaving home and surviving on his own. This line of escape took tremendous strength and resilience, at the same time that it failed to confront directly the monstrous acts of his father and brother. This failure to confront (as if he had a choice!) kept him in a passive position in relation to his traumas. That I was connected to the strength in him, that I could challenge him without the fear of his collapse, was perhaps what he most appreciated in our work together. My ability to see his strength allowed him to embrace his own strength without fearing the eruption of the sadism to which he had been subjected. What had changed was not that others could not harm him, but that he was no longer harming himself.

CONCLUSION

Our clinical and literary-biographical examples point to the mark that trauma leaves on its subjects. This mark coincides with our empirical findings that the most salient and lasting effects of trauma consist of a rupture in the sense of self which especially affects personal agency and one's sense of being in the world. This rupture can take the form of a repetition-compulsion, as in Don's case, or a breakdown in one's sense of personal intactness, and a breach in the sense of living in a relatively safe and predictable world, as in Kathy's case. We can also see, through Don's treatment and through the narratives of Zeitoun and Deng, the powerful effects of being able to speak to the trauma, not only in terms of conscious remembering and direct narrative, but through the capacity to experience the fullness of emotional experience of the trauma. Don's passive collapse into the position of victim was ameliorated through his treatment, where he could begin to access his rage and recover a sense of agency in the world. Zeitoun and Deng, fighters throughout their traumatic circumstances, were somehow able to retain a sense of agency. We speculate that through their ability to retain an active position and to hold on to hope, they were able to elude, to some extent, the psychic collapse that is common to many traumatized individuals. The return, recapturing, or creation of a sense of agency, within the self and in the world, is what the treatment of trauma may provide to shredded and broken selves.

NOTES

1. In the psychoanalytic literature, the spelling of fantasy/phantasy varies according to its usage. The Freudian conception of fantasy includes conscious thoughts and daydreams, while the Kleinian notion of phantasy is rooted in unconscious thoughts and feelings.
2. See, for example, O'Loughlin's (2012) discussion of the mark left by the Irish famine on succeeding generations. His point is that the denial of historical memory appears to represent a collective act of dissociation that we embody and live out in parts of our being without the conscious awareness of how historically located suffering structures our being in the world.
3. The clinical material reported here is Avigail Gordon's, and all clinical material has been used with consent and disguised to protect the patient's identity.

REFERENCES

American Psychiatric Association (1980). *Diagnostic and Statistical Manual of Mental Disorders, 3* Edition-Revised (DSMIII-R). Washington, DC: American Psychiatric Association.

American Psychiatric Association (2013). *Diagnostic and Statistical Manual of Mental Disorders, 5 Edition (DSM-V).* Arlington, Va.: American Psychiatric Association

Boulanger, G. (2007). *Wounded by Reality: Understanding and Treating Adult-Onset Trauma.* New York: Routledge.

Breslau, N. (2002). Epidemiologic Studies of trauma, Posttramatic Stress Disorder, and OtherPsychiatric Disorders. *Canadian Journal of Psychiatry, 47* (10), 923-929.

Breuer, J. and Freud, S. (1893–1895). Studies on Hysteria. In *The Standard Edition, Volume II.* London: Hogarth Press, 1955.

Derrida, J. (1994). *Specters of Marx: the State of the Debt, the Work of Mourning, and the New International.* New York: Routledge.

DuPont, J. (1988). The Concept of Trauma According to Ferenczi and Its Effects on Subsequent Psychoanalytical Research. *International Forum of Psychoanalysis, 7,* 235–240.

Eggers, D. (2006). *What Is the What?* New York: Vintage Books.

Eggers, D. (2009). *Zeitoun.* New York: Vintage Books.

Ferenczi, S. (1933). Confusion of Tongues between Adults and the Child. In *Final Contributions to the Problems and Methods of Psycho-analysis.* New York: Brunner/Mazel, 1955.

Fraiberg, S., Adelson, E., and Shapiro, V. (1975). Ghosts in the Nursery: A Psychoanalytic Approach to the Problems of Impaired Mother-Infant Relationships. *Journal of the American Academy of Child Psychiatry, 14*(3), 387–421.

Freud, S. (1915-1917). Introductory Lectures on Psychoanalysis. *The Standard Edition, Volumes XV-XVI.* London: Hogarth Press, 1955.

Freud, S. (1920). Beyond the Pleasure Principle. *The Standard Edition, Volume XVIII.* London: Hogarth Press, 1955.

Gordon, Avigail (2014). An Aetiology of Traumatization: A Consideration of Subjective and Objective Definitions of Trauma. Unpublished doctoral dissertation.

Janet, P. (1889). *L'automatisme psychologique.* Paris: Felix Alcan. Reprint: Societe Pierre Janet, Paris, 1973.

Khan, M. R. (1963). The Concept of Cumulative Trauma. *Psychoanalytic Study of the Child, 18,* 286–306.

Klein, M. (1946–1963). *Envy and Gratitude and Other Works.* London: Hogarth Press, 1975.

Lacan, J. (1966). *Ecrits.* New York: W.W. Norton, 2002.

Marmar, C.R., Weiss, D.S., and Metzler, T.J. (1997). The Peritraumatic Dissociative Experiences Questionnaire. In J.P. Wilson and T.M. Keane (Eds.), *Assessing Psychological Trauma and PTSD: A Handbook for Practitioners.* New York: Guilford Press.

O'Loughlin, M. (2013). Ghostly Presences in Children's Lives. In M. O'Loughlin (Ed.): *Psychodynamic Perspectives on Working with Children, Families, and Schools.* New York: Jason Aronson.

O'Loughlin, M, (2012). Trauma Trails from Ireland's Great Hunger: A Psychoanalytic Inquiry. In B. Willock, R. Curtis, and L. Bohm (Eds.). *Loneliness and Longing: Conscious and Unconscious Aspects.* New York: Routledge.

Winnicott, D.W. (1974). Fear of Breakdown. *International Review of Psychoanalysis, 1,* 103–107.

Yehuda , R. and McFarlane, A.C. (1995). Conflict between Current Knowledge about Posttraumatic Stress Disorder and its Original Conceptual Basis. *American Journal of Psychiatry, 152,* 1705–1713.

NINE

Sounding Home

Exploring the Use of Self-Selected Music as Meaningful Expression and Containment of Trauma with Patients Experiencing Psychosis

Trisha Ready

LYACONNIA

Just after finishing chart notes, I saw a frantic Lyaconnia standing at the nurses' station. Her pink hair was tangled and askew; she demanded in a loud voice: "Where is that woman who was trying to kill me?"

"There you are," she said, "Were you trying to kill me with that song? What were you doing?"

At that moment, all theories and aspirations about music's ability to serve a mothering function and to facilitate emotional expression evaporated. My initial response was panic: a combination of transference of Lyaconnia's terror of annihilation, mixed with my own fear that the hospital might terminate these pilot music sessions. Lyaconnia, and other participants described in this chapter have had their names changed, and their identities respectfully disguised to protect against recognition.

My intent to use music as an adjunct therapy on an acute psychiatric unit was not unique. Eventually this music project evolved into a research study involving listening to participant selected music for 10–30 minute sessions with patients who were experiencing early stages of psychosis. The focus of the study was to observe and measure, through the use of pre-and post-Rorschach assessment, whether music assisted in expression and containment of affect for participants, and facilitated building therapist and patient rapport. Oliver Sacks championed the use of music for numerous health issues, noting that "propensity to music shows itself in infancy, is manifest and central in every culture" and hails "back to the very beginning of time" (Sacks, 2007, p. x). Schneck and Berger (2006) proposed that music could bring about meditative, calming distractions that temporarily redirect limbic system responses away from fear, which could be triggered by early traumatic experiences.

The Death Cab for Cutie song we had listened to, "I Will Follow You into the Dark" (Gibbard, 2006, Track 1), contained longing, shadows and a quirky, cynical view of death. On the other hand, the song's simple rhythm and prosody had crossed the wall of her psychotic defenses.

"I didn't intend to cause pain, Lyaconnia." I apologized.

She stared at me, or past me, into the open door of the staff room. "Well, I hated it," she said. "Get me some hot water."

Lyaconnia's first admission to a psychiatric hospital was precipitated by unrelenting suicidal thoughts and hallucinations. Snakes came out of water faucets. God commanded her to pray for the restoration of New Orleans.

Lyaconnia was several months shy of 20. She had made a series of suicidal threats to her family as part of an ongoing, rage-induced struggle for love and attention. Her psychiatrist diagnosed her as experiencing a first break psychotic episode, fueled by fragments of childhood traumatic experiences including sexual exploitation, abandonment, and caregiver mis-attunements.

Lyaconnia told her doctor, "There is always yelling going on at home, from the moment I wake until they all leave for the day. It's hell in there."

Grotstein (1995) observed that people who experience psychosis are hypersensitive to their environments. Bion (1967, 1984) believed psychosis was forged by early years with too much tension, frustration and arousal with too little containment. Research shows that living in families who communicate with high expressed emotion (Hooley and Campbell, 2002; Hooley and Gotlib, 2000), marked by hostility, critical content and emotional impingement, can impact people with psychosis. Hostility in these studies was measured by the musical pitch, rate, and inflection of a relative's voice.

Lycaconnia's father, who drank heavily, had abandoned the family in order to live on the streets when Lyaconnia was seven. He was later diagnosed with paranoid schizophrenia. Lyaconnia, her mother, and her two younger half-brothers now lived in a two-bedroom apartment. She envisioned her mother's job in a foster care agency as constantly bringing home kids until there was no food and no place to sit.

On my second visit to Lyaconnia, she pulled off her cocoon of bed sheets. Her gaze was smoldering. "What are you still doing here?" she said, "I don't like your face."

On the third visit, she cooperated, "Okay. You want to get into my head? Go ahead." When I asked her what brought her into the hospital, she retorted disdainfully, "My Mother wanted to kill me. That's obvious."

After her physician transferred her to a higher functioning treatment unit, we started meeting for music listening sessions. We sat down with an iPod and portable speaker each day. I was hoping music could serve for her as the space where reverie could thrive and where raw primitive emotional material, as in Bion's (1967) beta elements, could be digested and returned as alpha elements in an organized, rhythmic way.

"I feel too ugly to start right now," she said. She asked me to leave. Psychoanalyst and musician Knoblauch (2005) insists that a therapist be available and receptive to all levels of communication—"intimate, primitive, poetic, or musical edges"—occurring during therapy so that there is "a broader and richer range of meaning and affect available for both analyst and patient to construct and inhabit" (p. 825). Listening to music with a patient experiencing psychosis requires a state of openness, much like Bion's (1967) suggestion for clinical therapists to suspend memory and desire.

Lyaconnia sat in the chair furthest from me, facing the door. She hugged her knees to her chest and rocked. I offered her the iPod. She gestured for me to choose. I chose Leonard Cohen's slow, sonorous, voice, hoping it would be comforting. She put her head on the table until the song ended. "That song reminded me of France. That's all I want to say."

The next song was "I Will Follow You Into the Dark" (Gibbard, 2006, Track 1). It completed one verse, before Lyconnia said, "I can't listen to that right now." She stood up abruptly. It was later that day that she accused me of trying to kill her.

A few days later, Lyaconnia's mother came to visit; she spoke in a loud, pressured voice. She believed that Lyaconnia's "anxiety-based" psychosis had started when Lyaconnia was dropped, as a child, by her drunken father, resulting in an injury to the back of her head. "It left her deaf in her left ear," her mother said, "and after that she was always oversensitive to sound, and to her environment."

Lyaconnia's name, her mother stated, was a combination of her own name (Connie) and Lyaconnia's father's name (Lyall). It also meant land of the wolves. Connie and her husband had worked as missionaries in Alaska when Lyaconnia was born. Lyaconnia was also a Biblical name.

Connie knew exactly what Lyaconnia needed—housing, medication, therapy, and a work-training program—components deemed essential and even urgent for young adult patients with psychosis (McGorry and Yung, 2003). Unfortunately, there were no such resources available in Billings, Montana. Connie wanted the hospital to treat her daughter until resources materialized.

When I told Lyaconnia that I had spoken with her mother, she got up abruptly and went into the bathroom, where I could hear her sobbing. I offered her the iPod when she returned.

She shrugged when asked to choose a song. I picked an improvised piano solo by Keith Jarrett. "That's okay," she said, "I don't love it. Something with words." She asked for Cohen's "Suzanne" (Cohen, 1975, Track 1). Her mood shifted between rage and depression.

I met with Lyaconnia's mother on a Friday afternoon. She spoke breathlessly in a high-pitched voice adding up tragedies: financial burdens, children with behavioral issues, and a demeaning boss. Taking Lyaconnia home was out of the question for her, even if it meant Lyaconnia had to go to a homeless shelter.

Lyaconnia's first response to the prospect of her mother's visit was dismissive, "I want to be called Gretchen. I don't want to think about wolves in Alaska or her first marriage when I say my name." I was surprised at her sudden shot at clarity and individuation. Lyaconnia asked about her discharge date. I reminded her that she was still not showering.

"Shut up," she said, "Mother, take me home." Two days later Lyaconnia's mother left a message reporting that Lyaconnia's father had died of uncertain causes the previous night on the streets of Anchorage. Her mother wanted to avoid giving bad news. Lyaconnia's physician and I were adamant about telling her the truth.

That afternoon a group of hospital staff met with Lyaconnia and her mother. Lyaconnia was unsettled by her mother's tears. "What's wrong? Did you forget my shampoo?" she asked.

"Ly honey," she said, "We received a call from the Anchorage police last night that your father is dead."

"That's fine," Lyaconnia said. "Can we talk about the shampoo now?"

"Honey" her mother stated, "I know the last time you saw your father you said something mean to him, but that doesn't matter now."

"I didn't," she replied. "He was an asshole."

Lyaconnia spoke loudly about fashion magazines and hair care products. Then she looked at her mother and said, "I don't know what to feel," and started to cry. Her mother took her hand. For the first time they seemed musically attuned, both their voices were equally soft and tender.

Lyaconnia asked her mother direct questions about the death of her father. Then, Connie started listing her burdens in a high pitched voice; Lyaconnia interrupted her to talk about red bumps on her feet.

I was scheduled to run a music group, so I asked Connie to join us. I started with several YoYoMa Bach pieces. Then I switched to Simon and Garfunkel's "Bridge Over Troubled Water" (Simon, Garfunkel, and Halee, 1970, Track, 1) a brief excerpt from Mozart's Requiem Mass, and ended with Leonard Cohen. Both women were tearful. Lyaconnia held her head in her hands. Her mother put her hand over her daughter's hands. Lyaconnia surprisingly tolerated her mother's touch.

Once her mother had left the unit, Lyaconnia asked, "Why did you play all of that really horrid music? I liked the River one. But the rest sucked." I translated that to mean that grieving about her father's death in proximity to her mother, while feeling rejected by her mother, was unbearable.

She continued to show sadness by focusing intensely on blemishes on her face, for which she requested special beauty products. She referred to staff members as zoo monkeys. She withdrew from groups.

After three days, Lyaconnia emerged with a clearer and more coherent presentation. During music listening sessions, she would mimic the varying pitch, volume, and tone of her mother's voice.

Connie called to tell me that she needed to bring some legal papers for Lyaconnia to sign regarding her father's burial. Lyaconnia was not fussed; she hoped her doctor would bless her leaving in two days.

"You'll need to wait and see about that group home," her mother said. "You'll stay higher on the list if you're here." Lyaconnia focused on a scar on the top of her foot. "Can you see it?" she asked. "It still really hurts."

"It must hurt also that you can't go home," I said.

"It's better for her to wait at the hospital," Connie interrupted. Their ensuing bickering voices sounded the way Lyaconnia had hummed them.

Lyaconnia said, "I want to apply for jobs and breathe fresh air again. " Lyaconnia went to her room and cried. Later, she asked for the iPod. We sat quietly listening to music. I put on Mendelssohn's Song Without Words. After several minutes she said, "I'm frustrated that I have had to stay here this long. I wish that my family were here for me." Then she selected Cohen's "Bird On a Wire." (Cohen, 1975, Track 7). "I feel like I've been left here and no one will ever come and get me." Lyaconnia said.

The evening she discharged from the hospital we revisited the Death Cab for Cutie song. She paced her room for hours in high heels and make-up. This was not typical discharge protocol, but it seemed like a healthy transition. The Death Cab for Cutie song reminded her of happier times, she said. It also made her think about her father, whom she didn't want to follow into a darkness that tugged at her mind.

STEVEN

Steven was a 23-year-old Southeast Asian male, diagnosed with Schizophrenia. He was tall and slender with a receding hairline. He spoke with a soft and pressured voice. Steven's mother and father, both born in Southeast Asia, had moved to Boise, Idaho, as teenagers. Steven was born in Boise. He dropped out of high school in the 12th grade. One-month prior to hospitalization, Steven stopped taking medications and visiting health providers. Instead, he tried to mediate his emotions by smoking cigarettes and $40 per day of marijuana. He had lost his job at a sports arena. Before that he had worked as a landscaper and caretaker for five years.

His family claimed that he became paranoid and delusional, expressing vague homicidal thoughts, after he went off medications. He had stopped sleeping and eating, and claimed that he could do 2000 push-ups per day. He was certain that his family had tried to conduct surgery and perform other nefarious acts on him. Steven was caught in a disturbance between his environment and personality, anticipating his own annihilation by abandonment (Bion, 1967).

Steven claimed that his father had formerly been an intravenous (IV) drug addict. Steven said, "He beat me with sticks and wires. He beat up everyone in our house." It was difficult to discern whether the abuse was actual or part of Steven's delusions. He had two younger sisters with whom he was close. He was also close to his mom.

It is likely that both Steven's parents struggled with untreated trauma from growing up in a war-torn country during a period of civil unrest and genocide (Mollica, Wyshak, and Lavelle, 1987). Steven's parents were undoubtedly impacted by frequent bombings and by the cruelties of holocaust (Kinzie, 1985; McKenzie-Pollock, 1996). PTSD and loss were common psychological issues affecting Southeast Asian families who arrived in the United States from Thai refugee camps between 1980 and 1989 (Mollica, Wyshak, and Lavelle, 1987). Danieli (1985) and Krugman (1987) described intergenerational trauma effects continuing into the third generation. MacDougall (1989) traced transmissions of traumas. She suggested taking into account all the people, such as "ancestors and living relatives, with whom the patient was related by means of various language games" and even "by the absence of all language of words and emotions." Steven had no words for the collection of traumas and untold stories he inherited from his family, some of which were communicated through his father's addictions and outbursts, and his mother's silence. Steven was also impacted by the loss of his birthright—due to his mental health issues, to the public shame of involuntary commitment, and to his banishment from the family home—as the first-born son in a Southeast Asian family (Rousseau, Drapeau, and Platt, 1999), Rather than having a traditional role in family leadership, Steven's place was usurped by his younger sisters.

The development of psychosis may be an unconscious strategy with which to face unbearable losses (Lewis, 2004). In their book *The Cognitive Psychotherapy of Schizophrenia,* researchers Kingdon and Turkington (2005) proposed trauma as one of the four predispositions that can lead to psychosis. In addition to the unspoken traumas of war, Steven was also subject to the unpredictability of his father's alcoholism. Studies in the

Netherlands and elsewhere point to links between parental problem drinking during childhood and psychiatric disorders in adulthood (Cuijpers, Langendoen, and Bijl, 1999; Greenfield, Swartz, Landerman, and George, 1993; Mathew, Wilson, Blazer, and George, 1993; Read, Mosher, and Bentall, 2004). Sons of fathers who are problem drinkers are at particularly high risk for developing psychiatric disorders (Cuijpers, et al., 1999).

Morrison and colleagues (2003) go so far as to suggest that PTSD and psychosis may lie on a spectrum of responses to trauma. Our current bio-psycho-social focus in the United States gives more weight to genetic and biological influences in the development of schizophrenia. Read et al., (2004) have proposed that social dysfunction, in addition to familial dysfunction, abuse and trauma may be the most important precursors of a psychotic disorder (Wittman and Keshavan, 2007).

When Steven started participating in the music listening sessions, he didn't know how to use the iPod, so he asked me to choose songs. We started with Frank Sinatra. "More like that," he said. When I chose "Close to You" (Bacharach and David, 1963, Track 6), performed by the Carpenters Steven said, "It reminds me of Mary Poppins or Willie Wonka with colors and people and cars floating in the air."

Steven preferred song familiarity, soft tone of voice, and simple melody, much like a young child prefers consonant melodies and the soft prosody of a mother's voice (Masataka, 2006; Trainor, Tsang, and Cheung, 2002). Steven grimaced at dissonant tunes.

He made slight eye contact during the sessions, and kept his sweatshirt hood pulled over his head. There was a cloud-like feeling in the room: songs drifting, his emotions drifting just beneath the surface.

Steven continued to respond positively to Karen Carpenter's voice. A music reviewer referred to her voice as "beautiful and neutral" and to The Carpenter's music as a mixture of "certitude and pliability" that offered sensual and "maternal comfort" (Jones, 2006). Another feature that attracted listeners to Carpenter's voice was her capacity to convey lived loneliness and suffering. When she died at the age of 32 due to complications from an eating disorder, she was beloved by fans but unable to receive their adoration.

Steven used Delilah's (2010) radio broadcasts as mothers use lullabies with infants, as sedatives to decrease stress (Nakata and Trehub, 2004; Trehub, 2000; Trehub, 2003, Patel, 2008). Delilah is a nationally syndicated radio host, and single mother of ten children, who links her love advice to songs. She described her show as a "safety zone where listeners take off armor, slip into a 'Mr. Rogers' cardigan, sit around the electronic hearth and share secrets" (Delilah, 2014).

Although Delilah's format seems formulaic, her radio programs serve an important reparative function for listeners. Her show provides Steven and other listeners with well-metabolized food (Bion, 1967/1984), a consistent feeding schedule, and the comfort of restful sleep. Delilah's radio show also seemed to assist in the reverse-inhibition of fantasies, potentially helping a person with psychosis remain calm while learning how to connect words to feelings (Bion, 1992).

For Steven, language was best served up with melody, thus making its emotional message clearer (Bleich-Cohen et al., 2009). Steven said that he saw film-like images with some songs, recalling a line from a film: "Sadness doesn't get through the cracks," with which he also stated his mistrust.

Before the fourth session, Steven returned to court where his parents testified against his return home, preferring placement in a group home. Steven felt betrayed but lacked the inner resources for processing thoughts and feelings about his family (Grotstein, 2007).

We started the fourth session by listening to Fleetwood Mac's "Landslide." "This is a really good song sometimes but I'm tired of the same music," he said. Later that evening, Steven got into a fight with a fellow patient who tried to steal his cigarette during smoke break. Since the court disappointment, he was more volatile. Later that night, he chose "Landslide" (Nicks, 1975, Track 8) again. Nicks' "coarse and tender" voice (Bruni, 1997) seemed to concretely articulate Steven's fear of standing at a precipice on the edge of arrival or annihilation in a landslide of crumbling infrastructures. He said, "It's something about not getting what you want so much." He requested the iPod on shuffle with the volume turned down. Steven had moved from paranoia to ambivalence (Grotstein, 1977); if he didn't anticipate a song, he could avoid disappointment.

Steven continued to take more active control of the iPod: scrolling through songs and searching for music. He selected the Hawaiian musician, Israel Kamakawiwo'ole (IZ). "This guy is good," Steven exclaimed. "If he was so fat how did he play that little guitar?" IZ had struggled until his early death with obesity, which seemed to be sequelae for other somatic issues with breathing, heart rhythms, etc. His voice, however, was a pure transcendence of pain: soft and inviting, not troubled by inner conflict or turmoil (Harada, 2010).

Steven stated, "I worked for this 103-year-old man 60 hours per week who was dying. The first time I came to this hospital was right before that guy died. It was too much for me." Steven talked about how the old man's family never visited.

While listening to IZ's "Somewhere Over the Rainbow" (Arlen and Harburg, 1939, Track 14), Steven talked about discontinuing medications due to lack of funds. His attention shifted: "My father will change his mind. They won't leave me here."

At the next session, Steven was depressed after arguing with his father. "He's an ass," Steven said. "He wouldn't talk to me that way if he was standing here. I'm bigger." We listened to several IZ songs and one song by Tupac Shakur: "All About U" (Shakur, 1996, Track 2). Steven was also angry about a recent Group Home interview. "It would be a bad place for me," he said, "with all those old drug guys." He had walked out of the interview, telling staff that he wasn't going to clean a toilet or make his bed if he didn't feel like it. Steven seemed to want to sustain a not-knowing in relation to the world around him, outside and inside the hospital, where it would be impossible to individuate. He would reject before being rejected (Bion, 1992).

Steven spent the next session listening to snippets of songs he chose for his CD . He was still confused by his family's decision. "They are the most important people to me," he said.

At the final session, Steven was in a fairly good mood. "Let's listen to my CDs again," he said. He was more comfortable operating the iPod. Steven said it was harder to meet for music sessions after his family's abandonment. He wasn't sure whom to trust.

Steven remained in the hospital for five more weeks, waiting for a group home placement. His feelings of persecution and betrayal after the court hearing extended beyond family to hospital staff. He was suspicious that we were colluding with his family, although, in truth, the staff had anticipated Steven's release from court.

Steven had encountered many factors that Wittman and Keshaven (2007) identified in a review of research regarding what contributes to depression for patients experiencing psychosis. The factors include feelings of loss and diminished self-worth, because the illness is such a destructive life event, and a sense of hopelessness or ambivalence about the future. The accumulation of numerous losses made grief and mourning necessary aspects of coming to terms with a psychiatric illness (Wittman and Keshaven, 2007). Besides mourning the loss of his family and home, Steven also seemed reluctant to let go of the psychotic symptoms that had provided a buffer from painful emotions (Lewis, 2004).

After Steven finished participating in the study, noted earlier in this chapter, he retreated to the point of lying in bed all day for ten days. Tait, Birchwood, and Trower (2003) observed that when depression following a psychotic episode does not lead to suicide, it may well lead to social withdrawal and disengagement from services.

It made sense that Steven, faced with layers of losses—loss of identity, of family, of personal agency, and of institutional opportunities—would return to the persecutory anxieties of a paranoid/schizoid position to postpone grief (Klein, 1946/1986c; Waska, 2003). He seemed flooded with feelings of abandonment, loneliness, envy, and rage. He was tired of hearing "the same music" of the hospital, the false note of my voice, or the treatment-urging voices of staff members. Non-verbal communications were not bringing Steven affective resonance as a form of nonphysical calming (Charles, 2002).

During the music sessions, Steven located his emotions and sense of identity in songs, moving from the regressive toward more sophisticated forms of symbolization (Benedetti, 1999). In this same vein of concreteness, Steven focused on objects still in his family's possession (i.e., white couch, big-screen TV). He worried that his family would keep his things, thus erasing him. During the final session, Steven admitted that he had experienced moments of wanting to intersperse intense hip-hop songs, such as Tupac Shakur's, that broke from his preference for ballads when he had spikes of anger, that he wanted to project outwards (Bion, 1958/1984; Grotstein, 1981). When Steven could no longer tolerate repressing his own anger he leaned into the vehicle of music, focused on such fiery topics as racial and socioeconomic inequalities and oppression. Listening to angry musical rants allowed him to participate in power and to construct a defense against the emotional chaos of his family.

A family-based approach would have been helpful to Steven's family, who had been so severely impacted by previous war traumas, substance abuse history, and Steven's illness. Family therapy might also have helped prevent relapse, which tends to be higher in unsupportive or stressful family environments (Carr, 2009; Kuipers, 2006).

Steven's case brings to mind the work of psychoanalyst Yrjo Alanen, in western Lapland, in Finland. In the 1970s and 1980s, Alanen and his colleagues focused on long-term treatment involving group family therapy, wherein the patient's case would be openly discussed with psychiatrists, psychologists, nurses, and family members, with the patient present and contributing (Whitaker, 2010). Alanen honored the patient's hallucinations and paranoid ideas as meaningful stories, which could be decoded by sensitive listeners (Alanen, 2009). The treatment model was designed to help patients build a new version of self-narrative to carry into the future. A similar treatment model, called open-dialogue therapy, was implemented and empirically measured by Jaakko Seikkula (2000, 2006) in Finland. His method involves family therapy, open dialogue, and minimal use of neuroleptics with early onset patients (Whitaker, 2010). Although recovery occurred at a slow pace, patients were able to return to their work, studies, and family. To return to a home that embraced him would have been rehabilitating for Steven.

KEVIN

Kevin walked into the music group wearing a pork pie hat. He was a 20-year-old mixed Caucasian and Cherokee male. He had been recently diagnosed with Bipolar Disorder and involuntarily hospitalized due to increased psychosis and suicidal ideation. Kevin had been hospitalized five times since the age of 18.

Kevin arrived at the hospital in a hyper-functional, albeit fragile, state. He acted out a fantasy that was a combination of martial arts master, hip-hop dancer, and Green Beret soldier. Mania and psychosis heightened his physical capabilities. He choreographed dance circles, with handstands and backflips, around other patients who struggled to stay awake.

Kevin was angry and paranoid about being detained against his will. He claimed super human special powers, such as manipulating kinetic energy. Once he realized magic could not undo legal detainment, he became cautious.

Kevin was first brought to an army hospital after making suicidal comments. His birth mother was a Master Sergeant in the army, soon to be stationed abroad. She had divorced Kevin's biological father when Kevin was ten. His biological father also had paranoia and PTSD (from Iraq). Kevin had a healthy mistrust of his mother who pretended to be a psychiatric nurse.

Kevin had lost weight and slept for weeks. He allegedly tried to burn his penis with a cigarette lighter because a brown recluse spider bit him and he wanted to draw the poison out. He had made physical threats to his parents and his little brother but had no history of suicide attempts or violent behavior.

Kevin had lived with an older girlfriend prior to hospitalization. The relationship ended with him reporting her to the police for fraud. He moved back in with his "smothering" parents, but dreamed of living with an artist aunt. Kevin had had four siblings, ranging in age from 15 to 30. His youngest brother was autistic. His maternal grandmother, a semi-retired college professor, sent a letter to the hospital reporting that Kevin's older siblings had run away from home as teens to live with her. She wrote about Kevin's mother: "I know my daughter has Borderline Personality Disorder. She causes chaos and conflict all around her. I'm worried that Kevin will take his own life and his mother's." Kevin described himself and his mother as sharing one unraveling mind. He said: "We're falling apart."

Initially, Kevin was manic and irritable, speaking in tangential, rambling, and nonsensical sentences. He told one staff member: "I could put you in a trance if I wanted. I see shadows and random spurts of gas pockets. I could make a tornado in here fast. I'm like an air bender." On his first few days on the unit he stated that he wanted to join the army to fight terrorists and to play football for the San Francisco 49ers.

Kevin was a classic example of early onset psychosis, in which a person's genetic vulnerability becomes exacerbated within the context of a dysfunctional family environment wherein communications are confusing and emotionally intense (Karon, 2003). He had then heightened his vulnerability to psychosis by experimenting with substances, beginning as a pre-adolescent (Malone, Hill, and Rubino, 2010). Kevin's case also seemed to carry elements of the type of intergenerational trauma that has been implicated in the etiology of psychotic disorders (Davoine and Gaudillière, 2004). His birth father had suffered from PTSD and his mother and stepfather each had been deployed to Iraq.

Kevin was bored in the hospital. He held himself aloof from everyone except young female patients. He agreed to be part of the music project as a distraction and as preparation for being a lead singer in an alternative band. "That's why I want to move to the city," he said. "Urban people are into music."

Kevin reported that he liked rappers such as T. I., DMX, Tupac Shakur, and Lil Wayne. He also listed his preferred bands: Cute is What We Aim For; Bad Light for Blue Eyes; From Autumn to Ashes; and As I Lie Dying. The predominant music Kevin selected could fit under the moniker "Emo," short for emotional music. This music typically expresses an outpouring of emotions associated with relationship break-ups or tragic events (Baker and Bor, 2008). In Emo music, the heart forever hurts and the ultra-ruminative songwriter pines for beautiful death (Sullivan, 2008). This music is the center of a popular youth subculture, featuring "overt demonstrations of emotions, feeling misunderstood" (Scott and Chur-Hansen, 2008). In the United Kingdom, studies have shown that Emo youth who listen to opera, heavy metal, industrial metal, punk, techno, and trance music and who glamorize suffering and death have increased attempts at deliberate self-harm and suicide (Baker and Bor, 2008).

One Emo band, Scary Kids Scaring Kids, consists of several young men, approximately Kevin's age, who became famous overnight singing emotionally charged love songs. Kevin held similar fantasies about sudden fame and romance. The band's lyrics expressed Kevin's lament for being locked up in the psychiatric hospital and his despair about childhood neglect.

I downloaded a few selections from each of Kevin's band choices. The metal music helped him to remain calm. "It's what I want here where it's like a jail," he said. He craved heavy metal after his mother visited or after speaking with her on the phone. "She gets so intense and controlling," he said. Kevin paced around while "Time" (Hackikyan and MacLean, 2008, Track 1) a Cute Is What We Aim For song played. "I could do this kind of thing, if I had the right studio," he said.

Kevin was manic at the third session. He thumbed through pages of his Bible. "I have this charisma," Kevin said. "People say I'm like Jim Morrison when my hair is long." He mimicked Jim Morrison, holding a microphone, then stood with arms outstretched like Jesus.

"Wherever I go," he said, "I'm the scene. I'm a musician. I wear tight pants. Other kids can imitate me. Younger kids want to be me." Developing a grandiose persona to magnify his true charisma and creative talent was part of Kevin's defense against being swallowed by the chaos of his childhood.

At the next session Kevin selected T. I., a hip-hop performer who had been described as "tightly wound, tense and somewhat paranoid, even in his most dynamic songs" (Carmanica, 2008, online). Kevin stood up to demonstrate his affinity with TI. "This is about dancing in the pit," he said, "but it's also called agro dancing. It's about fighting while you dance. You throw punches to the middle." He showed me how he used his elbows and feet to kick out to the beat of the music.

Kevin was in debate with his parents about where he would go after discharging from the hospital. He wanted to live with his aunt. His mother wanted him home, where she could monitor him. Kevin had increasing ineffable feelings of frustration and anger. He continued to let music express emotions for him, heavy metal music and Lil Wayne's "Drop the World" (Carter, 2009, Track 8).

Kevin wasn't sure if he could tolerate his parents visiting often, he considered asking them to back off. Popular music helped him with unsettling emotions, which seemed to worsen after his parents left. Kevin chose Michael Jackson's "Beat It" (Jackson, 1983, Track 5). He described fantasy images of himself performing on guitar, or singing and dancing with a backup band.

At the ninth session, Kevin told me that he was smarter than all of the hospital staff, doctors included. He said he wanted to hear a handful of songs on repeat. He first selected "I Will Follow You into the Dark," (Gibbard, 2006, Track 1), followed by Evanescence "Together Again" (Lee, 2010, Track 1), and "Watch Me Bleed" (Scary Kids Scaring Kids, 2007, Track 12). Kevin repeated the sequence twice.

Although "I Will Follow You into the Dark" (Gibbard, 2006, Track 1) has not been classified as Emo music, it shares common expressive characteristics. This is the kind of song a young person with a history of betrayals, confusions, and misattunements could identify with. It meets an abiding need to believe in a love that transcends physical and temporal obstacles.

In a review in the *New York Times* Sanneh (2005) referred to Death Cab for Cutie's songs as delicious and melancholy. "I Will Follow You into the Dark (Gibbard, 2006, Track 1) described an ideal world where love was an abiding force, and wherein someone might walk into the darkest place to find Kevin, as Searles (1979) suggested is the same psychological place where a clinician might find and best connect with patients.

Toward one of the later sessions, Kevin asked me what I would do for a job if mental illness didn't exist any longer. "You should think about that," he said. "My generation might decide all of this is just crap."

His warning was simultaneously an empty threat and a brief, brilliant vision. Kevin alternately masked and showed his tenderness, revealing a need for voice, nurturing, and structure. Kevin had a strong connection to music. He also had a difficult time tolerating the intimacy of listening to music with another person, within the repressive hospital environment.

For Kevin, the act of sitting still, listening to music together with me was precarious. His music selections were meant to express identity, not to be decoded, just as Kevin himself wanted to be experienced but not analyzed. His communications were more manic and anthem-like, allowing Kevin to wear the expert's mantle.

At the start of the tenth session, Kevin was calmer. He asked to bring the hospital guitar into the session. He played progressions of bar chords. "I'm not good with other people's music yet," he said. "I'm better when I'm playing my own." Kevin recited a fantasy about hitchhiking across the United States with his guitar. "I could pay my way by playing in coffee shops," he said. "I'd just like to get away from people who want to control my life." He described his older brothers and sisters running away: "I always felt like they were jumping from a sinking ship."

He put the guitar down on the tabletop and reached for the iPod. "I feel like listening to something different," he said. "Do you have any really good guitar songs?" I selected a song by Eric Clapton, which Kevin nodded that he liked.

Kevin had a concrete awareness of how music helped him to navigate the emotional landscape of his world and relationships. His "agro dancing" in the mosh pit seemed to symbolize a wish to establish, even violently if necessary, boundaries with his mother and with me so that he could make a space within which to move. He could articulate that he craved heavy metal music after seeing his mother, and he could state his affinity for the intense driving rhythms of Nigel Kennedy's violin pressing Vivaldi's "The Four Seasons" (Vivaldi, 1723, Track 1). Kennedy's playing matched the anger he felt inside but he could not yet allow his rage and urgency to be expressed through him.

The final song that Kevin selected, and which represented the more rebellious, angrier aspects of his identity, was T. I. singing "Whatever You Like" (T.I., 2008, Track 6). Kevin's attraction to T. I.'s music, as well as his heavy metal preferences, could allow for an exploration of the conflict within him between dependence and independence.

Kevin might have benefited from further exploration of his expressive talents, especially musical talents, in a therapeutic space. He was ready to explore his own music, but he was simultaneously locked in a kind of *Folie à Deux* with his mother. He was cautious about repeating that patterned enmeshment.

CONCLUSION

A psychiatric hospital is an effective and essential resource for addressing acute and critical psychological states. At the same time, it is not the ideal holding environment (Winnicott, 1971) or psychosocial environment (Kegan, 1982), wherein young people such as Kevin, Steven or Lyaconnia could rehabilitate effectively. Kevin perceived the hospital as secure but not psychologically safe. He found relief from suffering but he could not sufficiently trust hospital staff to embrace treatment. I believe that a clinical professional working with these three young people, using music or another safe portal of communication, would need to establish a meaningful connection to help them to resolve shame and trauma from childhood and inherited generational traumas, as well as the social failures they were experiencing in adulthood (Anastasi, 2005; Pollack and Reuter, 2007).

REFERENCES

Alanen, Y. (2009, September 7). Interview with Yrjo Alanen, Jukka Aaltonen, Viljo Rakkolainen. (R. Whitaker, Interviewer). Turku, Lapland, Finland: Crown.

Anastasi, A. (2005). Adolescent boys' use of Emo music as their healing lament. *Journal of Religion and Health, 44*(3), 303–319.

Arlen, H., and Harburg, E.Y. (1939). Somewhere over the rainbow. [Recorded by I. Kamakawiwo'ole and J. D. Mello, Conductor] On *Facing future* [CD]. Honolulu, HI: Mountain Apple. (1987).

Bacharach, B., and David, H. (1963). They long to be close to you. [Recorded by The Carpenters]. On *Close to you* [CD]. Los Angeles: A and M. (1970)

Baker, F., and Bor, W. (2008). Can music preference indicate mental health status in young people? *Australasian Psychiatry, 16*(4), 284–288. doi:10.1080/10398560701879589

Benedetti, G. (1999). Interpretation of schizophrenia. *Journal of the American Academy of Psychoanalysis, 27*(4), 551–562.

Bion, W. R. (1967). *Second thoughts*. London: William Heinemann.

Bion, W. R. (1984). *Learning from experience*. London: Karnac.

Bion, W. R. (1992). *Cogitations*. London: Karnac.

Bleich-Cohen, M., Hendler, T., Kotler, M., and Strous, R. (2009). Reduced language lateralization in first-episode schizophrenia: An fMRI index of functional asymmetry. *Psychiatry Research: Neuroimaging Section, 171*(2), 82–93.

Bruni, F. (1997, November 25). Going her own way, but slowly this time. *The New York Times* . Retrieved from http://www.nytimes.com

Carmanica, J. (2008, October 1). Facing time with plenty of swagger. *The New York Times*. Retrieved from http://www.nytimes.com

Carr, A. (2009). The effectiveness of family therapy and systemic interventions for adult-focused problems. *Journal of Family Therapy, 31*(1), 46–74.

Carter, D.M. (2009). Drop The world. [Recorded by Lil Wayne]. On *Rebirth* [Digital download]. New York: Cash Money Records.

Charles, M. (2002). *Patterns: Building blocks of experience.* Hillsdale, NJ: The Analytic Press.

Cohen, L. (1975). Suzanne. On *The best of Leonard Cohen* [CD]. New York: Columbia. (1967)

Cohen, L. (1975). Bird on A wire. On *The Best of Leonard Cohen* [CD]. New York: Columbia.

Cuijpers, P., and Langendoen, Y., and Bijl, R. V. (1999). Psychiatric disorders in adult children of problem drinkers: Prevalence, first onset. *Addiction, 94*(10), 1489–1498.

Danieli, Y. (1985). The treatment and prevention of long-term effects and intergenerational transmission of victimization: A lesson from Holocaust survivors and their children. In C. Figley (Ed.), *Trauma and its wake*. New York: Brunner/Mazel.

Davoine, F., and Gaudillière, J. M. (2004). *History beyond trauma*. (S. Fairfield, Trans.) New York: Other Press.

Delilah. (2010). Retrieved November 18, 2010, from http://www.Delilah.com/pages/about.html.

Delilah. (2014, January 10). *Delilah*. Retrieved January 31, 2014 from http:// http://www.premiereradio.com/shows/view/delilah.html.

Gibbard, B. (2006). I will follow you into the dark. [Recorded by Death Cab for Cutie]. On *Plans* [Digital download]. North Brookfield, MA: Atlantic.

Greenfield, S. F., Swartz, M., Landerman, L., and George, L. (1993). Long-term psychosocial effects of childhood exposure to parental problem drinking. *American Journal of Psychiatry, 150*(4), 608.

Grotstein, J. (1977). The psychoanalytic concept of schizophrenia: I. The dilemma. *International Journal of Psycho-Analysis, 58*, 403–425.

Grotstein, J.S. (1981). *Splitting and projective identification*. Lanham, MD: Jason Aronson.

Grotstein, J. (1995). Orphans of the "Real": I. Some modern and postmodern perspectives on the neurobiological and psychosocial dimensions of psychosis and other primitive mental disorders. *Bulletin of the Menninger Clinic, 59*(3), 287–311.

Grotstein, J.S. (2007). *A beam of intense darkness*. London, UK: Karnac.

Hackikyan, S., and MacLean, P. (2008). Time. [Recorded by Cute is What We Aim For]. On *Rotation* [Digital download]. Los Angeles, CA: Fueled by Ramen.

Harada, W. (2010, November 18). A late night for recording rainbow. *The Honolulu Advertiser*. Retrieved January 3, 2014 from http://iz.honoluluadvertiser.com

Hooley, J.M., and Campbell, C. (2002). Control and controllability: Beliefs and behavior in high expressed emotion relatives. *Psychological Medicine, 32*, 1091–1099.

Hooley, J.M., and Gotlib, I. H. (2000). A diathesis-stress conceptualization of expressed emotion and clinical outcome. *Applied and Preventive Psychology, 9*, 135–151.

Jackson, M. (1983). Beat it. On *Thriller* [Digital download]. Los Angeles, CA: EPIC.

Jones, C. (2006, December 18). The stuff of dreams: Karen Carpenter's voice. *The Chicago Tribune*. Retrieved April 11, 2010, from http://www.richardandkaren carpenter.com

Karon, B.P. (2003). The tragedy of schizophrenia without psychotherapy. *Journal of the American Academy of Psychoanalysis, 31*(1), 89–118.

Kegan, R. (1982). *The evolving self: Problem and process in human development*. Cambridge, MA: Harvard University Press.

Kingdon, D. G., and Turkington, D. (2005). *Cognitive psychotherapy of schizophrenia*. New York: Guilford.

Kinzie, D. (1985). Overview of clinical issues in the treatment of Southeast Asian refugees. In T. C. Owen (Ed.), *Southeast Asian mental health*. Washington, DC: National Institute of Mental Health.

Klein, M. (1986c). Notes on some schizoid mechanisms. In J. Mitchell (Ed.), *The selected Melanie Klein* (pp. 175–200). New York: The Free Press. (Original work published 1946)

Knoblauch, S.H. (2005). Body rhythms and the unconscious: Toward an expanding of clinical attention. *Psychoanalytic Dialogues, 15*(6), 807–827.

Krugman, S. (1987). Trauma in the family: Perspectives on the intergenerational transmission of violence. In B. van der Kolk (Ed.), *Psychological Trauma*. Washington, DC: American Psychiatric Press.

Kuipers, E. (2006). Family intervention in schizophrenia: Evidence for efficacy and proposed mechanisms of change. *Journal of Family Therapy, 28*(1), 73–80.

Lee, A. (2010). Together again. [Recorded by Evanescence]. On *United Nations: Haiti earthquake relief* [Digital download]. New York: Wind-Up Records.

Lewis, L. (2004). Mourning, insight, and reduction of suicide risk in schizophrenia. *Bulletin of the Menninger Clinic, 68*(3), 231–244.

Malone, D.T., Hill, M.N., and Rubino, T. (2010). Adolescent cannabis use and psychosis: Epidemiology and neurodevelopmental models. *British Journal of Pharmacology, 160*, 511–522.

Masataka, N. (2006). Preference for consonance over dissonance by hearing newborns of deaf parents and of hearing parents. *Developmental Science, 9*(1), 46–50.

Mathew, R.J., Wilson, W.H., Blazer, D.G., and George, L.K. (1993). Psychiatric disorders in adult children of alcoholics: Data from the epidemiologic catchment area project. *The American Journal of Psychiatry, 150*(5), 793–800.

McDougall, J. (1989). *Theaters of the body*. New York: Norton.

McGorry, P.D., and Yung, A.R. (2003). Early intervention in psychosis: An overdue reform. *Australian and New Zealand Journal of Psychiatry, 37*, 393–398.

McKenzie-Pollock, L. (1996). Cambodian families. In M. McGoldrick, J. Giordano, and J. Pearce (Eds.), *Ethnicity and family therapy* (pp. 307–315). New York: The Guilford Press.

Mollica, R.F., Wyshak, G., and Lavelle, J. (1987). The psychosocial impact of war trauma and torture on Southeast Asian refugees. *The American Journal of Psychiatry, 144*(12), 1567–1572.

Morrison, A.P., Frame, L., and Larkin, W. (2003). Relationships between trauma and psychosis: A review and integration. *British Journal of Clinical Psychology, 42*(4), 331–353.

Nakata, T., and Trehub, S.E. (2004). Infants' responsiveness to maternal speech and singing. *Infant Behavior and Development, 27*(4), 455–464.

Nicks, S. (1975). Landslide. [Recorded by Fleetwood Mac]. On *Fleetwood Mac* [CD]. Los Angeles, CA: Warner Bros.

Patel, A.D. (2008). *Music, language and the brain*. New York: Oxford University Press.

Pollack, H.A., and Reuter, P. (2007). The implications of recent findings on the link between cannabis and psychosis. *Addiction, 102*(2), 173–176.

Read, J., Mosher, L., and Bentall, R.P. (2004). *Models of madness: Psychological, social biological approaches to schizophrenia*. London: Brunner-Rutledge

Rousseau, C., Drapeau, A., and Platt, R. (1999). Family trauma and its association with emotional and behavioral problems and social adjustment in adolescent Cambodian refuges. *Child Abuse and Neglect, 23*(12), 1263-1273.

Sacks, O. (2007). *Musicophilia: Tales of music and the brain*. New York: Alfred A. Knopf.

Sanneh, K. (2005, August 28). Music: Nothing is certain but death and taxis. *The New York Times*, p. 22. Retrieved April 11, 2011 from http://www.nytimes.com/2005/ /08/28/arts/music/28sann.

Scary Kids Scaring Kids. (2007). Watch me bleed. On *Scary kids scaring kids* [Digital download]. Los Angeles, CA: Immortal

Schneck D.J., and Berger D.S. (2006). *The music effect: Musical physiology and clinical applications*. Great Britain: Atheneaeum Press.

Scott, L., and Chur-Hansen, A. (2008) The mental health literacy of rural adolescents: Emo subculture and SMS texting. *Australasian Psychiatry, 16*(5), 359–362

Shakur, T.A. (1996). All about u. [Recorded by T. Shakur, N. Dogg, and S. Dogg]. On *All eyez on me* [Digital download]. Los Angeles, CA: Death Row Records.

Searles, H.F. (1979). *Countertransference and related subjects*. New York: International Universities Press, Inc.

Seikkula, J. (2000). A two-year follow-up on open dialogue treatment in first episode pscyhosis. *Society of Clinical Psychology, 10*, 20–29.

Seikkula, J. (2006). Five year experience of first-episode nonaffective psychosis in open-dialogue aproach. *Psychotherapy Research, 16*, 214–228.

Simon, P., Garfunkel, A., and Halee, R. (1970). Bridge over troubled water. On *Bridge over troubled water* [Digital download]. New York: Columbia.

Sullivan, R. (2008). Hearts of darkness. *Architectural Digest*, 78–81.

T. I. (2008). Whatever you like. On *Paper trail* [Digital download]. Detroit, MI: Grand Hustle/Atlantic.

Tait, L., Birchwood, M., and Trower, P. (2003). Predicting engagement with services for psychosis: Insight, symptoms, and recovery style. *The British Journal of Psychiatry, 182*(2), 123–128.

Trainor, L.J., Tsang, C.D., and Cheung, V.W. (2002). Preference for sensory consonance in 2- and 4-month-old infants. *Music Perception, 20*(2), 187.

Trehub, S. (2000) Human processing predispositions and musical universals. In N. L. Wallin, B. Merker, and S. Brown (Eds.), *The origins of music* (pp. 427–448). E. Cambridge: Massachusetts Institute of Technology.

Trehub, S. (2003). The developmental origins of musicality. *Nature Neuroscience, 6*(7), 669.

Vivaldi, A. (1723). Concerto no. 1 in E. major: La Primavera, RV 269: III Allegro. [Recorded by N. Kennedy]. On *Vivaldi: The four seasons* [CD]. London, UK: EMI Records, Ltd.

Waska, R. (2003). Fragmented attachments: The paranoid-schizoid position of loss and persecution. *Bulletin of the Menninger Clinic, 67*(1), 50–64.

Whitaker, R. (2010). *Anatomy of an epidemic.* New York: Crown.

Winnicott, D.W. (1971). *Playing and reality*. London: Routledge.

Wittmann, D., and Keshavan, M. (2007). Grief and mourning in schizophrenia. *Psychiatry: Interpersonal and Biological Processes, 70* (2),154–166.

TEN

A Good Little Group

Recovering Lost Connections between Aboriginal Mothers and Infants

Cate Osborn[1]

So long as the past and present are outside one another, knowledge of the past is not of much use in the problems of the present.
—R.G. Collingwood (1939/2002)

In Australia there is a rupture between the truth about our colonial past and our present beliefs about our history and identity. The veracity of events such as massacres, frontier wars and the plight of the children of the Stolen Generations[2] is, even now, bitterly contested. The extent to which we are haunted by past events remains largely outside our consciousness. The true depth of the impact of dispossession, violence, loss of culture and separation from family on the lives of Aboriginal people, then and now, is largely unacknowledged. This is a traumatic legacy for both Aboriginal and non-Aboriginal Australians. We have not been able to come to terms with the cruel acts perpetrated by our recent ancestors. Instead, via a range of psychological and cultural devices, we have turned away from the reality and replaced it with a picture of heroism, benign "settlement" of "unclaimed" land, brave battles with the forces of nature, the "convict made good" and success against all odds. Our knowledge of the past remains unintegrated with our feelings about it. In this very important and fundamental way, we are unknowing.

Australian Aboriginal mothers and thus, also their children, are disadvantaged in a number of serious ways. Babies born to Aboriginal mothers are twice as likely as babies born to non-Indigenous mothers to be of a low birth weight. The Aboriginal infant mortality rate is twice that of non-Aboriginal infants. In 2006, nearly half of all Aboriginal children were living in jobless families and 45% of Aboriginal children were living in single-parent families. Added to this are the disproportionately high rates of imprisonment, suicide and hospitalizations for chronic disease. Along with these inequities in relation to physical and social health, are those impacting on mental health and the safety of children. The rate of hospitalization of Aboriginal people for mental health problems is nearly twice that of other Australians. In addition, in 2008–09, the rate of substantiated child protection notifications for Aboriginal children was close to eight times the rate of other children. (Australian Institute of Health and Welfare, 2011). These last two items, in particular, point to generational transmission of deprivation and trauma.

My aim in this chapter is to examine the traumas and difficulties (particularly the internal difficulties) that Aboriginal women are facing today. I will argue that it is the forgotten and unprocessed nature of this trauma that causes it to be passed on in largely unconscious ways, such that Aboriginal women are reliving, through their babies and young children, the experiences of their own pasts. I will describe the work of a mothers' group, designed around psychoanalytic principles, that was established in order to provide a space for women to develop healthier relationships with themselves and their children.

Traumatic experiences are unspoken, felt to be unspeakable, due to the destruction of the very psychic and cultural mechanisms needed to mitigate them. They weigh heavily on the hearts and minds of the women in ways that cannot always be known to them. Using clinical material from the group, I will show how these experiences are, nevertheless, communicated powerfully via projective identification and are, of necessity, received and held by the facilitator in the counter-transference. These communications illuminate some of the hidden traumatic experiences of the group members. I hope to demonstrate that the use of the psychoanalytic framework is a way of helping the women to build their capacity as mothers, as distinct from work that might take a more psycho-educational or didactic approach to the development of parenting skills.

THE MOTHERS' GROUP

The Mothers' Group is part of the Young Aboriginal Mothers Project at Gunawirra,[3] based in Redfern, Sydney. It is an early intervention service for Aboriginal mothers, their babies and pre-school children. The Project also offers psychoanalytic psychotherapy and social work services. The group is long term and open, with some members leaving and new members joining regularly. A "core" group has continued to attend since the beginning of the project eighteen months ago. There is a broad membership of fourteen women, with six to ten attending any given session. We meet weekly for three hours in the middle of the day and, along with the therapist, there are usually one or two volunteers and trainee social workers assisting. Other professionals attend on a sessional basis, depending on the activity that the group engages in. As the manager and senior therapist for the Project, my role is to coordinate the activities, facilitate group interactions and ensure that a therapeutic space is held. Through careful attention to both overt and unconscious communications within the group, I attempt to help the women put their feelings and actions into words and, thus, give them shape and meaning.

The group was born out of a wish expressed by a young Aboriginal mother known to us when she asked if there could be a type of "playgroup" that focused on meeting the needs of the mothers. She said, "there are lots of playgroups around for the kids, but what about the mothers?" Fractured families, poverty and dislocation, substance abuse and mental health problems often mean that there is no actual or perceived safe place for the women to seek the background support that all new mothers need. Fathers are absent, members of the extended family are dispersed or estranged, and much of the "mothering wisdom" has disintegrated.

On first meeting with the women, we asked them what they would want from such a group. Their responses were muted and they seemed to need a lot of support to even think that they had things like needs and interests that somebody might want to know about and respond to, let alone how some of these needs might be met. This was my first direct experience of the true depth of trauma and deprivation in the group and the inhibition (felt as *pro*hibition) of self-expression. Nevertheless, we managed to put together a program that included activities such as infant massage, cooking, art, ceramics, photography and music. Gradually a structure evolved whereby half the time is spent on any one activity, while the remainder is spent on sharing a meal and talking. The decision to provide activities was a deliberate one. It was felt that, without them, there would be too much openness that the women would find very difficult to tolerate. Where some groups might welcome a completely open agenda as an opportunity for exploration, experience told us that, where there is deep trauma, the openness becomes a terrifying emptiness or an unbounded space. Group members then feel overburdened by a perceived expectation that they must fill the space.

The center in Redfern, Sydney, provides a warm and containing atmosphere. The group room is furnished with comfortable couches and pillows. There are books and toys for the children and a courtyard area for them to play. The kitchen is adjacent and there is a space set up for painting and ceramics.

The program is not group therapy in the traditional sense. However, my role as facilitator is to find opportunities among the multitude of interactions to intervene in a therapeutic way. The aim is to help the group members forge links with the unknown and conflicted parts of themselves, with each other and with their children. The image of a "playgroup for mothers" stuck in my mind. I wondered if we could create a space where the women could begin to play with ideas of their own and that, along with the cooking and eating, there might be some "food for thought."

Comments and interpretations focus on the here-and-now interactions between the mothers and their children, each other, and within the transference. Sometimes it is possible to link these to earlier, unresolved conflicts. Care is taken to highlight and amplify healthy interactions, developments and success, helping to build up ego-strengths. Continuity and reliability are vital for the group and any perceived threat to this (e.g., a break) is felt as devastating. In describing work with very deprived patients, Winnicott (1965/1990) states that the patient may find this reliability in the analyst for the first time in his or her life and, in the early stages, this can be more important than interpretations. The group members have required a long period of reliability before they could find the courage to bring their concerns and worries forward more openly.

Frequently, situations arise within the group where it seems that the needs or wishes of the mother are in competition with the needs of the baby. This can create a great deal of pressure to intervene in an instructive way. Such an intervention might interrupt the current difficulty but does little to address what is usually a very deep and chronic state. I have found that focusing on the mother-baby relationship and/or the-baby-in-the-mother can provide a way through this dilemma.

From the very beginning of the program I was aware of powerful and, at times, unsettling and disorienting feelings. I knew from my experience as a therapist that I would need to hold negative projections and felt reasonably familiar and confident with this. However, I was unprepared for their rawness and intensity.

Initially, I was concerned that I would be seen by the group as yet another "colonizer," with a "superior" culture and knowledge. I worried that I would be unable to connect with the women when our worlds seemed so different. I understood this concern as both an echo of guilt in myself about our colonial past and a communication from the group related to their terror of making connections. The group has followed a developmental trajectory analogous to the growth and development of a baby, although it has not been a smooth path. During the early months, the transference was idealized and highly dependent. I decided not to interfere with this, believing that it was a necessary developmental step. "The presence in the mind of the good (ideal) object enables the ego to maintain at times strong feelings of love and gratification. The good object also affords protection against the persecuting object because it is felt to have replaced it" (Klein, 1975/1997, pp. 70–71). During this time I was aware of feeling overburdened and responsible, as well as, at times, experiencing feelings of warmth, protectiveness and pride. However, it wasn't long before the worm turned with the inevitable obstacles and frustrations. Initially, dissatisfaction, anger and hatred were expressed passively and in disguised form, for example, as complaints about meals or cold cups of tea. I experienced feelings of failure, emptiness and futility and there was, at times, an atmosphere of seething resentment. I understood this to be a communication about early experiences of deprivation and hunger that are expressed in the present as apparent greed and over-entitlement. Occasionally it was possible to put some of this into words, and gradually the women have become more open about their angry feelings, particularly about breaks.

A Very Vulnerable Time

It is well understood that a mother's circumstances and state(s) of mind during the early months and years of her child's life can have a profound effect on the ongoing development of her child. It could be said that there is an interface between the mother's emotional life (both conscious and unconscious) and the baby's needs, strivings, passions and fears out of which the child's personality begins to develop. Winnicott said that "(t)he infant and the maternal care together form a unit (and) . . .at the earliest stages the infant and the maternal care belong to each other and cannot be disentangled" (1965/1990, pp. 39–40). In thinking about the environment in which a baby develops, that environment must include the mother's mind.

Pregnancy and the early post-partum period bring enormous upheaval for the mother. There are the bodily changes and hormonal surges to adapt to. Some women may welcome these changes with pride in their body's ability to produce new life and as an affirmation of their sexuality and creativity. Others begin to feel that their body is not their own, that something is happening inside them that is now beyond their control. This is a particular sensitivity for women who have experienced sexual abuse or for whom the pregnancy has not been a conscious choice. The physical changes can prompt fears and fantasies about bodily integrity, body image and being attacked from inside. One woman in the group "hated getting fat" as the pregnancy progressed. (In fact she remained worryingly underweight throughout the pregnancy.) Another suffered severe morning sickness and had to be hospitalized several times during the pregnancy. She described herself as being "allergic" to the baby. Alongside the physical adjustments are the tremendous psychic shifts in identity and the reviving of the emotional conflicts and anxieties of past developmental stages.

Dinora Pines (1972) emphasizes that these upheavals are an expected and necessary part of the process whereby a woman comes to terms with the paradox that the developing baby is both an extension of herself physically and psychically and, at the same time, a separate individual with ongoing needs.

> One of the most impressive features to be observed. . . is the re-emergence of previously repressed fantasies into pre-conscious and consciousness—and their fate once the reality of the newborn baby has been established. These uneasy conflicts belonging to past developmental stages are revived, as is the case in any crisis point in life. . . (Pines, p. 333)

She goes on later to state that

> (t)he task a woman has to accomplish in pregnancy and motherhood is to integrate reality with unconscious fantasy, hopes and daydreams. She has, in addition, for the first time to meet the demands of a helpless dependent creature who represents strongly cathected areas of self and non-self, and many past conflictual relationships. (p. 342)

This hard psychological work is, ideally, carried out against a background of external support and security and relative internal confidence, trust and ego strength. It can bring opportunities for emotional growth and maturity but, for many of the women in the group, the backdrop is one of violence, poverty and isolation. Their early lives were frequently compromised by inadequate parenting, emotional and physical abuse, familial substance abuse and mental illness, racism in many forms, separation from parents, poor education and geographical dislocation. The revived conflicts and anxieties in pregnancy and early motherhood can be deeply traumatising and overwhelming, leaving both mother and child vulnerable. There is a heightened risk of insecure or disorganized attachment (Fonagy, 1999). A woman who has been deprived of adequate nurturing experiences will have little to call on in nurturing her own baby. The extreme helplessness and urgent demands of a new baby can reawaken the unmet dependency needs of the mother, leading to depression and rage. Many of the women have uneasy relationships with their own mothers and feel they have no positive figure with whom to identify. Significantly, they have all communicated the belief that they are perceived as inadequate parents and are subject to scrutiny and criticism. Internal and external doubts about their capacities and potentials undermine their very fragile sense of confidence and faith in themselves.

TRAUMA

One of the tragedies of severe and prolonged trauma is that it damages (and sometimes destroys) the very psychological and cultural mechanisms needed to mitigate it. All of us experience trauma to varying degrees throughout our lives where our sense of safety, security and meaning are ruptured by a physical or emotional catastrophe. Our usual ways of coping are lost to us. Everything we have known, trusted and believed in has been turned upside-down. Hopefully, following a period of crisis, disorientation and breakdown, there is some sort of recovery. Often, this recovery needs to be done with the help of family, friends or professionals and may take a long time. If the intensity of the trauma recedes and the victim is able to work through and make some sense of what has happened, then there can be a readjustment, an accommodation to what has happened, and the re-establishment of at least some trust in the world. However, when trauma is severe, pervasive and occurs early in life, the mind and personality can be so attacked and mutilated that the more ordinary process of recovery cannot take place.

In infancy and childhood, trauma can result from what Shengold (1991) calls too much *too muchness* or *too much not enoughness*. *Too muchness* means that the child has had to experience more than he or she can bear. This can take the form of physical, sexual or emotional abuse. *Not enoughness* means that the child is deprived of the care—physical and/or emotional—that is needed for his or her development. Deprivation and neglect aren't experienced only as a lack or an emptiness, but take on an active and persecuting presence. To a small baby, unrelieved hunger that goes on for too long can feel like a hostile, life-threatening internal attacker. In healthy enough circumstances the mother or caregiver is able to reflect on the baby's state of mind when distressed, imagine what the too much or not enough is, and respond accordingly, ameliorating the potential trauma. In Bion's terms, the mother takes in the baby's projected inchoate anxieties (beta elements) and, through thought and reflection (alpha function), transforms them into digestible pieces, thereby giving them meaning and making them bearable. This process of *containment* facilitates the beginning of thought in the baby and the process by which frightening sensations and emotions become bearable (Bion, 1962). It relies on the mother's capacity to tolerate the intensity of the baby's projections, her *desire to know* the source of the distress, and her capacity to imagine herself into the baby's experience. In Bion's model the baby not only takes in the comfort the mother provides. Through identifying with her, he or she introjects this process and begins to develop a mind that can think, dream, imagine, symbolize and discriminate between different states of being. I will give an account of the consequences of the breakdown of this vital process with an example from an early group session.

FIRST CLINICAL VIGNETTE

Anne is the mother of an eight-week-old girl and has come to the attention of child protection authorities due to her history of substance abuse and concerns that the baby is not putting on weight. Her partner is in prison and she lives with her mother with whom she has a very conflicted relationship. The little girl has been diagnosed as having "failure to thrive." Several years ago Anne had a little boy who died of SIDS and her oldest daughter is in the care of her grandmother. Many levels of support and treatment have been provided, as the pair is seen as being seriously at risk. As well as attending the group, Anne sees a psychotherapist at the Centre and is visited regularly at home by health workers. The baby needed a feed and Anne's breast milk supply is low so she is supplementing with bottle feeds. As she gave the baby the bottle, I saw that Anne had her knees slightly apart, so that the little bottom of the baby lying across her lap dipped down between them. The baby's neck was arched back and her head unsupported. Anne was not looking at the baby at all and she had a faraway, blank look on her face. I felt more alarmed as I noticed that the baby was not protesting at all, no struggle, no cry, just weak little sucks on the bottle. There was an urgent need to intervene but I was concerned that Anne could very easily feel criticized and undermined. I felt that I was watching a disaster unfold and was close to becoming a "failure to thrive" as a therapist. I simply said that I could see she was in another world and I wondered where she was. She didn't answer me but she did look at the baby and draw her knees together to make a safer lap. A little later I noticed her holding the baby firmly and protectively and making eye contact. I took this opportunity and said, "she looks very comfortable with you holding her like that." This time, Anne responded with a smile and continued to hold the baby lovingly.

The baby had already experienced too much *not enoughness* (specifically, not enough milk or firm holding and connection with her mother) and, overwhelmed by unthinkable anxieties (Winnicott, 1965/1990) or presymbolic dread (Mollon, 1998), had given up. One of the striking features of this interaction was that Anne *appeared* to have no concern or awareness for the baby's needs and I (along with my colleagues) held all the worry. At this time, she was not able to approach awareness of her own failure to thrive as a mother, nor her own early deprivation. She could not let herself imagine her baby's state of mind as this would have put her dangerously in touch with her own experiences. Having already lost two children, she was terrified of connecting to another.

Some weeks later, the group was discussing breast-feeding. There was talk about the importance of it for bonding and the health benefits for the baby. At this time, approximately half the group were breast-feeding their babies. There was some genuine acknowledgement and valuing of the breast-feeding relationship, but many of the comments were clichéd and glib, as if they knew what they were supposed to say and what I wanted to hear. I wondered with the group what it was like when breast-feeding didn't work out. I commented that it didn't always flow naturally and could be quite difficult. Some spoke of their disappointment, even a feeling of failure. There was acknowledgement from the group that "stress" can impact on breast-feeding but that sometimes it's hard not to worry. Anne said she was disappointed but at least she was breast-feeding some of the time. She then spoke with some anger about being "forced" to have a caesarean delivery and being "robbed" of the chance of a normal delivery. I wondered how much this persecuted state was connected to the feeding and attachment problems. Anne later showed me how she kept a record of how often and for how long her baby fed, as her health worker had showed her to do. This indicated that she now felt a little more able to touch on the reality of her situation with her baby.

ACROSS THE GENERATIONS

In her book *Trauma Trails,* Judy Atkinson (2002) describes the initial impact of colonization on Indigenous people and the ways that the repercussions of this have rippled outwards and downwards through the generations from the point of impact. She describes a collision of cultures and gives detailed accounts of the trauma experienced by individuals and, more widely, across whole communities. She shows that colonization and subsequent policies and practices have dismantled the vital relationship to land, traditional ceremony and ritual, and the rules and mores that mediate the relationships between people. Atkinson makes a case for the particular tragedy of collective or communal trauma as distinct from individual trauma. ". . .it has distinct and, in many cases, longer-lasting repercussions. It seeps slowly and insidiously into the fabric and soul of relations and beliefs of people as community" (Atkinson p. 53). Identity and one's place in the world are destroyed and replaced with shame. The traumatized individual then has no recourse to a healthy and intact community and the trauma is compounded.

Some of the women in the group are aware, at least to some degree, of the extent to which their lives have been affected by family histories that encompass domestic violence, separation from parents, mental illness and substance abuse. Lianne told the group about her daughters' father, his violence, and her decision to leave him. She said that her own father was violent and that she and her mother and sisters lived in fear. She said, "I don't want that for my girls. They're worth more than that." Hannah spoke about her fractured family life. Throughout their childhood she and her siblings were moved in and out of foster care as her mother struggled to deal with drug addiction. She said, "I remember what it was like. My whole family is fucked up. I'm not going to let that happen to him" (her son). There is an acknowledgement, within themselves, of their suffering as children and a determination that their own children not be afflicted. Pregnancy and motherhood can become the impetus for repair and a measure of healing.

For others in the group, the true nature of their plight as children is not recognized and they have only a dim awareness of the impact of their past. They may deal with past trauma through minimizing its seriousness—"everybody has problems," or even idealizing the experiences—"what doesn't kill you makes you stronger." Memories of events may be impaired. Where events are recalled, the associated feelings may be repressed or split off. In these circumstances, the women struggle to provide protection for their own children from the re-enactment of past deprivation and abuse.

Fraiberg, Adelson and Shapiro (1975), in their seminal paper "Ghosts in the Nursery," describe the ghosts of unremembered and unprocessed trauma in the parent's past and the multitude of ways that these can be unconsciously passed on to the infant and, ultimately, down the generations. In detailing their work with traumatized young parents and their at-risk infants, they conclude that where the child deals with the trauma by identifying with the aggressor and repressing her own terror and helplessness, this "provides motive and energy for repetition" (p. 1210). Once the feelings and their overwhelming nature are recovered, the parent is more able to imagine him or herself into the mind of the child and find a stronger protective capacity. "Through remembering they identify with an injured child (the childhood self), while the parent who does not remember may find himself in an unconscious alliance and identification with the fearsome figures of the past. In this way, the parental past is inflicted upon the child" (Fraiberg, Adelson and Shapiro, 1975, p. 1210)

These authors emphasize the *repressed* nature of childhood affects and the damage that can be done to relationships and personality when this necessary H is activated by trauma. It forecloses the opportunity to "work through" and heal. However, there is evidence from some interactions observed in the mothers' group that a more primitive and damaging defense is resorted to.

SECOND CLINICAL VIGNETTE

The following is taken from a session six months into the program. As the group arrived the older children ran ahead into the group room, calling out, "We're here! We're here!" They went straight to the table where morning tea was laid out and one child said, "there's nothing here I don't like!" There was a flurry of activity as cups of tea were organized, children were fed and then settled in to do some painting and crafts. The babies were playing on the floor in the middle of the circle of mothers. There was some talk about what everyone had been doing through the week and they compared notes on disrupted sleep and teething. April said proudly that her baby had "found his hands" and that he loved to play with them and stuff them in his mouth. With all this avid 'feeding' around, I said to the group that it had been a long wait through the week and they must be hungry to get here. Some smiled but they didn't take up the comment. I noticed that Sharon hadn't spoken, nor had she had anything to eat or drink. She was engrossed in looking at her phone. I said that she was very quiet today and might feel that there was too much going on. She said, "Oh I'm alright. I'm just tired." This is her catchphrase whenever there is an expression of concern or interest in how she might be feeling. I'm sure that she actually was very tired as she looks after three young children on her own.

Sharon often resorts to withdrawal and disconnection from her surroundings and in this case, I understood it to be a retreat from the overwhelming clamor of need and hunger expressed by the group. Her own needy and hungry feelings were dangerously close. She was irritated but otherwise unresponsive when one of her children spoke to her. He wanted to show her the painting he had just finished. He spoke to her again, becoming more urgent and insistent. She took a quick look at it and said, "That's good." Rather than feeling that she might engage with him and show interest and pleasure in what he had produced, she fobbed him off. In trying to reach her and draw her into the life of the group, I struggled with feelings of frustration and futility. I tried again, saying that I can see that sometimes all these demands were too much for her and she would like to be able to escape them. I noticed her little boy slump, all his enthusiasm gone. He then pushed another child, making her cry. Sharon reacted angrily, telling him to stop it. I asked her if she thought he might be trying to tell her something "like you're telling me something now about how you feel." She picked up her little boy and sat him on her lap.

Through repeatedly and gently drawing her attention to the pattern—"the kids, including her kid-self, can be so demanding" and "when it's too much, you want to escape," Sharon has gradually been able to develop more space in her mind for her children. She enjoys playing imaginative games with them and can respond to them more sensitively.

Sharon's early life was very deprived. Her mother, who spent much of her childhood in care, is hardened, embittered and depressed. She was unable to be emotionally responsive to Sharon's needs and feeding her was seen as a task to be completed without any of the associated warmth, holding and care. Without a responsive maternal mind, Sharon has not developed the capacity to bear and think about her own painful emotional states. Instead, they are experienced and expressed somatically as tiredness or in not feeding herself. (She is very underweight). While she was as a small baby, I imagine her frustrations were too great and she may have collapsed into despair. Mitrani (2008) has written that where the mother is not able to take in the baby's communications, the baby may internalize an object relationship that is obstructive and frustrating.

> If she (the mother) cannot digest what she receives, but is instead felt to add her own anxieties to those already overwhelming the infant. . ., then what she hurriedly gives back to the baby will be only suitable for some hyperbolic form of discharge. Consequently, the baby will develop a precocious mind as an instrument for evacuating or encapsulating experience rather than as an instrument for thinking thoughts. (Mitrani, 2008, p. 222)

Rather than undergoing thought, transformation and *repression*, the traumatic events and their associated affects are split off and enclosed. They remain raw, untouched and trapped in time. With no words to describe the experiences, they may be expressed through dissociative states, psychosomatosis, alexithymia, concrete thinking and autistic defenses. Sharon's use of her phone to hold herself together is an example of the latter.

This can be a very difficult area to work in. When members of the group have fallen into this state, the atmosphere is deadening and stultifying. I am often alerted to it when I begin to feel bored, frustrated and despairing. Many of the women in the group have communicated their terror of being in touch with their real feelings through blank stares, lapses in attention, "zoning out" and appearing to be in a dream state. This state is often precipitated by the children expressing their needs, anxieties, distress, hunger, joy or exuberance. It would seem that it is not only the painful nature of the feelings that is defended against but the very intensity and aliveness that is so frightening.

In a discussion of the relationship between disturbances in mother-infant attachment and dissociative disorders, Jon Allen (2001) cites a number of studies where dissociated states in the mother are linked to disorganized and disoriented attachment patterns. He relates disorganized attachment in the infant or young child to a process of compartmentalization. There are rapid and seemingly unconnected shifts in behavior, as if there is no continuity between the different parts of the child's self. Attachment disorientation is associated with detachment and dissociation. Allen suggests that dissociation in the mother or caregiver is a vehicle by which trauma is transmitted to the next generation:

> These post-traumatic dissociative states in the caregiver are frightening to the infant who, in turn, shows peritraumatic dissociative symptoms that are part and parcel of disoriented attachment. Disoriented attachment becomes a diathesis for dissociative pathology in adulthood,

which may then be perpetuated into the next generation. (Allen, 2001, p. 182)

THE SPARK OF CREATIVITY

After about six months, the group was introduced to an Aboriginal artist[4] who offered to run workshops in drawing, painting and ceramics using traditional Aboriginal symbols and other cultural elements. He spoke to the women about his own struggle to find a way of expressing himself through his art. He talked about his initial self-doubt, the gradual development of confidence in his work and the rewards he gained. The group members were cautiously interested and what has become a vital part of the group experience began. The women have gone on to produce a number of art works and ceramic pieces that have been exhibited at a local gallery. Although this is a great source of pride to them, the process has been painful and difficult. Their initial caution reflected grave uncertainty about their efficacy, terror at connecting with deeper parts of themselves and shame about exposing vulnerability. At this stage there was very little faith among the women that what they produced (be that paintings or babies) was good and would be welcomed with recognition and empathy. Instead, there was an expectation of indifference, disapproval and even hostility. Some of the women began paintings only to give up and lapse into boredom. Time and again we saw a little spark of interest and motivation, then paralysis and collapse into despair, meaninglessness and dejection.

Two important ideas helped me to understand and endure this very painful stage in the life of the group. The first is related to the fate of creativity and the capacity to symbolize when trauma has damaged psychic functioning. In order to form symbols, it is necessary to allow the experience of absence and loss in bearable doses. The baby, waiting for a feed, might imagine the breast in order to hold herself together for a short time. The toddler playing peek-a-boo is making a meaningful symbol of the experience of absence and joyful reunion. This process relies on a receptive mind in the mother or caregiver and the child's introjection of a containing object. As Segal notes, "The capacity to experience loss and the wish to recreate the object within oneself gives the individual the uncommon freedom in the use of symbols"(Segal, 1981, p. 56). However, if the absence and subsequent anxiety are too much to bear, this innate and powerful drive to form symbols is interrupted or the space is foreclosed. Symbol formation requires mental playfulness. There is a need for thinking to be nuanced, flexible, relatively uninhibited and free flowing. It is necessary to tolerate uncertainty and have faith that something might arise out of non-existence. I understood that, for many of the group members, these qualities were deadened and the pre-conditions corrupted by trauma. My artist colleague and I continued, doggedly, to provide the external support and interest in what might, potentially, be produced.

The second important idea concerned the apparent destructiveness within the process. Not only did they attack their own work with comments like, "I'm useless at this" or "This is crap." Myself, the other workers and our equipment also came under fire. There were bitter complaints from some of the group members about pencils that broke, paint that was too thick or too thin, water pots that weren't big enough, a table that was too wobbly. These obstacles seemed to spoil everything and the session would end with comments like, "I can't do it, I couldn't be bothered." This repeated experience sometimes felt so annihilating that it was as if we, and our work, had been hit by a wrecking ball. I thought about what it means to give and to receive and my initial anxieties about being felt by the group to be a superior "colonizer." In her 1993 paper, Elizabeth Bott Spillius offers a model to clarify different types of envy and their place in the giver-receiver relationship. Of course, it is not always the case that the giver gives freely and with pleasure and the receiver gratefully accepts. Among other permutations, Spillius describes the scenario where

> the giver may give with pleasure and in good faith, yet the receiver may misinterpret the gift as an attempt by the giver to establish superiority. A giver may have a reasonable expectation of gratitude. . ., but the receiver may be so resentful (of the inequity) that he reacts with hatred, contempt. . . (1993, p. 1209)

The giver and the gift are attacked as in the example above. Envy is a response to having to rely on another to provide something good and implies that there has been a good experience that is now frustratingly absent. However, where there has been no good experience, there can be little or no elaboration of presence and absence, as if there were no conception of anything to be envious of (Mitrani, 2008).

Although at times envious, I think that the complaints were primarily communications about desperate inner states that felt broken, wobbly, too much, too little and without adequate containment. They were also evidence of the pain and terror of feeling a spark of hope but believing that this will always be thwarted and extinguished. With all this in mind, my interventions were aimed at the despair rather than the attack. For example, "It's so hard to believe that you (or we) could make something good." Or, "Just when you get going, you get scared it won't work." One day—feeling particularly exasperated!—I said, "All these things that are wrong. I think you feel that we never get it right." There was some laughter around the table and one woman said, "No, it's not that bad. Actually, it's a good little group." Slowly and tentatively the group started to paint more freely. Their work is mainly around the themes of pregnancy, country, totems and their relationships with their children. Some paintings are very fresh and original. Others are copies of things they've been shown and may represent transitional borrowing or the beginning of a process of identification with a creative mind.

Over time, it seems that the stars have aligned such that the women are now more curious and ready to try new things. They are more able to bear uncertainty, tolerate "mistakes" and, rather than sink into hopelessness, try to find solutions. There is a cautious sense of pride and they have produced work that is worthy of exhibition. A more benign cycle has developed. There is some pleasure in creating and the expectation of hostility and indifference has been replaced by a little more trust and confidence. Growth in this area is reflected in the way the group members are more able to connect with each other, acknowledge painful and disturbing feelings and ask for help. The following material from a recent session shows the group becoming more cohesive and working together on common concerns. It traces a process of relative integration and thoughtfulness among the group, contact with pain, retreat into persecution and abuse and, finally, a recovery.

THIRD CLINICAL VIGNETTE

Janet missed the last two weeks and told us that she has had migraines and the baby has been sick with an infected rash. She talked about how the migraines cause dizziness and visual disturbances. It is very frightening and she worries about falling over while looking after the baby. Hannah asked if she has anyone to help her when she's sick and she said that sometimes her father-in-law comes over. Hannah said, "You have to make sure your family helps you." Janet then said she wants to ask something and maybe we can help. Her baby has been waking and "screaming" every two hours through the night for *the last two weeks*. She stops crying when Janet picks her up, it takes an hour to settle her, and then she wakes again an hour later. Janet has tried everything and can't work out what's going on. I asked her what she feels the screaming is like. Janet said, "It's a heart-breaking cry, like she's in pain and needs me straight away." She said she can't leave her to cry but she is now exhausted and desperate. I said that maybe she, too, was a bit heart-broken, missing out here over the last two weeks when she was feeling so overwhelmed and worried. Janet looked anxious and said that she felt bad that the baby might be picking up on her feelings. Anne said, "Yeah, they know exactly how you're feeling. If you're happy or sad or cranky." Janet agreed that this made sense. Anne said, "Maybe you could talk to her about it. Tell her you haven't been feeling well but that you're alright." Janet laughed and said, "She won't know the actual words but it might be reassuring for her."

The group talked about the "fine line" between letting babies settle themselves when they can and knowing when to attend to them straight away. They went on to complain about how they receive contradictory advice about how to manage crying and sleeping problems. The group became very angry about this. "Why can't the so-called experts get it together?" "They don't know what they're talking about." I thought this was partly a reference to the "so-called expert," me, who linked a mother's fears with her baby's in a way that felt guilt-inducing. I said to the group, "It's hard, isn't it, thinking about your emotional connection with your baby when you're feeling sad or cranky or scared. The guilt can take over." Sharon said, "Yes, you worry about doing lasting damage." Janet then spoke about a news program she had seen that was full of horror stories about child abuse, pedophilia and teenage prostitution. She wanted to know if anyone else had seen it.

Hannah had recently gone back to work two days a week and Janet asked her how it was going. She told us that she had quit her job yesterday because the baby was crying so much each time she left. She described sitting at the bus stop crying and knowing that the baby was at home with his grandmother, also crying. She said that she felt so miserable, she rang her boss to say she couldn't continue working and the boss was very understanding. Hannah said, "I thought I wanted to work but it was too soon. I want to be home with him and I want to be here." Janet said, supportively, "At least you gave it a go." They spoke about how working mothers are "pressured by society" to stay at home and yet mothers at home are pressured to go out to work. There was shared laughter about the absurdity of this. I was struck by the contrast to the earlier talk about the "experts." Acknowledging the guilt and sharing their heartbreaks had taken the sting out of what had been a very persecutory situation. I commented that they were actually working now, figuring out together what was best for themselves and their babies.

CONCLUSION

In this chapter I have described the work of a mothers' group for Aboriginal women conducted within a psychoanalytic framework. I have attempted to show that, through careful observation and attention to countertransference phenomena, it is possible to give words to previously unknown and unspeakable anxieties. When anxieties can be verbalized, understood and held, there is a possibility of release from the deadened space of trauma. As unconscious forces step into the light, they can be neutralized and there is less risk of projection onto the baby. The intimate relationship between mother and baby affords many opportunities for unconscious communication and it is only at this level that deeper and more lasting change can be effected. A formal study and evaluation of the program will be conducted in the near future. However, there is evidence from the material provided that the women are beginning to develop their capacity to be receptive containers for both their own and their children's experiences.

NOTES

1. My gratitude to my colleague Norma Tracey and my supervisor Dr. Louise Gyler for their help in guiding me through unchartered waters.

2. My gratitude to my colleague Norma Tracey and my supervisor Dr. Louise Gyler for their help in guiding me through unchartered waters. In 1997 the Human Rights and Equal Opportunity Commission published a report that concluded that from 1910 to 1970 between 10 and 30 percent of Australian Indigenous children were removed from their families and communities. These children are known as the Stolen Generations. Various State Acts of Parliament empowered police, welfare officers and even teachers to remove children they believed were in need of protection. The report draws on extensive personal testimony to detail the far-reaching traumatic impacts of these practices on the children and their families.

3. For more information about the work of Gunawirra, please see www.gunawirra.org.au

4. See Tracey, N and Toomey, G. (2014). The sense of loss and the search for meaning. In O'Loughlin, M (Ed.), *The Ethics of Remembering and The Consequences of Forgetting: Essays on Trauma, History and Memory.* (Vol.1). Lanham, MD: Rowman and Littlefield for an account of the use of art as a way through trauma.

REFERENCES

Allen, J.G. (2001). *Traumatic relationships and serious mental disorders.* Chichester, NY: John Wiley and Sons.

Atkinson, J. (2002). *Trauma trails, recreating song lines: The transgenerational effects of trauma in indigenous Australia.* Melbourne: Spinifex Press.

Australian Institute of Health and Welfare. (2011). *The health and welfare of Australia's Aboriginal and Torres Strait Islander people: An overview 2011.*

Bion, W. R. (1962). *Learning from experience.* London: Karnac.

Collingwood, R.G. (1939/2002). *An Autobiography.* New York:Oxford University Press.

Fonagy, P. (1999). *Attachment, the development of the self and its pathology in personality disorders.* Retrieved from http://www. psychomedia.it/pm/modther/fonagy-2.htm

Fraiberg, S., Adelson, E., and Shapiro, V. (1975). Ghosts in the nursery: A psychoanalytic approach to the problems of impaired infant-mother relationships. *Journal of the American Academy of Child Psychiatry, 14*(3), 1199–1211.

Klein, M. (1975/1997). *Envy and gratitude and other works 1946-1963.* London: Vintage.

HREOC. (1997). *Bringing them home: Report of the national inquiry into the separation of Aboriginal and Torres Strait Islander children from their families.* Sydney: Human Rights and Equal Opportunity Commission.

Mitrani, J. (2008). *A framework for the imaginary: Clinical explorations in primitive states of being.* London: Karnac Books.

Mollon, P. (1998). *Remembering trauma: A psychotherapist's guide to memory and illusion.* Chichester, NY: John Wiley and Sons.

Pines, D. (1972). Pregnancy and motherhood: Interaction between fantasy and reality. *British Journal of Medical Psychology, 45*(4), 333–343.

Segal, H. (1981). *The work of Hanna Segal: A Kleinian approach to clinical practice.* (6th ed.). NY: Jason Aronson.

Shengold, L. (1991). *Soul murder: The effects of childhood abuse and deprivation.* New York, NY: Ballantine Books.

Spillius, E. (1993). Varieties of envious experience. *International Journal of Psycho-Analysis, 74*, 1199–1211.

Tracey, N. and Toomey, G. (In press). The sense of loss and the search for meaning. In O'Loughlin, M. (Ed.), *The ethics of remembering and the consequences of forgetting: Essays on trauma, history and memory.* (Vol. 1). Lanham, MD: Rowman and Littlefield.

Winnicott, D. W. (1965/1990). *The maturational processes and the facilitating environment.* London: Karnac Books.

ELEVEN

"There's no trust at all, in anything"

Psychosocial Perspectives on Trauma in a Distressed African American Neighborhood

Annie Stopford

> It was a constant tremor and puzzlement to have right under my window this quasi-lunar urban landscape, with its unbelievable decay, misery, and violence, backed by a totally hermetic separation between the white, prosperous, and privileged world of the university and the abandoned African-American neighborhoods all around it.
> —Loic Wacquant (2011a, p. 83)

Drawing on notes and interviews from my fieldwork in Baltimore, Maryland, as well as research interviews with medical practitioners, criminal justice personnel, and community workers in Oakland and Philadelphia, in this chapter I will undertake a psychosocial exploration of the traumatic stress experienced by the residents of segregated, disinvested and unsafe neighborhoods in American cities. I will argue that while residents of distressed Baltimore (and other urban) neighborhoods should receive far more recognition and *effective* resources including intensive therapy for those who want it, the problem should be seen not in terms of individual pathology such as PTSD, but rather as symptomatic of a national condition of denial and dissociation about the historical creation and contemporary maintenance and exploitation of African American "ghettoes."

PSYCHOSOCIAL DISCUSSION

As I draw on both sociological and psychological discourses to describe and analyze the toxic stress and ongoing trauma associated with American ghettoes, I locate this discussion within the newly emerging field of psychosocial studies. Described by Sasha Roseneil, Birkbeck University Department of Psychosocial Studies as the study of "the interrelation between individual subjectivities and identities, and historical and contemporary social and political formations" (2013), psychosocial studies challenges the clear distinction between the psychological and the social, thereby encouraging interdisciplinary discussion. Psychosocial studies also includes a variety of investigative methods, including interviews, activism and documentary making. The aforementioned research interviews were conducted in 2013 by Llewellyn Smith and I for a documentary about trauma and young people of color, called *Wounded places: Confronting childhood PTSD in America's shell-shocked cities* (Smith and Blue Spark Collaborative, 2014) for which I was the director of research and development. Permission has been given for use of interview extracts.

My work in Baltimore is an independent project that has gradually developed since my first visit to the city in 2011. Since then I have made numerous visits, including a one month stint in early 2013. I describe it as fieldwork both because it is akin to the way sociologists and anthropologists conduct fieldwork through immersion in particular contexts, and also because I did not start out with a clearly formulated research question. Rather, my connection with particular people and locations in Baltimore began as a relational process (described presently) that developed into an ongoing discussion about trauma with my respondents. My four Baltimore respondents have read their interview transcripts, and have given permission for their narratives to be used, and for their names to be included (for two of them). Besides recording a series of interviews and conversations, I also took notes about phone conversations, visits to Safe Streets offices in East and West Baltimore, a block party in East Baltimore where I helped Safe Streets outreach workers serve food, community activist meetings that I attended, and several visits to Jessup men's and women's prisons. Due to space constraints I have been able to include only a very limited number of extracts from my Baltimore interviews and notes, but my experiences in Baltimore and connections with some of its brave and generous residents have been formative.

INTRODUCTION TO RESPONDENTS

Although Baltimore is my main focus, as I mentioned above, in this discussion I also draw on documentary film research interviews conducted in Philadelphia and Oakland in 2013 with men and women involved in trauma-informed work with young people of color in those two cities. While each location has its specificities, there are many similarities between parts of Philadelphia, Oakland and Baltimore, and extracts from interviews with Philadelphia and Oakland respondents, all of whom are deeply embedded in front line work with traumatized individuals, families and communities, add breadth to this discussion. My Philadelphia respondents are Dr. Sandra Bloom and Dr. John Rich, Drexel University Department of Public Health; Dr. Theodore Corbin, Drexel University College of Medicine; and Robert Reed, Assistant United States Attorney. Oakland respondents are Millie Burns, Deputy Chief of Programs for Catholic Charities of the East Bay, and Olis Simmons, Executive Director of Youth Uprising, East Oakland.

In Baltimore, two of my fieldwork interlocutors, Gardnel Carter and Greg Carpenter, are older men who direct safe streets and prison re-entry projects in East and West Baltimore. Both men are deeply connected to some of Baltimore's African American neighborhoods and communities, and, as they were both incarcerated for about 20 years in Maryland penal institutions, they are also involved with a number of projects and communities connected to prisons, including a community group called the Extra Legalese support group. This group was established to support the work of a group of men in Jessup Correctional Institution serving life sentences who have set up their own incorporated think tank called Extra Legalese (ELG), one of whose stated goals is to reduce gang related violence in the prison system and in Maryland neighborhoods. My husband's cousin is a founding member of ELG, and it was through this family connection that I made my first visit to Baltimore in October 2011.

I met Greg and Gardnel at an ELG support group meeting, where we had the first of many conversations about their work with young people on the streets and with men coming out of prison. We have also had numerous conversations about their own backgrounds, and their experiences in prison. My other two Baltimore respondents, who I will call Josie and Matt, are a young man and woman in their late twenties who grew up in one of Baltimore's most unsafe and disinvested neighborhoods, Middle East. I was introduced to Matt by Gardnel Carter, and Matt in turn introduced me to Josie.

Through visits to Safe Streets offices in East and West Baltimore I have also met and talked with some other men involved with the stressful and rewarding work of trying to make their neighborhoods safer through mediating conflicts and working with high-risk youth clients. Before they turned their lives around, most of these men (and some women) were incarcerated and/or involved in criminal gangs. They are not trained therapists, teachers, or mentors, but what they actually do when at their best is a combination of all of these roles. The first time I actually saw these 'street therapists' in action was in a documentary called *The Interrupters* (James and Kotlowitz, 2011), about the violence interruption work of the Ceasefire team (now called Cure Violence) in Chicago. Although the context could not be more different, I was struck by the similarity between some aspects of my work with my patients—most of whom have backgrounds of relational trauma—and the relationships between some of "the interrupters" and the people with whom they were working. Ameena Matthews, for example, the only woman in the Ceasefire team, and at one time a gang enforcer, showed extraordinary determination, insight and compassion in her efforts to stay connected with a troubled young woman with a history of severe abuse. The big difference of course (besides the fact that they are not trained therapists) is that Ameena and her fellow Ceasefire and Safe Streets workers operate in much more stressful conditions than most clinicians, and receive little financial remuneration.

TERMINOLOGY

Social scientists employ various terms including inner city neighborhoods, disinvested neighborhoods and ghettoes to describe the predominantly African American (and in some areas, Latino) communities that are most affected by community violence and its associated trauma. Reading sociological work clarified that "ghetto" is the term of choice for this discussion. In Loic Wacquant's words, the ghetto is "a spatially based implement of ethnoracial closure" (2011b, p. 2), which may or may not be dispossessed and dilapidated, just as areas that are economically disadvantaged are not *necessarily* ghettoes. In other words, ghettoes have been created to segregate and exploit an already devalued group; in this case, African Americans. Wacquant's elaboration of "a thick *relational* conception of the ghetto as a socio-spatial institution geared to the twin mission of isolating and exploiting a dishonored category" (2011b, p. 2) resonates with a relational conception of the traumatizing violence in African American communities as a symptom and an enactment of white America's historical and contemporary violence toward non elite African Americans. Also, although it is beyond the scope of this discussion to explore the "deadly symbiosis" (Wacquant, 2001) between ghettoes and prisons in the United States, and its implications in terms of trauma, it is important to note that as a result of the "war on drugs" and the associated mass incarceration of men of color (Alexander, 2010), over the last 30 years American penal institutions and probation and parole regulations have arguably developed into an even more efficient method (than ghettoes) for isolating, exploiting and discriminating against massive numbers of African American men.

PSYCHOANALYTIC CONCERNS

There are several ways in which psychoanalytic concerns shape discussion in this chapter. Perhaps the most important is the fact that I have been a psychoanalytic psychotherapist for over 20 years. Thus, although my fieldwork and film research interviews are not designed or intended to be psychoanalytic or therapeutic per se, I bring a certain sensibility to my interactions with respondents. As I have discussed elsewhere (Stopford, 2004), a psychosocial researcher with extensive clinical experience embodies a responsiveness to others that has been shaped through decades of clinical work, that impacts in often indefinable ways on the feeling tone of the conversations and interactions with our interlocutors, regardless of what one says or does not say. Likewise, my interlocutors embody decades of rich and often very challenging life experience in their spoken and affective responses to me.

In regards to psychoanalytic interpretation of narratives, for several reasons I do not include reflection on my subjectivity or analysis of fantasy, projection, possible transference and counter transference dynamics and so forth in this chapter. First, while psychoanalytic perspectives on trauma and the healing relationship are immensely valuable in the clinical context, I am less convinced of the usefulness of psychoanalytic interpretations of research interviews and narratives; that is, unless the psychoanalytic story is proffered as just one possibility, or respondents are offered the opportunity to respond to the researcher's interpretation and to contribute their own thoughts about the researcher. Otherwise, not only is there the problem of psychoanalysis as the "Master Discourse" (Parker, 2008), but the resultant text is likely to be of interest only to other academics and of less value for the people whose narratives were used to build the argument or discussion (not to mention the researcher's career). Psychoanalytic interpretation of interview texts and "in house" academic debate and discussion has its place of course. However, as I have tried to demonstrate in previous writing about intercultural and interracial research projects (for example, Stopford, 2004, 2006, 2008), if one is interested in forms of ethical relationality that destabilize rather than uphold the structures that create and perpetuate separation, segregation and inequality, the intersubjective quality of the relationship between researcher or fieldworker and respondents matters a great deal. Although my interests and perspectives inevitably dominate, I see my Baltimore fieldwork as a collaboration with my respondents, and to interpret their narratives without inviting them to respond to my analysis would be unconscionable.

Second, in this context the narratives of my respondents and interviewees are more important than psychoanalytic reflection on my subjectivity, or even analysis of transference and countertransference dynamics (usually the hallmark of psychoanalytic discussion). Since so many people seem to avoid direct contact with American ghettoes, what matters in this discussion is the endeavor to "give voice" to those who live and work in conditions of ongoing traumatic stress—conditions that are both created and ignored by wider society. Again, this is an ethical issue, and perhaps not of great concern to some psychoanalytic practitioners. But, as Donna Orange's work (Orange, 2010) shows, philosophical perspectives on ethical relationality can be of interest to psychoanalytic clinicians, and to psychosocial researchers. The ethics of Emmanuel Levinas, for example, shape the way some psychologists engage with clients in ghetto environments (see, for example, MacDonald, 2011).

Thirdly, there is the question of psychoanalytic insulation from the day to day realities of segregated, disinvested urban neighborhoods. Psychoanalytic and psychodynamic clinicians do significant work in distressed racially segregated communities in America (see, for example, Ainslie, 2013) and also in American prisons (for example, Kita, 2011). On the whole, however, the mainstream clinical psychoanalytic community in the United States has chosen to align itself with "the white, prosperous and privileged world" of the private clinic and academe, and has thus managed largely to ignore and deny the struggles of countless people of color in this country, including the millions who are incarcerated, or on parole or probation. Thanks to the work of some relational psychoanalytic writers (for example, Altman, 2000; Layton, 2006; Leary, 1995; Wachtel, 2002) I have long been aware of the race and class bias of (Anglo) American clinical psychoanalysis, and I've written about the racist, essentialist and colonialist discourse underpinning psychoanalytic responses to interraciality (Stopford, 2007) and intercultural and postcolonial contact zones (Stopford, 2006, 2008, 2013). It has only been since I began working on projects connected to African American communities, however, that the *degree* of psychoanalytic distancing from the challenges faced by many African American families has really hit home.

Let's not pull punches. When America imprisons more people than any country at any time in history, many of whom are African American, what does it say about the state of American clinical psychoanalysis that in the vast Psychoanalytic Electronic Publishing data base there are few mentions of incarceration, and then only in passing? And if we protest that psychoanalysis is interested only in the unconscious, Frantz Fanon's words about race relations and politics are as pertinent for the United States today as they were half a century ago:

> Since the racial drama is played out in the open, the black man has no time to 'make it unconscious.' The white man, on the other hand, succeeds in doing so to a certain extent, because a new element appears: guilt. The Negro's inferiority or superiority complex or his feeling of equality is *conscious*. These feelings forever chill him. They make his drama. In him there is none of the affective amnesia characteristic of the typical neurotic. (1967, p. 150)

Then there is the question of intergenerational trauma. In a country with a violent history of white oppression of African Americans starting with slavery, continuing with legalized segregation (Jim Crow) and the re-enslavement of African Americans from the Civil War to World War II (Blackmon, 2009), and manifesting today in grossly unfair drug laws and mass incarceration of (primarily) men of color (Alexander, 2010), how is it possible that in the plethora of psychoanalytic clinical literature about intergenerational transmission of trauma, apart from Janice Gump (2010) and Kirkland Vaughans' (2014) work, African American intergenerational trauma seems to have been ignored? Ironically, and sadly, the clinical discipline that provides some of the most sophisticated writing about trauma and dissociation is itself almost completely dissociated from both historical *and* contemporary African American trauma. A "totally hermetic separation" indeed. As Altman says; "We cannot succeed as psychoanalysts if we fail to examine how and why we insulate ourselves from so much suffering" (2013, p. 130).

The fact that American clinical psychoanalysis has developed as an exclusionary discourse and practice does not mean of course that psychoanalysis has little to offer the communities that are the focus of this discussion. On the contrary. Part of my motivation for doing this work is my own experience, both as a therapist and a patient, of the enormous value of intensive psychoanalytic therapy for people suffering from various forms of relational trauma. Although it is frequently noted that psychoanalysis is in decline (Stepansky, 2009)—and there is in no question that in some ways it is—there has never been a greater need for the kind of exploratory, compassionate and insightful "experience near" psychoanalysis practiced by many contemporary psychoanalytic clinicians, if only we can find effective ways to make it available to some of our most traumatized communities that are least likely to have access. And as Gill Straker and her colleagues in South Africa powerfully demonstrated (Straker, 1992), psychoanalytic perspectives on the violence and suffering caused by systemic injustice can make a significant impact well beyond psychoanalytic circles. In the words of Elizabeth Goren and Judie Alpert, "we as a profession have the knowledge and skills to take on the expansion of psychoanalysis beyond the individual and the office. . . analysts can and should work with the trauma of survivors of mass violence and natural disasters and with the multiple traumas of underserved and overstressed populations" (2013, p. 220). But psychoanalysts need the humility and honesty to recognize that many of us live in a privileged bubble, that we have as much (if not more) to learn from the people who live and work in America's ghettoes and prisons as we have to offer, and that if we want to stop insulating ourselves we have to be willing to leave our middle class offices and neighborhoods and work and even live in less comfortable conditions.

AMERICAN APARTHEID

While it has tragic outcomes, it is not surprising that many people avoid contact with the stressful conditions of the hood. According to Gardnel, "my informant, even the people who grew up in East Baltimore and still have family there, once they've "made it," almost never go back to visit. Characterized by high levels of violence, substance dependence, mental and physical health problems, food and housing insecurity, gang activity, few job opportunities and little access to good schools, these areas, described by Patrick Sharkey as "the spatial expression of social processes" (2013, p. 47), have been created over many decades through a combination of social and economic exclusion, disinvestment, exploitation and neglect. They are the product of what Douglas Massey and Nancy Denton (1998) call "American apartheid"; the creation in the early twentieth-century of urban ghettoes by whites determined to exclude and isolate the growing black population in cities across America. Government policy and action at all levels were instrumental in this process, including the underwriting practices of federal agencies that insured mortgages that led to the red lining of certain inner city areas, freezing African Americans out of affordable mortgages, and fueling white flight. Government funding for road and highway construction has also been used to isolate African Americans and perpetuate segregation (Katz, 2012, p. 52). The ghetto "is maintained today by a set of institutions, attitudes and practices that are deeply embedded in the structure of American life" (Massey and Denton, 1998, p. 217).

Statistics for homicides and gun violence in predominantly African American urban neighborhoods have improved over the last few years in most cities, but they are horrifying nonetheless. Nationally, homicide is the leading cause of death for African American males between the ages of 15 and 24 (Adams, 2014). Ninety percent of homicides are from gunshot wounds, and for every young man killed, another four are hospitalized for nonfatal gunshot wounds. Many of these incidents occur in ghetto communities, such as sections of north Philadelphia, East and West Oakland, and East and West Baltimore. In Philadelphia, for example, a dozen shootings were reported every weekend in the month of November, 2013, most of them in disadvantaged black neighborhoods (GunCrisis Philadelphia, 2013).

Children living in America's ghettoes grow up in an environment of constant threat. Many witness acts of violence including shootings and stabbings, and intimidating verbal exchanges in the street are common. They may see dead bodies in the street. Their homes may also be unsafe due to domestic violence, substance abuse, sexual abuse, untreated mental illness, or chronic anxiety and depression related to food, job, health and housing insecurity. One or both parents may be incarcerated, or on probation or parole. Researchers and professionals involved with children and young people growing up in violent communities regularly report statistics as high as 80% of children younger than 7 witnessing a homicide or shooting, or knowing someone who has been shot (Fitzpatrick, 1993; Kostelny and Garbarino, 2001; Roach, 2013). The psychological injuries to these children are immense. They include annihilation anxiety, hypervigilance, sleep disturbance, depression, feelings of powerlessness and hopelessness, the expectation of danger and violence, a sense of betrayal, loss of trust, a disposition for self-abuse, detachment and loss of bonding capacity (Parson, 1994; Wilson and Raphael, 1993). School disengagement and academic failure are common (Osofsky et al. 1993; Singer et al. 1995).

"THEY DON'T SEE A FUTURE": YOUNG PEOPLE LIVING IN URBAN TRAUMA ZONES

Many teenagers and young adults have lost so many friends to gun violence they do not expect to live long themselves, and cannot imagine a future beyond a month or two. Some respondents talked about the sense of hopelessness that they see in young people, their expectation that they will not live long:

> When I went back to working with kids 15 years ago, I'd never seen kids make a will. I'd never seen kids talk about how they wanted their funeral. I'd never seen kids go to a cemetery to visit 10, 15 graves of their friends. This is a new normality where their mortality is part of their identity. (Millie Burns)

You see sometimes the hopelessness in young people's eyes, people who are 14, 15, 13, 16, who seem to have lost all hope. (Rob Reed)

> We've had conversations like where do you think you're going to be in three years and when you look at them all they've got is a blank stare. . . in their neighborhood all they see is black people struggling, the addicts, the winos, the gratification they get from the now is all they're concerned about because they don't see a future. (Gardnel Carter)

This is not the whole story of course. No matter how disadvantaged and unsafe an area may be, residents may have affection for their neighborhood, parents try to create pockets of safety and peace for their children, and in the midst of hopelessness and despair there is also resilience, humor and creativity. Growing up in such challenging conditions can be strengthening for some. Josie, for example, had this to say about her experiences growing up in Middle East:

> When I got a real job I realized that some of the girls around my age didn't grow up being poor with their parents living from check to

> check and having to go through some of the circumstances that we went through in my life. Some of the things that they were really upset and stressed about I thought to myself "I wouldn't be so stressed out about that, I've been through so much worse in my life," so I didn't realize till I got to be an adult that we've been through some things really early that makes us stronger.

There is never one story that can do justice to the complexities of a particular place or phenomenon, and in the ongoing discussion about disadvantaged and unsafe neighborhoods in the United States, it is important not to objectify residents as powerless victims, or perpetuate ugly stereotypes of the "underclass" that generate fear and contempt and further entrench class and race boundaries. Nonetheless, by anyone's standards, neighborhoods like the one in Chicago described above by Loic Wacquant and like the ones in East and West Baltimore where two Safe Streets offices are located are highly stressful environments that thwart the development and potential of countless numbers of black and brown children. As John Rich said in his interview, "Just because some people can survive a toxic environment does not mean that we should allow that toxic environment to persist."

NO BEFORE OR AFTER: ONGOING TRAUMATIC STRESS

In fact, the degree of trauma experienced by residents of America's ghettoes can be so unrelenting, health professionals struggle to find appropriate terminology to describe it, calling it variously combat fatigue (Meets and Gordon, 1975), urban violence traumatic stress response syndrome [U-VTS] (Parson, 1998), ongoing traumatic stress response [OTSR] (Diamond et al., 2013), and continuous traumatic stress (Roach, 2013). Differences in the terminology used by psychologists and other health professionals to describe urban American trauma also reflect differing degrees of emphasis on individual pathology versus emphasis on the external and current conditions to which individuals must adapt in various ways. As Diamond and his colleagues point out, behaviors that may appear to reflect symptoms of PTSD or other disorders are actually adaptive and normative under extreme conditions.

Ethnographer Elijah Anderson's seminal study of young people in north Philadelphia (1999) and medical practitioner John Rich's work (Rich 2009; Rich and Grey, 2005) with young men of color in Boston demonstrate that adaptive and normative behaviors for young men living in the extreme conditions of ghetto environments may include observation of particular codes of honor, carrying weapons, joining gangs, and selling drugs, all of which increase the risk of violence. Massey and Denton (1998) show that the systematic segregation of African Americans, coupled with periods of economic downturn, inevitably leads to severe deterioration of social and economic conditions in particular neighborhoods. In response to the worsening conditions, long term residents may cope by medicating and numbing themselves with whatever drugs or substances they have access to, while the youngsters develop behaviors, dress codes and attitudes that shore up their sense of safety, identity and meaning but that also marginalize and alienate them even more from mainstream society, and, tragically, mean that their lives may be at great risk.

> They figure if they die in the streets they're gonna become a street legend, people are gonna love them for all of time. Getting shot is a badge of honor and then if you live, and you got shot that many times and you live, then everybody in the neighborhood got mad respect for you. (Gardnel Carter)

> They say "I'm willing to die if you just disrespect me because that's all I've got." (Millie Burns)

In regards to the impact of drugs in Gardnel's locality:

> You know, drugs, drugs has probably hit worse than the atom bomb in the black community. Drugs period, because when you look at it now, people are trying anything to mask their feelings, it ain't just the traditional heroin or cocaine, it's anything now, bath salts and all sorts of things. (Gardnel Carter)

What these narratives tell us is that the substance abuse and the traumatizing violence committed and experienced by young African American men and women (and children) is generated by the dangerous, impoverished neighborhoods that were created and "hermetically sealed" by white America. Similar to the apparently self-destructive behavior of some survivors of abuse (such as self-mutilation, disordered eating, drug abuse, risky sexual encounters) drug abuse and so-called black on black violence are both symptoms and an enactment of national historical and contemporary relational trauma. Past overt violence by white America toward African Americans has turned into contemporary white and middle-class indifference to the trauma, toxic stress and deep poverty of segregated neighborhoods in nearly all American cities, and contempt for the people who live in them (Scott, 1997).

SHAME AND RAGE, DESPAIR AND ALIENATION

While residents of ghetto neighborhoods are segregated from the mainstream in many ways and some may rarely venture beyond their immediate locality, they are affected in both conscious and unconscious ways by the combination of indifference, voyeuristic fascination, contempt and fear that the world "outside" feels toward them. Some become depressed and despairing, and increasingly numb, while others, especially the young, may become increasingly alienated. As Elijah Anderson writes; "When alienation becomes so entrenched, an oppositional culture can develop and flourish. . . Those who experience contempt from society often cannot enjoy self-respect without dishing out contempt in return" (1999, p. 318).

> We've had a generation or two of this incredible violence in the major cities, even though it's declining, it's still been going on and on, so that people within the inner cities I think have been dehumanized. Not only by themselves, they feel dehumanized, that people are actually dehumanizing them because they live in the war zones. There's all these stereotypes that are thrown against people living in certain communities. (Rob Reed)

> We know that many of these young people have grown up in a world of racism where they are seeing themselves depicted as without possibility. They go to schools where there's not much possibility that they'll emerge with a solid education. They're often treated in ways that erode their sense of self, and that also cuts them off from the sense of future. (John Rich)

Being aware of the huge difference between their material lives and those of middle-class mostly white communities has myriad detrimental outcomes, both psychological and social:

> There are a couple of things that I think the average American doesn't understand about the lived reality for young people in communities like East Oakland or disinvested communities any place in America. Poverty isn't just about not having; poverty is about the juxtaposition of not having to affluence...so the anger that people feel isn't because they don't have, it's because they see that other people have more than any one person can reasonably consume in a lifetime and that's where the rage comes from. (Olis Simmons)

In Baltimore, where past racially driven residential real estate practices including restrictive covenants, redlining, blockbusting, and predatory lending (Pietela, 2010) have created dramatically contrasting neighborhoods literally blocks from each other, residents of tough neighborhoods like East Baltimore see neighboring communities as another world.

> When you come up past Fayette Street, you see that's probably the dividing line right there, so that's probably 3 or 4 blocks over and you get here to South East and East Baltimore it's like you came into another city, and the people in the South east ain't gonna go to the Patterson Park community unless it's for crimes of opportunity, robbery and things of that nature. And then you have Canton, and all them that's

> down from the Patterson Park community, it's like two different worlds. (Gardnel Carter)

WHOSE LIVES MATTER? THE NORMALIZATION OF DEATH AND INJURY IN GHETTO NEIGHBORHOODS

Perhaps what is most disturbing and most damaging is the lack of interest mainstream America seems to have in the enormous death and injury toll of young people (particularly men) of color. According to statistics from the Centers for Disease Control and Prevention (CDC), in 2006, the homicide death rate was more than 19 times higher for young black men than young white men (Rich, 2009, p. ix). If homicide rates for young white men were as high, it is safe to assume that it would be viewed as a matter of national urgency. Only some lives are grievable and in America the loss of young white lives seems to count far more than the loss of young black and brown lives.

> My kid could get shot and it wouldn't be worthy of three lines in a newspaper because it happens all the time, and my kids know that. We were talking yesterday about the intense violence in East Oakland and one member of staff said "Why haven't we been seeing it in the newspapers?" Well, you're not going to because it's normal, it's not news. When a young black or brown man gets shot or killed, what's new? (Millie Burns)

Loss of life is a constant backdrop to the lives of my Baltimore respondents. Both Matt and Josie told me about recent murders of people in their lives; in Josie's case, a man was shot to death while having a haircut in a relative's back yard in Middle East, while Matt was traumatized by the shooting deaths of two young men from his neighborhood. Safe Streets workers hear about, and confront, constant violence. On many occasions the first thing Gardnel or Greg said after the initial greeting in our phone conversations was, "we had a shooting last night." I lost count of the numbers of shootings and murders they mentioned but one statistic stands out, largely due to the time period when I heard it and a particular conversation with Matt. Just before my longest visit to Baltimore thus far, from mid-March to mid-April, 2013, nine African American men and women were shot to death in West Baltimore over a two day period (*The Baltimore Sun*, 2013). The combination of the unusually high number of deaths in a very short period of time and the fact that I heard about them just before I was due to go to Baltimore to reconnect with respondents, one of whom, Greg Carpenter, was at that time the director of West Baltimore Safe Streets, made a strong impression on me.

But it was also what happened after I returned to Boston that ensured I would never forget these terrible statistics. A couple of days after I arrived back in Boston, four people tragically died in the Boston Marathon bombing, and Boston went into lockdown for days while police hunted for the perpetrators. A few days after the bombing, Matt called to express his condolences for the loss of life and for the dramatic disruption to daily life for many Bostonians. Poignantly, he said nothing about the much higher number of deaths in Baltimore in the preceding months, or the constant stress and fear that residents of East and West Baltimore endure as they try to go about their business. When I offered my condolences to him and fellow Baltimoreans and commented that some lives seem to be more grievable than others, Matt seemed surprised, but then started talking about his twenty one-year-old friend who had been shot dead the previous Tuesday by a fellow drug dealer. With Matt's support, this young man had been trying to get his life on track but in Matt's words he always got "sucked back in." I felt quite tearful hearing about the death of his friend; when I asked Matt how he felt, he said "numb."

Needless to say, the many deaths in Baltimore (and other similar contexts) receive only minimal local media attention, while the Boston Marathon deaths and injuries not only received saturation national and international media attention, according to The Centre for Research on Globalization (CRG), an independent research and media organization based in Montreal, many media outlets reported inflated numbers of injuries. Sadly, it's the reverse when it comes to the injuries of people from the 'hood. And if homicides don't get much attention, the non-fatal injuries inflicted by knives and guns are all but invisible to the wider world. In Philadelphia, trauma surgeon Ted Corbin says:

> So, monthly, through our emergency department, we see roughly about 30 to 40 people for intentional injury. So now we're talking knife stab wounds, assaults and gunshot wounds. That doesn't include homicides. And I want to stress that homicide as traumatic and as terrible as it is, it's just the tip of the iceberg.

Because many African Americans and other people of color are hurt or die from injuries inflicted by other people of color, it is easy for white and middle-class Americans to dismiss the violence and death as "self-inflicted"—the actions of antisocial and bad people—rather than recognizing the violence as a symptom of a national malaise. When society downplays, rationalizes or ignores the everyday violence of American ghetto communities, it becomes normalized both for those who are not affected by it, and those who are. In one of our discussions about his work with the West Baltimore Safe Streets team, Greg Carpenter said that one of his team members had asked him a question: "What is the universal language?" When Greg answered, "Laughter is the universal language," the young man responded, "No, no, that ain't it! Violence is the universal language." As Millie Burns puts it, "The young people in East Oakland live in a community where their exposure to violence is almost daily and the violence has been normalized because there's no cultural or societal response to their trauma."

VIOLENCE AS A PUBLIC HEALTH PROBLEM: A TRAUMA-INFORMED APPROACH

Fortunately, there are some health professionals, including medical practitioners, social workers, psychiatrists, community workers and psychologists who do not keep a distance from the day to day realities of America's urban war zones, and do not demonize the young people who are both perpetrators and victims. While most of America looks the other way, these dedicated professionals tend to the physical injuries of traumatized young people in hospital emergency rooms, and to their psychological injuries and the sorrows of grieving family members in health centers and community agencies. When violence is viewed as a public health problem, rather than the pathology of individuals or specific communities, and responses to the injured are informed by insight and empathy rather than blaming, it is known as a "trauma-informed response."

Fundamentally, a trauma-informed approach is driven by the belief that "Hurt people hurt people" (Bloom and Reichert, 1998, p. 162). In hospital and community health settings, to be "trauma informed" means having "a thorough knowledge of the complex biopsychosocial implications of exposure to toxic stress, adversity and traumatic life experiences" (Corbin et al., 2013, p. 515), so that victims of ghetto violence are not further traumatized by the judgmental and uncaring responses of medical staff, and are provided with ongoing resources and support to try to heal their physical and psychological injuries.

> We started seeing people not as sick, crazy, bad, but as injured and those injuries could encompass a wide variety of injuries it could be physical, it could be social, it could be spiritual. They could be injured in all those domains, but it is all about injury and that is really at the heart of what we call the paradigm shift. (Sandra Bloom)

In the criminal justice system, the adoption of a trauma-informed approach encourages prosecutors and police to recognize that the violent crime associated with ghetto neighborhoods is often the result of ongoing trauma and toxic stress.

> I think what trauma-informed care really teaches at its most basic is empathy. It is an understanding of how other people are living and suffering and I don' t think people in the criminal justice system really focus on that because we generally focus on the victim rather than on the whole process, on the whole community, on the whole society. (Rob Reed)

A trauma-informed lens is only one of a number of possible lenses through which to view the ongoing multiple stressors in America's ghettoes, but for some of those who live and work in America's segregated, severely disadvantaged urban neighborhoods, trauma-informed perspectives offer a critically different way of thinking about violence, and a welcome change from the usual viewpoint of young black men as dangerous and unworthy of our care. As the number of medical and mental health professionals involved in the treatment of trauma steadily increases and questions and controversies about the "trauma industry" intensify (see for example Golden and Bergo, 2009), it is important to keep in mind Judith Herman's (1992) argument that recognition of trauma can be a crucial dimension of political movements oriented toward social change and justice. To reiterate the point made earlier by Millie Burns, when there is no recognition by wider society of the trauma experienced by residents of ghetto neighborhoods, the violence and suffering are normalized. We need to take care therefore that academic questions about the politics of trauma do not inadvertently undermine this fledgling process of recognition.

"THIS TRAUMA THING": RE-TRAUMATIZING VERSUS HEALING RELATIONSHIPS

However, while there are many examples of effective trauma-informed programs in the United States today, including the projects in Philadelphia and Oakland that we researched for our documentary, I learned through my Baltimore fieldwork that having a "trauma-informed approach" does not in and of itself guarantee acceptance in distressed neighborhoods and communities. After I screened a cut of *Wounded places* at his Safe Streets office, I asked Gardnel whether the trauma-informed approach discussed in the film has any relevance for his team and the people in that neighborhood:

> G: I mean, it's something that Baltimore has been trying to do especially here in East Baltimore, they've been trying to do this trauma thing for about three and a half years.
> A: Who?
> G: Johns Hopkins and a couple of other organizations, but it's never got off the ground. I honestly can't say why, I think it's the investment of the people, they was trying to use people from the neighborhood to go back to their neighborhood, they've been training them
> A: To work as trauma informed?
> G: Yeah, they understand the trauma this neighborhood has experienced and gone through but it's getting people to actually come out and work with people in the neighborhood.
> A: That didn't happen?

> G: It hasn't happened yet and it's been in the process for three years now, the people aren't invested in it. . .It could be a combination of a whole lot of things you know, East Baltimore number one has been traumatized by Johns Hopkins for God knows how long, so every new thing that comes just looks like some kind of health initiative. . .lack of trust in anything, that's probably one of the biggest things, lack of trust in any services that's coming to communities that have been traumatized and they don't open up to a lot of things. There's no trust at all, in anything, and I think that's probably because that trauma unit and the Urban Health Institute has been trying to get that trauma thing off the ground for three years, basically all it is just rounds and rounds and rounds of meetings and meetings and meetings and meetings. People become tired of it, you know what I'm saying, especially when they're not seeing results.

Unpacking Gardnel's comments about the relationship between East Baltimore residents and Johns Hopkins University in any detail is beyond the scope of this discussion, but suffice it to say there is a tremendous amount of distrust, much of it well founded (see Markovitz and Rosner, 2013; Skloot, 2010;), and some of it, perhaps, more symptomatic of a deeply traumatized community's need to have a focus for its distress. Similar to the Chicago neighborhood described by Loic Wacquant at the beginning of this chapter, some of Baltimore's most disadvantaged African American neighborhoods are literally next door to one of America's most prestigious universities—a constant reminder of the massive differences in resources between communities, and the failure of the American political and economic system to ensure decent housing, education, health care and justice for the majority of its citizens.

The relationship between an institution like Johns Hopkins and its immediate neighbors is bound to be complex, but when Gardnel—who is very familiar with the multiple stressors of violence, poverty and substance abuse in East Baltimore—actually says "East Baltimore *number one* has been traumatized by Johns Hopkins for God knows how long" [emphasis added], it is clear that something is seriously awry. In fact, it tends to suggest that in their efforts to set up various programs in East Baltimore, Johns Hopkins personnel are re-traumatizing the residents. Perhaps there was once some hope that collaborations between community residents and university people would lead to substantive improvements, but according to Gardnel, in the eyes of local people the "rounds and rounds and rounds of meetings and meetings and meetings and meetings" have led to nothing, thus further eroding trust. Soon after this interview with Gardnel, I had a phone meeting with a former faculty member at Johns Hopkins who has been involved in trauma-informed violence prevention projects in East Baltimore. What was most striking for me about the conversation was this doubtless well-intentioned person's apparent lack of awareness that anyone associated with Johns Hopkins is bound to be viewed with great suspicion in East Baltimore, that failed past attempts by Johns Hopkins to set up similar trauma-related projects has had a psychological impact on residents, and that not keeping Safe Streets workers and their constituents informed about the erratic process of research grant applications has also had a negative impact.

Clinicians know that loss of trust is one of the most predictable outcomes of relational trauma: when there has been severe or ongoing abuse in a patient's background, it can take many years before he or she can trust that their therapist is genuinely committed to their healing. The same principle surely applies to relationships between a powerful institution like Johns Hopkins and a traumatized community like East Baltimore. Trying to set up trauma informed projects aimed at reducing violence may be well intentioned and may have some value for residents and for Baltimore as a whole, but *unless* Johns Hopkins personnel genuinely take account of the frequently destructive impact the university has had on East Baltimore, and unless the relationship between university employees and local residents is continuous, empathic, consistent, and genuinely collaborative, it is far more likely to be damaging than healing. Every time a new initiative fails or just stops, despair, cynicism and hopelessness may become even more entrenched and self-medication through substance abuse may increase, adding to ever deepening resistance to future programs and initiatives. In regards to communication and keeping local people informed about the progress of grant applications and so forth, while there are many reasons why Safe Streets workers and local residents have to be careful about what they say—they are the ones after all who live and work in the midst of gang activity and the threat of violence—it is incumbent on outside researchers and professionals (including me) to be as transparent and communicative as we possibly can about what we're doing, and why, and to understand that genuinely collaborative relationships require long term commitment.

Drexel University's Healing Hurt People and 11th St Family Health Center demonstrate that, when informed by trauma theory that includes insight into the ways professionals and organizations can and often do re-traumatize their patients and clients, relationships between large institutions and distressed neighborhoods can be very productive. At the same time it is important to remember that there are healing relationships in the 'hood, and in prisons, that do not involve a trained therapist or other health professional. Matt, for example, who endured very difficult childhood conditions, including chronic poverty, disrupted schooling and severe beatings from a stepfather, had this to say about his relationship with Josie:

> Well, I think now, before I met Josie I didn't think it was nothing, I didn't think I was traumatized, I thought it was supposed to happen. Even right now, with the beatings, I know it's traumatizing but by the

> same token I feel like I'm glad that I got someone to help me understand and to feel it because even then I'm learning that if it's pushed on you to learn something you're not going to learn it but if people can help you understand that this is wrong, it makes a difference.

And Gardnel, who got involved with a criminal gang in his early teens, attributes his transformation in prison largely to supportive relationships with other incarcerated men:

> Along the way I had a lot of helpful hands because one thing about incarceration some of the older guys that are incarcerated that maybe went through the same things so they recognize the changes you're making, they become guides, tell you what to read, who to stay away from, they help you educate yourself. A lot of mentors, a lot of mentors, so being mentored I became a mentor myself. . . I found that a lot of young people gravitated toward me because on the one hand who I used to be, and looking at me now, how did this brother make this change? You know what I mean.

Jama Adams writes that in the absence of job and educational pathways and ongoing accessible mentoring, young black men from distressed neighborhoods and homes often "embrace tutoring and validation from amoral persons occupying unsafe spaces" (Adams, 2014, p. 3). Gardnel, like the young men he mentors in East Baltimore, knows exactly what this means, and how transformative it can be to have what Adams calls "caring tutors of the imagination" (2014, p. 1).

CONCLUSION

In this chapter I have tried to show that far from being solely an individual or community problem, the violence and ongoing traumatic stress experienced by residents of America's ghettoes should be understood as large scale *relational* trauma, generated by national and local histories of social and economic exclusion and exploitation of non-elite African Americans. As such it can only be effectively addressed in genuinely collaborative healing and empowering relationships at the local level of interpersonal and intercommunity relationships, to state and federal political commitment to the prevention of exploitative and discriminatory practices and continuous provision of effective and appropriate resources and infrastructure to these highly disadvantaged neighborhoods. Segregation, exploitation and disinvestment cannot, happen without the participation of the majority of Americans. Whether that takes the form of overtly exploitative and discriminatory practices or the more discreet but no less damaging choices so many white and middle-class Americans seem to make—including the majority of psychoanalytic practitioners to avoid any direct contact with the black and brown ghetto, or with prisons, the damage wrought is inestimable. We must recognize that the violence and toxic stress experienced by traumatized ghetto communities is a *collective* problem caused by collective action and inaction. As John Rich writes; "if we want to make ourselves safe, if we want to end the high levels of violence affecting young black men (and, I would add, everyone in their neighborhood and community), we must focus on *their* safety. . . As difficult as it may seem, it is not their transformation that we must seek but ours" (2009, p. 201).

REFERENCES

Adams, J. (2014) The impact of neoliberalism on the psychological development of low-income black youth. *Psychoanalysis, Culture and Society,* 19(1): 39–46.

Ainslie, R. (2013). Intervention strategies for addressing collective trauma: Healing communities ravaged by racial strife. *Psychoanalysis, Culture and Society, 18,* 140–152.

Alexander, M. (2010). *The new Jim Crow: Mass incarceration in the age of colorblindness.* New York: The New Press.

Altman, N. (2013). Psychoanalysis in and out of the office. *Psychoanalysis, Culture and Society,* 18, 128–139.

Altman, N. (2000). Black and white thinking: A psychoanalyst reconsiders race. *Psychoanalytic Dialogues,* 10(4), 589–606.

Anderson, E. (1999). *Code of the street: Decency, violence and the moral life of the inner city.* New York: W.W. Norton.

Bloom, S.L. and Reichert, M. (1998). *Bearing witness: Trauma and collective responsibility.* Binghamton, NY: Haworth Press.

Corbin, T., Rich, J., Bloom, S., Delgado, D., Rich, L., and Wilson, A. (2011). Developing a trauma-informed, emergency-based intervention for victims of urban violence. *Journal of Trauma and Dissociation,* 12(5), 510–525. Cure Violence. http://cureviolence.org/

Diamond, G.M., Lipsitz, J.D., and Hoffman, Y. (2013). Nonpathological response to ongoing traumatic stress. *Peace and Conflict: Journal of Peace Psychology, 19*(2), 100-111. Extralegalese Group (ELG). http://www.extralegalese.com/

Fanon, F. (1967). *Black skins, white masks* (C. L. Markmann, Trans.). New York: Grove Press.

Fitzpatrick, K. (1993). Exposure to violence and presence of depression among low-income African American youth. *Journal of Consulting and Clinical Psychology, 61,* 528–531.

Golden, K. B. and Bergo, B.G. (Eds.). (2009) *The trauma controvers:Philosophical and interdisciplinary dialogues.* Albany, NY: State University of New York Press.

Gomez, M.B. (2012). *Race, class, power and organizing in East Baltimore: Rebuilding abandoned communities in America.* Lanham, MD: Lexington Books.

Goren, E. and Alpert, J. (2013). Conclusion to special issue on psychoanalysis, trauma and community: Psychoanalysts out of the office. *Psychoanalysis, Culture and Society, 18,* 217–221.

Gump, J. (2010). Reality matters: The shadow of trauma on African American subjectivity. *Psychoanalytic Psychology, 27*(1), 42-54. GunCrisis Philadelphia (2013, November 17). A dozen Philadelphia shooting victims reported for the fourth straight weekend. Retrieved December 2, 2013, from http://guncrisis.org/2013/11/17/a-dozen-philadelphia-shooting-victims-reported-for-the-fourth-straight-weekend

Herman, J. (1992). Complex PTSD: A syndrome in survivors of prolonged and repeated trauma. *Journal of Traumatic Stress, 5,* 377–391.

James, S. (Producer/Director), and Kotlowitz, A. (Producer). (2011). *The Interrupters* [Motion Picture]. United States: Kartemquin Films

Katz, M.B. (2012). *Why don't American cities burn?* Philadelphia: University of Pennsylvania Press.

Kita, E. (2011). Potential and possibility: Psychodynamic psychotherapy and social change with incarcerated patients. *Journal of Clinical Social Work 39*, 9–17.

Kostelny, K., and Garbarino, J. (2001). The war close to home: Children and violence in the United States. In D.J. Christie, R.V.,Wagner, and D. A. Winter (Eds.), *Peace, conflict, and violence: Peace psychology for the twenty-first-century* (pp. 110–119). Englewood Cliffs, NJ: Prentice-Hall.

Layton, L. (2006). Racial identities, racial enactments, and normative unconscious processes. *Psychoanalytic Quarterly 75*,237–269.

Leary, K. (1995). "Interpreting in the dark": Race and ethnicity in psychoanalytic psychotherapy. *Psychoanalytic Psychology, 12*(1), 127–140.

Markowitz, G., and Rosner, D. (2013). *Lead wars: The politics of science and the fate of America's children*. Berkeley, CA: University of California Press.

Massey, D. S. and Denton, N. (1993). *American apartheid: Segregation and the making of the underclass.* Cambridge, MA: Harvard University Press.

McDonald, H. (2012). Levinas in the hood: Portable social justice. *The Humanistic Psychologist, 39*(4), 305–311.

Meets, D.R., and Gordon, F. (1975). Traumatic and cultural distortions of psychoneurotic symptoms in a black ghetto. *Annual of Psychoanalysis, 20,* 580- 592.

Orange, D. (2010). *Thinking for clinicians: Philosophical resources for contemporary psychoanalysis and the humanistic psychotherapies.* New York: Routledge.

Osofsky, J.D., Werers, S., Hann, D.M., and Flick, A.C. (1993). Chronic community violence: What is happening to our children? *Psychiatrym 56,* 36–45.

Parker, I. (2008). Temptations of pedagogery: Seventeeen lures. *Subjectivity 24,* 376–379.

Parson, E.R. (1994). Inner city children of trauma: Urban Violence Traumatic Stress Response Syndrome (U-VTS) and therapists' responses. In J.P. Wilson and J.D. Lindy (Eds.), *Countertransference in the treatment of PTSD* (pp 157–178). New York: Guilford Publications, Inc.

Rich, J., (2009). *Wrong place, wrong time: Trauma and violence in the lives of young black men.* Baltimore, MD: The Johns Hopkins Press.

Rich, J., and Grey, C. (2005). Pathways to recurrent trauma among young black men: Traumatic stress, substance abuse, and the "code of the street". *American Journal of Public Health, 95,* 816–824.

Roach, C. (2013). Shallow affect, no remorse: The shadow of trauma in the inner city. *Peace and Conflict: Journal of Peace Psychology 19,* 150-163.

Roseneil, S. (2013). Department of Psychosocial Studies, Birkbeck University of London. Retrieved November 20, 2013, from http://www.bbk.ac.uk/psychosocial/

Scott, D.M. (1997). *Contempt and pity: Social policy and the image of the damaged black psyche, 1880–1996.* Chapel Hill: The University of Carolina Press.

Sharkey, P. (2013). *Stuck in place: urban neighborhoods and the end of progress toward racial equality.* Chicago: The University of Chicago Press.

Singer, M., Anglin, T., Song, L., and Lunghofer, L. (1995). Adolescents' exposure to violence and associated symptoms of psychological trauma. *Journal of the American Medical Association, 273,* 477–482.

Skloot, R. (2010). *The immortal life of Henrietta Lacks.* New York: Crown Publishers.

Smith, L. (Director) and BlueSpark Collaborative. (2014). *Wounded places: Confronting childhood PTSD in America's shell-shocked cities.* [Motion picture]. United States: California Newsreel.

Stepansky, P.E. (2009). *Psychoanalysis at the margins.* New York: Other Press

Stopford, A. (2004). Researching postcolonial subjectivities: The application of relational (postclassical) psychoanalysis to research methodology. *The International Journal of Critical Psychology 10,* 13–35.

Stopford, A. (2007). Psychoanalysis and interraciality: Asking different questions. *Psychoanalysis, Culture and Society, 12,* 205–225

Stopford, A. (2006). Hold the cloth that absorbs tears: Migration, marriage, and money in African Australian relationships. *Studies in Gender and Sexuality 7(1),* 15–30.

Stopford, A. (2008). Leaving "home": The challenges of living with radical cultural difference. *Contemporary Psychoanalysis, 45*(4), 444–466.

Stopford, A. (2013). Unconscious dominions: Psychoanalysis, colonial trauma, and global sovereignties [Book Review]. *Subjectivity, 6,* 445–446.

Straker, G. (1992). *Faces in the revolution: The psychological effects of violence on township youth in South Africa.* Cape Town: David Phillip Publishers (Pty) Ltd. The Baltimore Sun. (2013).Three dead in West Baltimore shooting. Retrieved April 15, 2013, from http://articles.baltimoresun.com/2013-03-19/news/bs-md-ci-triple-shooting-20130319_1_west-baltimore-gun-arrests-murder-rate.

The Center for Research on Globalization (2013). The Boston Marathon bombing's inflated injury tallies. Retrieved November 4, 2013, from http://www.globalresearch.ca/the-boston-marathon-bombings-inflated-injury-tallies/5334725

Vaughans, K. and Spielberg (2014). (Eds). *The psychology of black boys and adolescents.* (2 Vols). Westport, CT: Praeger.

Wachtel, P. (2002). Psychoanalysis and the disenfranchised: From therapy to justice. *Psychoanalytic Psychology, 19,* 199–215.

Wacquant, L. (2001). Deadly symbiosis. When ghetto and prison meet and mesh. *Punishment and Society. 3*(1), 95–134.

Wacquant, L. (2011a). Habitus as topic and tool: Reflections on becoming a prizefighter. *Qualitative Research in Psychology, 8,* 81–92

Wacquant, L. (2011b). A Janus-faced institution of ethnoracial closure: A sociological specification of the ghetto. In R. Hutchison and B.D. Haynes (Eds.), *The Ghetto: Contemporary global issues and controversies* (pp 1–32). Boulder, CO: Westview Press.

Wilson, J.P., and Raphael, B. (Eds.) (1993). *The international handbook of traumatic stress syndromes.* New York: Plenum Press.

TWELVE

Addressing Trauma and Identity in Teacher Education Spaces

Richard T. Johnson and Michael B. Salzman

We do not know if it is a fair comparison but we cannot help but wonder what we would do if we were teachers at Sandy Hook Elementary School when someone with loaded guns entered the school and started injuring and killing the children we serve and our colleagues on one particular day in time. Our thoughts are scattered when we consider this ordeal and compare it to other schools in different war-torn parts of the world that encounter traumatic disasters on a much more frequent basis. We consider how we would have handled the stress and trauma of these violent, life-threatening ordeals while attempting to educate our students. Of particular concern is how do traumatized children handle these psychological, social, emotional and physical traumatic concerns in the classrooms, schools, homes, and larger community settings where traumatic events impact their lives? This concern is highlighted by recent work (Wolmer et al., 2011) that notes that, "Teacher-delivered intervention following large-scale traumatic events is a relatively new approach to deal with massive psychological casualties" (p. 315).

Increasingly, research demonstrates that traumatic events involving life-threat, helplessness and horrifying scenes contribute a risk to mental health and developmental progress among children (Bettencourt, 2011; Bettencourt and Khan, 2008; Bornstein, 2013; Champion, 2009; De Young, Kenardy, and Cobham, 2011; *Science Daily*, 2010). As we follow the news on a daily basis, we witness these events on a global scale. Related news from this morning (1/10/14) revealed another child in Pakistan who lost his life at school while saving the lives of many of his school and classmates. The published story shared that,

> Aitzaz Hasan, a 15-year-old ninth grader, was late for school and rushing with two friends to make the morning assembly when they were stopped by a stranger wearing the same uniform as theirs, who curiously asked for directions. Aitzaz grew suspicious, and tackled the stranger as he tried to flee. Then the stranger blew himself up, killing them both. (Masood, 2014)

A few months ago, while catching up on the online *World News* that morning (11/21/13), we came upon yet another story about war and trauma from across the world that informed us that,

> A landmine blast in southeastern Afghanistan's Paktika province killed seven children and wounded five more playing in the area, officials said. The blast Monday in the Malizi area of the province's Khairkot district occurred when one of the children stepped on the explosive device, Mukhlis Afghan, a spokesman for the governor, told Pajhwok Afghan News. (http://www.upi.com/Top_News/ World-News/2013/11/19/Landmine-explosion-in-Afghanistan-kills-seven-children/UPI-19571384843620/#ixzz2lVYjQGiH)

Stories like those above are typical in war-zones and have become more and more common here in the United States, as well. It was just one year ago in Connecticut that Adam Lanza shot and killed his mother at the home they shared, then drove to Sandy Hook Elementary School with at least three of her guns, forced his way inside and opened fire in two classrooms. In a very brief time period he killed 20 children, six adults and himself. This story mirrors the 1999 Columbine school massacre and the Aurora movie theater shooting just a year earlier (Wolmer et al., 2011). For instance, just last week in a Pennsylvania high school, "A teenage boy wielding two kitchen knives went on a stabbing rampage at his high school in Murrysville, Pennsylvania, early Wednesday, before being tackled by an assistant principal" (Carter, Courson, and Brown, 2014).

In this chapter, we explore several different critical theoretical angles of trauma as we apply it to teacher-education research and teacher and caregiver practices in war-torn areas, such as Afghanistan (Peltonen and Punamäki, 2010), and in our respective U.S. schools and communities. We purposely move around the globe in this discussion to locate the various issues about trauma in different locations, to consider effective treatments of trauma, violence and their aftermath for children globally. For example, yesterday a student informed us that she is applying for a Department of Defense elementary education teaching job which could potentially relocate her to any U.S. military base school around the world. Her personal interactions with children in a military school will probably be quite different than those with children whose parents are not exposed to war.

In this work, we will use trauma studies as a theoretical standpoint to explore the complex realities of constructing, producing, and consuming traumatic violence in educational research and practice (Bartók, 2011). The idea of trauma studies has made tentative inroads into educational research as more studies are delving into critical inquiry and the theoretical, critical, and clinical aspects of the analysis and treatment of trauma, violence, and their aftermath (Carrington and Griffin, 2011; Luest, 2012; O'Loughlin, 2013a, 2013b).

WAR AND TRAUMA TODAY

A wealth of research findings (Flory et al., 2009; Overbeek et al., 2012) reveal that traumatic events such as those noted above, and occurring globally on a daily basis, threaten the mental health and developmental progress of children (Center on the Developing Child at Harvard University, 2010; Lieberman, Van Horn, and Ippen, 2005). For instance, in the currently war-torn country of Afghanistan, these types of violent events have reached epidemic proportions among children. Most of these children are physically and psychologically impacted in line with "a growing body of evidence that early traumatic experiences are associated with health problems throughout the lifespan" (Zimmerman and Mercy, 2011, p. 14). In 2009, over 1000 Afghani children experienced conflict-related violence and were killed or injured. In 2010, two Afghan children were killed in war every day (ARM, 2012). Our interests in Afghanistan and other war-torn environments grew out of Rich's recent personal work with the Ministry of Education in Afghanistan, as he evaluated and assessed the teacher education program and other aspects of education in that part of the world.

Beyond the horrific scope of the lives lost and bodies maimed, with each year of war and violence, thousands of children in Afghanistan have been killed or wounded, displaced from their homes and deprived of education and other essential services because of the war (ARM, 2012). It is not only the physical bodies of people that have been ravaged, but also the physical and psychological places they inhabit. Afghan children have had to deal with many different hurdles to receive an education, such as "militants burning schools down, poisoning students, and assassinating teachers and education officials" (Bezhan and Shinwary, 2012, p. 37).

Over the course of the past 30 years, the war in Afghanistan has been the world's longest-running major armed conflict. In just three years' time (2009–2011), more than 1,000 Afghani children were killed or injured in conflict-related violence. Of these children, 128 were killed by armed opposition groups; 55 were killed and 199 injured in land-mine accidents and 131 children lost their lives in aerial bombings conducted by international military forces in 2009 (Child Victims of War, 2012). In 2010 alone, a total of 1,396 children were killed or maimed, an increase of 35 percent from 2009 (Child Victims of War, 2012). According to the United Nations, 2011 was the deadliest on record for civilians in the Afghan war, with 3,021 people killed, averaging 8.3 deaths per day. Although the number of Afghan civilians killed dropped 36 percent in the first four months of 2013, as compared with the year before. Before, the violent acts continue, with physical, psychological, social, and emotional costs for children and adults alike.

For example, between 2006 and December 2008, 1,153 attacks on education targets were reported, including the damage or destruction of schools by arson, grenades, mines and rockets. Threats to teachers and officials were delivered by "night letters" or verbally, and students, teachers and other educational staff have been killed (Child Victims of War, 2012). These traumatic events continue to occur even after active efforts to improve education in Afghanistan by outside consultancy groups, such as the formal teacher education programs offered through the Teacher Education Division of the Afghanistan Ministry of Education, and efforts by various organizations (e.g., AusAID, UNICEF, UNESCO, World Bank/EQUIP, WUSC/Canada, JICA/Japan, Sweden, USAID/BESST, and Germany) to improve education from preschool to college.

In our extensive personal, theoretical and practicum-based work in formal teacher education programs at the undergraduate and graduate levels in Colleges of Education here in the United States and in war-torn countries like Afghanistan, we have noticed that little practical and research-based attention has been paid to how individuals in educational settings adopt or produce therapeutic practices or what role they can play in representing research or articulating trauma studies as an effective educational practice. Consequently, there has been little discussion concerning the epistemological or practical value of trauma studies to educational research and practice (Cho, 2008). During the past twenty years, our understandings of the impact of trauma on the mind and body has vastly increased, yet there appears to be a large gap in educational research and practice related respectively to modern violence and saturated cultural notions of trauma (Bartók, 2011; Salzman, 2001; Zlotnick et al., 2008).

THE EFFECTS OF WAR AND TRAUMA ON CHILDREN

Recently, the journal *Science Daily* provided research findings showing that "The truth is that violence is a contagious disease just like smallpox and typhoid, and children are particularly susceptible to catch it. In the

Mideast, violence has reached epidemic proportions among children, and most of them are infected" (*Science Daily*, 2010). A wealth of research evidence (Murrough et al., 2011; Zimmerman and Mercy, 2011; Zlotnick et al., 2008) reveals that early traumatic experiences are associated with health problems that occur throughout the lifespan, as these early life experiences are built into our bodies and "Abuse, neglect, and other traumatic events can take a serious toll, contributing to health problems over a lifetime" (Zimmerman and Mercy, 2011, p. 5).

Findings from several decades of research studies reveal,

> [t]he negative impact of abuse and neglect on children has been documented to include injuries, disabilities, and other physical health issues; low academic achievement; and emotional problems 'under the skin' that undermine health and development. Persistent stress produces excessive elevation in heart rate, blood pressure, and stress hormones that can impair brain architecture, immune status, metabolic systems, and cardiovascular function. (Shonkoff, Boyce, and McEwen, 2009, p. 2254)

Although a wealth of research clarifies the impact of traumatic experiences in conflict zones (Thabet et al., 2013), we still need more knowledge about how, as educational professionals inside and outside of elementary and secondary classrooms, we can assist those impacted by violence and aggression, such as the war-affected, displaced youth around the world (Panter-Brick et al., 2009; Van der Oord, Lucassen, Van Emmerik, and Emmelkamp, 2010). Research illustrates that cumulative exposure to traumatic stress in war and crises constitutes a predictor of the development of posttraumatic stress disorder (PTSD) (Weierstall et al., 2013), which has been quite prevalent among the men and women of different military services returning from service in Afghanistan over the past 12 years. Research studies show a clear dose-effect relationship between the exposure to differential stressful life events and the risk of development of post-traumatic stress disorder in various war-affected populations (Finzi-Dottan, et al., 2006; Weierstall, et al., 2013). For instance, while discussing the impact of war on children globally, the War Child organization (2012) recently noted that, "The treatment of children has been undeniably callous. Children and young people have been summarily massacred; illegally detained; sexually abused; used in combat; abducted and tortured, denied schooling and access to humanitarian aid; and deliberately targeted in violent attacks" (p. 5).

ADDRESSING EDUCATION IN WAR-TORN AREAS

In Afghanistan today, 42% of children remain out of school even though education has improved since the time of the Taliban. Progress in war-torn places like Afghanistan has been hampered by a shortage of qualified teachers, a lack of facilities (e.g., including school buildings), and ongoing threats posed by insurgents (Child Victims of War, 2012), leaving children increasingly bearing the brunt of that conflict: "One in five Afghan children suffers psychiatric disorder. Children who had experienced more than five traumatic events, such as domestic or community and war-related violence, were more than twice as likely as others to develop mental health problems" (Devlin et al., 2009, p. 3).

Like other research (Steele, 2009), Hasonovic et al.'s work also clarifies how children are the most vulnerable in these types of physical and emotional settings (2007). This work reveals that,

> Massive exposure to wartime trauma overwhelms most psychological defensive mechanisms in children, and that children may mitigate war effects in low-to-moderately intense wartime settings, which allows effective functioning after acclimatization. We found a high level of comorbidity between PTSD and depression among children exposed to war trauma who lost one or both parents. There was also highly positive correlation between PTSD, depression, and suicidal thoughts (Hasanović et al, 2006, pp. 90–91).

The World Health Organization (WHO) estimated in 2001 that, out of a population of 30 million, 5 million Afghan women and men suffered from mental distress such as PTSD, depression, anxiety disorders, and substance abuse and dependence (Panter-Brick, 2010; Thabet, et al., 2011a). Moving forward just a few years, Thabet and colleagues (2011b) noted that, "In 2009, there were two trained psychiatrists (neither practicing their profession due to other governmental obligations) and a smattering of psychologists and psychiatric nurses. Professional capacity in mental health is completely lacking" (p. 234). These findings are stunning given that "Severe traumatization stemming from violence can have effects for generations. The difficult conditions under which women and girls live and their social isolation have additional negative effects" (Thabet, Karim, and Vostanis, 2006, p. 155). These authors further discuss the impact of the continuing pervasiveness of domestic violence in Afghanistan and how this affects physical and mental health, productivity, and security not only of women but of society as a whole:

> Afghan males returning from long-standing wars are now at greater risk for developing aggression, hypervigilance, high levels of anxiety, flashbacks of traumatic memories, and other trauma-related symptoms. Left untreated, these have negative impacts not only on the normal functioning of men but also on their families. (Thabet, Karim, and Vostanis, 2006, p. 155)

When we view and further study images of active war zones and the rampant destruction, we then readily visualize how, "The consequences of military traumas are highly devastating including loss of close persons, demolition of homes, and witnessing of killing" (Peltonen and

Punamäki, 2010, p. 96). When we read about Afghanistan, each story speaks to these notions of devastation, demolition, and killing, and yet reading about it from afar can make it difficult to imagine what it must be like as a daily occurrence throughout a child's life. Research studies reveal that excessive fears and internalizing and externalizing symptoms are common consequences of traumatic events. Although teacher educators can recognize these types of sequelae in their students, trauma is not actively addressed in the formal curriculum plans and available teacher education program materials (i.e., syllabus and program standards) offered by university programs today.

Traumatic events have especially negative effects on regulative processes in cognitive (e.g., attention, memory and interpretation), emotional (soothing, recognition and expression) and functional (sleeping and eating) domains, which places traumatized children at increased risk for subsequent psychopathology (Keanne, Marshall, and Taft, 2006; Rosendal et al., 2011; Uguak, 2011). As with adults (Kerestes and Milanovic, 2006), "high co-morbidity between PTSD and depressive symptoms have been found among children and adolescents exposed to war and military violence" (Peltonen and Punamäki, 2010, p. 96). In certain parts of Afghanistan, "education has become both a target and a tool for terrorist attacks. . . as an estimated 238 schools have been destroyed since April 2006 and 650 have been rendered "inoperable as of March 2009" (JICA, 2009). Research from several decades of studies reveal "the negative impact of abuse and neglect on children has been documented to include injuries, disabilities, and other physical health issues; low academic achievement; and emotional problems" (Zimmerman and Mercy, 2011, p. 167). These extensive findings note that adversity can get "under the skin" and undermine health and development (Kohrt et al., 2011).

Current research findings exemplify that "In war and crisis, the cumulative exposure to traumatic stress constitutes a predictor of the development of post traumatic stress disorder (PTSD)" (Weierstall, et al, 2013, p. 140). Research by Peltonen and Punamäki noted that, "About a quarter (17–25 percent) of children exposed to severe collective trauma, such as natural and technical disasters, suffer from PTSD, whereas among victims of interpersonal trauma such as sexual abuse the rate is considerably higher, ranging from 40–58 percent" (Peltonen and Punamäki, 2010, p. 96). Peltonen and Punamäki's clinical work on PTSD then notes, "Personal exposure to severe violence and losses can result in prevalence as high as 58–69 percent (Palestinian children) or 80 percent (Iraqi children)" (2010, p. 96).

IMPLICATIONS FOR TEACHER EDUCATION PROGRAMS

From a teacher education perspective, we are left stifled by undergraduate and graduate teacher preparation curriculum that does not prepare us to consider what our kindergarten, 3rd or 5th grade, middle school or high school teachers would critically engage as discussion points individually and group-wise with the students they serve if tragedy were to happen in their personal school community. Our undergraduate teacher preparation curriculum requires only one class, *Educational Psychology*, that potentially might or might not address the numerous, varied issues that can arise. When we conducted a quick review of several syllabi available for that course, we did not see the word *trauma* even mentioned. Once in the classroom, our nation's focus on teaching to the standards (i.e., Common Core) and "Racing to the Top" allows little to no time to address trauma and identity and creatively work through how real-life issues impact the teacher and children as community members.

Similarly, when we studied the Afghanistan Ministry of Education's formal Teacher Education program a few years ago, we found that they offered almost identical coursework as our Teacher Education program in Hawai'i. We did not see the word trauma used in any formal capacity, and the content in related coursework was focused on subject delivery (e.g., science, mathematics, language and literacy) and foundational (e.g., education psychology and foundations of education) course content.

RESILIENCY AND PROTECTIVE FACTORS

Early interventions can be vitally important for later socio-emotional development, as our actions or lack thereof "sets either a sturdy or fragile stage for what happens" (Shonkoff and Phillips, 2000). As evidenced by the previous discussion and examples, multiple opportunities present themselves to both the child and the caregiver(s) (whether parent, teacher, babysitter, etc.) for the promotion of effective socio-emotional development. Given what we know of the deep connections between emotion and cognition (Lewis, 2005; Phelps, 2006), and how they are "interactive and integrated or mingled in the brain" (Izard et al., 2008, p. 3), our role as teachers and caregivers of young children must include developmentally effective promotion of these capacities (Andreassen and West, 2007; Damasio, 1999). Other related findings typify that how siblings, peers, classmates, parents and teachers interact influences "neural systems and mental processes involved in emotion feelings, perception, and cognition" (Izard et al., 2008, p. 369).

Children's learning opportunities and experiential background around socio-emotional development contribute to their growth. Adults play a pivotal role in this development, as they have the potential to provide children with the necessary experiences that will assist in the provision of constructive and effective means for self-expression (Aikens, Coleman, and Barbarin, 2008; Spagnola and Fiese, 2007). Not recognizing and taking advantage of the possible positive growth opportunities here can lead to a "cascade of psychological, neurobiological, and genetic processes that interfere with the acquisition of adaptive self-regulatory capacities in youngsters and increase children's risk for future emotion regulation" (Maughan et al., 2007, p. 699).

When children's life experiences fall out of the normative structure of what a so-called "typical" infant, toddler, or preschool child is accustomed to, this can potentially impact their development in negative ways (Dyson, 2003). For example, when a child experiences continuous traumatization (e.g., child abuse; ongoing ineffective foster care placement; parental separation or divorce; bullying by a peer or sibling) and other aversive interpersonal incidents (Nesdale and Pickering, 2006) and has no effective healthy interventions provided, these ongoing negative interactions can lead to high levels of aggressive cognition and impulses in children (Bigatti, Cronan, and Anaya, 2001; Francis and Wolfe, 2008; Slep and O'Leary, 2001). Statistics reveal that as many as 60% of school-age children may at some time be a victim of bullying. If left untreated, these neglected aggressive tendencies potentially increase and continue to manifest themselves in negative ways for both the recipient (i.e., the child) and the transgressor (i.e., adult, peer, sibling) (Aikens, Coleman, and Barbarin, 2008; Larson et al., 2008; NICHD Early Child Care Research Network, 2004). It is therefore critical that such aversive experiences are addressed in the early years and that children are able to build a repertoire of effective, proactive strategies.

Traumatic interactions will likely impact the child's experiences in school (Pianta and Stuhlman, 2004). For instance, if a child is abused at home, this could lead to difficulties in actively engaging in the classroom. Neglect, such as that found, for example, with depressed mothers, can also impede the child's ability to actively engage (Aikens, Coleman and Barbarin, 2008). The unknowing teacher or potential friend might label avoidant or anxious behaviors in ways that lead to interpersonal conflict and social exclusion on the playground or during group work.

Again, these have far-reaching consequences as "these types of stressors may reduce children's participation in collaborative learning activities and adversely affect achievement" (Duncan et al., 2007, p. 1430). Research reveals that negative socio-emotional interactions impact children's self-control, interpersonal skills, aggressive behavior and worries, and that children experiencing these interactional patterns are reported to feel unloved and sad, cry more often, and to be more anxious, depressed, antisocial, stubborn, less cooperative and worried (Duncan et al., 2007). The negative potential of these feelings and behaviors then influence how a child interacts with peers and adults in school, including self-concept and motivation for learning (Greenberg et al., 2003; Heins et. al., 2011). It is not necessarily the number or frequency of these traumatic events that impacts children and adults. Even "a single traumatic event, as in the case of the recent Japanese tsunami or the September 11 terrorist attacks in the United States, can be the cause of PTSD in thousands of individuals" (Jain et al., 2012, p. 543). Again, this is where teacher educators can play an important role as we work with pre-service and professional teachers in our undergraduate and graduate education programs. Research shows that "emotional, behavioral and social problems of children and adolescents, including anxiety, depression, disruptive behavior problems, and substance abuse, can be prevented or ameliorated through the use of school-based interventions" (Urbis, 2011, p. vii). The role of the teacher(s) in environments where school counselors and other professionally educated officials do not exist (e.g., Afghanistan, Syria, Palestine), becomes even more notable as we consider from a teacher-education perspective the courses and practicum experiences that might assist them in effectively intervening in the multitude of children's lived experiences.

CONCLUSION

As we are all well aware, in today's world traumatic events continue to demand our attention. The *WorldNews* on ABC a few months ago (1/15/14) began with a lead story about a middle school here in the United States. The report shared that on that particular day (1/14/14) in a school in New Mexico, a 12-year-old boy with a loaded shotgun walked into his school and opened fire in the cafeteria wounding at least 2 students before his gun was removed from his possession. The news report later shared related statistics about the number of shootings in schools in the United States since 2000. Between 2000 and 2008, the number of shootings in schools averaged 5 per year, and since 2009 the numbers have tripled to average about 16 per year over the past 5 years.

Statistics like these, along with the research presented previously (van Dam et al., 2012; Varese et al., 2012), represent how child trauma remains a serious global concern requiring a wealth of technical assistance and education to service providers that has not been provided to date (Luest, 2012). We need critical research-based work to support our clinical practices with children and educational curriculum work given the scarcity of current "research on interventions with children and youths traumatized by war and organized violence (Erti et al., 2011). "All too often, we see that children are left in situations of prolonged, interpersonal and repeated abuse and neglect, impacting their worldview, neurobiology, developmental momentum, mental and behavioral health, and subsequently, their ability to engage in healthy relationships" (Luest, 2012, http://www.witnessjustice.org/advocacysta/issue_brief.pdf).

As educators working with pre-service and veteran teachers and school administrative staff, we have much active work to do in effectively addressing the many related current education and community issues (e.g., loss of power, bullying, exposure to stress, child abuse, PTSD, a view of the self as vulnerable) discussed here (Berger and Gelkopf, 2009; Gelkopf and Berger, 2009; Urbis, 2011). Our failure to address these many topics on education and trauma effectively (Tyrka et al., 2009) makes it more difficult to recognize and address the deleterious effects of continued exposure to violence in school, home, and community settings, such as those "associated with dramatic increases in post-traumatic stress symptoms and increases in aggressive behavior directed at peers" (*Science Daily*, 2010). Repeated exposure to these violent and traumatic acts also results in difficulty in sustaining attention, an incapacity to listen, failure to complete duties, difficulty in organization, avoidance of mental tasks, memory dysfunction, irritability and restlessness, all of which impede cognitive development and school performance (Thabet et al., 2011a).

The role of educators in all parts of the world is critical, as parents and families might not be effectively dealing with the wide variety of issues that impact children's "ability to recover from the damaging impact of traumatic events" (Lieberman, 2004, p. 338). If we do not somehow address this timely work in our diverse global communities and schools (Kohrt et al., 2011; Steele, 2009), then trauma will be allowed to continue to be "strongly predictive of psychotic experiences" (Kelleher et al., 2013) for those children whom our work is meant to serve and assist. Lieberman's work (2004) on traumatic stress speaks to this notion quite powerfully as she notes:

> When the child does not have an opportunity to process, give meaning, and learn to cope with the sequelae of the traumatic experience with a trusted adult, the trauma can have a devastating impact not only on the child's mastery of stage-specific developmental tasks at the time of the trauma but also on the course of subsequent development. (p. 339)

As clinical educators, we need to personally recognize the "different kinds of traumatic stressors and associated fear or dissociative reactions in considering the mechanisms of posttrauma mental health" (Rosendal et al., 2011, p. 636). Moving forward from there, we need to inform our students and ourselves so that we can more effectively provide and critique different theoretical and research-based perspectives and also oversee clinical experiences of our pre- and inservice teachers working with children who experience these stressors (Steele, 2009; Steele and Kuban, 2011). The findings presented here affirm the urgent need for more comprehensive prevention and intervention strategies against childhood trauma in the community, from war zones to abuse at home and bullying at school.

REFERENCES

ABCNews. (2014). *Young guns: New numbers on kids and guns.* Retrieved January 28, 2014, from http://abcnews.go.com/WNT/video/hidden-camera-experiment-children-drawn-guns-found-classroom-22258370

Aikens, N.L., Coleman, C.P., and Barbarin, O.A. (2008). Ethnic differences in the effects of parental depression on preschool children's socioemotional functioning. *Social Development, 17*(1), 137–160.

Andreassen, C., and West, J. (2007). Measuring socioemotional functioning in a national birth cohort study. *Infant Mental Health Journal, 28*(6), 627–646.

ARM. (2012). *Two Afghan children killed in war everyday in 2010.* Retrieved July 7, 2012, from http://www.arm.org.af/ idex.php?page=en _Latest + News+05

Bartók, M. (2011). *The memory palace: A memoir.* New York: Free Press.

Berger, R., and Gelkopf, M. (2009). School-based intervention for the treatment of tsunami-related distress in children: A quasi-randomized controlled trial. *Psychotherapy and Psychosomatics, 78*(6), 364–71.

Bettencourt, T. (2011). Attending to the mental health of war-affected children: The need for longitudinal and developmental research perspectives. *Journal of the American Academy of Child and Adolescent Psychiatry, 50*(4), 323-325.

Bettencourt, T., and Khan, K. (2008). The mental health of children affected by armed conflict: Protective processes and pathways to resilience. *International Review of Psychiatry, 20*, 317-328.

Bezhan, F., and Shinwary, H. (2012). *System tests Afghan graduates' resistance to radicalism.* Radio Free Europe. Retrieved July 12, 2012 from http://www.afghanistannewscenter.com/news/2012/may/may312012.html#a3

Bigatti, S.M., Cronan, T.A., and Anaya, A. (2001). The effects of maternal depression on the efficacy of a literacy intervention program. *Child Psychiatry and Human Development, 32*, 147–162.

Bornstein, D. (2013, November 3). Protecting children from toxic stress. *The New York Times.*

Carrington, K.L., and Griffin, S. (2011). *Transforming terror: Remembering the soul of the world.* Berkeley: University of California Press.

Carter, C.J., Courson, P., and Brown, P. (2014). *Four school stabbing victims in critical condition: Teen suspect charged as adult.* Retrieved April 10, 2014, from http://www.cnn.com/2014/04/09/justice/pennsylvania-school-stabbing/

Center on the Developing Child at Harvard University. (2010). *The Foundations of Lifelong Health Are Built in Early Childhood.* National Scientific Council on the Developing Child and the National Forum on Early Childhood Policy and Programs.

Champion, M. (2009). *Afghan children under war trauma.* Retrieved July 23, 2013, from http:southasia.oneworld.net/todaysheadlines/afghan-children-under-war-trauma/

Child Victims of War. (2012). Promoting peace—protecting children. Retrieved March 23, 2014, from http://childvictimsofwar.org.uk/

Cho, G.M. (2008). *Haunting the Korean diaspora: Shame, secrecy, and the forgotten war.* Minneapolis: University of Minnesota Press.

Damasio, A. (1999). *The feeling of what happens: Body and emotion in the making of consciousness.* New York: Harcourt Brace.

Devlin, L., Rinck, J., Dennys, C., and Zaman, I. (2009). Conflict analysis: Kunduz city, Kunduz province. *Cooperation for Peace and Unity.* Retrieved January 3, 2014, from http://www.cmi.no/pdf/?file=/afghanistan/doc/ACF178.pdf

De Young, A.C., Kenardy, J.A., and Cobham, V. E. (2011). Diagnosis of posttraumatic stress disorder in preschool children. *Journal of Clinical Child and Adolescent Psychology, 40*(3), 375–384.

Duncan, G.J., Claessens, A., Huston, A.C., Pagani, L.S., Engel, M., Sexton, H., Dowsett, C.J., Magnuson, K., Klebanov, P., Feinstein, L., Brooks-Gunn, J., Duckworth, K., and Japel, C. (2007). School readiness and later achievement. *Developmental Psychology, 43*(6), 1428–1446.

Dyson, L. L. (2003). Children with learning disabilities within the family context: A comparison with sibling in global self-concept, academic self-perception, and social competence. *Learning Disabilities Research and Practice, 18*(1), 1–9.

Erti, V., Pfeiffer, A., Schauer, E., Elbert, T., and Neuner, F. (2011). Community-implemented trauma therapy for former child soldiers in Northern Uganda. *JAMA, 306*(5), 503–512.

Finzi-Dottan, R., Dekel, R., Lavi, T., and Su'ali, T. (2006). Posttraumatic stress disorder reactions among children with learning disabilities exposed to terror attacks. *Comprehensive Psychiatry, 47*, 144–151.

Flory, J.D., Yehuda, R., Grossman, R., New, A.S., Mitropoulou, V., and Siever, L.J. (2009). Childhood trauma and basal cortisol in people with personality disorders. *Comprehensive Psychiatry*, 50, 34–37.

Francis, K.J., and Wolfe, D.A. (2008). Cognitive and emotional differences between abusive and non-abusive fathers. *Child Abuse and Neglect, 32*, 1127–1137.

Gelkopf, M., and Berger, R. (2009). A school-based, teacher-mediated prevention program (ERASE-Stress) for reducing terror-related traumatic reactions in Israeli youth: A quasi-randomised controlled trial. *Journal of Child Psychology and Psychiatry, 50*(8), 962–971.

Greenberg, M.T., Weissberg, R.P., O'Brien, M.U., Zins, J.E., Fredericks, L., Resnik, H., and Elias, M.J. (2003). Enhancing school-based prevention and development through coordinated social, emotional, and academic learning. *American Psychologist, 58*, 466–477.

Hasanović, M., Sinanović, O., Selimbašić, Z., Pajević, I., and Avdibegović, E. (2006). Psychological disturbances of war-traumatized children from different foster and family settings in Bosnia and Herzegovina. *Croatian Medical Journal, 47*, 85–94.

Heins, M., Simons, C., Lataster, T., Pfeifer, S., Versmissen, D., Lardinois, M., Marcelis, M., Delespaul, P., Krabbendam, L., van Os, J., and Myin-Germeys, I. (2011). Childhood trauma and psychosis: A case-control and case-sibling comparison across different levels of genetic liability, psychopathology, and type of trauma. *American Journal of Psychiatry, 168*, 1286–1294.

Izard, C.E., King, K.A., Trentcosta, C.J., Morgan, J.K., Laurenceau, J.P., Krauthamer-Ewing, E. S., and Finlon K. J. (2008). Accelerating the development of emotion competence in Head Start children. *Developmental Psychology, 20*(1), 369–397.

Jain, S., McMahon, N.C., Hasen, P., Kozub, M.P., Porter, V., King, R., and Guarneri, E.M. (2012). Healing touch with guided imagery for PTSD in returning active duty military: A randomized controlled trial. *Military Medicine, 177*.

Japan International Cooperative Agency (JICA). (2009). *The difficulty and perils of education in Afghanistan*. Tokyo, Japan: Japan International Cooperation Agency (JICA).

Keane, T.M., Marshall, A.D., and Taft, C.D. (2006). Posttraumatic stress disorder: Etiology, epidemiology, and treatment outcome. *Annual Review Clinical Psychology, 2*, 161–197.

Kelleher, I., Keeley, H., Corcoran, P., Ramsay, H., Wasserman, C., Carli, V., Sarchiapone, M., Hoven, C., Wasserman, D., and Cannon, M. (2013). Childhood trauma and psychosis in a prospective cohort study: Cause, effect, and directionality. *American Journal of Psychiatry, 170*(7), 734–41.

Kerestes, G., and Milanovic, A. (2006). Relations between different types of children's aggressive behavior and sociometric status among peers of the same and opposite gender. *Scandinavian Journal of Psychology, 47*(6), 477–483.

Kohrt, B.A., Jordans, M., Tol, W.A., Luitel, N.P., Mahargan, S.M., and Upadhaya, N. (2011). Validation of cross-cultural child mental health and psychosocial research instruments: Adapting the depression self-rating scale and child PTSD symptom scale in Nepal. *BMC Psychiatry, 11,* 127–144.

Larson, K., Russ, S.A., Crall, J.J., and Halfon, N. (2008). Influence of multiple social risks on children's health. *Pediatrics, 121*(2), 337–344.

Lewis, M. (2005). Bridging emotion theory and neurobiology through dynamic systems modeling. *Behavior and Brain Science, 28,* 169–245.

Lieberman, A.F. (2004). Traumatic stress and quality of attachment: Reality and internalization in disorders of infant mental health. *Infant Mental Health Journal, 25*(4), 336–351.

Lieberman, A.F., Van Horn, P., and Ippen, C.G. (2005). Toward evidence-based treatment: Child-parent psychotherapy with preschoolers exposed to marital violence. *Journal of the American Academy of Child and Adolescent Psychiatry, 44,* 1241–1248.

Luest, H. (2012). Addressing the mental health of violence and trauma on children. *Coalition Addressing Trauma.* Retrieved January 13, 2014, from http://www.witnessjustice.org/advocacysta/issue_brief.pdf

Masood, S. (2014). *Call to honor Pakistani boy in fatal tackle of a bomber.* Retrieved January 11, 2014, from http://www.nytimes.com/2014/01/10/world/asia/call-to-honor-pakistani-boy-in-fatal-tackle-of-a-bomber.html)

Maughan, A., Cicchetti, D., Toth, S.L., and Rogosch, F.A. (2007). Early-occurring maternal depression and maternal negativity in predicting young children's emotion regulation and socioemotional difficulties. *Journal of Abnormal Child Psychology, 35,* 685–703.

Murrough, J.W., Czermak, C., Henry, S., Nabulsi, N., Gallezot, JD., Gueorguiva, R., Planeta-Wilson, B., Krystal, J.H., Neumaier, J.F., Huang, Y., Ding, YS., Carson, R.E., and Neumeister, A. (2011). The effect of early trauma exposure on serotonin type 1B receptor expression revealed by reduced selective radioligand binding. *Archives of General Psychiatry, 68*(9), 892–900.

Nesdale, D., and Pickering, K. (2006). Teachers' reactions to children's aggression. *Social Development, 15,* 109–127.

NICHD Early Child Care Research Network. (2004). Trajectories of physical aggression from toddlerhood to middle childhood: Predictors, correlates, and outcomes. *Monographs of the Society of Research in Child Development, 69*(4, Serial No. 278).

O'Loughlin, M. (2013a). Introduction. In M. O'Loughlin (Ed.), *Psychodynamic perspectives on working with children, families, and schools.* Lanham, MD: Jason Aronson.

O'Loughlin, M. (Ed.). (2013b). *Psychodynamic perspectives on working with children, families, and schools.* Lanham, MD: Jason Aronson.

Overbeek, M.M., deSchipper, J.C., Lamers-Winkelman, F., and Schuengel, C. (2012). The effectiveness of a trauma-focused psycho-educational secondary prevention program for children exposed to interparental violence: Study protocol for a randomized trial. *Trials Journal, 13,* 12. Retrieved January 2, 2014, from http://www.trialsjournal.com/content/13/1/12

Panter-Brick, C. (2010). Conflict, violence, and health: Setting a new interdisciplinary agenda. *Social Science and Medicine, 70*(1), 1–6.

Panter-Brick, C., Eggerman, M., Gonazalez, V., and Safdar, S. (2009). Violence, suffering, and mental health in Afghanistan: A school-based survey. *The Lancet, 374,* 807–816.

Peltonen, K., and Punamäki, R-L. (2010). Preventive interventions among children exposed to trauma of armed conflict: A literature review. *Aggressive Behavior, 36,* 95–116.

Phelps, E.A. (2006). Emotion and cognition: Insights from studies of the human amygdala. *Annual Review of Psychology, 57,* 27–53.

Pianta, R.C., and Stuhlman, M.W. (2004). Teacher-child relationships and children's success in the first years of school. *School Psychology Review, 33,* 444–458.

Rosendal, S., Salcioglu, E., Andersen, H.S., and Mortensen, E.L. (2011). Exposure characteristics and peri-trauma emotional reactions during the 2004 tsunami in Southeast Asia—what predicts posttraumatic stress and depressive symptoms? *Comprehensive Psychiatry, 52*, 630–637.

Salzman, M. (2001). Cultural trauma and recovery: Perspectives from terror management theory. *Trauma, Violence and Abuse: A Review Journal, 2*(2), 172–191.

Science Daily. (2010, September 16). How Palestinian and Israeli children are psychologically scarred by exposure to war. *Science Daily*. Retrieved August 19, 2013, from http://www.sciencedaily.com/releases/2011/03/110329095742.htm

Shonkoff, J., Boyce, W.T., and McEwan, B.F. (2009). Neuroscience, molecular biology, and the childhood roots of health disparities: Building a new framework for health promotion and disease prevention. *JAMA, 301*(21), 2252–2259.

Shonkoff, J., and Phillips, D., (Eds.). (2000). *From neurons to neighborhoods: The science of early childhood development*. Committee on Integrating the Science of Early Childhood Development, Board on Children, Youth, and Families. National Research Council.

Slep, A.M.S., and O'Leary, S.G. (2001). Examining partner and child abuse: Are we ready for a more integrated approach to family violence? *Clinical Child and Family Psychology Review, 4*, 87–107.

Spagnola, M., and Fiese, B. H. (2007). Family routines and rituals: A context for development in the lives of young children. *Infants and Young Children, 20*(4), 284–299.

Steele, W. (2009). An evidence-based intervention for trauma victims. *Reclaiming Children and Youth, 18*(1), 20–23.

Steele, W., and Kuban, C. (2011). Trauma-informed resilience and posttraumatic growth (PTG). *Reclaiming Children and Youth, 20*(3), 44–46.

Thabet, A.A.M., Tawahina, A.A., Sarraj, E.E., Henely, D., Pelleick, H., and Vostanis, P. (2013). Comorbidity of posttraumatic stress disorder, attention deficit with hyperactivity, conduct, and oppositional defiant disorder in Palestinian children affected by war on Gaza. *Health (1949–4998), 5*(6), 994–1002.

Thabet, A.A.M., Tawahina, A.A., Sarraj, E.E., Henely, D., Pelleick, H., and Vostanis, P. (2011a). Post-traumatic stress disorder and attention-deficit hyperactivity disorder in Palestinian children affected by the war on Gaza. *International Psychiatry, 8*(4), 90–91.

Thabet, A.A.M., Matar, S., Carpintero, A., Bankart, J., and Panos, V. (2011b). Mental health problems among labour children in the Gaza Strip. *Child: Care, Health and Development, 7*(1), 89–95.

Thabet, A. A. M., Karim, K., and Vostanis, P. (2006). Trauma exposure in pre-school children in a war zone. *The British Journal of Psychiatry, 188*, 154-158.

Tyrka, A.K., Wyche, M.C., Kelly, M.M., Price, L.H., and Carpenter, L.L. (2009). Childhood maltreatment and adult personality disorder symptoms: Influence of maltreatment type. *Psychiatry Research, 165*, 442–447.

Uguak, U.A. (2011). The importance of psychological needs for the posttraumatic stress disorder (PTSD) and displaced children in schools. *Journal of Instructional Psychology, 37*(4), 340–352.

Urbis. (2011). *The psychological and emotional wellbeing needs of children and young people: Models of effective practice in educational settings*. Final Report. Retrieved November 13, 2013, from http://www.urbis.com.au/

Van Dam, D.S., van der Ven, E., Velthorst, E., Selten, J.P., Morgan, C. and de Haan, L.. (2012). Childhood bullying and the association with psychosis in non-clinical and clinical samples: A review and meta-analysis. *Psychological Medicine, 42*(12), 2463–74.

Varese, F., Smeets, F., Drukker, M., Lieverse, R., Lataster, T. Viechtbauer, W., Read, J. van Os, J. and Bentall, R.P.. (2012). Childhood adversities increase the risk of psychosis: A meta-analysis of patient-control, prospective-and cross-sectional cohort studies. *Schizophrenia Bulletin, 38*(4), 661–71.

WarChild. (2012). *Syria: A war on childhood*. Retrieved July 11, 2012, from www.warchild.org.uk

Weierstall, R., Hinsberger, M., Kaminer, D., Holtzhausen, L., Madikane, S., and Elbert, T. (2013). Appetitive aggression and adaptation to a violent environment among youth offenders. *Peace and Conflict: Journal of Peace Psychology, 19*(2), 138–149.

Wolmer, L., Hamiel, D., Barchas, J.D., Slone, M., and Laor, N. (2011). Teacher-delivered resilience-focused intervention in schools with traumatized children following the second Lebanon war. *Journal of Traumatic Stress, 24*(3), 309–316.

Zimmerman, F., and Mercy, J.A. (2011). *A better start: Child maltreatment prevention as a public policy priority. Zero to Three*. Retrieved July 15, 2012, from http://www.zerotothree.org/maltreatment/child-abuse-neglect/30-5-zimmerman.pdf

Zlotnick, C., Johnson, J., Kohn, R., Vicente, B, Rioseco, P., and Saldivia, S. (2008). Childhood trauma, trauma in adulthood, and psychiatric diagnoses: Results from a community sample. *Comprehensive Psychiatry, 49*, 163–169.

THIRTEEN

Making Sense of the Senseless

Feeling Bad, Being Mad, Getting Charged Up

Judy Atkinson

COLONIZATION, TRAUMATIZATION, AND HEALING

I am an Aboriginal[1] Australian woman, of Jiman and Bundjalung heritage, as well as Anglo-Celtic German ancestry. In 2006, I won the Carrick Neville Bonner Award for my curriculum development and innovative teaching practice in response to generational trauma stemming from the violence of colonization and the healing/recovery of Indigenous peoples from such trauma. In 2011 I was awarded the Fritz Redlick Memorial Award for Human Rights and Mental Health from the Harvard University program for Refugee Trauma. My book, "*Trauma Trails: Recreating Songlines: The transgenerational effects of trauma in Indigenous Australia,*" provides context to the life stories of people who have been moved from their country in a process that has created trauma trails, and the changes that can occur in the lives of people as they make connection with each other and share their stories of healing. In retirement, as well as the work I do across Aboriginal Australia, I am presently volunteering my time to skill a trauma informed workforce in Papua New Guinea, which can respond to the needs of people who have experienced violence within Papua New Guinea society.

In this chapter I narrate the stories, in part, of Aboriginal Australian men and women who have been both alcohol and drug dependent, and who have had what Western mental health practitioners would label as mental illness. This narration helps to show the effects of trauma through an Aboriginal lens that contextualizes the transgenerational experience that contributes to people's present circumstances. I will show the links between the traumatic experiences of the colonial processes, with alcohol and drug misuse by Aboriginal Australians, interconnected with the increasing incidence of physical, emotional, mental and spiritual distress, including self-harm and harm of others. With their permission, I am using these stories, in their words, linking them to the theory base of healing from trauma.[2] These healing steps are: 1. Establishing safe cultural and spiritually safe places for trauma-healing work to occur; 2. Finding and telling the stories; 3. Making sense of the stories; 4. Feeling the feelings in safety to self and others; 5. Moving through the layers of loss and grief to acceptance; 6. Reclaiming cultural and spiritual identities.[3]

I will include myself in the narrative. What was happening for me in our relationship, as we worked together and with others in our group through the pain of their trauma, is relevant to the bigger story. I will demonstrate the need for workers to always check in with themselves, to be about their own healing work if they desire to work effectively with others. In the context of trauma healing, in this chapter I will then present concepts of Indigenous[4] therapeutic practice presently offered as contributing to the essential healing needs of Indigenous (and in the spirit of Dadirri—non-Indigenous) lives as we work together to repair the traumatic distress of our collective colonization.

IN THE BEGINNING: THE PAST

Stanner has summarized the cultural and spiritual beliefs and practices of Aboriginal people, both in day to day living and in sacred ceremonial practice as: "uniting hearts and establishing order,"[5] in relationship to both the natural world and to other humans. Relationship is of central importance to Aboriginal people. There is no relationship without feeling. People have deep and abiding relationships with their country, which also defines people's relationships with other people. Such relationships define all that it means to be Aboriginal.

Within both the natural world and in human relationships, there is always the potential for disorder and disharmony. Natural disasters such as flood, fire, drought, and cyclone are a normal part of the extreme Australian climate. Relationships with the natural world, and in particular the distressed feelings that accompany a natural disaster, were processed through ceremony and ritual so that healing could occur in the land, with other living species and between the land and the people. Order was maintained in relationship with the natural world by the rituals and ceremonies conducted to ensure species increase and the healing of the environment which was essential for survival. Order was also ensured in human relationships by such ceremonies and rituals. It was as if Aboriginal people knew then what we know now, that after a disaster—either manmade or natural—the psyche or soul of the human has to be healed, otherwise the trauma that results from violence will be enacted on other humans and on the earth itself.[6]

In previous times, when the conflict normal to all human relationships occurred, ceremonial processes were used to bring the contending parties together to manage the conflict and to mediate ways in which people could live with each other. Then and today, there was and is a continuing tension between the rights of an individual and responsibility to the group, the role and place of women, and the role and place of men within the whole as *community*. As men and women came together in ceremony, both in separate gender groups and in the context of *community*, relationships were renegotiated, redefined and healed on an ongoing basis. This is in keeping with an ethic that respects moral authority and honors *community* and which places great emphasis on, and effort in, the maintenance of relationships. Through dance, art, music, theater, and story telling, used and acted out in day-to-day secular and sacred ceremony, relationships were established, maintained, re-affirmed, strengthened, and healed.

The disasters of colonization brought disorder and disharmony. Today, some Aboriginal families reflect the pain and disorder that came with the disasters of the colonial process: large scale epidemics; massacres; removals of whole populations to detainment or refugee camps; removal of children; physical and cultural genocide. Many of these experiences are now understood to induce traumatic stress in human beings.[7] In fact, through these trauma-inducing actions, the relationships between the people and their land and among themselves were willfully destroyed.

TRAUMATIZATION AND TRAUMA TRAILS

The human trauma experiences that are implicit in human acts of violence result in trauma behaviors.[8] In tracing some of these experiences, patterns I began to call *trauma trails* became apparent, running through particular families across five and six generations. These trauma trails show the increase of so-called mental illness, alcohol and drug misuse, sexual and physical abuses, suicide and suicide attempts that reflect the pain of people's day-to-day life experiences. They are experiences both of the individual and of the collective.

Collective social trauma describes the psychological blow resulting from traumatic events shared by a group of people, including whole social groups. It may involve collective or shared traumatic memory. Kai Erikson defines collective trauma as a "blow to the basic tissues of social life that damage the bonds attaching people together and impairing the prevailing sense of community."[9] The applicability of this thinking has been explored in relation to understanding Aboriginal Australian people's traumatic experience across generations. Such trauma, when experienced by an entire society, can engender collective feelings resulting in a shift in that society's culture and mass actions. Ratnavale proposes a series of signs and symptoms common to collective trauma:

> Deep mistrust of self, others, even within family; self-directed violence-suicide, risk-taking behavior; substance misuse; violence against women; unremitting grief; shame and humiliation; intergenerational conflict; role diffusion, including sexual abuse and other boundary violations; cultural genocide, losing traditional values, desecrating land and institutions; leadership crisis; a conspiracy of silence—an overall attitude of secrecy.[10]

This list of signs and symptoms is consistent with the experience of some Aboriginal communities, suggesting that the concept of collective trauma is relevant to the experiences of Aboriginal Australian peoples. It differs from the individualistic nature of Post Traumatic Stress Disorder and requires an approach with collective and community components.

Following from this work, Indigenous peoples have named their experiences as historic and cultural trauma. Historical-cultural trauma can be defined as "the collective emotional and psychological injury both over the life span and across generations,"[11] the subjective experiencing and remembering of events in the mind of an individual or the life of a community, passed from adults to children in cyclic processes. Salzman and Halloran describe the destruction of cultural worldviews that have sustained Indigenous peoples for millennia: a collective experience across diverse cultures and peoples: "the Yup'ik of Alaska; Navajos and Athabaskan Indians; Hawaiian Natives; Maori in New Zealand, and Aboriginal Australians, all having experienced similar physical, social, behavioral and psychological symptoms (e.g., high rates of suicide, alcoholism and accidental deaths)." [12] Duran and Duran[13] also suggest that historic trauma becomes embedded in the cultural memory of a people and is passed on by the same mechanisms by which culture is transmitted more generally, and therefore becomes normalized within that culture. Milroy concurs:

> The trans-generational effects of trauma occur via a variety of mechanisms including the impact on the attachment relationship with caregivers; the impact on parenting and family functioning; the association with parental physical and mental illness; disconnection and alienation from extended family, culture and society. These effects are exacerbated by exposure to continuing high levels of stress and trauma including multiple bereavements and other losses, the process of vicarious Traumatization where children witness the on-going effect of the original trauma, which a parent or other family member has experienced. Even where children are protected from the traumatic stories of their

> ancestors, the effects of past traumas still impact on children in the form of ill health, family dysfunction, community violence, psychological morbidity and early mortality.[14]

The theory that current levels of violence are a result of trauma experienced since colonization and passed through the generations is supported by Ralph, Hamaguchi and Cox,[15] who found that the high rates of suicide among the young Aboriginal people of the Kimberley Region of Western Australia, which were previously thought to be a result of depression, are more likely caused by exposure to trauma.

> It was contended that Aboriginal youth in the Kimberley region might experience several layers of trauma, through their own direct and secondary exposure as set against a backdrop of historical unresolved trauma and grief. These layers of trauma are thought to be cumulative in the manner in which they inform the adolescents' experience, and continue to adversely reinforce the basic assumptions that are violated by chronic trauma exposure; that the world is meaningful and safe, that the self is worthy, and that others can be trusted. It was thought that the current rate of suicide amongst Aboriginal adolescents in the Kimberly region may be the youths' contemporary expression of distress in response to chronic trauma exposure, as underpinned by the legacy of historical unresolved trauma and grief. [16]

In fact, Ralph, Hamaguchi and Cox found a clear link between levels of trauma exposure, post-traumatic stress and suicide, particularly for young Aboriginal girls, generally resulting from a complex of childhood experiences of abuse.

Complex trauma has been described by Herman, van der Kolk and others[17] as the pervasive effects that exposure to repeated or chronic trauma sometimes has on an individual's physical, emotional, intellectual, and psychological functioning. Such trauma exposure includes child removals, child abuse and neglect, living in poverty, and witnessing violence. It is important to understand the pervasive effects that trauma can have on biological functioning. More recent research shows that trauma is a complex mixture of psychological, physiological and social responses to highly stressful experiences, which overwhelm an individual or a group's ability to cope.[18] The common factor linking people to these complex traumas is the pain, and behaviors arising from the pain; pain of violation and loss; pain of anger and grief; pain of feeling helpless and powerless; pain of despair; and fear of more pain. Such family and community trauma has repercussions on the total well-being of Aboriginal families and communities across generations as people feel bad about who they are what has been and is being done to them, and what they do to themselves and others.

To survive, many Aboriginal people have had to suppress and deny their feelings of distress and despair, of hopelessness and powerlessness.

The pain becomes internalized within the family and community. To focus on the abuse so it can be dealt with feels like a betrayal of other family members who, it is understood, also carry this pain. Denial requires the pain be pushed down further. This denial results in physical, mental, emotional and spiritual distress and ill-health. For such people, the only reality is the mantle and demeanor of pain. They eventually come to a situation where they neither see nor feel their own experiences as harmful or that they are hurting others through their own damaging behaviors. Children growing up in such situations become emotionally numb or emotionally chaotic and, as adults, are unable to provide emotional nurturing to their children. Thus, the cycle repeats itself.

Merida Blanco, as cited by Peter Levine, suggests that the trauma of colonization in South America is best understood in relation to its generational effects. In the 1st generation, colonised males are killed, and imprisoned, females are sexually misused. In the 2nd generation, men turn to alcohol or drugs as their cultural and spiritual identity is damaged their self-worth eroded. In the 3rd generation, spousal assault becomes more prevalent. In the 4th generation, abuse moves from spousal assault to child abuse or both. The group then enters the violence trauma violence vortex,[19] This type of cross-generational account of the effects of trauma is also relevant to Aboriginal people.

THE STORY: IN THE PRESENT

The extracts from stories presented here were told over the years 1993-97. During that time, I was running We Al-li workshops.[20] An exercise we do is called Past Present Future using art, music and dadirri—deep listening in reflective discussion.[21] Participants are asked, "When I say 'childhood' what is it you most remember?" One Elder woman's immediate response was:

> Running when they killed my family. I was six years old. (this was at the Mistake Creek Massacre, just out of Turkey Creek Western Australia).

Her memory of the terror she felt over seventy years ago is caught in time. Another eighty year old woman, living in the same community, said:

> My father, the sound of the stockwhip as he was beaten, chained to a boab tree.

The most dominant childhood memory of this Elder woman, living in a remote part of Australia, is focused on the sound of the stockwhip. These were the massacre times, held within living experience and memory of those alive today. The following accounts of childhood belong to young people who, in age, could be the grandchildren of those two Elders from

Western Australia. They substantiate the changing face of trauma across generations.

> In the them days, I remember getting under the bed. . . in cupboards. . . hiding. . . just putting heaps of blankets on me and laying as still as I could, trying not to even breathe so nobody, whoever it was that was in the fights, would find me.

> I was fearful in my childhood, always afraid. I felt very insecure, so alone. I got beaten a lot of times. I was too young to have any memory but when I was one-and-a-half I ended up in hospital for two weeks from a beating. I was sexually abused when I was only . . . I can't remember the exact age. . . between ages of three and six.

> I've seen my mother being bashed and I was always afraid for her. I felt for her. I remember one time I tried to help her and I ended up getting bashed up myself. He just backhanded me. He had broke her nose and jaw and when I tried to stop him, he just backhanded me, and mum and me, we ended up on the floor together holding onto each other—blood everywhere.

> I was one that was sexually abused as a child . . . Nobody would listen to me, to my problems. . . about the violence. . . the blood on the floor, the blood on the walls, the blood on my grandparents.

> A leather belt or cane. Pretty scary. He was a big man and when I did something wrong if he didn't hit me over the head straight away I would be sent to wait for him and sometimes it would take hours for him to come and that was the most scary. Always waiting for him. Never a chance to explain.

> A lot of my childhood was . . . has been practically blanked out. A man once . . .(crying) I get funny when I watch movies like the one the other night (a documentary on sexual assault in the boy's homes) and I get angry, really angry. I rang the TV station and abused them for putting it on. I felt bad in myself for days afterward.

All of these comments come from Aboriginal people. They each had diverse childhood parenting experiences: Aboriginal parents, Aboriginal/non-Aboriginal parents, single parent, foster care, institutional care. Their common link today is that they all have extended alcohol and drug problems, diagnosed "mental illness" and all but one had been convicted of criminal behavior. They have all named childhood experiences we now know to be traumatic, that leave long-lasting scars on the psyche or soul.

There are clear links between the experiences of one generation and another that affect the behaviors of people in the present.[22] While I have not conducted prolonged controlled studies, what I can say is that almost 95 percent of the Aboriginal men and women I have listened to in prison and who have been diagnosed mental illness, in their stories of childhood, say they saw what I would classify as extreme acts of violence. Just over 85% experienced sexual violence as a child. In one alcohol and drug treatment center with which I am familiar, just over 83 percent of the people in the center, both the "clients" and the "counsellors," claimed they had experienced sexual assault as a child. These levels of abuse were both in family situations (that is where families were functioning in pain and with difficulty) and in institutional settings, to which they had been removed "for their own protection" by the state.

MAKING SENSE OF THE STORY

Aboriginal history is an oral one, stories stretching beyond the level of personal knowledge to "grandmother's grandmother." This history is less concerned with precise chronology than with recalling important events that have relevance in the lives of people today. Such an approach to the past seeks to explain why things are as they are in the present. Those important events would generally be those with the greatest emotional charge, the things we most remember, or events we may not remember because our psyche has blocked them out but our unconscious has stored. Our body, with its billions and billions of cells, holds this memory, which is our individual and collective history. This is the *Dreaming*.[23] Thus, significant events get passed from one generation to another in both the collective conscious and collective unconscious.

When there has been violation, the person feels fear, anxiety, rage—deep feelings. Generally, if it is unsafe to express these feelings near those who have violated, the feelings build up and the story is pushed down. The intense feelings continue into adult life and, internalized, can become so great the person feels unsafe with the flooding of emotion or the knowledge of his or her own potential for violence. The body holds the memory and carries the burden.

> The fear—it takes over your whole body—you're hiding and running, yeah running. . . running forever. Oh Judy the dreams! I ran—full of fear—always looking behind. Jeez I've never put this into words before.
>
> I can't feel—I can't talk about it—if I did I'd get mad—go really mad and kill someone.

At other times, the rage finds release in violence on others. Once the trauma enters the body, it must be expressed in some way. The unconscious reliving of traumatic violent experiences will often trigger violent behavior in the home and the community. When there are no outlets for that expression, in ceremony, dance, or ritual, the conscious and unconscious feelings of *being mad* are stored and emerge at times of further stress.

> I was afraid—always afraid—fearful for my life and when it came to fighting, I tried to avoid getting into fights. I had my first bashing by the police when I was fourteen, before I started drinking. I started drinking when I was sixteen. It was when I was drinking that I got into my first fight, and I won and I realised how much anger and strength I had inside me. So it happened then on a regular basis I would get into a fight. I wouldn't have had the guts to fight when I was sober. Sometimes I can remember, but most I can't remember what they were about. I wouldn't go out with the intention of fighting but I would feel so stirred up inside and I would just be waiting for somebody to do something wrong and I would just take all my anger out on this innocent person. Now I can see that, I am finding other ways of getting rid of this anger in me.

Sometimes, however, the story is so painful it cannot be acknowledged until there is a place of safety for the telling.[24] Often the story gets buried in the psyche to emerge in ways that do not make sense to the individual or to observers. Some people dissociate themselves from the feelings of anger and rage and, when these feelings are not owned, they can become self-destructive or act out in ways that induce labels of "mental illness" or criminal behavior.

> Kinda of—hung myself. I was really upset and angry. A few people around me had done the wrong thing, what I thought anyway. I was sick of people doing this to me, of being alone. I went and hung myself. I was lucky, the rope broke. I broke a couple of ribs. I still have this scar around my neck. I've also cut myself a good few times, with razor blades.

> I've destroyed a lot of things. Once I smashed the car—yeah I've destroyed a lot of cars, me in them—and I come home and kicked every piece of fibro wall, smashed the washing machine, broke all the windows—must've been a good noise. Fell on the bed and when they woke me in the morning and asked me why I did it I said I hadn't. Wasn't half obvious (laughs) there was blood everywhere, my blood.

> I stopped carrying a knife after my last attempt. I had a fight and I had this man up against a wall, a very good friend, a brother, and I was

> completely off my face. Had him by the neck, off the ground, I was ready to open his belly and I'm glad somebody pulled me off him.

> Something would happen that would hurt me and I would punch the walls. As I got older and I was drinking and drugging more and more, I started walking out in front of cars hoping I would get killed. I didn't want to live anymore. I didn't like myself. My suicide attempts were anything from what I said running out into cars, slashing my wrists. I would just stick a needle into me or cut myself to feel the pain. I was killing myself very slowly by my drinking and drugging and the other things I was doing to hurt myself.

In many instances getting charged up [drunk], or the use of alcohol and other drugs, becomes a form of self-medication, a coping mechanism.

> I began drinking when I was eight, and got on drugs by the time I was twelve. Eighteen years, I sniffed glue, smashed up mogodoms, serapax, valium and snorted them up my nose. Speed, mushrooms, all kinds of different hashes, yandie, cannabis, ever since I was twelve years old. That was how I coped in them days.

Alcohol and other drugs, with the flooding of feelings and the behaviors that result, combine as *cause* across generations, escalating dimensions of family violence that become *effect*.

> I seen my mother slapped around and choked and physically mangulated and I thought that was the way to live too, so when I got a girlfriend, when I was charged up, I'd just get her on the ground and kick her head in and smash her up against the wall, like she was a rag doll.

Labelling, an aspect of colonization, enforces separation. Mental health professionals and society generally use labels as a coping mechanism. Such labels box people into treatment situations that are inappropriate. In many instances, the treatment re-traumatizes the individual and the community without beginning to address the root causes of the trauma.

> They said I was schizophrenic. I got sent to a doctor. He didn't want to listen to me. They expect sick people to go to them and listen to them and they say "Well this is what you should do. Take this tablet in the morning and this tablet at night." I was already taking everything I could lay my hands on. I just wanted somebody to listen to me.

> They said I was paranoid schizophrenic. I was put in the ward up at the hospital. One time I went off, I was yelling and screaming, it took six of them to hold me down and inject me. It is only now that I can see what had happened to me in there was what happened to me as a child:

> being held down and abused. And I was fighting them nurses off in the same way I'd fought (my other abusers) off.

Sometimes making sense of the story means suspending all assumptions, acknowledging there are many things we do not know. A young man I was working with entered a "dissociated" state, coming toward me as if he had been drinking (which I knew he had not). He had taken on the persona of a woman as he stumbled around the room. He appeared to be searching for something. This lasted for approximately 20 minutes. After a while, he entered another state in which it appeared that he was giving birth. Elders present at that time were upset until I told them to stay with what was happening, and just allow the story, whatever needed to emerge, to unfold. Again, after some time, he settled down to rest, and some hours later entered another state of "dissociation." This time, I could not understand what was happening, but he was extremely distressed. Over a period of eight hours, he acted out three separate and distinct stories. When the night ended, I was exhausted and in crisis. What was happening here? Was I responding in the right way to what was presenting? As usual, I checked in with a supervising psychiatrist for advice the next morning, and was told I had done all I could under the circumstances. However, some weeks later, the young man came to see me. He told me that after this experience, with its deep impression on him, he felt the need to check into the Stories he acted out on that night with his grandparents. They told him that the stories he had felt and acted out belonged to his great grandmother: she had been raped on the frontier; she gave birth to a girl child; the child was taken from her by the state; and she spent the rest of her life wandering around that area, trying to find her child, and drinking to sustain her distress.

Today I am still perplexed by what I saw and heard. I have no capacity to make any comment except to say the lesson I learned was to stay with the story, to suspend judgment, and just to be present in a supportive role to help the person make sense of what had happened.

FEELING THE FEELINGS: CLIENT AND WORKER, STUDENT AND TEACHER

I would like, now, to take the narrative into a deeper dimension, this time using labels as I describe what I observed was happening for a person, and also naming my own feelings, thoughts and actions, what was happening for me as a worker and teacher, at the time the events were occurring. It is important for us to understand what is happening for us in any communication between ourselves and those we are working with. In the narrative that follows, my own feelings are enclosed in brackets.

We had a new person start within in our workplace, a "man with a bit of paper," a psychologist, a white man. This new person's presence in the workplace triggered "psychotic" behavior in a client. Early one morning, during the residential component of a course I was running, I received a call to say "he had gone off". [I felt an initial panic—how much had he "gone off"?]. When I found him, he had regressed into a child state, sucking his thumb, talking child talk: "the bogey man, he's come to get me—take me away."

For some seconds I felt fear, not fear of him but fear of what would happen if people found out I had *this* happening. What if we were wrong? Maybe he should be in that hospital where others had said he should be? All my knowledge—all the theory and practical skills—flew out the window as I sat watching him stumble toward me. Then I started to worry. What am I going to do now? My mind was working in overdrive, only half listening, watching him, creating labels to fit what I was seeing and hearing, dissociation, transference, psychosis, trying at the same time to figure out what I should do. Finally, reason returned. I knew what had triggered the behavior. What was the story behind it?

I got him to a safe place and began to listen as he talked. Often, he was not making sense except to repeat that "white men with bits of paper hurt you." An hour later, he was settled enough for us to be able to continue with the program for the day, although he remained, to an extent, unbalanced and was not able to participate fully. That night I was at the craft table.[25] He came down the stairs in a child tantrum, jumping up and down, screaming, "Why can't I do anything right?" as he beat himself with his fists. I felt a flash of pure anger. "Not again! I'm tired and I don't need this now, not tonight. It's been too long a day," I thought, before I settled on the floor to wait for the tantrum to subside. By this time I was starting to feel inadequate. Nothing seemed to be working. One of our participants came up dragging a mattress, saying, "Come on. Let's get him breathing," and we settled the young man on the mattress and into connected breathing [Question to myself: Who is the teacher, who is the student here? Thank you for students who teach].

MOVING THROUGH THE LAYERS OF LOSS AND GRIEF TO ACCEPTANCE

And there, in the breath, the story came in its multiple layers. As the tangle of confused feelings dropped away, we began to hear what he had not spoken about before. First layer: The men who came to his mother and abused her and him (*I never seen or experienced sex when I was a child without it being violent*); second layer: the man who came with a bit of paper to take him away from his family and put him into a home where he was further violated (*they never told me why they took me, but somebody told me later. . . it was because I was stupid, that was why they put me in the home*); third layer: a man with the bit of paper who took his own child from him. Clear, strong anger was expressed toward those (including me) whom he felt had allowed violation of his safety at different times in his childhood and young adult life. After an hour or so of the connected breathing exercise, he became clear and reasonably balanced and we were all able to go off and have a good night's sleep. We had earned it. Healing, I am always reminded, is hard work.

Two weeks later I am again with this young man, visiting him at his home, and he tells me, "it's still there," the feeling of resentment against the "white man with the bit of paper." [My feelings—a flash of impatience, frustration: "Come on, when does this 'victim' stuff end? How many times do we have to keep going back to the same old stories?"]. I start to go over with him what we had come to know of the story associated with these feelings.

Q. Is it because of the men in your mother's life?

A. No, it's not that—but it's something—it's still sitting in my gut.

Q. Well, those fellas involved when you were taken to the boy's home?

A. No Jude, that's not it.

Q. The man who took baby away?

He looks at me stunned. "When did I tell you that?" he asks. I tell him, "In the connected breathing session two weeks ago. Don't you remember?" He goes into his bedroom and brings out a pile of papers and hands them to me. The top paper is a letter from a solicitor, dated 1993, outlining the results of a DNA test that was done on the baby girl he sang to in his girlfriend's womb, at whose birth he attended, played with and loved as a father should. The girl left him and, as he attempted to see his child, to gain visitation rights, she used the Western legal and medical system to deny him right of access. The letter said, in cold clear legal medical terms that the baby was not his. DNA proved that. Yet, in Aboriginal cultural beliefs, the physiological conception of the child is less important than the spiritual links we have with those who come into our lives for us to parent on our combined life journeys. Under this letter were a large number of letters from Canberra, the Australian National Capital, demanding he pay maintenance for this child. With tears in his eyes he says, *"they just keep sending me these letters saying I have to pay them money."*

He is clearly upset and has been unable to do anything about the letters he was getting from the Commonwealth government. Each letter had been a source of renewed trauma for him—white men with bits of paper, hurting him, controlling his life. I offered to sort it all out but he declined. He said he would now attend to it himself. He did, the next day, beginning the long process of having the bureaucrats in Canberra rectify the fear and distress they sent to him with each demanding letter in regard to maintenance for a child that was not biologically his. And that was the end of the resentment toward the white man with the bit of paper working in our organization.

I have often heard judgmental comments by professional workers and bureaucrats about Aboriginal clients. In fact, in relating this story, I had a person say with an impatient tone, "well he could have just gone and fixed up the paper work," as if it were that simple. I am not sure if I can explain adequately what I saw and felt, the depth of pain, the fear, the confusion, the paralysis that the letters generated in him, letters that for him did not make sense and only triggered other painful memories, allowing more of a whole story to resurface. Once he made sense of what was happening for him, he himself acted to rectify the problem.

I have used this story to show the complexity that is part of the multiple trauma experience, sometimes expressed in behaviors that don't make sense until the whole story begins to be put together. I also wanted to stress the responsibility we have as workers to know what is happening for us in any interaction with others. The interaction I have described above taught me many things about myself as I reacted to the situations at the time. Over and over again, I am reminded to ask: What is the story? I use it as a mantra. Listen to the story, what is the story behind this behavior? How can we, this person and I, work together to find ways to help the story to be told, to hold the story, as together we work to make sense of the senseless? Do I have the patience and tolerance to stay with the layers of pain to the full extent of the feelings? It is only then that resolution is reached to enable acceptance so that the person comes to a knowing that, yes this has happened to me. I have survived. I am strong. I can to be responsible for my own healing work. I can move on.

RECLAIMING THE SACRED SELF-MOVING INTO THE FUTURE

In Indigenous therapeutical processes, we use many tools to help facilitate healing: narration or story-mapping, art, music, dance, drama, emotional release, body work, all skilled tools based in traditional healing practice and now seen to be of value within contemporary therapeutic processes. I would like to finish by telling the story of a young woman and how she was able to unconsciously allow me to participate in her healing journey through her art.

When I first met this young woman, she had just been released from a mental health ward at the local hospital and was resident in a local alcohol and drug education and treatment center. She made a commitment to come to the workshops but she was not sure how she could participate. We talked a little about the negative experiences she had with the social worker who was assigned to her, as well as her experiences in the hospital where she had been labelled as paranoid schizophrenic and manic depressive. After the second workshop, she began to participate. She was asked to role play a father in a family violence situation while we were doing theater. During the role play she was frozen. She could do nothing except be there. afterward I was at the craft table and she came up to me holding her head, which she said was going to burst. I asked her if she could talk about it and she said no, it was too big, she didn't have words for what she was feeling. "If I talked about it I would go really mad and I would kill someone." I gave her some paper and pencils, and asked her if she could draw how she was feeling for me. Some time later, she came back with a drawing of a hand clutching a heart dripping blood. Above the heart, were clouds with words in them: kill, hate, suicide, stab, punch—twenty-two negative words and one glimmer of hope, the word *love*, which enabled me to understand what was happening inside her—the pain she was unable to talk about, the flashes she continued to have of the violence she saw as a child.

The next day I went out and bought canvas, paint brushes, paper and pastels, and went to see her. "Paint for me," I said. And she did and each time I came down to a new painting I would said in front of it and say: "this is so . . . tell me about it." Some months later, we were doing a group painting and I watched as she painted a clown with no head and its hands lifted up as if in surrender or juggling. I thought, "well this will be an interesting story." Some days later, she went back and put the face on, a painted white face, grinning as clowns do, juggling four balls. I asked her to tell me about the painting, and she said she felt like this clown, with a stupid smile on its face while inside she felt like dying. At that time, she did not have a good feeling about being Aboriginal, and in her painting she described juggling her identity as she struggled with who she was.

She continued to come to the workshops and was participating more and more at deeper levels in the activities and discussions. She enrolled in a course of study I was running at the university, and during the next year spent most of the time listening to others and occasionally putting some gems of observation into the group discussions. Often she would be up all night listening to music and painting. One morning, I came down and on the wall was a painting of a woman's face split in half—multiple tones of blue, white and black—one side of the face exquisite in its beauty, the other side distorted, computerized, fractured. I asked her to tell me about the picture, and she told me it was how she felt. She explained she felt split in two, the past and the present, the black and white—the strength and peace of being Aboriginal and the computerized fast world of being white. I could still feel her struggle but something was being resolved.

Some time later, I came down one morning and on the wall was a painting of two hands holding a globe of the world. I asked, who did this, and she said *"I did. That's me. I'm holding the world in my hands. That's how I feel anyway."* And indeed she was. Not only was she getting on with her own life drug free but, by what she has done, she has influenced her family at many levels. Her mother entered alcohol rehabilitation later in the year. She became foster parent to her brother's three children until he was able to receive custody again. She was enrolled in university again the following year, and her art work continued to grow in strength and depth.

Five years after I first met her, she asked me if I would go for a walk on the beach with her. As we walked together, she told me it was finished. I asked: "What is finished?" She then told me that she had now stopped the man who had come into her room as a small child, into her teenage years, into her adult years, and took advantage of her sexually against her will. It was finished. She herself had taken the action necessary to stop his violations.

CONCLUSION

I began this chapter by quoting William Stanner, referring to the ceremonial processes used by Aboriginal people to *unite hearts and establish order.* This is what we must be about again as we work to repair the damage created by the colonial disasters in our lives and on our lands. Working with my own people in therapeutic processes that I call educaring, recreating the ceremonies of healing we use, has become a journey of self-discovery as I have been confronted with the need to put aside previous beliefs that came from my colonized construction. I have been challenged to replace such beliefs with new understandings and knowledge. As the individual stories are heard and put together to make the collective story, I have learned more about history, sociology, anthropology, and psychology in the context of colonization than from any formal course of study I have undertaken at a university. More importantly, I have learned about people's pain and how healing from pain can be transforming. I have learned what it really is to be Aboriginal, and about relationship at a deep level. I have taken responsibility for my own learning, my own "consciousness development, self-knowledge, as I am more and more able to participate without fear in the intense and extraordinary experiences of others and am willing to face new observations and situations that do not fit any of my previous theory frameworks."[26]

As a worker, I am coming to trust more and more the inner healing mechanisms that are there for us all. What we have to do is to create safe places, without drugs and restraints, for the stories to be told, for the feelings to be felt, and for the healing to happen. As a worker, I have the responsibility to be there, to give a friendly hand, provide a listening ear, share a little of my own healing story with some of the insights I gained along the way and, always, to honor the other's journey. And never to pathologize the human story. It is sacred. It is our stories that link us to each other, that build the bridges between our creative diversity to our humanizing commonality. Sure, we can have it both ways, so long as we always ask: Where am I in this process? What is my contribution to the whole? How can I make a difference?

NOTES

1. The word Aboriginal refers to those people of the Australian mainland, who are of Aboriginal descent, who are recognized as such by the community in which they live, and who identify as Aboriginal.
2. All identities are disguised to protect the privacy of the people who share their stories.
3. Atkinson, J. (2002). *Trauma trails—Recreating song lines. The transgenerational effects of trauma in Indigenous Australia*. Melbourne: Spinifex Press.
4. The word Indigenous honours the United Nations Declaration of the Rights of Indigenous Peoples and recognizes their collective experiences as colonised people, and also recognizes the relevancy of Indigenous trauma healing approaches.
5. Stanner, W.E.H. (1979). *White man got no dreaming: Essays 1938–1973,* Canberra: Australian University Press (p. 143).
6. A number of studies now show that after a natural or manmade disaster violence against women and children increases. For example the Report of the British Columbia Task Force on Family Violence (1992).
7. Figley, C. (1985). *Trauma and it's wake: The study and treatment of post traumatic stress disorder,* and (1987) *Trauma and it's wake* (Vol. 11). New York: Brunner-Mazel.
8. Ibid.
9. Erikson, K. (1994). *A new species of trouble: The human experience of modern disaster*. New York. Norton and Company. (p. 233). Erikson, K. (1976). *Everything in its path*. New York: Simon and Schuster.
10. Ratnavale, D. (2007, March). An understanding of Aboriginal experience in the context of collective trauma: A challenge for healing. Presented at the *Aboriginal and Torres Islander Mental Health Services of CNAHS.*
11. Muid, O. (2006). *Then I lost my spirit: An analytical essay on transgenerational theory and its application to oppressed people of color nations.* Ann Arbor: UMI Dissertation Services/ProQuest (p. 36).
12. Salzman, M. B., and Halloran, M.J. (2004). Cultural trauma and recovery: Cultural meaning, self esteem, and the reconstruction of the cultural anxiety buffer. In J. Greenberg, S. L. Koole, and T. Pyszczynski (Eds.), *Handbook of experimental existential psychology* (pp. 231–246). New York: Guilford.
13. Duran, E. and Duran, B. (1995). *Native American post-colonial psychology*. Albany: State University of New York Press.
14. Milroy. H. (2005). Preface. In S. R. Zubrick, S. R. Silburn, D. M. Lawrence, E. G. Mitrou, R. B. Dalby, E. M. Blair (Eds.), *The Western Australian Aboriginal child health survey: The social and emotional wellbeing of Aboriginal children and young people*. Perth: Curtin University of Technology and Telethon Institute for Child Health Research. (p. xxi)
15. Ralph, N., Hamaguchi, K. and Cox, M. (2006). Transgenerational trauma, suicide and healing from sexual abuse in the Kimberley region, Australia. *Pimatisiwin, A Journal of Aboriginal and Indigenous Community Health,* 4(2), 118–136.
16. Ibid p. 123.

17. Herman, J. (1992). *Trauma and recovery.* London: HarperCollins. Herman; J. (1997). *Trauma and recovery: The aftermath of violence, from domestic abuse to political terror.* New York: Basic Books; Van der Kolk, B.A., Roth, S., Pelcovitz, D., Sunday, S., and Spinazzola, J. (2005). Disorders of extreme stress: The empirical foundation of a complex adaptation to trauma. *Journal of Traumatic Stress , 18*(5), 389–399.

18. Scaer, R. (2001). *The body bears the burden: Trauma, dissociation, and disease.* New York: The Haworth Press; Van der Kolk, B. A. (2005). Developmental trauma disorder: toward a rational diagnosis for children with complex trauma histories. *Psychiatric Annals , 35*(5), 401–408; Van der Kolk, B. (2007). Developmental impact of childhood trauma. In L. Kirmayer, R. Lemelson, and M. Barad (Eds.), *Understanding Trauma: integrating biological, clinical and cultural perspectives.* New York: Cambridge University Press.

19. In Levine, P. and Kline, M. (2007). *Trauma through a child's eyes.* Berkeley, CA: North Atlantic Books.

20. *We* is the word for fire in Woppaburra Language, while *al'li* means water. In 1993 a group of us established programs for healing, and in finding a name we realised most people were coming to our workshops with deep anger (fire) and grief (water). Fire and water are both essential elements for life. Over the years the programs was taken up to form university course of study. We Al-li continues however in the work we do at community levels. www.wealli.com.au.

21. Dadirri from Ngangikurungkurr people of Daly River Northern Territory is "a special quality, a unique gift of the Aboriginal people, it is inner deep listening and quiet still awareness. Dadirri recognises the deep spring that is inside us. It is something like what you call contemplation." I used this deep listening as the cornerstone of my PhD research. Also see www.creativespirits.info/aboriginalculture/education/deep-listening-dadirri.

22. Edward, Prager, Hantman, Shira, and Zahava, Solomon, How the Gulf War affected aged Holocaust survivors, *Clinical Gerontologis. 14*(3), 1994, 27–37. Vogal, M. L. (1994). Gender as a Factor in the Transgenerational Transmission of Trauma, in *Women and Therapy, 15*(2) Haworth Press. Danieli, Y. (1988c). Treating survivors and children of survivors of the Nazi Holocaust. In F. Ochberg (Ed.), *Post traumatic therapy and victims of violence* (pp. 278-294). New York: Brunner/Mazel. Danieli, Y. (1989). *Mourning in survivors and children of survivors of the Nazi Holocaust: The role of group and community modalities,* in D.R. Dietrich and P.C. Shabad (Eds.), The problems of loss and mourning: Psychoanalytic perspectives (pp. 427–457). Madison: International Universities Press.

23. For further discussion on the Dreaming see Nicholls, C. (2014) Dreamtime and the dreaming—An introduction, in *The Conversation,* 23 January 2014.

24. See Herman's work (1992) on *Trauma and recovery,* cited above, for discussion about the need to create safety for the trauma story to be told and healed.

25. We have a craft table during the residential unit of the course, which becomes a de-briefing place where people sit at night and make things while they talk together about issues that may have come up during the day.

26. Sparks, T. and Sparks, C. (1989). *Doing not doing.* Unpublished manuscript.

FOURTEEN

To Unchain Haunting Blood Memories

Intergenerational Trauma among African Americans

Kirkland C. Vaughans

In this chapter I have several immodest goals that are intricately connected, as well as independently complex and encompassing. First, I will attempt to give representation to the voice of ordinary people who were enslaved and perished. But for a few who wrote narratives of their lives, or wrote letters to their families and loved ones, or who were later interviewed by the Works Progress Administration, they are mostly forgotten. I will represent some of the thematic content from those writings as they are manifested today within the African American community as a sort of "cultural introject." I also intend to differentiate what I refer to as a cultural introject from the notion of internalized racism which is the main construct used to 'explain' negative behavioral patterns within American Black communities today. By cultural introject I mean internalization of something without quite knowing why. It is not quite identification but a disturbing amplification of unknown fears. In addition, I am proposing to describe some of the historical responses to the aftermath of slavery by both Whites and Blacks that inhibited the resolution of its traumatic aftermath. Lastly, I will attempt to describe some of the current impediments to working through the traumatic legacy of slavery within the African American community.

While space will not permit me to elaborate on all of the circumstances of slavery, what I will make note of is the traumatic legacy of American slavery on American White society. Toni Morrison (1992) takes up an aspect of this issue in her study of the impact of Blackness in White literature. While I view this subject matter as extremely important for the psychological well-being of African Americans and our nation, like the historian John Hope Franklin, I claim no more than a glimmer of insight into these powerful dynamics.

HISTORY

With very few exceptions (Fanon, 1967; Gump, 2010; Pinderhughes, 2004), psychoanalysis has only tentatively considered the impact of slavery on the psyche of the African American community. Between the sixteenth and nineteenth centuries, Berlin (2010) estimates that at least 11 million Africans were forcibly transported from across the Atlantic through what has come to be known as the Middle Passage. Black scholars have named this Black Diaspora *Maafa*, a Swahili term meaning the "Great Sorrow or Tragedy" (Ani 1994). Africans identified themselves by tribe and ethnicity, so their treacherous voyage through the Middle Passage would thus constitute both a "death and birth canal." For them, the voyage constituted the death of a whole way of life and the birth of a new culture and racial identity (Gomez 1998). The American brand of slavery dehumanized the subjects of this predatory system legally, politically, economically, and socially. Sociologist Orlando Patterson (1982) characterized it as a social death, meaning that the enslaved had lost their membership in the universal family of humanity. Until this time, slaves across the world had maintained their identity as human, but the American experience would be qualitatively different. Slaveowners sought not only to enslave them physically, but also to enslave their very souls. This attempt at soul murder is reflected in the writings of Frederick Douglas (1845/2003) who describes his struggle with a slave breaker: "Mr. Covey succeeded in breaking me. I was broken in body, soul, and spirit. . . the dark night of slavery was upon me" (p. 75).

Today American slavery is viewed erroneously as that part of American history that occurred solely in the southern states. What is not understood is that America was in fact a slave nation, meaning that its total economic growth was thoroughly dependent upon slavery. Patterson distinguishes nations that hold people in slavery from nations whose economic well-being is dependent upon slavery, he refers to the latter as slave nations. Slavery was such a powerful part of the American credo that most of the Presidents, from the founding of the United States until the Civil War, were large slave holders. This included Washington, Jefferson, Madison, Jackson, Tyler, Polk, and Taylor. In addition, during this period, a majority of members of the Supreme Court and of the U.S. Congress were also slave holders (Berlin, 2003). Thus, as it is today, those with economic wealth wielded the most political power. American slavery was therefore embedded within the historical and cultural marrow of the United States. It played a significant part in igniting the Revolutionary War, in uniting northern and southern colonies to form one union, as well as serving as a major cause of the Civil War.

Despite the fact that African Americans have historically spent less time emancipated than they did in slavery, the historian Rushdy (2001) warns us that slavery is very distant in the American imagination, and it has remained so because: "slavery is the family secret of America." (p. 2) By calling it "secret," Rushdy does not mean that slavery is concealed from the public. It is a secret because it remains on the periphery of the national imagination. It remains the national paradox, the stain on our founding ideals of freedom, liberty, and justice. The cruel, dehumanizing and violent nature of slavery can no longer be denied as earlier writers had sought to do. It was not just the institution of slavery, and its effects on those who lived through it, that has resulted in a traumatic legacy but also the collective memory of slavery by those who endured it, by their offspring, as well as the national response in its aftermath, that have contributed to the traumatic legacy of slavery (Eyerman, 2001; Morrow, 2003; Vaughans, 2014). Writing from the perspective of cultural trauma, Eyerman (2001) articulates this position: "The trauma in question is slavery, not as an institution or as a personal experience, but as a collective memory: a pervasive remembrance that grounded the identity-formation of a people" (p. 1). This construct in no way negates the individual or group psychological trauma experienced by those who were subjected to it. It simply views the experience from a different vantage point. Nor by examining Black experience through this lens do I mean to suggest that all Africans arriving on American shores came as slaves, as Sertima (1976) has documented. Eyerman (2001) describes cultural trauma as a "dramatic loss of identity and meaning, a tear in the social fabric" (p. 2a) for a people who previously were cohesive. In addition, it is not necessary for individual members or any member of the group to directly experience or acknowledge the trauma. This view in no way is to be considered a counter assertion of the actual trauma experienced by those who were enslaved.

VOICES OF THE ENSLAVED

The history of American slavery has largely been told from the vantage point of those who did the enslaving, through their personal records, memoirs, biographies, and public documents. What was missing was the voice of those who had been enslaved. Any documentation that did become available was largely discredited or ignored, and the vast amount of it was lost through years of neglectful storage. During the 1920s, a number of Black scholars began documenting the personal experiences of those who had been enslaved and later, in the 1930s, the Federal Writers Project began interviewing thousands of the formerly enslaved and recording their interviews. The legitimacy of these narratives would be repeatedly contested on the grounds of their subjectivity and supposed bias and inaccuracy, and due to the alleged failing memories of the narrators (Berlin 1998). The end result was the perpetuation of the benign and humanitarian view of slavery propagated, for example, by the historian Ulrich Phillips (1929). This damaging stereotype would remain dominant and largely unchallenged until the 1960s. As Berlin (1998) noted, the struggle regarding whose memory of slavery would prevail was just about as fierce as the actual conflict over slavery. Almost anticipating this struggle over the legitimacy of the enslaved voices, John Little, who had escaped bondage and fled to Canada, stated in 1855 that "Tisn't he who had stood and looked on, that can tell you what slavery is—tis he who has endured" (Yetman 1970, p. 1).

The slave narratives and biographies do not always speak with one unified or collective voice, with the possible exception of those written during slavery, that most often made appeals to abolitionists to protest the institution of slavery and to seek its demise. In the narratives, there are discussions of the daily struggles of working on a plantation, whether or not they were worked too hard, and even if they had good or bad masters. Other prominent issues reflected upon were sexual exploitation of young girls by the master and his sons, colorism, loss and longing for family members, and being whipped. Very often the women reported being partially or fully stripped of their clothing on these occasions. As Berlin (1998) points out, their stories reflect a strong capacity for love and forgiveness. In addition, their stories do not reflect the simple dichotomy between the house slave and that of the field Negro, so popular in today's Black culture and as it is depicted in the film *Django Unchained* (Tarantino, 2013) in which the actor Samuel Jackson, the house servant, was extremely identified with his master. He identified with the aggressor, in opposition to a slave played by Jamie Foxx, who played the role of the rebel or field Negro, who stood in opposition to White supremacy. In some narratives, slaves speak of the "kindness" of their masters. In most instances, however, this referred to reluctance on the master's part to sell them. Priscilla Joiner spoke to this sentiment, stating, "My old mistress was the best woman in the world. She may have owned slaves, but she never sold any. She brought me up just like one of her own children until I was twelve years old. Then she paid for me to go to a colored school with my own people" (Perdue, Barden and Phillips, 1976, p. 90). Other examples of masters who were considered kind were those who allowed their slaves to stay with their chosen mates, those who fed them well, and those who did not beat them. In many instances, the power of the master is acknowledged, something that is also constantly challenged and often renegotiated. Examples of resistance include slaves running away rather than be beaten, and remaining hidden until word from the owner reached them with a report that they would forgo the lash only if they returned within a specified time or the beating would be increased. A second example (Berlin 1998) of this is where husbands living on different plantations visited their wives despite orders from their owners not to. Martha Spence offers an example. She describes how her father was sold away from the family when she was small and how the rest of the family lived in fear of being sold as well. She explains,

> My father sho did hate to leave us. He missed us and us longed for him. He would often slip back to our cottage at night. Us would gather around him and crawl up on his lap, tickled slap to death, but he give us these pleasures at a painful risk. When his Mars missed him he would beat him all the way home. Us could track him the next day by de blood stains. (p. 145)

A similar story is related by Vinnie Busby who lived on a plantation in Mississippi but whose father lived on a different plantation and whose owner also refused him permission to visit his family. She reports that at night her father would slip over and visit the family and would sometimes be caught by his owner who was on the lookout for such: "When he would cathch him he would beat him so hard till we could tell which way he went back by de blood. But pa, he would keep a coming to see us and takin de beatins" (Berlin, 1998, p. 144).

Another very powerful and frequently reported issue pertained to that of parental authority over the children of the enslaved. The contest between the master and the mother could reach dangerous levels for the enslaved mother, as the master by law had no obligation to respect their parental standing or the marriage, but rather, as Berlin stated, he had preeminent authority. In her autobiography, *Incidents in the life of a slave girl* (1861/1987), Harriet Jacobs shares her personal thoughts on this issue after being threatened by her owner Dr. Flint, who stated, "These brats will bring me a handsome sum of money one of these days. . . I thought to myself that, God being my helper, they would never pass into his hands. It seemed to me I would rather see them killed than have them given up to his power" (p. 80). John Boggs, who was formerly enslaved, echoed similar views: "That is what our people dread the most. The idea is like this. When a man goes out in the morning, he may have a wife and a parcel of children, and maybe when he comes back at night, he will find nobody who will tell him anything about them. If a woman ask about her children that had been sold, she would be whipped or knocked and slashed about" (Blassingame 1977, p. 422). In recalling her childhood, Fannie Moore spoke of the love and protection displayed by her mother. She states, "I never see how my mammy stan sech had work. She stan up for her chillum tho. De ol overseeah he hate my mammy, case she fight him for beatin her chilun. Why she get more whippins for dat den anything else. She had twelfe chillum" (Berlin 1998, p. 133).

Although they realistically feared the whip, they probably feared being sold away from their families even more. Hence the verbal threat by the master, "I'll put you in my pocket" (Stuckey 1987), meaning they would be sold off, was more than enough to win obedience. Thomas Jefferson was well aware of these fears and believed the most severe punishment that he could exert over incorrigible slaves was to sell them away from their families (Berlin 1998). This struggle to maintain family was unrelenting for two and one half centuries, and the odds against doing so were pathetically unforgiving. As Berlin (1998) points out, "Few enslaved parents could expect to nurture their children to maturity, see their grandchildren grow up, or succor their own parents in their last years" (p. xxvi). But the relentless loss of family and community, a half a century before the Civil War, ushered in what Berlin (2010) described as the "second middle passage." This entailed the greatest change in movement that the enslaved had endured since arriving on North America's shore. The vast shipment of millions of enslaved from the eastern seaboard to the Deep South constituted wholesale disruption of families and communities. The civilization that had been developed was now all but lost, and both those left behind and those that were scattered were forced to begin anew. With the end of slavery, four million people were finally liberated. The moment of their emancipation was noted by Booker T. Washington:

> For some minutes there was great rejoicing, and thanksgiving, and wild scenes of ecstasy. But there was no feeling of bitterness. In fact, there was pity among the slaves for our former owners. The wild rejoicing on the part of the emancipated colored people lasted but for a brief period. . . .there was a change in their feelings. The great responsibility of being free, of having charge of themselves, to think and plan for themselves and their children, seemed to take possession of them. (1901/1989, p. 21)

Despite incredible disappointments at the short span of the Reconstruction Period, the newly freed exploited it to their fullest. First and foremost came education, not only as a pragmatic investment but also as a moral crusade to uplift and redefine a people. It also included reconstituting families and searching for long lost members.

LOSS, SORROW, AND CULTURAL AMNESIA

As Black newspapers were quickly developed, they contained numerous announcements seeking to reunite families. An example of such an ad appeared in the *Colored Tennessean* in 1865 stating:

> Information is wanted of my two boys. James and Horace. One of whom was sold in Nashville and the other was sold in Rutherford County. I, myself, was sold in Nasville and sent to Alabama, by Wm Boyd. . . . Ps. Any information sent to the Colored Tennessean office, Box 1150 will be thankfully received." (Williams, 2012, p. 186)

Thornton Cope would search for his mother for more than twenty years and Charity Moss ventured to find her sons despite her journey of many miles since she last saw them (Williams, 2012). Despite many years of determined searching, most searches ended in sorrowful disappointment. Much progress was, nonetheless, achieved by Black people and their vision was forward looking, as slavery was now a thing of the past. As Booker T. Washington (1901/1989) noted, slavery was "something to be forgotten and left behind like a dead skin" (p. 19). This forgetting of slavery would quickly become culturally sanctioned and motivated by Blacks and Whites for different reasons that would ultimately cause a revision to the meaning of slavery for the nation. Black churches served as the bedrock for cultural advancement, moral support, and political liberation for Black people, and they were quite insistent that the "ole spirituals" sung during slavery be removed from their hymn books (Berlin 1998). Du Bois had referred to these as the "Sorrow Songs," which he described as the ". . .echo of haunting melody from the only American music which welled up from Black souls in the dark past" (1961, p. xiv). Later, this exclusion would also come to include the gospel blues (Harris, 1992) and ragtime blues, constituting a kind of cultural purging of the collective memory of slavery. In interview, Sarah Debro noted, "I's lived near about 90 years, and I's seen and heard much. My folks don't want me to talk about slavery, they's shame niggers ever was slaves. . ." (Hurmence, 1984, p. 61) The abrupt end and failure of Reconstruction, in effect, was an economic compromise between the North and the South (DuBois, 1935; Foner, 2005). Dreams of full participation in American democracy were violently suppressed by institutional terrorism, including loss of the right to vote, massive imprisonment for those without work, physical destruction of self-sustaining Black communities, birth of the Ku Klux Klan, and the lynching of thousands. Once again, the might of the nation's scientific, religious, academic, and arts establishments was used to denigrate and humiliate Black people as innately inferior. It is this sequestering of the collective memory, together with the abject failure of Reconstruction, as well as its humiliating and terrorizing aftermath, that set the tone for the unresolved trauma of African Americans today. In *Trauma and recovery,* Herman (1992) explains that trauma shatters connections among people and their communities, resulting in a crisis of faith. She insists on three basic requirements for recovery from trauma: the establishment of safety; reconstruction of trauma narrative; and reconnecting survivors to each other and to their community. Herman also describes how silence is the usual response to atrocity and, as is well established in trauma literature, this leads to trauma symptoms and intergenerational transmission. The immediate goals of Black people were physical and psychological survival. Many of those who could, moved north, fearing the re-institution of slavery (Painter, 1976), and the bulk of their energies went into carving out a new racial identity against both the history of their enslavement and against the new national tsunami of racial denigration. One of the ways public opinion was fashioned against Blacks during this period was through the construction of national and state memorials, monuments, and statues honoring their respective military leaders and battlefields (Eyerman, 2001). No monuments were ever built to acknowledge those who were enslaved and their accomplishments. Volkan (1977) views the building of monuments and the like after traumatic events as a psychological necessity. Their perceived indestructibility affords those who were victimized a psychological containing function that also sustains and regulates emotions. Thus, the collective memory of slavery was consigned to entombment as America's "skeleton in the closet" (Frederickson, 2000).

The crucial importance of collective memory is actively demonstrated in the refusal of Jewish people to allow the Holocaust to fall into a universal amnesia, as expressed in the aphorism, "Never forget," as well as in the construction of Holocaust memorials and museums. Prior to claiming this legacy, Jews who survived the Holocaust were subjected to a conspiracy of silence resulting in additional clinical trauma by having their voices muted. Volkan (1997) suggests that children become the reservoir for unresolved and unacceptable mental representations of the trauma of previous generations who have been unable to come to terms with issues of humiliation and loss. The children absorb their elders' traumatized parts and then bear the burden of completing the task that their forebears were unable to resolve. These mental representations or traumatized self-images are continuously passed from one generation to the next and are constituted by shared feelings, perceptions, fantasies, and interpretations of the calamity. In what may be viewed as a radical approach to generational transmission of trauma, Abraham and Torok (1994) suggest that, during treatment, psychoanalytic inquiry must move beyond the individual patient because they believe that some patients have inherited the "secret psychic substance" of their ancestors. Thus the analyst must listen for phantom voices from different generations in the patient under treatment. The process of therapy includes uncovering shameful secrets and understanding nameless and undisclosed suffering. This, Abraham and Torok believe, will assist the patient in remembering the past, recalling what was taken, and understanding and mourning what was lost, so that healing can begin. The group psychoanalyst Earl Hopper seems to have a similar notion in mind when he asserts, "People and groups must always be located within their foundation matrices. It is necessary to think in terms of horizontal depth. Within the infinite context of time and space, the self belongs mostly to others, who may have lived far away and long ago" (2003, p. 19). Through their narratives, the voices of those who were formerly enslaved speak painfully of loss, shame, and grief as well as of a profound need to develop a positive identity in a "land without sanctuary" due to their "unforgiveable Blackness."

The accomplishments of African Americans are significant, but some aspirations remain unfulfilled to this day. Each succeeding generation has in some form championed these tasks; however, their legacy has not been successfully redeemed. That which remains unclaimed, without a collective narrative, constitutes a breach with our past, and it is filled with haunting blood memories, whose lease must expire for the well-being of the African American community to be realized. From a psychoanalytic perspective, I suggest we first appreciate what impediments may deter our thinking about slavery and how that may be made manifest psychosocially. It is also important to understand racism as a major organizing principle in American society, as Pinderhughes (2004) explains. Because of the imperative of survival, we, Black Americans, have colluded in our own invisibility by shrouding painful and degrading aspects of our past and placing our faith in the future. However, it is also important to note as Grand (2000) stated, that ". . .forgetting is the first condition of evil's dissociative contagion" (p. 153). While teaching at Howard University in the 1950s, the Black sociologist E. Franklin Frazer requested those students who were descendants of slaves to raise their hands. He acknowledged that no student ever raised their hand.

I recall sixty years ago my father's painful confrontation with the past when a picture of my White maternal great-grandfather arrived in the mail. He violently threw it in the garbage, saying that no picture of a White bastard that had preyed on Black women would ever hang in his house. My White great-grandfather had eighteen children by several different Black women, and their descendants are largely divided by color cleavage to this day. Those who pass as White, and those who are very light, go by his surname of Arbuthnot, and the others, including me, are known as Vaughans. It is only now that I am finally able to reach back into that garbage and reclaim that picture as a part of my heritage and as a part of my own identity. One may be tempted to relegate these two examples to ancient history, but please do not. Ten years ago, while conducting research on Black boys, a den mother at Jack and Jill (an upper class social club for Black children), reported the following effort to raise racial consciousness among the Black boys in her care (Vaughans, 2014). She presented them with a very festive lunch, but she divided the group in half, and designated one half as servers, who had to not only serve the other half their lunch, but also could not begin their own lunch until the other half was finished. When it was over, she inquired as to what it was like for them and what social implication it might have. They all agreed that it was totally wrong and unfair and equated it to anti-Semitism and gender bias. None of these children were from economically or academically impoverished backgrounds. A confrontation with my own son challenged my own comforting illusion that I had worked through these issues in my multiple therapies and two personal analyses. The fact of the matter is that the topic of race and the trauma of slavery was never broached in any of those therapies. In chastising my young son David over some misdeed, I asked him "if he was out of his cotton-picking mind." He responded with the perplexed inquiry, "Dad, why would my mind have to be cotton picking?" I apologized to him and assured him that it was my mind that was still "cotton picking," not his; that some injuries just take an awful long time to heal, especially when we are unaware of our wounds. Recall the struggle Black mothers endured over losing parental rights to their own children from having them sold away. For the more economically disadvantaged in the Black community in the United States today, that very struggle continues, as evidenced in the over-representation of Black families in family court, special education, child protective services, as well as the school-to-prison pipeline in the United States While these agencies can constitute a real threat to the survival of the family and to Black youth, I sense that Black people's fears become confounded by residual anxieties arising from slavery. Often today, when Black parents become highly threatened about their ability to protect or guide their children, you will hear the expression, "I brought you into this world, I will take you out." In the film *The Butler* (Daniels, 2013), the surviving son joins the Black Panther Party and, when the father is unable to dissuade his son, he barks this very threat at him. It is my sense that through this expression Black parents are unknowingly expressing grievances to earlier unacknowledged losses as well as proffering a manic defense against a felt sense of helplessness about the fate of their children, as their forbears had done earlier. During slavery, Black women worked in the fields right beside Black men. However, they were expected to pull double duty by bearing children for the profit of the owner. They continued performing hard labor until the last quarter of the pregnancy. In some of the narratives, enslaved women reported their ability to perform work the equal of any man on the plantation. Today, double duty is still expected of Black Women. They are expected to bear up under any odds and be known as resilient. An analyst colleague of mine commented on "the phantasy that Black women have been through so much, that they are like tempered steel" (Adams, 2004). Clinically, this sometimes appears during the course of treatment with the complaint, "I feel like I am getting weaker."

TREATMENT IMPLICATIONS

It is paradoxical that Blackness constitutes a most significant element in the lives of Black youth, and that psychoanalytic psychotherapy is the tool for examining one's internal and external world, and yet I am informed by White therapists and by Black boys that race is rarely discussed in treatment. While resistance to such exploration is probably present on both sides of the racial dyad, it is the responsibility of the therapist to acknowledge and invite the oppressed "otherness" into the treatment. Failure to do so constitutes the formulation and maintenance of an "as if" relationship. Hence, the sources of social trauma, degradation, and shame remain outside the purview of the therapeutic situation. This is a modern day version of what Danieli (1984) referred to as a "conspiracy of silence" and is a quiet message to the Black patient that ghosts from past social trauma are too powerful to engage here. These powerful unconscious communications also serve to reinforce stereotypes regarding the toughness of Black males, that Black males should be able to take it if they are man enough. This notion also serves to deny Black boys a crucial developmental stage of "boyhood." Research by Goff et al., (2014) confirms that Black boys in many instances are seen as about four and a half years older than their actual age. Pinderhughes (1989) emphasizes that it is not clinically possible to help patients examine their own cultural identity without therapists having done similar self-examination for themselves. I strongly concur with her definition of race "as entrapment for everyone" (p. 71). I also believe that while the exploration of the impact of living in a racist society is painful and frightening, it is also liberating for the patient, as well as for the therapist.

CONCLUSION

African Americans proudly celebrate Kwanza, a holiday that combines many African customs and beliefs (Riley, 1995). During this celebration, many Blacks adorn themselves in their finest African garb. This celebration is excellent for acknowledging our African ancestry and the wisdom in its value systems. However, it fails to address the sacrifice, courage, strength, and loss of those who were enslaved on these shores. In order to so, my colleague Dr. Michael Harris (2006) advises that we would have to adorn ourselves in knapped cotton or burlap in their honor, something my more fashion conscious colleague, Dr. Owens, informs me is not likely to happen, regardless of the worthiness of the cause. While I graciously concede her point, I do not yield on my own point at all. The honoring of our African Heritage appears to highlight a gap in African American consciousness regarding the honoring of those who were enslaved. It is my belief that much stands to be gained from the study of African

American slavery, for both Blacks and Whites, that can positively expand how we see ourselves and each other. Fraiberg (1987) talked about ghosts in the nursery, and I have been speaking of ghosts in African American culture whose presence needs acknowledgement in order for us to be truly strengthened by them. Therapeutically, Dimen (1998) describes the psychoanalytic session as an opportunity for the unspeakable to be spoken and the unthinkable to be thought by imagining what was never known and could not be thought. It is time for that silence to be broken and those muted voices be allowed to tell their stories. Examining history from a different perspective can also help facilitate this process. The Black historian John Henrik Clarke (1998) contends that,

> History is a clock that people use to tell their political and cultural time of day. It is also a compass that people use to find themselves on the map of human geography. History tells a people where they have been, what they have been, where they are, and what they are. Most important, history tells a people where they still must go and what they still must be. The relationship of history to its people is the same as a mother to her child.

Such a perspective can help significantly to alleviate some of the disavowed shame that haunts today's Black youth and can transform the traumatic emotional scars that they bear into a source of new-found strength.

REFERENCES

Abraham, N. and Torok, M. (1994). *The Shell and the kernel.* Chicago: University of Chicago Press.

Adams, M.V. (2001). Personal communication.

Ani, M. (1994) *Let the circle be unbroken*. New York: Nkonimfo Publications.

Berlin, I.(2010). *The making of African America: The four great migrations.* New York: Penguin.

Berlin, I. (1998). *Remembering slavery.* New York: The New Press.

Berlin, I. (2003). *Generations of captivity: A History of African American slaves,* Cambridge: Belknap Press.

Blassingame, J.W. (1977). *Slave testimony: Two centuries of letters, speeches, interviews, and autobiographies.* Baton Rouge: Louisiana State University Press.

Clarke, J.H. (1998). *A Great and Mighty Walk.* (DVD) WBAI Radio 99.5 fm. New York: Dot Media: Cinema Guild.

Danieli, Y. Psychotherapists' participation in the conspiracy of silence about the Holocaust. *Psychoanalytic Quarterly. 1984, 1,* 23–42.

Daniels, L. (Director) (2013). *The Butler*. (DVD). The Weinstein Company www.leedanielsthebutlermovie.com

Dimen, M. (1998). Strange hearts: On the paradoxical liaison between psychoanalysis and feminism. In M. Roth (Ed.), *Freud: Conflict and culture: Essays on his life, work and legacy*. New York: Knopf.

Douglas, F. (1845/2003). *Narrative of the Life of Fredrick Douglas: An American slave.* New York: Barnes and Noble.

DuBois, W.E.B. (1935). *Black reconstruction in America.* New York: Russell and Russell.

Eyerman, R. (2001). *Cultural trauma: Slavery and the formation of African American identity.* Cambridge: Cambridge University Press.

Fanon, F. (1967). *Blacks skin, white masks.* New York: Grove Press.

Foner, E. (2005). *Forever free: The Story of emancipation and reconstruction.* New York: Knopf.

Fraiberg, L. (1987). *Selected writings of Selma Fraiberg.* Columbus: Ohio State University Press.

Franklin, J.H. (2006). Black Men, America and the Twenty-First-Century. Conference keynote Address: *Black Male Youth: Creating a Culture of Educational Success.* Cuny.

Fredrickson, G. (2000). The Skeleton in the Closet. *New York Review of Books, 47, .17.* 61-66.

Gomez, M. (1998). *Exchanging our country marks. The transformation of African identity in the colonial and ante-bellum South.* Chapel Hill: University of North Carolina Press.

Goff, P., Jackson,M., Brooke, A., Cullotta, C. and DiTomasso, N. (2014). The essence of innocence: Consequences of dehumanizing black children. *Journal of Personality and Social Psychology. 4,* 526-545.

Gump, J. (2010). Reality matters. *Psychoanalytic Psychology. 27,* 42–54.

Harris, M. (2006). Personal Communication.

Harris, M. (1992). *The Rise of gospel blues.* New York: Oxford University Press.

Herman, J. (1992). *Trauma and recovery.* New York: Basic Books

Hopper, E. (2003). *The Social unconscious: Speaking the unspeakable: Selected papers of Earl Hopper.* London: Jessica Kingsley Publishers.

Hurmence, B. (1984). *My folks don't want me to talk about slavery.* Winston-Salem: John F. Blair Publisher.

Jacobs, H.A. (1861/987). *Incidents in the life of a slave girl.* Cambridge: Harvard University Press.

Morrison, T. (1992). *Playing in the dark: whiteness and the literary imagination.* Cambridge: Harvard University Press.

Morrow, A. (2003). *Breaking the curse of Willie Lynch.* Florrissant: Rising Sun Publications.

Painter, N. (1976). *Sojourner Truth: A Life, A Symbol.* New York: Norton.

Patterson, O. (1982). *Slavery and social death.* Cambridge: Harvard Press.

Perdue, C., Barden, T. and Phillips, R. (1976). *Weevils in The Wheat.* Charlottsville: University of Virginia Press.

Phillips, U. (1929). *Life and labor in the old South.* New York: Grosset and Dunlap.

Pinderhughes, E. (1989). *Understanding race, ethnicity and power.* New York: Free Press.

Pinderhughes, E. (2004). The multigenerational transmission of loss and trauma: The African American experience. In F. Walsh and M. McGoldrick (Eds.), *Living beyond loss* (pp. 161–181). New York: Norton.

Riley, D.W. (1995). *The complete Kwanza: Celebrating our cultural harvest.* New York: Harper Collins.

Rushdy, A. (2001). *Remembering generations: Race and family in contemporary African American Fiction.* Chapel Hill: University of North Carolina.

Sertima, I.V. (1976). *The African presence in Ancient America: They came before Columbus.* New York: Random House.

Tatrantino, Q. (Director). 2013. *Django unchained.* (DVD). (Available from Anchor Bay Entertainment, LLC, 9242 Beverly Blvd. Beverly Hills, CA 90210).

Vaughans, K. (2014). Disavowed fragments of the intergenerational transmission of trauma from slavery among African Americans. In K. Vaughans and W. Spielberg (Eds.), *The Psychology of Black Boys and Adolescents, v. 2.* 189–208. New York: Praeger.

Volkan, V. (1997). *Blood lines: From ethnic pride to ethnic terrorism.* New York: Farrar, Straus and Giroux.

Washington, B.T. (1901/1989). *Up from slavery: An autobiography.* Williamstown: Corner House Publishers.

Williams, A.H. (2012). *Help me to find my people.* Chapel Hill: University of North Carolina Press.

Yetman, N. (1970). *Voices from slavery*. New York: Holt, Rinehart and Winston.

FIFTEEN

"Thinking beyond Our Means"

Engendering a Depth Understanding of Trauma

Michael O'Loughlin and Barbara Ann McLeod

I usually begin my first class in my doctoral clinical elective *Bearing witness to trauma.*[1] by writing the word "Trauma" on the board and drawing a large "X" through it to signify to my students, fourth-year clinical psychology candidates who are well grounded in a medicalized clinical psychology worldview, that trauma, this reified term that is so taken for granted in clinical psychology and psychiatry, is open to contestation.[2] While it is hardly a surprise that a psychoanalytically informed depth pedagogy has made little headway—and is actually losing whatever ground—it may have held in mainstream university education—I have found it striking that the education of clinical psychologists has also remained relatively untouched by depth pedagogy. The push for therapeutic eclecticism, the pressure from the American Psychological Association Committee on Accreditation for "evidence-based practices," and often the demand from students for practical know-how that "works," creates demand for didactic techniques that reduce knowledge to positivist certitudes to be dispensed and ingested. My own experiences as a student and instructor in psychoanalytic institutes suggest that positivist, didactic pedagogy is too often the norm there, too. The richness and depth of analytic education typically comes from the requirements for personal supervision and analysis. This chapter is about importing a depth sensibility more directly into a pedagogical setting in which the aim is to assist students in developing clinical intuitions about the suffering that constitutes experiences of trauma. By definition, this challenge requires shifting the epistemological core of trauma studies away from a positivist epistemology of inert "trauma knowledge" toward a much greater emphasis on the contribution of the knower, and particularly the role of unconscious knowing, in the development of an understanding of what it means to suffer and what it means to heal.

My decision to pursue depth pedagogy has been influenced not only by my psychoanalytic training but also by the writings of a number of pedagogical writers.[3] One of the writers who most influenced me to approach trauma pedagogy from a depth perspective is Shoshana Felman (1987, 1992). In this chapter, I will give an overview of Felman's distillation of Lacanian theory and illustrate from my course the ways in which such a pedagogy holds out the promise for students "to think beyond their means" (Felman, 1987, p. 15). Barbara Anne McLeod, a student in my class in Fall 2013, wrote a final paper for my class that nicely illustrates some elements of Barbara's capacity to "think beyond her means" while participating in the class, and the chapter closes with Barbara's final piece of writing for the class. She wrote her paper as an intentional response to the class and at that time she was not aware that I was planning to write this chapter.

THE BLINDNESS OF INSIGHT AND THE VALUE OF IGNORANCE

What distinguished Jacques Lacan's life, as well as his work, was a profound impatience with the sovereign order of things (Benvenuto and Kennedy 1986; Roudinesco, 1997, 2014). As Felman (1987) notes, Lacan's work underlines the importance of recognizing systems of signification and challenging them. Lacan was particularly critical of the foreclosure of exploration in the discourse of the university. The predetermined "insight" that is proffered and taken in by students is indeed blind insight: the words are empty (*la parole vide*), and instead of ignorance presenting an opportunity to develop authentic questions and full speech (*la parole pleine*), students are left with the illusion of understanding. While this is problematic for students in all disciplines, how much more problematic is this for students whose life work as therapists ought to be about entering into dialogue with people who are experiencing foreclosure of meaning, to enable them to begin the journey back to full speech? Drawing on Freud's work on education as one of the "impossible professions," as well as Lacan's reworking of Freud, Felman notes that a crucial component of a learning encounter is factoring in the implicit knowing that is hidden beneath each student's ostensible effort after meaning. Extending to pedagogy the old therapist's shibboleth: "It is not what the patient is saying that matters, it is what the patient is *really* saying," Felman notes:

> Indeed, *the unconscious itself*, is a kind of unmeant knowledge that escapes intentionality and meaning, a knowledge spoken by the lan-

> guage of the subject (spoken for instance by his [sic] slips or by his [sic] dreams), but that the subject cannot recognize, assume as his [sic], appropriate; a speaking knowledge nonetheless denied to the speaker's knowledge. In Lacan's own terms, the unconscious is "knowledge that cannot tolerate one's knowing that one knows. (1987, p. 77)

Returning to Freud, then, Felman notes that ignorance is rooted in resistance to coming to know the unthought knowns (Bollas, 1987) of one's own unconscious experience. Crucially, then, a Lacanian-informed pedagogy, mirroring the discursive properties of a Lacanian analysis, is one in which the teacher re-punctuates the narrative of the teller such that those points of resistance create conditions for the possibility of new knowledge-making. In a pedagogical situation, therefore, questions about points of resistance can be posed either about the student's own dispositions of ignorance or about the potential for foreclosure embodied in the material to which students are exposed:

The pedagogical question crucial to Lacan's own teaching will thus be: Where does a text (or a signifier in a patient's conduct) precisely make no sense, that is, resist interpretation? Where does what I see and what I read resist my understanding? Where is the ignorance—the resistance to knowledge—located? And what can I learn from the locus of that ignorance? How can I interpret *out of* the dynamic ignorance I analytically encounter? How can I turn ignorance into an instrument of teaching? (1987, p. 80).

Felman argues that the task of a teacher practicing a depth pedagogy is to become a student of the student's unconscious. "It is. . . out of the patient's active ignorance, out of the patient's speech which says much more than it itself knows, that the analyst will come to learn the patient's own unconscious knowledge, the knowledge that is inaccessible to itself because it cannot tolerate knowing that it knows" (1987, p. 82).

Reminiscent of Paulo Freire's (1970) notion of "teachers-as students and students-as teachers," Felman invokes Lacan's refusal of the distinction in analysis between "the one who suffers and the one who cures" (1987, p. 89) and in education between "the one who knows and the one who does not know" (1987, p. 90). What is critical here, as Freud had noted, is that analytic knowledge is built around ephemeral wisps of knowledge (e.g., dreams, slips, archaic remnants, embodied knowledges) that inherently undermine any attempt at authoritative or omniscient interpretation. This aspect of Freud's work receded while ego psychology was the dominant order of the field in North America, and Lacan's 'return to Freud' was driven by a desire to reclaim this fundamental analytic posture. A pedagogy of uncertainty, and perhaps even incomprehension is therefore called for—a pedagogy that can only move forward through mutual inquiry:

> Lacan's unprecedented *poetic pedagogy* always implicitly opens up onto the infinitely literary, infinitely teaching question: What is the "navel" of my own theoretical dream of understanding? What is the specificity of my incomprehension? What is the riddle I pose here under the guise of knowledge? (1987, p. 96)

BEARING WITNESS TO TRAUMA AS A PEDAGOGICAL DEVICE

It is only as I reread Felman's "Education and crisis, on the vicissitudes of teaching" (1992) that I realize how much her struggle with trauma pedagogy has saturated my practice of teaching trauma. A key concern for Felman is understanding the role of witness in addressing trauma.[4] In this essay, she poses the question whether the process of bearing witness can be of pedagogical use. She asks: "Is the act of *reading* literary texts itself inherently related to the act of *facing horror*?" (1992, p. 2). Felman discusses her thoughts about a course she taught, *Literature and testimony,* in which students confronted the necessary gaps in the testimony they read, and were drawn into performing acts of witness in order to grapple with the lacunae in the texts. As Felman discovered, it was the lack of closure in the texts—their *strangeness*—that provided the invitation for the enactment of witnessing among her students:

> to . . . progressively discover, how the testimony cannot be subsumed by its familiar notion, how the texts that testify do not simply *report facts* but, in quite different ways, encounter—and make us encounter—*strangeness*: how the concept of testimony, speaking for a stance of superimposition of literature, psychoanalysis and history, is in fact quite unfamiliar and *estranging*, and how, the more closely we look at texts, the more they show us that, unwittingly, we do not even know what testimony is, and that, in any case, it is not simply what we thought we knew it was. (1992, p. 7)

It was only when Felman raised the stakes, however, by introducing historical and autobiographical testimony from the Fortunoff Video Archive for Holocaust Testimony[5] that students made the leap from a cognitive engagement with the class to an encounter with the unconscious. Felman and her students, all equally surprised by the emotional crisis produced by the intensity of the videotaped testimony, were forced to regroup. Felman, however, recognized the mutative analytic potential of this pedagogical moment and held her nerve:

> I was myself in turn taken by surprise, and worried by the critical dimensions of the crisis which the class was obviously going through, and which was gathering momentum. I realized at the same time, that the unpredicted outcome of the screening was itself a psychoanalytical enhancement of the way in which the class felt actively *addressed* not

> only by the video tape but by the intensity and intimacy of the testimonial encounter throughout the course. (1992, p. 18)

Here Felman underlines a key issue in any depth pedagogical experience: In what way does the pedagogical experience constitute an address to the unconscious of the students? Contrary to humanistic notions of teaching which tend to privilege *comfort* over all else, Felman suggests that the induction of some sense of *crisis* appears necessary to engage the archive of the unconscious and precipitate some kind of awakening in students.[6] Experiences of dissonance need to be structured so as to invite students to engage performatively with the possibilities of coming to know their own depths through experience with a testifying other:

> There is a parallel between this kind of teaching (in its reliance on the testimonial process) and psychoanalysis (in its reliance on the psychoanalytic process), insofar as both this teaching and psychoanalysis have, in fact, *to live through a crisis*. Both are called upon to be *performative*, and not just *cognitive*, insofar as they both strive to produce, and to enable, *change*. Both this kind of teaching and psychoanalysis are interested not merely in new information, but, primarily, in the capacity of their recipients to *transform themselves* in function of the newness of that information. (1992, p. 53)

CREATING A CRITICAL ADDRESS TO THE UNCONSCIOUS: TEACHING AND TESTIFYING

In the fall semester of 2013, twelve of a possible twenty PhD students signed up for my elective, *Bearing witness to trauma*. The students were in their fourth and last year of academic study before embarking on a required year-long internship. Derner Institute is one of the oldest psychoanalytically-oriented clinical psychology doctoral programs in the United States. Programs such as this are heading rapidly toward extinction as capitalist forces eliminate anything but short-term and supposedly "evidence-based" therapies. The students in my class were eminently well prepared and were sophisticated clinicians. I knew some of them very well, and some I had never met before. Aware of the level of their prior preparation and their challenging expectations, I prepared a syllabus with a wide range of readings covering autobiography, intergenerational trauma, therapeutic issues, and therapist self-care. I also added a heavy dose of testimony—most of it in the form of video testimony—to address the unconscious directly. We followed the suggested course sequence from the syllabus,[7] as summarized in the attached appendix.

Despite the academic tone of the syllabus, the pedagogical address of the course was explicitly to the unconscious. I spoke with the students at our first session about the course as an exercise in building stamina. The hallmark of their capacity to do difficult work, I proposed, would be in their capacity to be comfortable in the presence of trauma narrative, and hence a primary focus of the course would be immersion in trauma testimony. While this seemed to send a shiver of apprehension through the class, the students also knew that that was precisely why they had chosen this elective. In their weekly writings to me, many students repeatedly voiced worry about being able to develop this kind of stamina: Would they have the right stuff when confronted with horror? I use the word "horror" advisedly here, since their conceptualization of trauma at the beginning of the course was largely congruent with Felman's notion of *facing horror,* discussed earlier. Over the course of the semester, I hoped to engender a shift from this totalizing concept of horror to an understanding of social suffering and the possibility that by bearing witness they could in some ways break down the monolith implied by "horror" to get to the human anguish underneath. Their anxiety about horror also spoke to an awakening of the unconscious. While Felman suggests that a *crisis* is necessary to provoke an address to the unconscious, I think perhaps it is a bit more subtle: Students, just like analytic patients, know when intimations of dread are making their presence felt. They just need to be in the company of someone who presents, not as a fearless leader or omniscient interpreter, but as somebody who has visited such places before and can, with humility, take them as far down the road to as deep a place as they are comfortable venturing.

During the semester, we also had an opportunity to visit the issue of understanding. A discussion of Lanzmann's article *The obscenity of understanding* (Appendix: Week #9, Lanzmann, 1995) created a space for a counter-narrative to the notion that therapy is about understanding the patient—or, indeed, that learning is about understanding texts—and that therapeutic interpretation is about communicating that understanding back to the patient, or that regurgitation of material constitutes learning. Lanzmann's counterintuitive suggestion that to seek understanding of an event such as the Holocaust is obscene, created a limit space in which students had the freedom to explore more deeply analytic ideas such as cultivating a disposition of *receptivity* (Epstein, 2004) to trauma as opposed to developing a posture of inquiry accompanied by an urge to formulate concrete interpretations.

My course began—as all of my courses do—with an autobiographical invitation. The students could not be expected to embark on the journey from any point other than their own starting points. To emphasize that that this was a journey where the only tools required were humility and a capacity for exploring their own vulnerability, I began by sharing with them some aspects of my own autobiography. I shared some writings (Appendix: Week #2, O'Loughlin, 2007b, 2009) that revealed my own struggles seeking to ward off—and ultimately to embrace cautiously—the nameless anxieties and formless dread that have been my constant companion probably at least since birth. I purposely chose for them writings by Marilyn Charles, Dori Laub, and Annie Rogers (Appendix: Week #3, Charles, 2003; Week #9, Laub, 1992, 1995; Weeks #11–12, Rogers, 2006) because these writers model beautifully the necessity of inner work and an address to the unconscious as key to mutative depth-therapeutic work with people who have suffered greatly. My hope was that witnessing this kind of inner journeying among seasoned therapists would give them permission, if they needed it, to view the learning experience I offered as primarily a space for internal work, rather than a place for intellectual understanding and omniscient interpretation. Students were invited to write to me weekly, and this became a private conversational space that many students used to begin working though the interaction between their own unconscious archive—the "tattered script" of the inheritances littering their archive (Fraiberg, Adelson and Shapiro, 1975)—and the evocative testimony to which we bore witness.

The heart of the course, then, was extensive viewing of videotaped testimony in a wide variety of narrative styles, each one chosen for its capacity to produce the kind of emotional impact that creates an address to the unconscious. A variety of formats was used in order to trouble the possibility of students either taking comfort in privileging a certain presentation as what should constitute trauma narrative, or in privileging any one type of narrative as representing a prototypical victim tale. I encouraged the students, to the extent possible, to "experience the experience" rather than to dissect, analyze, or intellectualize the experience of the testimony. I was interested in students reacting to their own visceral reactions to the material, and in allowing themselves to free associate so that material from their unconscious archive had an opportunity to surface. We spoke, of course, of the parameters of confidentiality regarding the disclosure of information. Some students shared personal feelings in class. Others conversed with me privately in their weekly writings. Others took the material to their own therapists for further work. However, echoing Felman's experience with her class, the group experience each week was characterized by intensity. This intensity included deep emotional resonance with the suffering witnessed, surfacing of personal material and decisions as to how to manage that in our classroom context, and courageous sharing and mutual support as we began to construct a collective response to the awfulness of human evil and the resilience, grace, and sometimes abjectness (Appendix: Weeks #4–5, Langer, 1991) of human responses to painful experiences. Here are a few key points from the semester. All of the video testimony materials discussed below are listed in the Appendix.

Sex in a cold climate offers compelling survivor testimony from women who had been imprisoned in Magdalene Laundries[8] in Ireland during their adolescence. The testimony is very compelling and, in the language of psychoanalysis, much of it could be described as well metabolized. These women obviously had engaged in careful reflection on their experience and they offered thoughtful meditations on the effects of their incarceration. The extract from *The forgotten Maggies,* another documentary on the same subject, however, presents a stark contrast. Mary Collins, the witness, presents as a woman who, while determined to testify, is obviously still suffering serious adverse consequences from the brutality she experienced during her childhood. Viewers get to experience her raw, unmetabolized trauma, and reaction shots of the filmmaker allow the viewer to identify vicariously with his evident traumatization. Comparison of the testimonies leads to fruitful discussion of our feelings about the different presentations of trauma and raise the thorny problem of the implicit normative notions of what constitutes goodness in testimony.

The students find Shosh Shlam's depiction of life in a hostel in Israel for octogenarian Holocaust survivors, depicted in her documentary *Last journey into silence,* very hard to bear. The elderly residents evoke painful images of mortality. The film depicts people entering senescence, grappling with dementia, and weighed down by Holocaust losses we can only imagine. The return of three daughters to visit three of the women residents raises the stakes further. We can sit in judgment on the daughters for having abandoned their mothers many years before. But then we learn of the daughters' struggles growing up in the shadow of deeply wounded mothers, and how the abandonment of their mothers arose from a desire to protect themselves and their children in the next generation from such damage, and the full scale of the tragedy is revealed. I have had students in the past sometimes request that the viewing of this film be stopped, but this year's class was stoic, and we watched all the way through. As is my practice, I seek to avoid dissection or any flight toward intellectual interpretation, so students mostly absorbed the sensibility of the testimony into their bone marrow.

Students always approach Holocaust testimony with anxiety about exposure to horror. Claude Lanzmann's *Shoah,* with its elliptical and polyphonic style, surprised them and provoked considerable debate about his intentions. This debate extended, too, to the narrative of Menachem S, whose testimony from the Fortunoff Archive we viewed. Some students seemed to feel that he was too fluent, perhaps even slick, and that his dream of the conveyor belt was too neatly packaged. These two types of testimonies led to more fruitful discussion of how we approach trauma with implicit normative notions of what constitutes goodness in testimony. What would happen, I wondered, if we could divest ourselves of all such notions and simply assume a receptive posture?

Viewing *Long night's journey into day: South Africa's search for truth and reconciliation,* a documentary about South Africa's truth and reconciliation process offered yet another window into the unconscious. This film provides interviews with those who perpetrated atrocities, as well as their victims, and offered a space where students could begin to talk about some of the complexities of concepts such as "perpetrator" and "victim," especially in complex political contexts such as apartheid-era South Africa. Bishop Desmond Tutu's discussion of the choice between restorative and retributive justice was also of great interest to students living in the United States, a society where retributive justice is often valorized as a tool for "moving on" from trauma. We then engaged with Jon Alpert's *War torn*, a film that complexifies the notion of post-traumatic stress disorder, and how the reality of the experience differs markedly both from the public rhetoric around PTSD and the reductionist characteristics embedded in the diagnostic categories used in the DSM classifications. Finally, on impulse, seeking another mode of address, I proposed viewing Lina Wertműller's *Seven beauties* because it refuses simplification and offers an anti-hero with decidedly venal moral qualities. "Oh yea!"

> Inspired by Shoshana Felman's experience, my invitation to the students to reach within themselves to produce something meaningful to draw the class to a close was phrased as follows. "An exploration of the importance of 'memory work' ands 'witnessing' in addressing individual and collective trauma in human society."
>
> I would like you to use your final paper for a meditation on the human condition, and the effects of taking this course on your understanding and your emotions. A primary purpose of the course was to expose you to multiple ways of telling about trauma and suffering [memoir, theory, poetry, documentary, fictional movie, eyewitness testimony, video testimony, etc.]. As I noted above,
>
> > A fundamental clinical purpose of the courses is to engage students with the experience of *being with* trauma, embodied in the idea of therapist as *witness* to trauma narrative. We will explore memory. . . the nature of traumatic memory. . . attempts at extermination of memory. . . struggles with the preservation of memory. . . the role of witnessing in the preservation of memory and alleviation of trauma. . .
>
> I would like you to travel across the narrative genres we explored and talk about what specifically you experienced with each one. It is not helpful to just praise a genre or dismiss it. Every genre has advantages and shortcomings, and the response you experienced was most likely an artifice of the particular choices a particular author or filmmaker chose to use. For each work you discuss, please be specific. Do not make sweeping generalizations. Discuss concrete examples and instances. While psychoanalysts remain committed to the importance of testimony as part of the *working through* of trauma, Lawrence Langer claims that "Holocaust memory is an insomniac faculty" (1991). Do you agree?
>
> I would like you to think of this project very much in the psychoanalytic sense as a *working through* of the emotions produced by all that you met and were exposed to this semester. Try to understand the moments

when you engaged with traumatic narrative, and the moments when you mobilized your defenses to avert your eyes or turn your face away. Shoshana Felman, who taught a course like this one [exclusively on the Holocaust] at Yale some years ago, described her final paper as quoted below. This may give you some guidance as to what I ultimately want you to strive for:

I invite you to write a paper on your experience of the testimony and on your experience of the class. To do that, you need to think of the Holocaust videotapes in the context of the significance of the entire course, and in relation to the other texts we studied. I want you to work on precisely what you said was so difficult for you to achieve: you felt a disconnection, and I want you to look on the contrary for the connections. What has this experience taught you in the end? What did it change in your perception of those other texts? What difference did it make in your global perception of the class.

What I am suggesting is that you view this paper as your testimony to this course. I admit that it would be a precocious testimony. I know you feel you are not ready. . . I am inviting you, in turn, to 'shoot ahead of yourselves' . . and to give, in turn, your precocious testimony. (Felman, 1992, pp. 51-2)

Felman reminds us that "teaching and psychoanalysis are interested not merely in new information, but, primarily, in the capacity of their recipients to *transform themselves* in function of the newness of that information (p. 53). I would like you to address that process of transformation in yourself. You might find it worthwhile to conceptualize this project in personal ways, either through autobiographical exhumation of parts of your own personal and familial histories, or through your interest in/ involvement with some world, national, or local trauma. In addition, I would like you to play with presentation and format. What follows is Barbara Ann McLeod's response to this invitation.

SMOKE SIGNALS: A PROCESS OF MOURNING AND TRANSFORMATION

I have argued that the evolution of relational thinking places increased demands on the analyst. Always we produce and are exposed to more than we can master, know, or manage. However you use your countertransference, it is both crucial and only ever imperfectly masterable. That mix of powerlessness, shame, and insistent demand is actually a terrible combination, a prescription for dissociation and trauma. I think this may be one of the indissoluble, irreducible conditions of analytic work (Harris, 2009, p. 6).

The project is, you ask us to mark the transformation process we have experienced in this course *Bearing Witness to Trauma*. My paper is an

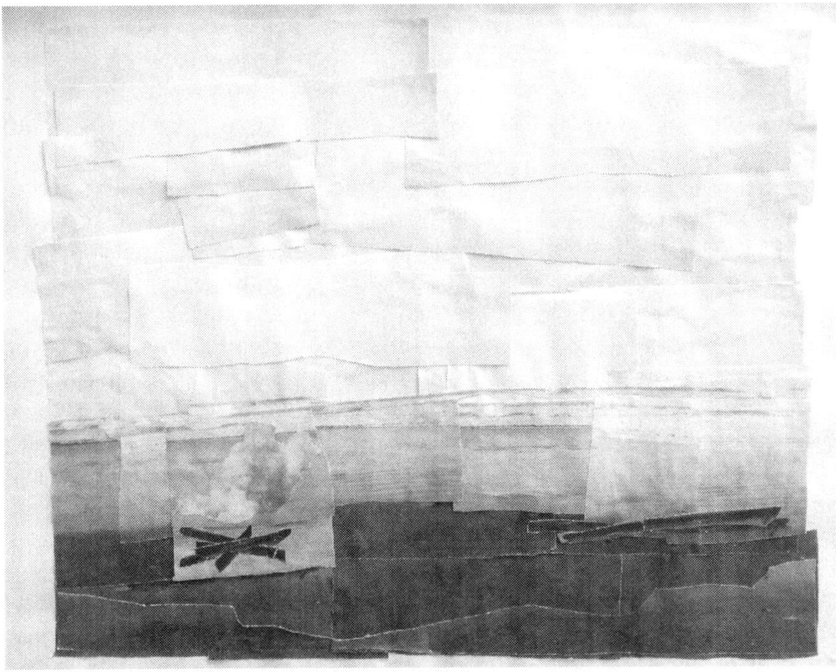

Figure 15.1. Smoke Signals By Barbara Ann McLeod

effort to map that transformation by bridging analytic and autobiographical material with our coursework.

When I think about the semester, I have to hold it alongside three processes that, although distinct, shaped one another: the trauma course, internship applications, and my clinical practice.

Transitioning from graduate school into an internship signals the interruption to a way of life I have sought out in New York City and in psychoanalysis. With so much end in sight, it is no surprise I have experienced a fair amount of regression: missed deadlines, witnessing my patient's hospitalization, writer's block, and the endless barrage of self-reproach. The pairing of this course with internship application season created a further reworking of experiences that highlighted limitations. This paper is an effort to describe those limits and perhaps transcend them or at least transform them from something punishing into something meaningful—even redemptive.

I remember when we first began this course, you marked out the word trauma and asked us to remember it as something else. You wanted us to expand our capacity to experience with our patients. We were called upon to mark our desire to flee or turn away and to work on the capacity to stay. As in Harris's quote above, we were asked to grapple with "a terrible combination" and an impossible task. For me, this course has been about working at the limits: the limits of experience, understanding, tolerability, capacity. It has been about having to work with the effects of breaching my own limits—the shame, the reproach, the denial, and mustering the courage to continue despite knowing there would be more than I could manage.

The opening quote of this paper comes from Harris's (2009) article "You must remember this." It is a moving paper partly because it points to the difficult truth that analysts have more in common than not with those they seek to treat. Her piece focuses on those psychic points of resonance and dissolution. When there is too much psychic equivalence to bear what we witness, we flee or dissociate or deny. We use whatever tricks we employ not to experience that unbearable truth or terror we sense about ourselves or our objects in the other. This flight is a place Harris explores as an important cause for therapeutic impasse. It seems to me this course is of a similar nature. By creating questions and experiences from which we cannot or are asked not to flee, we were encouraged to explore what it is in us, in our histories, that incites this flight rather than passing it off to the patients we treat.

Harris (2009) calls upon us to consider the role of the analyst in therapeutic impasses, those points when change stalls or becomes impeded. She bravely asks the analyst to understand the interlocutions within a treatment of the patient and analyst, the moments of impasse being attributed to those places within an analyst where she cannot tolerate the expressions of the patient. Harris sources research that looks at the commonality between analysts and the avoided histories of disorganized attachment, of caretaking for dissociated, terrorized parents, of our shared experiences of archaic shame and the loss from our earliest rejections. While these places of unmetabolized trauma and grief hinder our ability, she also points to them as potential openings and places where we can "tumble into the abyss" (Harris, 2009, p. 18). For Harris, part of this tumbling involves circling back, something she describes as *nonlinear dynamic systems (NDS).*

Borrowed from chaos theory, NDS is a way of experiencing temporality in an all-at-once or a few-pieces-at-a-time kind of way. It suggests that, in the unconscious, we feel things not in the order in which they *happened* but as they are happening, combined with what they call up from past experiences and fantasies. This nonlinear order is a place of reworking, where time is changed by "experience, and history, and recognitions" (Harris, 2009, p. 13). This funny kind of time changes us, develops us.

There are many access points to the unconscious and many ways to work with it.

Annie Rogers (2006) writes about the role of responsibility in developing and listening to the unconscious—her responsibility and the patient's. Her child analysis work posits the subject with a responsibility as well as a subjectivity. How the child fits into her world is in part determined by the degree of receptivity she encounters in those close to her and also determined by her reaction to whatever receptivity she finds. The child brings her own ways of responding that alters the course of the story. For Rogers, Lacanian analysis is a way of listening to the unconscious of the person. By looking at the patient as a subject rather than a victim or survivor, she is locating within the child a way out of her anguish. There is some way this view puts aside a sense of blame, and allows the participants to encounter their responsibilities and make corresponding decisions.

In *The Unsayable*, Rogers concludes her story of Ellen with the question, "What makes it possible for a child to speak and be truly heard when speaking has been impossible in the family?" (2006, p. 196). Rogers writes that the Lacanian unconscious is an extension of Freud's unconscious, where the logic is dynamic and revealed through dreams, jokes, word play, and unintended actions, and proceeds to describe the Lacanian unconscious as a linguistic container of the repressed. Those sounds, images, and thoughts have to be censored and held back because they are believed (rightfully or not) to go unrecognized or refused by the other. This process creates an inner split. The speaker is not aware of the repressed because she needs to focus on what she is saying so she can affect the listener. This process creates a gap between what is said and unsaid. The speaker cannot hear the unconscious signifiers that emerge in her language.

Although Rogers (2006) does not make the relational aspect of her work with Ellen primary, relationality is implicit in her approach to the unconscious. She aims to allow Ellen to hear herself through how Ellen speaks to Rogers. But it is Rogers who hears and then amplifies the signifiers. What Rogers hears depends on what she can hear, her receptivity, which again is determined by a host of histories outside of Ellen. While relationality is a piece of the story, it is not the piece Rogers attends to in her work. She pays more attention to object relations, as she underscores. "[Ellen's] speaking depends upon my hearing and, even more critically, how *she* hears me hearing her." *Her* hearing is her multi-determined subjectivity.

ON SUBJECTIVITY

In a nod to both subjectivity and intersubjectivity, Harris (2009) locates problems of clinical impasse in the difficult affects of sadness and shame. Her investigations of therapeutic stalemates sent her to analysts' early experiences of interruptions and loss. These painful experiences arouse an unbearable sadness with an attendant and automatic shame response:

shame at having lost what we so deeply mourn. This shame is unbearable and rouses the powerful defense of omnipotence. For me, as for many therapists, the stories of my early interruptions cannot be considered outside of my capacities (and limitations) for this job.

When I was a child, I often had this visual memory of a beachside motel. I could recall the outdoor peach stucco hallways and the ice machine. There was a parking lot and metal stairways and doors that opened into suites. I never really thought much of the images. I figured they must have been a dream. When I became a young adult and was trying to make sense of confusing feelings of loss, my mother began telling me stories in an attempt to help me make sense of myself.

One such story goes that when I was about three, my family went to Florida for a beach holiday. My mother was at the hotel with my brother, then about ten, and my father had taken me to the beach to play. Later in the afternoon he returned to the room and my mom asked where I was. My father had forgotten he was watching me. My mother flew down to the beach to find me playing alone and heading toward the water. When I asked her later if I seemed upset, she said I didn't seem to realize what had happened. It had only been a short time between when my father left me and she found me. This memory has been important to me in approaching how I have responded to this course because its content serves as a backdrop from which my difficulties with clinical work and witnessing trauma emerge.

I see this story as a screen memory and an allegory for my clinical impasses. I can play and work in the world safely but more than likely it will be insufficiently supervised, and with a looming sense that something dangerous could happen. Nothing dangerous did happen to me in the story, but the events reveal a deeper vulnerability that, although I survived and was unharmed, I was forgotten and forgettable.

As Rogers concedes, my symptoms, my problems, are a result of my deep attachment to being forgotten and making myself forgettable. Harris might argue that omnipotent defenses protect me from the humiliation and rage of loving someone who could leave me to be harmed. As Garland (1998) writes, in the internal world there is no such thing as an accident or forgetting. Our inner worlds find places and people to hold to account. In approaching this trauma course, I have been unable to avoid the cost of carrying around my introjected father. It is partly what made it so painful to witness *Last Journey into Silence* (Shlam, 2001). Images and stories that arouse being forgotten cut too close.

In Lear's book on radical hope (2006), he references Plato and Freud who wrote of how people are born into the world as longing creatures. Our original natures seek out what we hold to be beautiful, evocative, and good. Lear notes that these longings could be mistaken, and that is for me what ties this work to the course. This is the dynamic that arouses archaic object relations that make future traumatic experiences so painful.

The innocence of longing later becomes wretched and unbearable—a dreaded aspect of experience. But Lear also speaks to us of courage. He writes that our longing causes us to reach out and, perhaps, in the reaching we find others or even cultural ideas that nurture us. Those ideas give us a way of conceptualizing what it is we are longing to receive. Although Lear's idea of courage is in relation to pursuing the question of hope in the face of devastating cultural loss, it feels as though there could also be something for the analytic mind, something speaking to what beats back the refusal of the other.

Trying to return to this task, I travel backward from the present and land on a time somewhere between eight and ten. It's after church. My father is telling me a story about a Native American princess who is seated with her father, the head of the tribe, at a ceremonial feast. During this important event, a bee stings the princess's hand. She shows her great loyalty and love by not crying out, as that would show her weakness and cause great shame to her father and her tribe. It strikes me that, in this story, the mentalizing function belongs to the child. It is the daughter who considers her impact on the father and tribe, and she responds with benevolent stoicism.

Several years ago, I made a collage in response to the story about my father losing me and as a response to his princess story. I called it *Smoke Signals*. This image is confounded with another beach memory of a family bonfire. In it, I was also around three. Apparently, we did not have a permit to have a beach fire, and the authorities came to tell my parents to extinguish it. I remember the confusion of adults buzzing around, our dogs running and barking, and horseflies swarming. My mother was trying to pour sand over the fire and a horsefly flew at me. I tried to run away from the fly, but instead I ran into the fire. As my mother screamed, I jumped over the embers. This work represents a habitual retreat from pain to an inner landscape free from other humans and the irony of running from danger but becoming more embroiled in it. This beach represents a space I have created within myself, both a longing for connection and the belief that it will not come.

SMOKE SIGNALS

Thinking back over the course, there were some moments of watching that stood out more than others. Of course, my reactions are projections and identifications based on my own internal world but elaborating them is part of my process of transforming myself based on my involvement with these images and sounds, for instance, the art therapy scene from *Last Journey into Silence*, where the woman is making the repetitive drawings and the therapist begins first encouraging and then insisting she work with different materials and make a new image. I identified with both the impossible frustration of rejection and the aggressive reaching out as a therapist when a person is so lost in an internal world and refusing new contact. I also felt the intrusion and sadism of the therapist humiliating the patient in front of the other group members, patients and staff, pointing out her lack. Then there was the testimony of A-63, Menachem S[9] which moved me greatly. My reaction spoke to my transformation as a witness to trauma. His consideration for and love of his wife and daughter pointed toward my radical hope, while also touching on my earliest losses and longings. His respect for their thoughts was palpable and offered me an experience approaching mourning and transformation.

Analytic work requires we push past our clinical impasses through a continued circling back onto our histories and sore spots. It demands the recognition that it will at times be more than we can bear. My efforts here to approximate a transformation have merely pointed toward a source, a potential narrative of subjectivity. That effort alone exceeded my capacity. These words are still frozen and my story stuck somewhere I cannot access. It is a pain that can make it hard to write, hard to work, hard to come close. It is a life's work and an imperative if I am to live it, if I am to learn to remember and not to forget.

NOTES

1. To view the syllabus please see michaeloloughlinphd.com/
2. See, for example Fassin and Rechtman (2009) and Leys (2000) for critical interrogation of the origins and usage of the term "trauma" and for an overview of the issues see O'Loughlin (2014).
3. For depth pedagogy see Felman (1987), the writings of Deborah Britzman (1998, 2003, 2006, 2009, 2010), my own work in this area (O'Loughlin, 2009), and the writings of the many writers whose work appears in O'Loughlin (2013a, 2013b), and O'Loughlin and Johnson, (2010).
4. For the development of my own view on bearing witness see O'Loughlin, (2007a).
5. http://www.library.yale.edu/testimonies/
6. Note again the parallel here also to Freire, who speaks of conventional didactic education as anesthetizing. See also the disucssion of revivifying education in O'Loughlin (2009, 2013c) and of therapy that animates subjectivity in O'Loughlin and Merchant (2012).
7. For complete current syllabus, please see michaeloloughlinphd.com/. The sequence of readings and testimonies used in the fall of 2013 version of the course is presented in the appendix to this chapter.
8. For a history of abuse in Irish institutions for children including Ireland's Magdalene Laundries see McCarthy (2010), Raftery and O'Sulivan, (1999), Smith, (2007).
9. http://www.library.yale.edu/testimonies/education/singlewitness.html

REFERENCES

Benvenuto, B., and Kennedy, R. (1986). *The works of Jacques Lacan: An introduction.* London: Free Association Books.

Bollas, C. (1987). *The shadow of the object: Psychoanalysis of the unthought known.* New York: Columbia University Press.

Britzman, D. (1998). *Lost subjects, contested objects: Toward a psychoanalytic inquiry of learning.* Albany: SUNY Press.

Britzman, D. (2003). *After education: Anna Freud, Melanie Klein and psychoanalytic histories of learning.* Albany: SUNY Press.

Britzman, D. (2006). *Novel education: Psychoanalytic studies of learning and not learning.* New York: Peter Lang Publishing.

Britzman, D. (2009). *The very thought of education: Psychoanalysis and the impossible professions.* NY: SUNY Press.

Britzman, D. (2010). *Freud and education.* New York: Routledge.

Epstein, M. (2004). *Thoughts without a thinker: Psychotherapy from a Buddhist perspective.* New York: Basic Books.

Fassin, D., and Rechtman, R. (2009). *The empire of trauma: An inquiry into the condition of victimhood.* Princeton, NJ: Princeton University Press.

Felman, S. (1987). *Jacques Lacan and the adventure of insight: Psychoanalysis in contemporary culture.* Cambridge, MA: Harvard University Press.

Felman, S. (1992). Education and crisis: On the vicissitudes of teaching. In C. Caruth (Ed.), *Trauma: Explorations in memory* (pp. 1–56). Baltimore: Johns Hopkins University Press.

Fraiberg, S., Adelson, E., and Shapiro, V. (1975). Ghosts in the nursery. *Journal of the American Academy of Child Psychiatry, 14,* 387–421.

Freire, P. (1970). *Pedagogy of the oppressed.* New York: Continuum.

Garland, C. (Ed.). (1998). *Understanding trauma: A psychoanalytic approach.* London: Karnac.

Harris, A. (2009). You must remember this.*Psychoanalytic Dialogues, 19*(1), 2–21.

Lear, J. (2009). *Radical hope: Ethics in the face of cultural devastation.* Cambridge, MA: Harvard University Press.

Leys, R. (2000). *Trauma: A genealogy.* Chicago: University of Chicago Press.

McCarthy, R. (2010). *Origins of the Magdalene laundries: An analytical history.* Jefferson, NC: Mcfarland.

O'Loughlin, M. (2007a). Bearing witness to troubled memory. *Psychoanalytic Review, 94*(2), 191–212.

O'Loughlin, M. (2007b). On losses that are not easily mourned. In L. Bohm, R. Curtis, and B. Willock (Eds.), *Psychoanalysts' reflections on deaths and endings: Finality, transformations, new beginnings.* New York: Routledge.

O'Loughlin, M. (2009). *The subject of childhood.* New York: Peter Lang Publishing.

O'Loughlin, M. (Ed.). (2014). *The ethics of remembering and the consequences of forgetting: Essays on trauma, history and memory.* Lanham, MD: Rowman and Littlefield.

O'Loughlin, M. (Ed.). (2013a). *Psychodynamic perspectives on working with children, families and schools.* Lanham, MD: Jason Aronson.

O'Loughlin, M. (Ed.). (2013b). *The uses of psychoanalysis in working with children's emotional lives.* Lanham, MD: Jason Aronson.

O'Loughlin, M. (2013c). Reclaiming genealogy, memory and history: The psychodynamic potential for reparative therapy in contemporary South Africa. In C. Smith, G. Lobban, and M. O'Loughlin (Eds.), *Psychodynamic psychotherapy in contemporary South Africa: Contexts, theories, practices.* Johannesburg, SA: Wits University Press.

O'Loughlin, M., and Johnson, R. (Eds.). (2010). *Imagining children otherwise: Theoretical and critical perspectives on childhood subjectivity.* New York: Peter Lang Publishing.

O'Loughlin, M. and Merchant, A. (2012). Working obliquely with children. *Journal of Infant, Child and Adolescent Psychotherapy, 11,* 149-159

Raftery, M. and O'Sullivan, E. (1999). *Suffer the little children: The inside story of Ireland's industrial schools*. Dublin: New Island Books.
Rogers, A. (2006).*The unsayable: The hidden language of trauma*. New York: Random House.
Roudinesco, E. (1997). *Jacques Lacan*. New York: Columbia University Press.
Roudinesco, E. (2014). *Lacan in spite of everything*. London: Verso.
Shlam, S. (2001). *Last journey into silence* [Motion picture]. Waltham, MA: Brandeis University: National Center for Jewish Film: http://www.jewishfilm.org/Catalogue/films/lastjourney.html
Smith, J. (2007). *Ireland's Magdalen laundries and the nation's architecture of containment*. Notre Dame, IN: University of Notre Dame Press.

Appendix

Course Texts and Film Testimony

Memoirs/Novels

Students will select a memoir/novel to read and follow the outlined weekly schedule below

Jelinek, E. (2004). *The piano teacher*. New York: Grove Press.
Laguna, S. (2009). *One foot wrong*. New York: Other Press.
Tyler, C. (2009). *You'll never know, Book One: A good and decent man. New York: Penguin.*
van Dis, J. (1994). *My father's war*. New York: New Press.

Week #1

Video Testimony: Sex in a cold climate, 1997. Steven Humphries, Director.
The forgotten Maggies, 2009, Stevcen O'Riordan, Director:
Siebert, C. (2006, October 8). An elephant crackup? *New York Times Magazine.*

Week #2

Video Testimony: Last journey into silence (2001). Shosh Shlam, Director.
Fraiberg, S., Adelson, E., and Shapiro, V. (1975). Ghosts in the nursery. *Journal of the American Academy of Child Psychiatry, 14,* 387–421.
O'Loughlin, M. (2007). On losses that are not easily mourned. In L. Bohm, R. Curtis, and B. Willock (Eds.), *Psychoanalysts' reflections on deaths and endings: Finality, transformations, new beginnings.* New York: Routledge.
O'Loughlin, M. (2009). The curious subject of the child. In O'Loughlin, M. (Ed.), *The subject of childhood*. New York: Peter Lang Publishing.

Week #3

Video Testimony: *Salad Fingers*
http://www.youtube.com/playlist?list=PL9383CC2C6DBD902F
Auerhahn, N. and Prelinger, C. (1983). Repetition in the concentration camp survivor and her child. *International Review of Psychoanalysis, 10,* 31-46.
Charles, M. (2003).The intergenerational transmission of unresolved mourning: Personal, familial, and cultural factors. *Samiksa: Journal of the Indian Psychoanalytic Society, 54,* 65–80.
Kaplan, L. (1996). Images of absence, voices of silence. In *No voice is ever wholly lost: An exploration of the everlasting attachment between parent and child*. New York: Simon and Schuster.

Weeks #4 and 5

Video Testimony: Waltz with Bashir. (2009). Ari Folman, Director.

Abraham, N. (1994). "Secrets and posterity. . ." "Notes on the phantom: A complement to Freud's metapsychology." In Abraham, N. and Torok, M., *The shell and the kernel.* Edited, translated and with an Introduction by N. Rand, Chicago: University of Chicago Press.

Faimberg, H. (1988).The telescoping of generations: Genealogy of certain identifications. *Contemporary Psychoanalysis, 24,* 99–117.

Garon, J. (2004). Skeletons in the closet. *International Forum of Psychoanalysis, 13,* 84-92.

O'Loughlin, M. (2007b). Bearing witness to troubled memory. *Psychoanalytic Review.*

O'Loughlin, M. (2012). Trauma trails from Ireland's Great Hunger: A psychoanalytic inquiry. In L. Bohm, R. Curtis, and B. Willock (Eds.), *Loneliness and Yearnings.* New York: Routledge.

Langer, L. (1991). *Holocaust testimonies: The ruins of memory.* New Haven: Yale University Press.

Volavková, H., (1993).(Ed.). . . .*I never saw another butterfly: Children's drawings and poems from Terezin Concentration Camp,* 1942–1944. New York: Schocken.

Weeks # 6 and 7

Video Testimony: *Shoah.* (1985), Claude Lanzmann, Director.

Davoine, F. and Gaudillière, J. (2004). *History beyond trauma.* New York: Other Press.

Week #8

Video Testimony: Unseen tears (2009). Ron Douglas, Director.
http://blip.tv/free-speech-tv/unseen-tears-4290810

Erikson, K. (1976). Loss of community at Buffalo Creek. *American Journal of Psychiatry, 133,* 302–305.

O'Loughlin, M. (2008). Radical hope or death by a thousand cuts? The future for Indigenous Australians. *Arena Journal, 29/30,* 175–202.

O'Loughlin, M. (2013). Reclaiming genealogy, memory and history: The psychodynamic potential for reparative therapy in contemporary South Africa. In C. Smith, G. Lobban, and M. O'Loughlin (Eds.), *Psychodynamic psychotherapy in Contemporary South Africa: Contexts, theories, practices.* Johannesburg, SA: Wits University Press.

Week #9

Video Testimony: Fortunoff Video Archive for Holocaust Testimonies. A-35, Helen K; A-63, Menachem S.
http://www.library.yale.edu/testimonies/

Lanzmann, C. (1995). An evening with Claude Lanzmann. In C. Caruth, *Trauma: Explorations in memory.* Baltimore: Johns Hopkins University Press.

Laub, D. (1992). Bearing witness or the vicissitudes of listening. An event without a witness: Truth, testimony and survival. In S. Felman and D. Laub, *Testimony: Crises of witnessing in literature, psychoanalysis, and history.* New York: Routledge.

Laub, D. (1995). Truth and testimony: The process and the struggle. In C. Caruth, *Trauma: Explorations in memory.* Baltimore: Johns Hopkins University Press.

Week #10

Testimony: Lawson, G. (2004). The Rwanda witness. *New York Times Magazine.*

Rubin, E. (1998, March 23). Letter from Uganda: "Our children are killing us," *The New Yorker.*

Gartner, R. (1999). Betrayed as boys. Psychodynamic treatment of sexually abused men. New York: Guilford Press.
Herman, J. (1995). Child abuse. In *Trauma and recovery*. New York: Basic Books.

Weeks #11 and 12

Video Testimony:. (2000). F. Reid and D. Hoffman, Directors.
Ferenczi, S. (1988). Confusion of tongues between adults and the child. *Contemporary Psychoanalysis*, 24, 197–206.
Rogers, A. (2006). *The unsayable: The hidden language of trauma*. New York: Random House.

Weeks #13 and 14

Video Testimony: *War torn*. (2010). Jon Alpert, Director.
Bell, D. (1998). External injury and the internal world. In C. Garland (Ed.). *Understanding trauma: A psychoanalytical approach*. London: Karnac.
Garland, C. (1998). Introduction: Why psychoanalysis?, Thinking about trauma, Issues in treatment: A case of rape. In C. Garland (Ed.), *Understanding trauma: A psychoanalytical approach*. London: Karnac.
Taylor, D. (1998). The psychodynamic assessment of post-traumatic stress. In C. Garland (Ed.), *Understanding trauma: A psychoanalytical approach*. London: Karnac.

Week #15

Testimony: Deidentified human rights affidavits from asylum evaluations performed by M. O'Loughlin
Seven beauties, (1975). Lina Wertműller, Director.
Danieli, Y. (1996). Who takes care of the caretakers? The emotional consequences of working with children traumatized by war and communal violence. In R. Apfel and B. Simon (Eds.), *Minefields in their hearts: The mental health of children in war and communal violence*. New Haven: Yale University Press.
McWilliams, N. (2005). Preserving our humanity as therapists. *Psychotherapy: Theory, Research, Training.*, 42(2), 139–151.
Wiese, E. B. (2007). I think he is still inside me: Mother/child psychotherapy with a Kosovar family. In B. Droždek and J. Wilson (Eds.), *Voices of trauma: Treating survivors across cultures*. New York: Springer.

REFERENCES

Felman, S. (1995). Education and crisis, or the vicissitudes of teaching. In *Trauma: Explorations in memory*, ed. C. Caruth. Baltimore & London: Johns Hopkins University Press, pp. 13-60.
Fraiberg, S., Adelson, E., & Shapiro, V. (1975). "Ghosts in the nursery," *Journal of the American Academy of Child Psychiatry, 14*, 387-421.
Morrison. T. (1987). *Beloved*. New York: Vintage
Morrison. T. (1970). *The bluest eye*. New York: Vintage

Index

About the Contributors

Judy Atkinson, Emeritus Professor is a Jiman (central west Queensland) and Bundjalung (northern New South Wales) woman, with Anglo-Celtic and German heritage. Her academic contributions to the understanding of trauma related issues stemming from the violence of colonisation and the healing/recovery of Indigenous peoples from such trauma has won her the Carrick Neville Bonner Award in 2006 for her curriculum development and innovative teaching practice. In 2011 she was awarded the Fritz Redlick Memorial Award for Human Rights and Mental Health from the Harvard University program for refugee trauma. In retirement she is working across Australia, and in Papua New Guinea to skill up a trauma informed workforce, responding to violence and its relational trauma in populations, with a focus on whole-of community change. For further information please go to www.wealli.com.au.

Claude Barbre, M.S., M.Div., Ph.D., L.P., is Associate Professor, The Clinical Psychology Psy.D. Department, The Chicago School of Professional Psychology. He is Course Stream Coordinator of the Psychodynamics Orientation at The Chicago School, and also teaches in the Psychology and Spirituality Studies, and the Child and Adolescent Track. Dr. Barbre has counseled children, adults, and families for over 25 years, and served for 12 years as Executive Director of The Harlem Family Institute, a New York City school-based, psychoanalytic training program working with children and families in low-income, high-needs neighborhoods. He also taught psychology and religion at Manhattan College and Fordham University before his appointment at The Chicago School. A former Associate Editor of the *Journal of Religion and Health: Psychology, Spirituality, and Medicine* (Springer Press) for fifteen years, Dr. Barbre is an award-winning author of articles, books, and poetry, among them *Creative Dissent: Psychoanalysis in Evolution* (Praeger-Greenwood Press, 2003), edited with Alan Roland and Barry Ulanov; and *Psychotherapy and Religion: Many Paths, One Journey*, edited with Marcella Weiner and Paul C. Cooper (Rowman and Littlefield, 2005). He is a certified hospital chaplain and a licensed psychoanalyst in private practice.

Marilyn Charles is a staff psychologist at the Austen Riggs Center and a psychoanalyst in private practice in Stockbridge, MA. She is affiliated with Harvard University and several psychoanalytic institutes, and serves as Contributing Editor of *Psychoanalysis, Culture, and Society* and on the editorial boards of a number of psychoanalytic journals. As the Co-Chair of the Association for the Psychoanalysis of Culture and Society (APCS) and President-Elect of Division 39 (Psychoanalysis) of the American Psychological Association, she is actively engaged in mentoring and promoting community involvement for those in the helping professions, and supports psychoanalytic training, outreach, and research initiatives. Her own research focuses on creativity, psychosis, and resilience. Marilyn has presented her work nationally and internationally, publishing over 80 articles and book chapters and four books: *Patterns: Building Blocks of Experience, Constructing Realities: Transformations Through Myth and Metaphor, Learning from Experience: a Guidebook for Clinicians,* and *Working with Trauma: Lessons from Bion and Lacan*. Currently in progress: *The Stories We Live: Life, Literature, and Psychoanalysis*.

Avigail Gordon is currently a PhD candidate in clinical psychology at the Derner Institute of advanced Psychological Studies at Adelphi University. She was among the first to earn a Master's degree in Trauma and Violence Transdisciplinary Studies from New York University. Avigail's research explores trauma in a variety of ways, from an examination of trauma as a theoretical construct to studies focusing on the repercussions of trauma in specific communities, including women and Orthodox Jews. Her clinical and theoretical endeavors are both shaped by the ever-present influence of her patients' and participants' traumatic experiences

Marie C. Hansen is currently a Clinical Psychology doctoral student at Long Island University in Brooklyn. She received a BA in Women's Studies from Stony Brook University and an MA in Clinical Psychology from Teachers College, Columbia University. Marie is a member of the Maternal Psychology Lab at Teachers College, a Recovery Coach at the Lieber Recovery and Rehabilitation Clinic, and an active supporter of the Hearing Voices Movement in New York City. Marie's clinical and research interests include psychosis and the psychotic spectrum; psychiatric stigma; women's mental health; reproductive mental health; phenomenological research; and the application of psychodynamic thought to social issues.

Richard T. Johnson is a professor at the University of Hawaii at Manoa where he is on the faculty in Curriculum Studies. His recent research and field-based work includes no-touch policies in education and sports, risk, childhood subjectivity and visual culture. He has taught and served extensively in various field-based preservice early childhood/elementary teacher education programs for over 20 years. He earned his EdD at Vanderbilt University.

Ingo Lambrecht Ph.D., is a clinical psychologist for over twenty years, and has practiced in South Africa and New Zealand. He works in the public sector and has a private practice. Besides his PhD in psychology and MA in Comparative Literature, he has been the clinical leader of the Child and Adolescent Mental Health Service in Hawke's Bay (HBDHB) in New Zealand. He worked as a senior clinical psychologist with people struggling with severe psychosis at the Buchanan Rehabilitation Centre in Auckland District Health Board (ADHB), and for years been at the specialist service for personality disorders, called Segar House (ADHB). Furthermore, he is currently providing clinical leadership at Manawanui Māori Mental Health Service (ADHB). As a clinical advisor to He Kamaka Oranga (Māori Health Service, ADHB), he is a consultant and project leader on the integration of various Māori mental health services. He has presented internationally, and lectured widely on the complex clinical work regarding the cultural-clinical interface for indigenous people. He has also published various book chapters, and is the author of *Sangoma Trance States: Exploring Indigenous Consciousness Disciplines in South Africa* (2014) that weaves personal experiences of being trained as a sangoma, a South African shaman, together with the complex relations of clinical psychology, anthropology, and indigenous knowledges.

Karen L. Lombardi is a Professor at the Derner Institute of Advanced Psychological Studies at Adelphi University in Garden City, New York where she teaches and supervises doctoral candidates in clinical psychology, as well as Faculty and Supervisor in the Postgraduate Programs, Derner Institute. She has published over 30 articles on childhood subjectivity, psychoanalytic theory, and critical social theory. She is also author, with Naomi Rucker, of *Subject Relations*, published by Routledge. She maintains a private practice in psychoanalysis and psychotherapy on Long Island, New York.

Barbara Ann McLeod is completing her doctoral degree in clinical advanced psychology at the Derner Institute of advanced Psychological Studies at Adelphi University, where she researches the influence of gender identity on interpersonal dependency. A graduate of Pratt Institute's Creative Arts Therapy program, she has worked as an art therapist with adults and children recovering from complex trauma. She is a previous visiting faculty member at Pratt Institute, where she worked as a thesis advisor for graduate students. In her clinical practice, she listens for the long reach of traumatic influence.

Jeff Moore is a research and training associate for Immigrant Counseling and Psychotherapy and Jigsaw program coordinator with Headstrong, the National Center for Youth Mental Health (icap). Until recently he was the Director of Welfare for the London Irish Centre where he managed the operation of the largest welfare service for Irish migrants. Jeff holds a MA from Goldsmiths College, University of London and is currently a PhD candidate with Saint Patrick's College, Dublin City University. In 2012 he co-authored a large scale empirical study on Irish migrants to London. He has also published research on the impact of UK welfare reform on the Irish community in London and research methods with Irish migrant communities.

Cate Osborn is an accredited Mental Health Social Worker and psychoanalytic psychotherapist. She trained at the University of NSW. Cate has had twenty years experience as a clinician and program manager in the drug and alcohol field. She has also worked in domestic violence and HIV prevention and as a teacher in drug and alcohol work. Cate is currently in private practice in Sydney, seeing couples, adolescents and adults in psychotherapy. She has a special interest in the impact of early trauma. She provides clinical supervision for counseling and psychotherapy, and seminars in the psychoanalytic understanding of addictions and substance abuse. Cate is also the manager and therapist for the Gunawirra Young Aboriginal Mothers' Program, an early intervention service for Aboriginal women and their children, based in Redfern, Sydney.

Michael O'Loughlin PhD, is professor in the School of Education and clinical and research supervisor in the PhD program in Clinical Psychology at Adelphi University. He is co-chair of the Association for the Psychoanalysis of Culture and Society. He published *The Subject of Childhood* in 2009 and edited *Imagining Children Otherwise: Theoretical and Critical Perspectives on Childhood Subjectivity* with Richard Johnson in 2010. He is coeditor with Cora Smith and Glenys Lobban of *Psychodynamic Psychotherapy in Contemporary South Africa: Contexts, Theories, and Applications* (2013), and in 2013 he edited two books on children's emotions: *The uses of psychoanalysis in working with children's emotional lives* and *Psychodynamic perspectives on working with children, families and schools*. He also edited a companion volume to this book: *The Ethics of Remembering and the Consequences of Forgetting: Essays on Trauma, History and Memory,* also available from Rowman and Littlefield. He has a private practice for psychotherapy and psychoanalysis on Long Island, New York. Website: michaeloloughlinphd.com.

Trisha Ready is a psychotherapist at an acute psychiatric hospital in Seattle where she directs the Partial Hospitalization Program. Trisha has conducted psychoanalytic based research in using music as an adjunct therapy with hard-to-reach patients. Her particular focus has been on the use of self-selected music as a means of emotional containment and expression for people experiencing early stages of psychosis. She has articles published in the*American Journal of Hospice and Palliative Medicine,*

Music and Medicine, and *Psychoanalysis, Culture, and Society,* as well as a chapter in *Music and Medicine: Integrative Models in Pain Medicine.* Trisha serves as co-chair of the Early Career Committee of Division 39 of the American Psychological Association, and as an at-large Board Member of the Association for Psychoanalysis, Culture and Society (APCS). Outside of academic venues Trisha has published numerous social justice and arts based articles, and essays in various magazines and newspapers.

Michael B. Salzman is a professor and Chair of the Department of Educational Psychology at the University of Hawaii at Manoa. He is a licensed psychologist and has published in the areas of cross-cultural psychology, cultural psychology, intercultural conflict, intercultural sensitivity training, multicultural counseling and cultural trauma and recovery among indigenous peoples. He has worked with diverse populations as a teacher, clinician and researcher in urban and rural settings and has been at UH since 1997. He recently contributed a chapter entitled "Ethnocultural Conflict and Cooperation in Hawaii" in the *Handbook of Ethnic Conflict: International Perspectives* and a chapter in the just published *Internalized Oppression: The Psychology of Marginalized Groups.*

Cora Smith is an Adjunct Professor and Chief Clinical Psychologist at the Child, Adolescent and Family Unit, Charlotte Maxeke Johannesburg Academic Hospital, Department of Neurosciences, Division of Psychiatry, School of Clinical Medicine, Faculty of Health Sciences, University of the Witwatersrand, South Africa. She holds a MA (Clinical Psychology) and a PhD. She has worked in the Child and Family Unit for 30 years and focused on child trauma, disrupted and disadvantaged families, HIV/AIDS orphans and the development of personality problems in children and parents. She has published and presented numerous papers at conferences on child trauma, attachment and psychodynamic interventions in the South African context. She is co-editor with Glenys Lobban and Michael O'Loughlin of *Psychodynamic Psychotherapy* in *South Africa: Contexts, theories and applications* WITS University Press, 2013. Prof. Smith is a member of the South African Psychoanalytic Confederation and chairs the Johannesburg Contemporary Psychoanalytic Reading and Supervision Group.

Annie Stopford PhD is a psychoanalytic psychotherapist in private practice and director of research and development for BlueSpark Collaborative, a film and research company based in Boston www.bluesparkcollaborative.com. Annie is an adjunct research fellow at the School of Medicine, University of Western Sydney; fellow, Psychology and the Other Institute, and contributing editor for *Psychoanalysis, Culture and Society.* In nearly 30 years of clinical work Annie has specialized in working with different forms of relational trauma, while her psychosocial research over fifteen years has primarily explored intercultural and interracial relationality, particularly African-Western contact zones. Since moving to the United States from Sydney, Australia in 2011, Annie's focus has expanded from clinical work and psychosocial research to include collaborative film projects that challenge racial injustice in the United States, including a series of films on America's incarceration crisis.

Christine Thornton is a group analyst and organizational consultant in private practice, and was until recently Clinical Director of icap, which offers culturally sensitive psychotherapy to Irish people throughout the UK, particularly to those who grew up in the Industrial Schools and others who experienced trauma in early life; an independent study (2012) found icap particularly effective in working with people who normally find it hard to access and sustain psychotherapy, including survivors of institutional abuse. Christine holds an MSc in Psychology as well as her clinical qualifications, and has had a professional interest for many years in the interplay of professional and personal life in the caring professions. She is author of several books and papers, and is currently focusing on supervision and on writing. Her latest book, *Group and team coaching* (Routledge, 2010) has been translated into both European and Asian languages. Address for correspondence: hello@thorntonconsulting.org.

Kirkland C. Vaughans, PhD is a clinical psychologist/psychoanalyst and the founding editor of the journal of infant, child, and adolescent psychotherapy. He is also first editor of the upcoming 2-volume series entitled, *The psychology of Black Boys and Adolescents.* He is an associate professor of psychology at the Derner Institute of Advanced Psychological Studies: Adelphi University, professor in the Postgraduate Program in Child and Adolescent Psychotherapy at Adelphi, and clinical supervisor at the National Institute of Psychotherapies. He has presented and written on trauma within the African American community, treatment issues for conduct disordered youth, and cultural issues in psychotherapy. He is a school psychologist in Hempstead High School, New York, and maintains a private practice in New York City.

Janice A. Walters, PhD is a Psychoanalyst and Associate Professor of Psychology at the Borough of Manhattan Community College of the City University of New York. She is also a visiting scholar within the Department of Anthropology at the University of Sydney. Dr. Walters lives in New York but her research interests lie in her country of origin where she conducts a longitudinal investigation of the impact of trauma on the Stolen Generation Aboriginal People. Specifically, her interest is in the role that intergenerational trauma plays in the lives of the Stolen Generation and the ways in which silent messages are passed onto future generations, as well as the impact that this has and continues to have on the psychological, social and cultural well-being of the Aboriginal people and their communities. She is also interested in the role of women as the current matriarchs of the Aboriginal culture in circumventing the impact of intergenerational trauma. Other interests are in the social construction of race and the ways in which race becomes embedded into the fabric of a nation causing a splitting of groups based on race and culture.

CPSIA information can be obtained at www.ICGtesting.com
Printed in the USA
BVOW04*1434311014

373072BV00004B/4/P

9 781442 231856